NINTH EDITION

MANAGEMENT MISTAKES AND SUCCESSES

Robert F. Hartley
Cleveland State University

BICENTENNIAL
1807
WILEY
2007
BICENTENNIAL

John Wiley & Sons, Inc

ASSOCIATE PUBLISHER	Judith Joseph
ACQUISITIONS EDITOR	Kimberly Mortimer
MARKETING MANAGER	Amy Scholz
DESIGN DIRECTOR	Harry Nolan
SENIOR DESIGNER	Kevin Murphy
SENIOR PRODUCTION EDITOR	Patricia McFadden
SENIOR MEDIA EDITOR	Allison Morris

Wiley 200th Anniversary logo designed by: Richard J. Pacifico

This book was set in by Laserwords and printed and bound by Courier/Westford. The cover was printed by Lehigh Press, Inc.

This book is printed on acid-free paper. ⊗

To order books or for customer service please, call 1-800-CALL WILEY (225-5945).

Library of Congress Cataloging-in-Publication Data:

Hartley, Robert F., 1927–
    Management mistakes and successes / Robert F. Hartley.—9th ed.
        p. cm.
    Includes index.
    ISBN 978-0-470-08700-8
1. Management—Case studies.   I. Title
    HD31.H3485 2008
    658.4—dc22

                                    2007016754

ISBN-13: 978-0-470-08700-8

Printed in the United States of America.

10 9 8 7 6 5 4 3 2

PREFACE

Welcome to this ninth edition of *Management Mistakes and Successes*. It has now been around for almost 25 years, and its sister book, *Marketing Mistakes*, for over 30 years. Who would have thought that interest in mistakes would have been so enduring? I know that many of you are past users, and hope that you will find this new edition a worthy successor to the earlier ones.

After so many years of investigating mistakes, and more recently some successes as well, it might seem a monumental challenge to keep these new editions fresh and interesting and still provide good learning experiences. But the task of doing so, and the joy of the challenge, has made this an intriguing endeavor through the decades. It is always difficult to abandon interesting cases that have stimulated student discussions and provided good learning experiences, but newer case possibilities are ever competing for inclusion. Examples of good and bad handling of problems and opportunities are always emerging. But sometimes we bring back an oldie, and with the updating a new perspective and new learning insights often result.

For new users, I hope the book will meet your full expectations and be an effective instructional tool. Although case books abound, you and your students may find this one somewhat unique and very readable, a book that can help transform dry and rather remote concepts into practical reality, and lead to lively class discussions, and even debates amid the great arena of decision making.

NEW TO THIS EDITION

In contrast to the early editions, which examined only notable mistakes, and based on your favorable comments about recent editions, I have again included some well-known successes. While mistakes provide valuable learning insights, we can also learn from successes, and we can learn by comparing the unsuccessful with the successful.

We have continued Managing Ebbing Performance and Crisis, as well as Merger Pitfalls, but have reduced each of these parts to three cases from five and four respectively. This enabled us to reintroduce Great Comebacks, which had been deleted from recent editions. From your comments, Great Comebacks with its three inspiring examples may be one of the best sections. I didn't dare delete

Entrepreneurial Adventures, and even added an additional case. Some of you have recommended that we add additional cases so as to provide more choice for classes where you need fresh material. So, from the last edition we have added six new cases, and deleted five. Some of the cases are so current that we continued updating until the manuscript left for the production process. We have tried to keep all cases as current as possible with Postscripts, Later Developments, and Updates.

A number of you have asked that I identify which cases would be appropriate for the traditional coverage of topics as organized in typical management texts. With most cases it is not possible to truly compartmentalize the mistake or success to merely one topic. The patterns of success or failure tend to be more pervasive. Still, I think you will find the following classification of cases by subject matter to be helpful. I thank those of you who made this and other suggestions.

Classification of Cases by Major Management Topics

Topics	Most Relevant Cases
Change and Crisis Management	Scott Paper, Sunbeam, Perrier, MetLife, United Way, Maytag, Firestone/Ford, Boeing, Herman Miller, Euro Disney, Gateway
Mergers	Snapple, Newell Rubbermaid, DaimlerChrysler, Kmart and Sears, Hewlett-Packard, Maytag
Great Comebacks	Continental Air, Harley-Davidson, IBM, Boeing
Planning	Euro Disney, Boeing, Vanguard, Kmart and Sears, Hewlett-Packard, Southwest Air, Boston Beer, OfficeMax, Wal-Mart
Leadership and Execution	Continental Air, Harley-Davidson, IBM, Vanguard, Kmart/Sears, Hewlett-Packard, Wal-Mart, Southwest Air, Maytag, Boston Beer, OfficeMax, United Way, Herman Miller
Controlling	United Way, Maytag, MetLife, Firestone/Ford, Wal-Mart, Boeing
Global Applications	Euro Disney, Boeing, Harley-Davidson, Perrier, DaimlerChrysler, Maytag, Firestone/Ford, Wal-Mart
Entrepreneurial	Boston Beer, OfficeMax, Gateway
Ethical	United Way, MetLife, DaimlerChrysler, Scott Paper and Al Dunlap, Wal-Mart
Customer Relations	Vanguard, Maytag, Euro Disney, Boston Beer, Harley-Davidson, Firestone/Ford, United Way, Southwest Air, Continental Air, IBM, MetLife, OfficeMax, Wal-Mart
Outsourcing	Boeing, Wal-Mart, Herman Miller, Maytag, Gateway

TARGETED COURSES

As a supplemental text, this book can be used in a variety of courses, both under-graduate and graduate, such as introduction to business, principles of management, management skills, and strategic management. It can also be used in courses in busi-ness ethics and organizational behavior. It certainly can be used in training programs and even may appeal to nonprofessionals who are looking for a good read about well-known firms and personalities.

TEACHING AIDS

As in the previous editions, you will find a plethora of teaching aids and discussion material within and at the end of each chapter. Some of these will be common to several cases, and illustrate that certain successful and unsuccessful practices are seldom unique.

Information Boxes and Issue Boxes are included in each chapter to highlight relevant concepts and issues, or related information. Learning insights help students see how certain practices—both errors and successes—cross company lines and are prone to be either traps for the unwary or success modes. Discussion Questions and Hands-On Exercises encourage and stimulate student involvement. A recent pedagogical feature is the Team Debate Exercise, in which formal issues and options can be debated for each case. New in some cases is the *Devil's Advocate* exercise, in which students can argue against a proposed course of action to test its merits. A new pedagogical feature in this edition, based on a reviewer's recommendation, appears at the end of the Analysis section: students are asked to make their own analysis, draw their own conclusions, and defend them, thereby having an opportunity to stretch themselves. Where a case involves considerable updating, a new feature invites students to *Assess the Latest Developments*. Invitation to Research suggestions allow students to take the case a step further, to investigate what has happened since the case was written, both to the company and perhaps to some of the individuals involved. In the final chapter, the various learning insights are summarized and classified into general conclusions.

An Instructor's Manual written by the author accompanies the text to provide suggestions and considerations for the pedagogical material within and at the ends of chapters.

ACKNOWLEDGMENTS

It seems fitting to acknowledge everyone who has provided encouragement, infor-mation, advice, and constructive criticism through the years since the first edition of these *Mistakes* books. I hope you all are well and successful, and I truly appreciate your contributions. I apologize if I have missed anybody, and would be grateful to know so that I can rectify this in future editions. I welcome updates of present affiliations.

Michael Pearson, Loyola University, New Orleans; Beverlee Anderson, University of Cincinnati; Y. H. Furuhashi, Notre Dame University; W. Jack Duncan, University of Alabama—Birmingham; Mike Farley, Del Mar College; Joseph W. Leonard, Miami University (OH); Abbas Nadim, University of New Haven; William O'Donnell, University of Phoenix; Howard Smith, University of New Mexico; James Wolter, University of Michigan, Flint; Vernon R. Stauble, California State Polytechnic University; Donna Giertz, Parkland College; Don Hantula, St. Joseph's University; Milton Alexander, Auburn University; James F. Cashman, University of Alabama; Douglas Wozniak, Ferris State University; Greg Bach, Bismark State College; Glenna Dod, Wesleyan College; Anthony McGann, University of Wyoming; Robert D. Nale, Coastal Carolina University; Robert H. Votaw, Amber University; Don Fagan, Daniel Webster University; Andrew J. Deile, Mercer University; Samuel Hazen, Tarleton State University; Michael B. McCormick, Jacksonville State University; Neil K. Friedman, Queens College; Lawrence Aronhime, John Hopkins University; Joseph Marrocco, Boston University; Morgan Milner, Eastern Michigan University; Souha Ezzedeen, Pennsylvania State University, Harrisburg; Regina Hughes, University of Texas; Karen Stewart, Stockton College; Francy Milner, University of Colorado.

Also: Barnett Helzberg Jr. of the Shirley and Barnett Helzberg Foundation, and my colleagues at Cleveland State University: Ram Rao, Sanford Jacobs, Andrew Gross, and Benoy Joseph. From Wiley: Judith Joseph, Jamie Heffler, Jennifer Conklin, and Carissa Marker.

Robert F. Hartley, Professor Emeritus
College of Business Administration
Cleveland State University
Cleveland, Ohio
R.Hartley@csuOhio.EDU

ABOUT THE AUTHOR

Bob Hartley is Professor Emeritus at Cleveland State University's College of Business Administration. There he taught a variety of undergraduate and graduate courses in management, marketing, and ethics. Prior to that he was at the University of Minnesota and George Washington University. His MBA and Ph.D. are from the University of Minnesota, with a BBA from Drake University.

Before coming into academia, he spent 13 years in retailing with the predecessor of Kmart (S. S. Kresge), J. C. Penney, and Dayton-Hudson and its Target subsidiary. Positions held included store management, central buying, and merchandise management.

His first textbook, *Marketing: Management and Social Change*, was published in 1972. It was ahead of its time in introducing social and environmental issues to the study of marketing. Other books, *Marketing Fundamentals, Retailing, Sales Management*, and *Marketing Research*, followed.

In 1976, the first *Marketing Mistakes* book was published, and it brought a new approach to case studies, making them student-friendly and more relevant to career enhancement than existing books. In 1983, *Management Mistakes* was published. These books are now in the tenth and ninth editions respectively, and have been widely translated. In 1992, Professor Hartley wrote *Business Ethics: Violations of the Public Trust*, and *Business Ethics Mistakes and Successes* was published in 2005. He is listed in *Who's Who in America* and *Who's Who in the World*.

CONTENTS

V LEADERSHIP AND EXECUTION 223

VI CONTROLLING 299

VII ENTREPRENEURIAL ADVENTURES 343

CHAPTER ONE

Introduction

$\mathbf{A}$t this writing, *Management Mistakes* is nearing its twenty-fifth anniversary. The first edition, back in 1983, was 254 pages and included such long-forgotten cases as World Football League, Korvette, W. T. Grant, Montgomery Ward, Edsel, Corfam, A. C. Gilbert, Robert Hall, and STP.

In this ninth edition, we have added six new cases from the eighth edition, several of these being modified from earlier editions. Five other cases have been dropped to make room for the new entries, with the rest revamped and updated, and in some instances reclassified. One new part, Great Comebacks, is brought back by popular demand from an earlier edition. Many of these cases are as recent as today's headlines; some have still not come to complete resolution.

We continue to seek what can be learned—insights that are transferable to other firms, other times, and other situations. What key factors brought monumental mistakes for some firms and resounding successes for others? Through such evaluations and studies of contrasts, we may learn to improve the batting average in the intriguing, ever-challenging art of management decision making.

We will encounter examples of the phenomenon of organizational life cycles, with an organization growing and prospering, then failing (just as humans do), but occasionally resurging. Success rarely lasts forever, but even the most serious mistakes can be (but are not always) overcome.

As in previous editions, a variety of firms, industries, mistakes, and successes are presented. You will be familiar with most of the organizations, although probably not with the details of their situations.

We are always on the lookout for cases that can bring out certain points or caveats and that give a balanced view of the spectrum of management problems. We have sought to present examples that provide somewhat different learning experiences in which at least some aspect of the mistake or success is unique. Still, we see similar mistakes occurring time and again. The prevalence of some of these mistakes makes us wonder how much decision making has really improved over the decades.

Let us then consider what learning insights we can gain, with the benefit of hindsight, from examining these examples of successful and unsuccessful management practices.

1

LEARNING INSIGHTS

Analyzing Mistakes

In looking at sick companies, or even healthy ones that have experienced difficulties with certain parts of their operations, it is tempting to be overly critical. It is easy to criticize with the benefit of hindsight. Mistakes are inevitable, given the present state of decision making, and the dynamic environment facing organizations.

Mistakes can be categorized as errors of omission and of commission. *Mistakes of omission* are those in which no action was taken and the status quo was contentedly embraced amid a changing environment. Such errors, which often typify conservative or stodgy management, are not as obvious as the other category of mistakes. They seldom involve tumultuous upheaval; rather, the company's fortunes and competitive position slowly fade, until management at last realizes that mistakes having monumental impact have been allowed to happen. The firm's fortunes often never regain their former luster. But sometimes they do, and we describe the cases of Continental Airlines, Harley-Davidson, and even IBM, which all fought back successfully from adversity.

Mistakes of commission are more spectacular. They involve bad decisions, wrong actions taken, misspent or misdirected expansion, and the like. Although the costs of the erosion of competitive position coming from errors of omission are difficult to calculate precisely, the costs of errors of commission are often fully evident. We have devoted Part III to a particularly costly class of errors of commission, those involving unwise mergers and acquisitions. But errors of commission are seen in many other cases throughout the book. Looking at a few such examples, the costs associated with the misdirected efforts of MetLife in fines and restitution totaled nearly $2 billion. For Euro Disney, in 1993 alone the loss from a poorly planned venture was $960 million; it improved in 1994 with only a $366 million loss. For Maytag's overseas Hoover Division, the costs of an incredibly bungled sales promotion brought a loss of $315 million (10.4 percent of revenues) in 1992, with losses continuing to mount after that.

Although they may make mistakes, organizations with alert and aggressive management show certain actions or reactions when reviewing their problem situations:

1. Looming problems or present mistakes are quickly recognized.
2. The causes of the problem(s) are carefully determined.
3. Alternative corrective actions are evaluated in view of the company's resources and constraints.
4. Corrective action is prompt. Sometimes this requires a ruthless axing of the product, the division, or whatever is at fault.
5. Mistakes provide learning experiences. The same mistakes are not repeated, and future operations are consequently strengthened.

When a company is slow to recognize emerging problems, this indicates that management is incompetent or that controls have not been established to provide prompt feedback at strategic control points. For example, a declining competitive position in one or a few geographical areas should be a red flag to management that something is amiss. To wait months before investigating or taking action may mean a permanent loss of business. Admittedly, signals sometimes get mixed, and complete information may be lacking, but procrastination is not easily defended.

Just as problems should be quickly recognized, the causes of these problems—the "why" of the unexpected results—must be determined as quickly as possible. It is premature, and rash, to take action before knowing where the problems really lie. To go back to the previous example, the loss of competitive position in one or a few areas may reflect circumstances beyond the firm's immediate control, such as an aggressive new competitor who is drastically cutting prices to "buy sales." In this situation, all competing firms will likely lose market share, and little can be done except to stay as competitive as possible with prices and servicing. However, closer investigation may reveal that the erosion of business was due to unreliable deliveries, poor quality control, noncompetitive prices, or incompetent sales staff.

With the cause(s) of the problem defined, various alternatives for dealing with it should be identified and evaluated. This may require further research, such as obtaining feedback from customers and from field personnel. Finally the decision to correct the situation should be made as objectively and prudently as possible. If drastic action is needed, there usually is little rationale for delaying. Serious problems do not go away by themselves: they tend to fester and become worse.

Finally, some learning experience should result from the misadventure. The president of one successful firm told me:

> I try to give my subordinates as much decision-making experience as possible. Perhaps I err on the side of delegating too much. In any case, I expect some mistakes to be made, some decisions that were not for the best. I don't come down too hard usually. This is part of the learning experience. But God help them if they make the same mistake again. There has been no learning experience, and I question their competence for higher executive positions.

Analyzing Successes

Successes deserve as much analysis as mistakes, although admittedly the urgency is less than with an emerging problem that requires quick remedial action. Any analysis of success should seek answers to at least the following questions:

Why were such actions successful?

- Was it because of the nature of the environment, and if so, how?
- Was it because of particular research and planning efforts, and if so, how?
- Was it because of particular engineering and/or production achievements, and if so, can these be adapted to other aspects of our operations?
- Was it because of any particular element of the strategy—such as service, promotional activities, or distribution methods—and if so, how?
- Was it because of the specific elements of the strategy meshing well together, and if so, how was this achieved?

Was the situation unique and unlikely to be encountered again?

- If the situation was not unique, how can we use these successful techniques in the future or in other operations at the present time?

ORGANIZATION OF THIS BOOK

In this ninth edition we have modified the classification of cases somewhat from earlier editions. Part I has been renamed and reduced from five cases to three as we study firms that faced major changes and crises and mishandled them. Part II has been reinstated and reinvigorated, with three inspirational examples of great comebacks. Part III still deals with costly mistakes resulting from an eagerness to merge, but we have reduced the cases from five to three. The next three sections are mistakes and successes classified under traditional management functions. Finally, we have continued Entrepreneurial Adventures and follow the progress of two entrepreneurs we first encountered in an earlier edition, as well as the roller-coaster ride of a third entrepreneur. Let us briefly describe the cases that follow.

Managing Ebbing Performance and Crises

Albert Dunlap had a well-deserved reputation as the premier hatchet man, the one who would come into a sick organization and fire enough people to make it temporarily profitable—he was known as "Chainsaw Al." Somehow, with Sunbeam this seemingly proven downsizing strategy did not work, and Dunlap himself was fired by the board of directors. Later investigations brought fraud suits for accounting misdeeds.

Perrier, the bottled water firm, encountered adversity when traces of benzene were found in some of its product. Responsibly, the company ordered a sweeping recall of all bottles in North America and, a few days later, in the rest of the world while it tried to correct the problem. For five months Perrier was off the market, thereby allowing competitors an unparalleled windfall and savaging its market share. Added to this was public recognition that the claims regarding the purity of its product were false.

Product safety lapses that result in injury and even loss of life of users are among the worst ethical and social-responsibility abuses. Even more reprehensible is when such risks are allowed to continue for years, with no responsibility admitted. Ford Explorers equipped with Firestone tires were implicated in more than 200 deaths from tire failures and vehicle rollovers. After revelations about the accidents surfaced, Ford and Firestone each blamed the other for the deaths. Eventually, inept crisis management brought a host of lawsuits resulting in massive recalls and billions in damages.

Great Comebacks

The comeback of Continental Airlines from extreme adversity and devastated employee morale to become one of the best airlines in the country is an achievement of no small moment. New CEO Gordon Bethune brought human relations management skills to one of the most rapid turnarounds ever, overcoming a decade of raucous adversarial labor relations and a reputation in the pits.

In the early 1960s, Harley-Davidson dominated a static motorcycle industry. Suddenly, Honda burst on the scene, and Harley's market share dropped from 70 percent to 5 percent in only a few years. It took Harley nearly three decades to revive, but now it has created a mystique for its heavy motorcycles and gained a new customer base while attracting hundreds of thousands of bikers to rallies across the country.

In an earlier edition, we classified IBM as a prime example of a giant firm that had failed to cope with changing technology. Along with many other analysts, we thought that the behemoth could never rouse itself enough to regain its status as a major player. But we were wrong, and IBM once again has become a premier growth company.

Merger Pitfalls

Snapple, a marketer of non-carbonated fruit-flavored and iced tea drinks, was acquired by Quaker Oats in late 1994 for $1.7 billion. As sales declined and losses mounted, it soon became apparent to all but the CEO of Quaker that far too much had been paid for this acquisition. No business plan was able to turn Snapple around. In 1997, Snapple was sold for $300 million, a loss of $1.4 billion in only three years.

Newell, a consumer-products firm, successfully geared its operations to meet the demands of giant retailers, particularly Wal-Mart, whereas Rubbermaid had in recent years been unable to meet those stringent requirements. In 1999, Newell acquired Rubbermaid, confident of turning its operation around, only to find that Rubbermaid's problems were not easily corrected and that they had a negative impact on the fortunes of Newell as well.

The merger of Chrysler with Daimler, the huge German firm that makes Mercedes, was supposed to be a merger of equals. But Chrysler's management quickly found this was not so, and the top Chrysler executives were soon replaced by executives from Germany. Problems of assimilation and coordination plagued the merger for years. Adding to the problems, the industry and the economy soured.

Planning

In April 1992, just outside Paris, Disney opened its first European theme park. It had high expectations and supreme self-confidence (critics called it arrogance). The earlier Disney parks in California, Florida, and more recently Japan were spectacular successes. But the rosy expectations soon became a delusion as a variety of planning miscues showed Disney that Europeans, and particularly the French, were not carbon copies of visitors elsewhere.

Boeing had an interesting dilemma: too much business. It was unable to cope with a deluge of orders in the mid- and late 1990s. Months, and then years, went by as it tried to make its production more efficient. In the meantime, a foreign competitor,

Airbus, emerged to oust Boeing in 2003 as number one in the commercial plane industry. But by 2006, Boeing had turned the tide and had Airbus on the ropes.

Vanguard fought Fidelity to become the largest mutual fund firm. Vanguard's business plan has been to walk a road less traveled, to downplay marketing and shun the heavy advertising and overhead of its competitors. It provided investors with better returns through far lower expense ratios, relying on word of mouth and unpaid publicity to gain new customers, while old customers continued to pour money into the best values in the mutual fund industry.

Two faltering retail chains, Kmart and Sears, merged under the auspices of a hedge fund manager, Edward Lampert. Whether two weaklings could become one strong operation to compete with the likes of Wal-Mart and Target was uncertain, though investors bid both stocks up to extravagant levels in anticipation. The real estate could be worth quite a bit if the retail business does not succeed, though this would hardly warrant present stock prices. A crap shoot, or a calculated gamble by a very savvy turnaround expert? We shall see.

Leadership and Execution

In July 1999, Hewlett-Packard, the world's second-biggest computer maker, chose Carly Fiorina to be its CEO. Thus she became the first outsider to take the reins in H-P's 60-year history. Three years later she engineered the biggest merger in the high-tech industry, with Compaq Computer. Only a year later, H-P was able to boast that this merger had become a model for effectively assimilating two giant organizations. But growth in profitability did not follow, and early in 2005, the board fired Fiorina.

With a business plan of offering customers the lowest prices, Wal-Mart is by far the largest retailer in the world and reflects the genius of its founder, Sam Walton, who did this in his lifetime. But size can bring coercive power, especially in respect to smaller suppliers. It can also destroy competitors and even change the social structure of small towns. Some observers are suggesting that Wal-Mart has gotten too big.

Southwest Airlines found a strategic window of opportunity as the lowest-cost and lowest-price carrier between certain cities. And how it milked this opportunity. Its CEO, Herb Kelleher, was a charismatic leader, and built it to become the nation's sixth-largest airline, a feared competitor to major airlines on many of their domestic routes, and the only one to be profitable for more than 30 consecutive years.

Herman Miller, maker of top-of-the-line office furniture, had long been extolled in management books and classrooms for successfully melding good business operations and altruistic employee and environmental relations. In recent years these policies were seriously tested as demand for its high-price products declined and harsh realities pitted altruism against viability.

Controlling

United Way of America is a not-for-profit organization. The man who led it to become the nation's largest charity perceived himself as virtually beyond authority. Exorbitant spending, favoritism, conflicts of interest—these went uncontrolled and uncriticized until investigative reporters from the *Washington Post* publicized the scandalous conduct. Amid the hue and cry, contributions nationwide drastically declined.

The problems of Maytag's Hoover subsidiary in the United Kingdom almost defy reason. The subsidiary planned a promotional campaign so generous that the company was overwhelmed with takers; it could neither supply the products nor grant the prizes. In a miscue of multimillion-dollar consequences, Maytag had to foot the bill while trying to appease irate customers.

The insurance firm MetLife, whether through loose controls or tacit approval, permitted an agent to use deceptive selling tactics on a grand scale, and enrich himself in the process. Investigations of several state attorneys general forced the company to cough up almost $2 billion in fines and restitutions.

Entrepreneurial Adventures

Boston Beer burst on the microbrewery scene with Samuel Adams beers, higher priced even than most imports. Notwithstanding this—or maybe because of it— Boston Beer became the largest microbrewer. It showed that a small entrepreneur, Jim Koch, could compete successfully against the giants in the industry, and do so on a national scale.

OfficeMax, an office-supply category-killer chain, grew to $2.5 billion in sales in only a few years. The dedication and creative efforts of its founder serve as a model for any would-be entrepreneur who aspires to make it big. Yet it was number three in its industry, with the heady years of profitable growth seemingly over. In October 2003, Michael Feuer, the founder, agreed for his firm to be acquired by Boise Cascade, a giant lumber firm.

Ted Waitt's Gateway Computer, after its heady growth in the early days of the PC, found itself unable to compete with the low prices of Dell Computer. It desperately sought ways to bring its costs down and still survive in the PC industry. Finally selling all of its Gateway stores, it attempted to develop relationships with high-tech retailers. Its viability still remains in doubt.

GENERAL WRAP-UP

Where possible, the text depicts the major personalities involved in these cases. Imagine yourself in their positions, confronting the problems and facing choices at their points of crisis or just-recognized opportunities. What would you have done differently, and why? We invite you to participate in the discussion questions, the hands-on exercises, the debates appearing at the ends of chapters, and the occasional devil's advocate invitation (a devil's advocate is one who argues an opposing position for the sake of testing the decision). There are discussion questions for the various boxes within chapters. And, new to this edition, you are invited to make your own analysis and conclusions at the end of the analysis section.

While doing these activities, you may feel the excitement and challenge of decision making under conditions of uncertainty. Perhaps you may even become a better future executive and decision maker.

QUESTIONS

1. Do you agree that it is impossible for a firm to avoid mistakes? Why or why not?

2. How can a firm speed up its awareness of emerging problems so that it can take corrective action? Be as specific as you can.

3. Large firms tend to err on the side of conservatism and are slower to take corrective action than smaller ones. Why do you suppose this is so?

4. Which do you think is likely to be more costly to a firm, errors of omission or errors of commission? Why?

5. So often we see the successful firm eventually losing its pattern of success. Why is success not more enduring?

PART

ONE

MANAGING EBBING
PERFORMANCE AND CRISES

CHAPTER TWO

Tough Love: Dunlap's Approach to Troubled Companies

Al Dunlap was hired in July 1996 by two large Sunbeam investors to turn Sunbeam around. He had gained a reputation as a turnaround artist extraodinaire, most recently from his efforts at Scott Paper. His philosophy was to cut to the bone, and the press frequently called him "Chainsaw Al." But he met his comeuppance with Sunbeam. In the process, his philosophy as well as his character came under bitter attack. How far do you cut into an organization, and to the living, breathing people involved, before you cross the line? Opinions differ on this, but the telling blow was his cooking the books to make his performance look far better than it really was.

ALBERT J. DUNLAP

Dunlap wrote an autobiography, *Mean Business: How I Save Bad Companies and Make Good Companies*, describing his business philosophy and how it had evolved. The book became a best seller. Dunlap grew up in the slums of Hoboken, New Jersey, the son of a shipyard worker, and was imbued with the desire to make something of himself. He played football in high school and graduated from West Point. A former army paratrooper, he was known as a quick hitter, a ruthless cost cutter, a tough boss. But he got results, at least in the short term.

In 1983, Dunlap became chief executive of Lily Tulip Co., a maker of disposable cups that was heavily in debt after a buyout. He quickly exhibited the management philosophy that was to make him famous. He slashed costs by decimating the headquarters staff, closing plants, and selling the corporate jet. When he left in the mid-1980s, the company was healthy. In the latter 1980s, Dunlap became the number-one operations man for Sir James Goldsmith, a notorious raider of corporations. Dunlap was involved in restructuring Goldsmith's acquisitions of Crown-Zellerbach and International Diamond. In 1991, he worked on a heavily debt laden Australian conglomerate, Consolidated Press Holdings. Two years later, after his "chainsaw approach," Consolidated Press was 100 divisions lighter and virtually free of debt.

By then, Dunlap was a wealthy man, having made close to $100 million on his various restructurings. Still, at 56, he was hardly ready to retire. When the board of Scott Paper heard that he was available, they wooed him, even purchasing his $3.2 million house in Florida from him.

SCOTT PAPER—A SICK COMPANY— AND DUNLAP'S RESULTS

An aged Scott Paper was reeling in the early 1990s. Per-share earnings had dropped 61 percent since 1989 on flat sales growth. In 1993, the company had a $277 million loss.

Part of the problem stemmed from Scott's commercial paper division, S. D. Warren. In 1990, the company spent heavily to increase capacity at Warren. Unfortunately, the timing could not have been worse. One of the worst industry slumps since the Great Depression was just beginning. Three subsequent "restructurings" had little positive effect.

Table 2.1 shows the decline in sales from 1990 through 1993. Table 2.2 shows the net income and loss during these four years. Of even more concern was Scott's performance relative to the major competitors, Procter & Gamble and Kimberly-Clark, during these four years. Table 2.3 shows the comparisons of profits as a percentage of sales, with Scott again showing up most poorly. Undoubtedly this was a company needing fixing.

In characteristic fashion, Dunlap acted quickly once he took over as CEO on April 19, 1994. That same day, to show his confidence and commitment, he invested $2 million of his own money in Scott. A few months later, after the stock had appreciated 30 percent, he invested another $2 million.

After only hours on the job, Dunlap offered three of his former associates top positions in the company. On the second day, he disbanded the powerful management committee. On the third day, he fired nine of the eleven highest-ranking executives.

TABLE 2.1. Sales of Scott, 1990–1993 (billions)

1990	$3.9
1991	3.8
1992	3.9
1993	3.6
Total change, 1990–1993	(7.7%)

Source: Company annual reports.

Commentary: The company's deteriorating sales come at a time of great economic growth and advancing revenues for most firms.

TABLE 2.2.   Net Income of Scott and Percent
of Sales, 1990–1993

	(millions)	% of sales
1990	$148	3.8%
1991	(70)	(1.8)
1992	167	4.3
1993	(277)	(7.7)

Source: Company annual reports.

Commentary: The company's erratic profit picture, culminating
in the serious loss of 1993, deserved and received deep concern.

TABLE 2.3.   Profit as a Percentage of Sales: Scott,
Kimberly-Clark, and Procter & Gamble, 1990–1993

	1990	1991	1992	1993
Scott	3.8%	(1.8%)	4.3%	(7.7)
P&G	6.6	6.6	6.4	(2.1)*
Kimberly-Clark	6.8	7.5	1.9	7.3

*Extraordinary charges reflecting accounting changes.

Source: Company annual reports.

Commentary: Scott again shows up badly against its major competitors,
both in the low percentage of earnings to sales and their severe
fluctuations into earnings losses.

To complete his blitzkrieg, on the fourth day Dunlap destroyed four bookshelves
crammed with strategic plans prepared by previous administrations.

Can such drastic and abrupt changes be overdone? Should change be introduced
more slowly and with more reflection? See the Issue Box: How Soon to Introduce
Drastic Change? for a discussion of these questions.

ISSUE BOX

HOW SOON TO INTRODUCE DRASTIC CHANGE?

Some new administrators believe in instituting major changes as quickly as possible.
They reason that an organization is expecting this and is better prepared to make the
adjustments needed than it will ever be again. Such managers are often referred to as
gunslingers because they "shoot from the hip." Other managers believe in moving more

slowly, gathering more information, and taking action only when all the pros and cons have been weighed. But sometimes such delays can lull an organization into a sense of false calm, and make for even more trauma when the changes eventually come.

Relevant to the issue of moving swiftly or slowly is the health of the entity. If a firm is sick, in drastic need of help, we would expect a new manager to move more quickly and decisively. A firm doing well, although perhaps not as well as desired, should not reasonably require drastic and abrupt disruption.

It has always baffled me how a fast-acting executive can acquire sufficient information to make such crucial decisions as who to fire and who to retain, what operations to prune and which to support, all within a few days. Of course, operating statistics can be studied before formally taking charge, but the causes of the problems or successes—the whys—can hardly be understood so soon.

Boards, investors, and creditors want a fast turnaround. Waiting months before taking action to fix a sick company is not acceptable. However, not all companies are easily fixable; some can defy the best efforts of past and new managers.

Do you think Dunlap acted too hastily in his initial sweeping changes? Playing the devil's advocate (one who takes an opposing view for the sake of debate), argue the position that he did indeed act far too hastily.

At the annual meeting in June 1994, barely two months after assuming command, Dunlap announced four major goals for the first year. First, he vowed to divest the company of nonstrategic assets, most notably S. D. Warren, the printing and publishing papers subsidiary, which had received major expansion funding only a few years before. Second, he would develop a core team of accomplished senior managers. Third, Scott was to be brought to "fighting trim" through a one-time-only global restructuring. Last, Dunlap promised to develop new strategies for marketing Scott products around the world.

In one of the largest relative restructurings in corporate America, more than 11,000 positions out of a total of 25,900 worldwide were eliminated. This included 71 percent of the headquarters staff, 50 percent of the salaried employees, and 20 percent of the production workers. Such draconian measures certainly cut costs. But were they overdone? Might such cuts have detrimental long-term consequences? See the Issue Box: How Deep to Cut? for a discussion of these topics.

ISSUE BOX

HOW DEEP TO CUT?

Bloated bureaucratic organizations are the epitome of inefficiency and waste, whether in business corporations or in governmental bodies, including school systems. Administrative overhead might even exceed actual operating costs. But corrections can be overdone—they can go too far. In Scott's case, was the axing of 11,000 of 25,900 employees overdone?

Although we are not privy to the needed cost/productivity records, we can raise some concerns. Did the massive layoffs go well beyond fat and bloat into bone and muscle? If so, future operations might be jeopardized. Other concerns ought to be: Does an organization owe anything to its loyal and senior employees, or should they simply be considered pawns in the pursuit of maximizing profits? Where do we draw the line between efficiency and responsibility to faithful employees? And even to the community itself?

You may want to consider some of these questions and issues. They are current in today's downsizing mindset.

In addition to cutting staff, Dunlap sought to reduce other costs, including outsourcing some operations and services. If these could be provided cheaper by other firms, should they be farmed out? Dunlap announced that with the restructuring completed by year-end, pretax savings of $340 million were expected.[1]

By late fall of 1994, Dunlap's plans to divest the company of nonstrategic assets bore fruit. S. D. Warren was sold for $1.6 billion to an international investment group. Other asset sales generated more than $2 billion. Dunlap was able to lower debt by $1.5 billion and repurchase $300 million of Scott stock. This led to the credit rating being upgraded.

The results of Dunlap's efforts were impressive indeed. Second-quarter earnings rose 71 percent; third-quarter earnings increased 73 percent, the best quarterly performance for Scott in four years. Fourth-quarter earnings were 159 percent higher than in 1993, establishing an all-time record. For the whole year, net income increased 82 percent over the previous year, and the stock price performance, since Dunlap took over, stood at the top 1 percent of major companies traded on the New York Stock Exchange.[2]

Still, the cost slashing was not helping market share. In the fiscal year ended April 2, 1995, Scott's bath-tissue sales in key U.S. markets slipped 1 percent, and paper towels sales fell 5.2 percent.[3]

On July 17, 1995, Dunlap's efforts to make Scott an attractive acquisition candidate were capped by Kimberly-Clark's $7.38 billion offer for the firm. In the process, Dunlap himself would be suitably rewarded, leaving far richer than after any of his seven previous restructuring efforts. But Dunlap insisted, "I am still the best bargain in corporate America."[4]

---

[1] *The New Scott 1994 Annual Report*, p. 5.

[2] *Ibid.*, p. 6.

[3] Joseph Weber and Paula Dwyer, "Scott Rolls Out a Risky Strategy," *Business Week*, May 22, 1995, p. 45.

[4] Joann S. Lublin and Steven Lipin, "Scott Paper's 'Rambo in Pin Stripes' Is on the Prowl for Another Company to Fix," *Wall Street Journal*, July 18, 1995, p. B1.

THE SUNBEAM CHALLENGE

Sunbeam was a maker of blenders, electric blankets and gas grills. These old-line products had shown little growth, and revenues and profits languished. After the well-publicized turnaround success of Dunlap at Scott, it was no surprise when he was courted for the top job at Sunbeam, and he entered the fray with gusto.

The day Dunlap was hired, Sunbeam stock rose 50 percent, "on faith." It eventually rose 300 percent. With his customary modus operandi, he terminated half of Sunbeam's 12,000 employees and cut back its product offerings. Gone were such items as furniture and bed linens, and efforts were concentrated on things like grills, humidifiers, and kitchen appliances. In 1996, he took massive write-offs amounting to $338 million, of which almost $100 million was inventory.

In 1997, it looked like Dunlap was accomplishing another of his patented "miracles." Sales were up 22 percent to $1.168 billion, while income had risen from a loss of $196 million the previous year to a gain of $123 million in 1997. For stockholders this translated into earnings per share of $1.41 from a $2.37 loss in 1996. Table 2.4 shows the trend in revenues and income of Sunbeam through 1997.

In October 1997, after barely a year on the job, Dunlap announced that the turnaround was complete and he was seeking a buyer for Sunbeam. Stockholders had much to be pleased about. From a low of $12 a share in 1996, the price had risen to $50. Unfortunately, there was a serious downside to this, as Dunlap was soon to find. The high price for Sunbeam stock took it out of the range for any potential buyer; $50 gave a market capitalization of $4.6 billion, or four times revenues, a multiple reserved for only a few premier companies. So for the time being, the stockholders were stuck with Dunlap.

Since he was not able to sell the company, Dunlap went on a buying spree. He began talking about his "vision" in such words as "We have moved from constraining categories to expanding categories. Small kitchen appliances become

TABLE 2.4. Trend of Sunbeam Revenues and Income, 1991–1997

	1991	1992	1993	1994	1995	1996	1997
			(Millions $)				
Revenues	886	967	1,066	1,198	1,203	964	1,168
Net Income	47.4	65.6	88.8	107	50.5	−196	123

Source: Company annual reports.

Commentary: Dunlap came on the scene in July 1996, the year that Sunbeam incurred $196 million in losses. The $123 million profit for 1997 showed a remarkable and awesome recovery, and would seemingly make Dunlap a hero with his slash-and-burn strategy. Unfortunately, a reaudit did not confirm these figures. The inaccurate figures were blamed on questionable accounting, including prebooking sales and incorrectly assigning costs to the restructuring. The auditors said that the company had overstated its loss for 1996, and had overstated profits for 1997. The revised figures showed a loss of $6.4 million for 1997 instead of the $123 million profit. (Sources: Martha Brannigan, "Sunbeam Audit to Repudiate '97 Turnaround," *Wall Street Journal*, October 20 1998, p. A3; "Audit Shows Sunbeam's Turnaround Really a Bust," *Cleveland Plain Dealer*, October 21, 1998, pp. 1-C and 2-C.)

kitchen appliances. We'll move from grills to outdoor cooking. Health care moves from just a few products to a broad range of products."[5]

So Dunlap bought Coleman Company, Signature Brands and its Mr. Coffee, and First Alert for an aggregate of approximately $2.4 billion in cash and stock. Part of this was financed with $750 million of convertible debentures, and $60 million of accounts receivable that were sold to raise cash. Critics maintained that he had paid too much, especially the $2.2 billion for money-losing Coleman. The effect of these acquisitions on Sunbeam's balance sheet would have been sobering if any stockholders had looked closely.

When Dunlap took over Sunbeam, it was performing poorly, but had only $200 million in debt. By 1998, Sunbeam was over $2 billion in debt, and its net worth had dropped from $500 million to a negative $600 million.[6]

THE DEBACLE OF 1998, AND THE DEMISE OF DUNLAP

The first quarter of 1998 showed a complete reversal of fortunes. Revenues were down, and a first-quarter loss was posted of $44.6 million—all this far below expectations. Sunbeam's stock price plunged 50 percent, from $53 to $25. By midsummer, it was to reach a low of $4.62.

Dunlap conceded that he and top executives had concentrated their attention too much on "sealing" the acquisitions of Coleman and the two smaller companies, allowing underlings to offer "stupid, low-margin deals" on outdoor cooking grills. He pointed to glitches with new products, a costly recall, and even El Nino. "People don't think about buying outdoor grills during a storm," he said. "Faced with sluggish sales, a marketing executive offered excessive discounts," he further said. More job cuts were promised, through eliminating one-third of the jobs at the newly acquired companies.[7]

On Monday, June 15, 1998, after deliberating over the weekend, Sunbeam's board abruptly fired Al Dunlap having "lost confidence in his ability to carry out the long-term growth potential of the company."[8] A legal fight ensued as to what kind of severance package, if any, Dunlap deserved. A severance package for him would be "obscene—an obscenity on top of an obscenity, capitalism gone crazy," said Michael Cavanaugh, union leader.[9] Other comments were reported in the media; a sampling is in the following Information Box.

---

[5] As quoted in Holman W. Jenkins, Jr., "Untalented Al? The Sorrows of a One-Trick Pony," *Wall Street Journal*, June 24, 1998, p. A19.

[6] Matthew Schifrin, "The Unkindest Cuts," *Forbes*, May 4, 1998, p. 45.

[7] James R. Hagerty and Martha Brannigan, "Sunbeam Plans to Cut 5,100 Jobs as CEO Promises Rebound from Dismal Quarter," *Wall Street Journal*, May 12, 1998, pp. A3 and A4.

[8] Martha Brannigan and James Hagerty, "Sunbeam, Its Prospects Looking Ever Worse, Fires CEO Dunlap, *Wall Street Journal*, June 15, 1998, pp. A1 and A14.

[9] Martha Brannigan and Joann S. Lublin, "Dunlap Faces a Fight over His Severance Pay," *Wall Street Journal*, June 16, 1998, p. B3.

INFORMATION BOX

THE POPULARITY OF "CHAINSAW" AL DUNLAP

Not surprisingly, the slashing policy of Dunlap did not bring him a lot of friends, even though he may have been admired in some circles. Here are some comments reported in the press, immediately after his firing:

"He finally got what he's been doing to a lot of people. It was a taste of his own medicine." (union representative)

"I'm happy the son of a bitch is fired." (former supervisor)

"Somebody at that company finally got some sense." (small-town mayor)

"I couldn't think of a better person to deserve it. It tickled me to death. We may need to have a rejoicing ceremony." (small-town mayor)

"I guess the house of cards came tumbling down ... when you reduce your workforce by 50 percent, you lose your ability to manage." (former plant manager)[10]

Is there a lesson to be learned from such comments? Perhaps it is that the human element in organizations and communities needs to be considered.

Taking a devil's advocate position, defend the philosophy of Dunlap.

Allegations of Fraud

At the end of a three-month audit after Dunlap's departure, auditors discovered accounting irregularities that struck down the amazingly high reported profits for 1997, the first full year of Dunlap's leadership. Rather than a turnaround, the good results came from improper accounting moves that adversely affected the 1996 and 1998 results. The restated numbers showed that Sunbeam actually had a small operating loss in 1997, while 1996 showed a modest profit.

On May 15, 2001, the Securities and Exchange Commission (SEC) formally charged that Dunlap and some of his executives had violated security laws to make Sunbeam look healthier and more attractive for buyers. This was done by fraudulently shifting revenue to inflate losses under the old management and boosting income to create the false impression of the rapid turnaround in financial performance for 1997. Furthermore, revenue was increased in 1997 at the expense of future results by inducing retail customers to sell merchandise more quickly than normal, a practice known as channel stuffing. By the next year, the company was desperate to hide its mounting financial problems and misrepresented its performance and prospects in quarterly reports, bond offerings material, press releases, and statements to stock

---

[10] *Sources:* Thomas W. Gerdel, "Workers at Glenwillow Plant Cheer Firing of 'Chainsaw Al'," *Cleveland Plain Dealer*, June 16, 1998, 2-C; and "No Tears for a Chainsaw," *Wall Street Journal*, June 16, 1998, p. B1.

analysts. Dunlap denied any involvement or knowledge of such matters and said that any accounting changes by the auditors were "judgment calls" on matters subject to interpretation.[11]

The company was forced to restate its financial results for 18 months; it filed for bankruptcy protection in February 2001.

In early September 2002, Dunlap agreed to settle the SEC suit by paying $500,000 and agreeing never to be an officer or director of another public company. He neither admitted nor denied the SEC's claim that he had masterminded the accounting fraud. A month earlier, Dunlap also paid $15 million in settlement of a class-action suit filed by shareholders for their losses due to Sunbeam's fraudulent business practices.[12] All thoughts of a severance package for Dunlap after his firing were long forgotten.

The SEC also came to believe that there was funny accounting at Scott Paper when Dunlap was running it. But this suspicion came at the height of the Enron furor, and the SEC had bigger game to pursue.[13]

Later Developments

Dunlap's exploits brought turmoil to the executive-search industry. Major search firms checking his employment history before he was hired by Sunbeam failed to uncover that he had been fired from two previous positions. He was terminated at Max Phillips & Sons in 1973 after only seven weeks. Three years later, in 1976, he had been fired as president of Nitec Paper Corp. under circumstances of alleged fraud involving misstated profits, a situation not unlike his departure from Sunbeam.

While these episodes took place 20 years before the recruiting for Scott Paper and Sunbeam, and were apparently overlooked because of Dunlap's supposedly strong track record in recent years, significant and pertinent omissions in his job history were not caught by search firms expected to conduct thorough background checks. Along the way, Dunlap erased both jobs from his employment history, and no one who checked his background discovered the omissions.[14]

The Final Fate of Scott and Sunbeam

Dunlap left both Scott and Sunbeam in shambles, easy acquisition preys with their battered stock prices and demoralized organizations. In 1995, Scott Paper was acquired by Kimberly-Clark Corporation, which continues to use the Scott brand name. Scott Paper Limited, formerly a subsidiary, was acquired by Kruger Inc., a Montreal-based pulp and paper producer, and now operates four papermaking mills in Canada.

---

[11] Martha Brannigan, "Sunbeam Slashes Its 1997 Earnings in Restatement," *Wall Street Journal*, October 21, 1998, p. B23.

[12] Jill Barton, "Sunbeam's 'Chain Saw Al' to Pay $500,000 Judgment," Associated Press, as reported in *Cleveland Plain Dealer*, September 5, 2002, p. C1.

[13] Floyd Norris, "Fraud Surrounded 'Chainsaw Al', Yet Little Was Done," *New York Times*, as reported in *Cleveland Plain Dealer*, September 8, 2002, p. G3.

[14] Joann S. Lublin, "Search Firms Have Red Faces in Dunlap Flop," *Wall Street Journal*, July 17, 2001, pp. B1 and B4; and Floyd Norris, "Uncovering Lost Years of Sunbeam's Fired Chief," *New York Times*, reported in *Cleveland Plain Dealer*, July 17, 2001, pp. C1 and C4.

Sunbeam and its ill-fated acquisitions, Coleman, Mr. Coffee, and First Alert, were grabbed at fire-sale prices by Jarden Corporation, headquartered in Rye, New York. Jarden is a global provider of market-leading branded consumer products, firms usually obtained by strategic acquisitions. The company was ranked by the*Wall Street Journal* as the number-one performing stock in the consumer products sector over the last five years, with a compound return for shareholders of 59 percent.[15]

So these brand names appear to now be in strong hands, even though their original stockholders may rue the devastation wrought by Dunlap.

ANALYSIS

Was Dunlap's Management Style of "Slash and Burn" Appropriate?

We see conflicting evidence in the Scott and Sunbeam cases. Without doubt, Dunlap achieved his goal of making Scott an attractive acquisition candidate and thus rewarding shareholders and himself (although suspicions later arose that the sterling results may have been tainted). That he did this so quickly seemed, at the time, a strong endorsement of his strategy for turning around sick companies—simply decimate the organization, sell off all ancillary units, cut costs to the bone, and virtually force the company into increased profitability.

The flaw in this reasoning is that it tends to boost short-term performance at the expense of the longer term. Morale and dedication of surviving employees are devastated. Vision and innovative thinking may be impaired, because the depleted organization lacks time and commitment to deal effectively with more than day-to-day basic operations.

Dunlap's strategy backfired with Sunbeam. When he couldn't sell the company after manipulating the performance statistics for 1997, he was left with a longer-term management challenge that he was by no means equal to. It is ironic that his reputation for turning around sick companies acted against him with Sunbeam. Confident of his ability to quickly turn the company around, investors bid the price up so high that no other firm would buy it. And they were stuck with Dunlap.

Did the Adversity Require Such Drastic Changes?

Sales of Scott and Sunbeam were flat, with profit performance deteriorating. Stock prices were falling counter to a bull market, and investors were disillusioned. Did such situations call for draconian measures?

Neither company was in danger of going belly-up. True, they were off the growth path, but their brands continued to be well regarded by consumers. On the other hand, many firms become too bureaucratic, burdened with high overhead and chained to established policies and procedures. Such organizations desperately need paring down, eliminating bloated staff and executive levels, and—not least—cutting the red tape that destroys flexibility and creativity.

---

[15] *2005 Jarden Annual Report*, p. 2.

The best answer lies in moderation, cutting the deadwood, but not bone and muscle. The worst scenario is to cut with little investigation and reflection. This cost-cutting climate may degenerate to the extent that worthy operations and individuals are cut regardless of their merit and future promise. We would expect better long-term performance in an organization that is not decimated with shattered morale.

Dunlap quickly sold off the S. D. Warren unit of Scott, and this added $1.6 billion to Scott's coffers. The company's former management had invested heavily in what seemed a reasonable diversification into commercial paper, only to encounter an unexpected industry downturn. How could this have been predicted? Was Warren worth keeping? Research and investigation might have found that it was.

Creeping Bureaucracy

Bureaucratic excesses often come about after years of reasonable success and viability. Bureaucracy seems to have been rampant at pre-Dunlap Scott. After all, Dunlap eliminated 71 percent of the headquarters staff and four bookshelves crammed with strategic plans of previous administrations. Too many administrators and staff people bring higher overhead costs than leaner competitors, thus placing the firm at a competitive disadvantage. Some pruning needed to be done.

Was the same thing true at Sunbeam? Perhaps not to the same extent, although without more specific information we cannot know for sure. We can suspect, however, that Dunlap, caught up in his success at Scott, simply transferred his strategy to Sunbeam with no consideration of their differences. We might call this slashing by formula, and it suggests a rigid mind-set devoid of flexibility or compassion.

Paying Too Much for Acquisitions

Dunlap made three questionable acquisitions, and burdened Sunbeam with several billions of dollars of debt. In particular, the $2.2 billion paid for money-losing Coleman, seems to have been a shoot-from-the-hip decision. Such questionable research in an acquisition decision followed the pattern of his personnel-slashing decisions and the quick sale of S. D. Warren. Furthermore, the reckless accumulation of debt for these acquisitions almost suggests a masochistic mind-set. Or did Dunlap think that if the share price now dropped drastically, the firm would become attractive for an acquisition?

Detection of Fraud Destroys Any Perception of Management Competence

Dunlap apparently had a long history of manipulating records to make himself look better. While this fraud pales in comparison with the massive misdeeds of Enron, Tyco, WorldCom, and others because Dunlap's were much smaller firms, it can no more be condoned than their fraudulent practices. Dunlap may yet face jail time, if the SEC decides to turn its attention to less publicized cases.

❊ ❊ ❊

An Invitation to Draw Your Own Analysis and Conclusions

How do you think Scott and Sunbeam's adversities could have been better handled? Use your good judgment, and support your position.

❊ ❊ ❊

WHAT CAN BE LEARNED?

How can we jumpstart a languid organization?—How can we stimulate an organization that is not performing up to potential? Or maybe even inspire it to perform beyond its potential? The challenge is similar to that of motivating a discouraged and downtrodden athletic team to rise up and have faith in itself and recommit itself to quality performance.

In athletics and business, personnel changes are the usual solution. Dunlap introduced the idea of severe downsizing. But this is controversial and, in view of Dunlap's problems with Sunbeam, now almost discredited. How much should be cut, how quickly should changes be made and how sweeping should they be, and what kind of information is most vital in making such decisions? Furthermore, there is the question of morale and its importance in any restoration.

We find more art than science in this mighty challenge of restoration. In particular, the right blend or degree of change is crucial. Let us look at some considerations:

How much do we trim?—In most revival situations, some pruning of personnel and operations is necessary. But how much is too much, and how much is not enough? Is an ax always required for a successful turnaround? One would hope not. Certainly, personnel who are not willing to accept change may have to be let go. And weak people and operations that show little probability of improvement need to be pruned, just as the athlete who can't perform up to expectations may have to be let go. Still, it is often better to wait for sufficient information as to the why of poor performance before assigning blame for the consequences.

How long do we wait?—Mistakes can be made both in taking action before all the facts are known and in waiting too long. If the change maker procrastinates for weeks, an organization that at first was psychologically geared to major change might find it more traumatic and disruptive.

What should be the role of strategic planning?—Major actions should not be taken without some research and planning, but strategic plans too often delay change implementation. They tend to be the products of a fumbling bureaucracy and of some abdication of responsibility. (Despite the popularity of strategic planning, it often is a vehicle for procrastination and blame-dilution; e.g., "I simply followed the strategy recommendations of the consultants.") Dunlap had an aversion to strategic planning; he saw it as indicative of a top-heavy bureaucratic organization. Perhaps he was right, when it is carried to an extreme. But going into an organization and heedlessly slashing positions without considering the individuals involved and their promise is akin to shooting from the hip, with little regard for careful aiming. Then there is the matter of morale.

Morale considerations.—Major restructuring usually is demoralizing to the organizations involved. The usual result is massive layoffs and forced retirements, complete reassignment of people, traumatic personnel and policy changes, and destruction of accustomed lines of communication and authority. This is hardly conducive to preserving stability and morale and any faint spark of teamwork.

Moderation is usually best.—Much can be said for moderation, for choosing the middle position, say, between heavy cost-cutting and light cost-cutting. Of course, the condition of the firm is a major consideration. A business on the verge of bankruptcy, unable to meet its bills, needs drastic measures promptly. But the problems of Scott and Sunbeam were by means so serious. More moderate action could have been taken.

It is better to view the restoration challenge as a *time for building rather than tearing down.* This focuses attention more on the longer view than on short-term results that may come back to haunt the firm as well as the change maker, someone like Dunlap.

Periodic housecleaning produces competitive health.—In order to minimize the buildup of deadwood, all aspects of an organization ought to be objectively appraised from time to time. Weak products and operations should be pruned, unless solid justification exists for keeping them. Justification might include good growth prospects or complementing other products and operations or even providing a desired customer service. In particular, staff and headquarters personnel and functions should be scrutinized, perhaps every five years, with the objective of weeding out the redundant and superfluous. Most important, these axing evaluations should be done objectively, with decisive action taken where needed. Sometimes layoffs result, but they may not be necessary if suitable transfers are possible.

Ethical considerations should be involved in downsizing.—The impact severe downsizing has on people and communities is usually overlooked in making decisions. These matters are considered subordinate to the best interests of the firm (and its investors). Still, ethical issues sometimes arise at the extremes of downsizing. They may pertain not alone to the severity of the job cuts but to how they are handled. For example: Is the decision made with due research and reflection, or is it made quickly, ruthlessly, and perhaps by formula, such as cut 20 percent or 30 percent, or, as was done, 50 percent of Sunbeam's employees? Is any attempt made to help fired employees find alternative employment or retraining? How fair is the severance package and/or the notice of termination?

In Dunlap's handling of Scott Paper and Sunbeam, we see an absence of humanity. This doesn't necessarily make his actions unethical in the eyes of many people, provided that the greater good of the business was fostered. Later developments, however, showed that the business did not benefit, because the reported profitability during the Dunlap years was based on fraudulent accounting.

CONSIDER

Can you add any other learning insights?

QUESTIONS

1. Was Dunlap's management style of "slash and burn" appropriate?
2. Did the adversity require such drastic changes?
3. "Periodic evaluations of personnel and departments aimed at pruning cause far too much harm to the organization. Such axing evaluations should themselves be pruned." Argue this position as persuasively as you can.
4. Now marshal the most persuasive arguments for axing evaluations.
5. Describe an employee's various stages of morale and dedication to the company as it goes through a restructuring, with massive layoffs expected and realized, but with the employee finding himself or herself one of the survivors. How, in your opinion, would this affect productivity and loyalty?
6. Is it likely that any decades-old organization will be bloated with excessive bureaucracy and overhead? Why or why not?
7. What decision guides should be used to determine which divisions and subsidiaries are to be divested or sold?
8. In a time of restructuring, what arguments would you make for keeping your particular business unit? Which of the arguments are likely to be most persuasive to an administration committed to a program of heavy pruning?
9. Do you see any ethical problems in heavy downsizing of a sick company? How about one not so sick?
10. Dunlap quickly sold off the S. D. Warren unit of Scott, and this added $1.6 billion to Scott's coffers. Do you think this was a wise action? Why or why not?

HANDS-ON EXERCISES

1. You are one of the nine high-ranking executives fired by Dunlap his third day on the job. Describe your feelings and your action plan at this point. (If you want to make some assumptions, state them specifically.)
2. You are one of the two high-level executives kept by Dunlap as he sweeps into office. Describe your feelings and your likely performance on the job.
3. You are one of the three outsiders brought into Scott vice-presidential jobs by Dunlap. You have worked for him before and must have impressed him. Describe your feelings and your likely performance. What specific problems, if any, do you foresee?

4. *Devil's advocate position.* Several board members are concerned about the operational and ethical aspects of Dunlap's downsizing plans. Argue as persuasively as you can that these plans are essentially ill-advised and even unethical.

TEAM DEBATE EXERCISES

1. It is early 1996. The board of Sunbeam is considering bringing in a turnaround team. Dunlap's team argues for major and rapid change. Clarence Ripley's advocates more modest immediate changes. Which team should be selected? Array your arguments and present your positions as persuasively as you can. Attack the recommendations of the other side as aggressively as you can. We are talking about millions of dollars in fees and compensation at stake for the winning team.

2. Debate the issue of the ethics of Dunlap's severe downsizing. (For purpose of the debate, disregard the subsequent fraud charges from deceptive accounting.)

INVITATION TO RESEARCH

What has Dunlap been up to since being fired by the Sunbeam board in mid-1998? Has he gracefully retired or is he running scared pending legal charges? Is he still fighting for severance pay? Who replaced Dunlap, and how well is he doing? How is Jarden Corporation—the little-known company with the big consumer brands—doing?

CHAPTER THREE

Perrier: Overreacting to a Crisis

On a Friday in early February 1990, the first news reached Perrier's executive suite that traces of benzene had been found in its bottled water. Ronald Davis, president of the Perrier Group of America, ordered a sweeping recall of all bottles in North America. Just a few days later, Source Perrier S.A., the French parent, expanded the recall to the rest of the world while the company sought to identify the origin of the problem and correct it.

Although at first view the firm's reaction to this unexpected crisis seems zealous and the ultimate in customer concern and social responsibility, a deeper study reveals mistakes of major proportions.

BEFORE

In late 1989, Ronald Davis, 43-year-old president of Perrier's U.S. operations, had reason to be pleased. During his 10-year tenure, Perrier's U.S. sales had risen from $40 million to more than $800 million at retail, which was a significant 25 percent of the company's worldwide sales. He was also proud of his firm's being depicted in a May 1989 issue of *Fortune* as one of the six companies that competed best. *Fortune* captioned: "These are companies you don't want to come up against in your worst nightmare. In the businesses they're in, they amass crushing market share."[1]

A company report in 1987 described the French source, a spring in Vergeze, as follows:

> One of Perrier's identifying qualities is its low mineral (particularly sodium) content. This is because the water spends only a short time filtering through minerals. While flowing underground, the water meets gas flowing vertically through porous volcanic rocks. This is how Perrier gets its fizz ... the company assured us that production has

[1] Bill Saporito, "Companies That Compete Best," *Fortune*, May 22, 1989, pp. 36 ff.

never been limited by the source output. The company sells approximately one billion bottles of which 600 million are exported.[2]

Davis recognized that he was in two businesses, albeit both involved bottled water: (1) sparkling water, in the famous green bottle, which he had successfully positioned as an adult soft drink with a French mystique, an alternative to sodas or alcohol; and (2) still water, a tap-water replacement, with the product delivered to homes and offices and dispensed through water coolers. This latter business he saw as more resembling package delivery such as UPS and Federal Express, and less akin to pushing soft drinks. Accordingly, he emphasized quality of professional service for his route drivers. While best known for the green-bottled Perrier, a mainstay of most restaurants and bars, the company owned nine other brands of bottled water, including Poland Spring, Great Bear, Calistoga, and Ozarka.

At a price 300 to 1,200 times that of tap water, bottled water was the fastest-growing segment of the U.S. beverage industry (see Table 3.1). Perrier controlled 24 percent of the total U.S. bottled-water business. In the imported bottled-water sector, the green bottle dominated with almost 50 percent of the market, although its market share had fallen when new competitors attempted to push into the rapidly growing market. In the 1980s more than 20 firms had taken a run at the green bottle, but without notable success; these included such behemoths as Coca-Cola, PepsiCo, and Anheuser-Busch. Now Davis was more concerned with expanding the category and was trying to shift the brand's image from chic to healthy, so as to make the brand more acceptable to the "masses."

THE CRISIS

The North American Recall

Davis, as he prepared his five-year plan in early 1990, wrote that competing in the 1990s would require not strategic planning, but "flexibility planning."[3] In retrospect, he seemed to be prophetic.

As Davis was fine-tuning his plan, the first news trickled in that a lab in North Carolina had discovered traces of benzene, a carcinogen, in some of the bottles. That same day, February 9, he ordered Perrier removed from distribution in North America.

Source Perrier officials were soon to inform reporters that the company believed the contamination had occurred when an employee mistakenly used cleaning fluid containing benzene to clean the production-line machinery that fills bottles for North America. Frederik Zimmer, managing director of Source Perrier, said that the machinery in question had been cleaned and repaired over the weekend. But at another news conference, Davis announced that he expected Perrier to be off the market for two or three months.

---

[2] B. Facon, *Source Perrier—Company Report*, November 13, 1987, p. 4.
[3] Patricia Sellers, "Perrier Plots Its Comeback," *Fortune*, April 23, 1990, p. 277.

TABLE 3.1. **Average Annual Growth of Beverage Sales,
1985–1989**

Beverage Type	Percent of Growth
Bottled water	+11.1
Soft drinks	+3.2
Milk	+1.5
Tea	+1.2
Beer	+0.4
Coffee	−0.4
Wine	−2.0
Distilled spirits	−2.6

Source: Beverage Marketing Corporation, as reported in *Fortune* April 23, 1990, p. 277.

Such a long absence was seen by some observers as potentially devastating to Perrier, despite its being the front-runner of the industry. Al Ries, chairman of a consulting firm and well-known business writer, was quoted in the *Wall Street Journal* as saying: "If I were Perrier, I would make a desperate effort to reduce that time as much as possible, even if I had to fly it in on 747s from France."[4]

Without doubt, competitors were salivating at a chance to pick up a bigger share of the $2.2 billion annual U.S. sales. Major competitors included Evian and Saratoga, both owned by BSN of France, and San Peligrino, an Italian import. In 1989 PepsiCo had begun test marketing H2OH!, and in January 1990, Adolph Coors Company introduced Coors Rocky Mountain Sparkling Water. The Perrier absence was expected to accelerate their market entry.

Despite competitive glee at the misfortune of Perrier, some in the industry were concerned. They feared that consumers would forsake bottled water altogether, now that its purity was being questioned. Would the public be as willing to pay a substantial premium for any bottled brand? See the following Information Box for a discussion of the relationship between *price* and *quality*.

Worldwide Recall

A few days later, on February 14, the other shoe fell. After reports of benzene being found in Perrier bottles in Holland and Denmark, Source Perrier expanded its North American recall to the rest of the world and acknowledged that all production lines for its sparkling water had been contaminated in recent months by tiny amounts of benzene.

At a news conference in Paris, company officials acknowledged for the first time that benzene occurs naturally in Perrier water and that the current problem had

---

[4] Alix M. Freedman and Thomas R. King, "Perrier's Strategy in the Wake of Recall," *Wall Street Journal*, February 12, 1990, p. B1.

come about because workers failed to replace filters designed to remove it. This was a critical reversal of previous statements that the water was tainted only because an employee had mistakenly used cleaning fluid containing benzene to clean machinery. Zimmer went even further, revealing that Perrier water naturally contains several gases, including benzene, that have to be filtered out.

The company insisted that its famous spring was not polluted. But now questions were being raised about this and other contradictory statements about the problem. For example, how widespread was the contamination? Was benzene a naturally occurring phenomenon, or does it represent man-made pollution? Suspicions were tending toward the man-made origin. While benzene occurs naturally in certain foods, it is more commonly found as a petroleum-based distillate used in many manufacturing processes.

Particularly surprising was the rather nonchalant attitude of Perrier executives. Zimmer, the president, even suggested that "all this publicity helps build the brand's renown."[5]

Ronald Davis was quick to point out that the company did not have to recall its entire 70-million-bottle U.S. inventory. After all, health officials in both the United States and France had noted that the benzene levels in Perrier did not pose significant health risk. The major risk really was to the image of Perrier: it had gone to great lengths to establish its water as naturally pure. And while it was not particularly dangerous, it was certainly not naturally pure—as all the world was now finding out from the publicity. Add to this the undermining of the major attraction of bottled water—the belief that it was safer than ordinary tap water—and the recall and subsequent publicity assumed more ominous proportions.

INFORMATION BOX

IS QUALITY BEST JUDGED BY PRICE?

Consumers today have difficulty in judging the quality of competing products. With their complex characteristics and hidden ingredients, we cannot rely on our own expertise to determine which is best. What sources of information can we use? We can rely on our past experiences with the brand; we can be swayed by our friends and neighbors, we might be influenced by advertising and salespeople (but more and more we become skeptical of their claims); we can study *Consumer Reports* and other consumer-information publications. But all of these sources are flawed in that the experience and information usually are dated, and are a limited sample—usually of one—so that we can seriously question how representative the experience is.

Most people judge quality by price: the higher the price, the better the quality. But a price/quality perception sets us up. While it may be valid, it also may not be. With the

---

[5] Alix M. Freedman and Thomas R. King, "Perrier Expands North American Recall to Rest of Globe," *Wall Street Journal*, February 15, 1990, p. B1.

publicity about the impurity of Perrier, we are brought to the realization that paying many times the price of tap water gives us no assurance of better quality as measured by purity.

Is a price/quality misperception limited mostly to bottled water, do you think? How about liquor? Designer clothes? Perfume?

THE COMEBACK

It took until mid-July before Perrier was again widely available in the United States; this was five months rather than the expected three months. Still, Davis was confident that Perrier's sales would return to 85 percent of normal by the end of 1991. Actually, he was more worried about short supply than demand. He was not sure that the one spring in Vergeze, France, would be able to replace the world's supply before the beginning of 1991.

Davis's confidence in the durability of the demand stemmed from his clout with retailers, where the brand did a majority of its business. He believed that the brand's good reputation, coupled with the other brands the firm distributed that had replaced some of the supermarket space relinquished by Perrier, would bring quick renewal. To help this, he wrote letters to 550 CEOs of retail firms, pledging heavy promotional spending. The marketing budget was increased from $6 million to $25 million for 1990, with $16 million going into advertising and the rest into promotions and special events. A highly visible discount strategy was instituted, which included a buy-two, get-one-free offer. Supermarket prices had dropped, with bottles now going for $0.89 to $0.99, down from $1.09 to $1.19. To win back restaurant business, a new 52-member sales force supplemented distributor efforts. However, a setback of sorts was the Food and Drug Administration order to drop the words "naturally sparkling" from Perrier labels.

Still, a consumer survey indicated that 84 percent of Perrier's U.S. drinkers intended to buy the product again.[6] Davis could also take heart from the less-than-aggressive actions of his competitors during the hiatus. None appeared to have strongly reacted, although most had improved their sales considerably. The smaller competitors proved to be short of money and bottling capacity, and apparently were fearful that a beleaguered Perrier would negatively affect the overall market. Big competitors, such as PepsiCo and Coors, who were introducing other bottled waters, somehow also appeared reluctant to move in aggressively.

CONSEQUENCES

By the end of 1990, however, it was clear that Perrier was not regaining competitive position as quickly and completely as Davis had hoped. Now more aggressive

[6] Sellers, p. 278.

competitors were emerging. Some, such as Saratoga, La Croix, and Quibell, had experienced major windfalls in the wake of the recall. Evian, in particular, a non-sparkling water produced by the French firm BSN S.A., was the biggest winner. Through aggressive marketing and advertising it had replaced Perrier by the end of 1990 as the top-selling imported bottled water.

Perrier's sales had reached only 60 percent of pre-recall levels, and its share of the imported bottled-water market had sunk to 20.7 percent from the 44.8 percent of one year earlier. While the Perrier Group of America expected to report a sales gain for 1990 of 3.7 percent, this was largely because of the strong performance of its domestic brands, Calistoga and Poland Spring.

Particularly worrisome for Davis was the slow return of Perrier to bars and restaurants, which had formerly accounted for about 35 percent of its sales. A sampling of comments by restaurant managers, as reported in such prestigious papers as the *Wall Street Journal* and the *Washington Post*, was far from encouraging. For example:

> The manager of the notable Four Seasons restaurant in New York City said his patrons had begun to shift to San Pellegrino: "I think Perrier is finished," he said. "We can write it off."[7]

> The general manager of the Spago Restaurant in Los Angeles said: "Now consumers have decided that other brands are better or at least as good, so Perrier no longer holds the monopoly on water." And Spago no longer carried Perrier.[8]

> Le Pavillon restaurant in Washington, D.C., switched to Quibell during the recall, and had not gone back to Perrier. "Customers still ask for Perrier, but it's a generic term like Kleenex, and customers aren't unhappy to get a substitute."[9]

EVIAN

David Daniel, 34, had been Evian's U.S. CEO since June 1988. He joined the company in 1987 as the first director of marketing at a time when the American subsidiary was a two-person operation. By 1990 there were 100 employees.

Daniel came from PepsiCo, and his background was marketing. He saw Evian's sphere to be portable water that is good for you, a position well situated to capitalize on the health movement. He was particularly interested in broadening the distribution of Evian, and he sought out soft-drink and beer distributors, showing them that their basic industries were only growing at 1 to 3 percent a year, while bottled water was growing at over 10 percent per year. In 1989, Evian's sales doubled to $65 million, with $100 million in sight for 1990. The attractiveness of such growth to these distributors was of no small moment.

Daniel made Evian the most expensive water on the market. He saw the price as helping Evian occupy a certain slot in the consumer's mind—remember the

---

[7] Freedman and King, "Perrier's Strategy," p. B3.

[8] Alix M. Freedman, "Perrier Finds Mystique Hard to Restore," *Wall Street Journal*, December 1, 1990, p. B1.

[9] Lori Silver, "Perrier Crowd Not Taking the Waters," *Washington Post*, July 4, 1990, p. 1.

price/quality perception discussed earlier. For example, at a fancy grocery in New York City's West Village, a 1-liter bottle of Evian sold for $2.50; the city charged a fraction of a penny for a gallon of tap water[10]—a lot of perceived quality in that! This type of pricing along with the packaging that made Evian portable—plastic nonbreakable bottles and reusable caps—were seen as keys in the selling of bottled water. See the following Issue Box for a discussion of Are Bottled Water Claims Bunk?

Then, late in 1990, Evian benefited greatly from the Persian Gulf War, with free publicity from several newspapers and from all three national TV networks: GIs were shown gulping water from Evian bottles.

UPDATE

Latest on Perrier

Perrier was purchased in 1992 by Nestlé, the world's largest food company. Nestlé, headquartered in Vevey, Switzerland, had more than 500 factories and 230,000 employees worldwide, and produced such brands as Nestlé chocolate, Nescafe coffee, Stouffer's frozen foods, Contadina pastas, and Nestea iced tea products. Perrier, in the Nestlé Waters division, became just one bottled water brand among 70 brands worldwide. This division was the world's largest bottled-water company, although in the last few years, Coca-Cola and Pepsi had been making inroads in the market share position of Nestlé in the United States.

The Industry

Despite occasional publicity about the rip-off perpetrated by the bottled-water industry—charging exorbitant prices for water little better than tap water—public demand continued to grow. By 2003, bottled water had become the fastest-growing sector of the beverage industry. Americans, for example, consumed 60 percent more bottled water in 2002 than they did five years before; the increase was even greater in India and China. Furthermore, bottled water carried hefty markups. Pepsi's Aquafina became the leading brand and was enhanced by a multimillion-dollar promotional campaign. Coke, through acquisitions, amassed such brands as Dannon, Evian, and Dasani, although plans to make Dasani into a global brand were slowed by an aborted launch in Europe after elevated levels of bromate, a cancer-causing substance, were detected in bottles in Britain. The industry leader was Nestlé with its many regional brands, including Poland Spring and Deer Park. Perrier was only a minor player now. By summer 2003, competition among the major beverage companies became more intense as consumers leaned toward less-expensive private-label brands. The result? A water price war. Some would say that it was about time for the exorbitant markups to be curbed.[11]

---

[10] Seth Lubove, "Perched Between Perrier and Tap," *Forbes*, May 14, 1990, p. 120.
[11] Sherri Day, *New York Times*, and reported in *Cleveland Plain Dealer*, "Water War," May 13, 2003, p. C2.

ANALYSIS

Was the massive recall overkill, or was it a prudent necessity? Did it show a concerned corporate citizen, or a panicked executive? Were consumers impressed by the company's responsiveness, or were they more focused on its carelessness? Was the end result on public image favorable, neutral, or unfavorable?

Perrier did not have to recall its product. It was a North Carolina county laboratory that first noticed the excessive amounts of benzene in Perrier and reported its findings to the state authorities. The state agriculture and health departments did not believe that a recall was necessary, although they issued a health advisory warning that Perrier should not be consumed until further tests could be made. It was the state's plan to issue the health advisory that was reported to Davis on the afternoon of the critical day, February 9. He announced the recall later that same day.

ISSUE BOX

ARE BOTTLED-WATER CLAIMS BUNK?[12]

The bottled-water industry came under serious attack in April 1991. As if the massive Perrier recall was not enough, a congressional panel with wide media coverage accused the Food and Drug Administration of "inexcusably negligent and complacent oversight of the bottled-water industry." Despite its high price, the panel said, bottled water may be less safe than tap water. The panel noted that although consumers pay 300 to 1,200 times more for bottled water than for tap water, 25 percent of all bottled water comes from public drinking water sources. For example:

Lithia Springs Water Company touts its "world's finest" bottled mineral water as "naturally pure" and recommends its special Love Water as an "invigorator" before bedtime. But, it was found to be tainted with bacteria.

Artisia Waters, Inc., promoted its "100% pure sparkling Texas Natural Water." But it comes from the same underground source that San Antonio uses for its municipal water supply.

Furthermore, the FDA released a list of 22 bottled-water recalls because of contaminants such as kerosene and mold. For the most part, these went unnoticed by consumers, being overshadowed by the Perrier recall.

Critical studies still found bottled water no cleaner or safer than big-city tap water; a third of the bottles sampled were contaminated by synthetic chemicals, bacteria, and arsenic. Out of the average $1.50 spent for a bottle of water, 90 percent went for bottling, packaging, marketing, retailing, and other expenses. The industry, in defense, claimed that the federal Centers for Disease Control had never found a U.S. outbreak of disease or illness linked to bottled water.

---

[12] *Source:* Examples are taken from Bruce Ingersoll, "FDA Finds Bunk in Bottled-Water Claims," *Wall Street Journal*, April 10, 1991, p. B1. Also, Lance Gay, "Bottlers Tap Profits from Designer Water," Scripps Howard, as reported in *Cleveland Plain Dealer*, September 11, 2001, pp. Al, A8.

At issue: Are we being hoodwinked? Debate two positions: (1) the bottled-water industry really is a throwback to the snake-oil charlatans of the last century; and (2) a few unscrupulous or careless bottlers are denigrating the image of the entire industry, an industry that is primarily focused on health and purity.

We are left to wonder: Perhaps a complete recall was not needed. Perhaps things could have been worked out entirely satisfactorily with less drastic measures. Given that a recall meant a 3- to 5-month absence from the marketplace, should it not have been the action of last resort?

But let us consider Davis's thought process on that ill-fated afternoon in February. He did not know the source of the problem; he certainly had no reason to suspect that it emanated from the spring in southern France or that it was a worldwide problem. He probably considered it of less magnitude. Perhaps he thought of the total North American recall as a gesture showing managements' concern to preserve their products' reputation for health and purity and, yes, its status. Only after the fact do we know the error of this decision: that it was to bring a 5-month absence from the hotly competitive market; that it was to result in revelations far more serious than a simple employee error or even a natural occurrence largely beyond the company's control.

Perhaps Davis's drastic decision was fully justified and prudent. But it was confounded by circumstances he did not envision.

A lengthy absence from the marketplace is a catastrophe of monumental proportions. This is all the more true for a product that is habitually and frequently consumed—in Perrier's case, sometimes several times daily. Such an absence forces even the most loyal customers to establish new behavior patterns, in this case switching brands. Once behavior becomes habituated, at least for some people, a change back becomes less likely. This is especially true if the competitive offerings are reasonably similar and acceptable. Anything that Perrier could have done to lessen the time away from the market would have been desirable—regardless of expense.

Perhaps the biggest problem for Perrier concerned the false impressions, and even outright deception, that the company had conveyed regarding the purity of its product. Now, in the wake of the total recall and the accompanying publicity, all was laid bare. Company officials in France had to own up that the contamination had occurred "in recent months," and not suddenly and unexpectedly on February 9.

But more than this, under intense pressure from the media to explain what had caused the problem, Source Perrier ultimately conceded that its water does not bubble up pure, already carbonated and ready to drink, from its renowned spring in southern France. Instead, contrary to the image that it had spent tens of millions of dollars to promote, the company extracts the water and carbon dioxide gas separately, and must pipe the gas through charcoal filters before combining it mechanically with the water to give the fizz. Without the filters, Perrier water would contain benzene and, even worse, would taste like rotten eggs.

Finally, the public relations efforts were flawed. Source Perrier officials issued a confusing series of public statements and clarifications. Early on, the company tried to maintain Perrier's mystique by concealing information about the cause of the contamination and by blaming it on a mistake by cleaning personnel in using an oily rag, which could have contained some benzene, to wipe equipment used for bottles to be shipped to the United States. But the spokespeople knew the problem was more fundamental than that.

An aura of nonchalance was conveyed by corporate executives and reported in the press. This was hardly in keeping with a serious problem having to do with the possible safety of customers. Furthermore, Source Perrier relied mainly on media reports to convey information to consumers. Misinformation and rumors are more likely with this approach to public relations than in a more proactive strategy of direct company advertisement and statements.

The reputation of Perrier was on the ropes. And top management seemed unconcerned about the probability of severe public-image damage. The following Information Box discusses the topic of ignoring possible image damage.

❖ ❖ ❖

Invitation to Make Your Own Analysis and Conclusions

How do you think Perrier's public relations efforts could have been better handled? Use your good judgment and support your rationale.

❖ ❖ ❖

INFORMATION BOX

IGNORING POSSIBLE NEGATIVE-IMAGE CONSEQUENCES

Several factors induce a firm to ignore public-image considerations until sometimes too late. First, a firm's public image often makes a nonspecific impact on company performance. The cause-and-effect relationship of a deteriorating image is virtually impossible to assess, at least until and unless image problems worsen. Image consequences may be downplayed because management is unable to single out the specific profit impact.

Second, an organization's image is not easily and definitively measured. Although some tools are available for tracking public opinion, they tend to be imprecise and of uncertain validity. Consequently, image studies are often spurned or given short shrift relative to more quantitative measures of performance.

Third, it is difficult to determine the effectiveness of image-building efforts. While firms may spend thousands, and even millions, of dollars for institutional and image-building advertising, measures of the effectiveness of such expenditures are inexact and also of questionable validity. For example, a survey may be taken of attitudes toward a product before and after the image-building campaign is run. If a few more people profess to be favorably disposed toward the company after the campaign than before, this is presumably an indication of its success. But an executive can question whether this really translates into sales and profits.

Given the near impossibility of measuring the effectiveness of image-enhancing promotion, how do you account for the prevalence of institutional advertising, even among firms that have no image problems?

WHAT CAN BE LEARNED?

Beware exiting a market for months, particularly with a regularly consumed product?—Such an absence allows new habits to be established and new loyalties to be created among dealers as well as consumers, and complete recovery may be impossible. This is especially true if competing products are comparable, and if competitors are aggressive in seizing the proffered opportunity. Since a front-runner is a target anyway, abandoning the battlefield simply invites competitive conquest.

Deception discovered destroys a mystique.—No mystique is forever. Consumer preferences change, competitors become more skilled at countering, or perhaps a firm becomes complacent in its quality control or innovative technology. These conditions nibble away at a mystique and eventually destroy it. In the case of Perrier, long-held beliefs in the healthfulness and purity of the product were suddenly revealed to be false—and its advertising was shown to be less than candid and even deceptive. Similarly, any mystique may come tumbling down, unlikely ever to be regained. This scenario can only be avoided if the publicity about a deception or misdeed is not widespread. But with a popular product such as Perrier, publicity reaches beyond business journals to the popular press. Such is the fate of large, well-known firms.

Consumers often have a price/quality misperception.—Without doubt, most consumers judge quality by price: the higher the price, the higher the quality. Is a $2.50 liter of Evian better quality than a gallon of tap water costing a fraction of a cent? Only maybe. But is it a hundred times better? And yet many people embrace the misconception that price is the key indicator of quality, and are consequently taken advantage of every day.

A few unscrupulous firms can damage an industry catering to health?—The general public is vulnerable to claims for better health, beauty, and youthfulness. We want to reach out, hopefully, to achieve what is promised about our important personal concerns. We become gullible in our desire to find ways to change our condition. And so we have been victims of quacks and snake-oil charmers through the ages. Governmental agencies try to exercise strong monitoring in these areas, but budgets are limited, and all claims cannot be investigated. As congressional scrutiny has revealed, the bottled-water industry had long been overlooked by governmental watchdogs. Now this may change, perhaps at least partly because of the Perrier recall. Still, one wonders whether there has been any positive long-term effect.

Should an organization have a crisis-management team?—Perrier did a poor job of crisis management. Would a formal organizational unit devoted to dealing with catastrophes have handled things better than top executives unskilled in such matters? The issue can hardly be answered simply and all-inclusively. Crises occur rarely; and some organizations may never experience a serious crisis. This means that the crisis team would have to be composed of executives and staff who have other primary responsibilities, so their decisions and actions under fire might be no better than less formal arrangements. For severe crises—and Perrier's was certainly that—top executives who bear the ultimate responsibility have to be the final decision makers. Some will be cooler under fire than others, but this usually cannot be fully ascertained until the crisis occurs. More desirable for most organizations would be contingency plans formulated in advance for various foreseeable occurrences, including the worst scenarios. With action plans drawn up under more normal conditions, better judgments are likely to result.

CONSIDER

Can you think of other learning insights from this case?

QUESTIONS

1. Discuss the desirability of Perrier's price-cutting during its comeback.
2. Who are the primary customers for Perrier? For Evian? For other bottled waters? Are these segments likely to have an enduring commitment to bottled water?
3. Why do you think the big firms, such as Coca-Cola, PepsiCo, and Coors, were so slow to enter the bottled-water market?
4. Are you a regular user of bottled water? What induces you to buy it?
5. "The success of bottled water in the United States, unlike the situation in many countries of the world where bottled water is often essential for good health, attests to the power of advertising." Evaluate this statement.
6. Is the appeal of bottled water largely attributable to an image of sophistication and status?

HANDS-ON EXERCISES

1. Put yourself in the position of Ronald Davis on the afternoon of February 9, 1990. The first report of benzene found by a Carolina lab has just come in. What would you do? Be as specific as you can, and describe the logic behind your decisions.
2. How would you attempt to build up or resurrect the mystique of Perrier after the recall?

TEAM DEBATE EXERCISES

1. Debate the issue of extreme measures (a massive recall) undertaken in a product-safety situation versus more moderate reactions (a modest recall). Consider as many aspects of this issue as you can, and make educated

judgments of various probable consumer and governmental reactions. (Do not be swayed by what actually happened; this extreme reaction may be criticized.)

2. Debate Ronald Davis's decision to discount prices as he sought to reestablish Perrier in the marketplace.

INVITATION TO RESEARCH

Assess the popularity of bottled water today? Has it increased or lessened since the events described? How prominent does Perrier seem to be in grocery stores, in restaurants, at sporting and outdoors events? From your observation, what are the characteristics of the major customers for bottled water? Are they younger, more elderly, more athletic, more affluent . . .?

Ford Explorers with Firestone Tires: Ill-Handling a Killer Scenario

A product defect that leads to customer injuries and deaths through manufacturer carelessness constitutes the most serious crisis that any firm can face. In addition to destroying brand reputation, ethical and social responsibility abuses are involved, and then legal and regulatory consequences. Managing such a crisis becomes far worse, however, when the manufacturer knew about the problems and concealed or denied them.

The case in this chapter is unique in that two manufacturers were culpable, but each blamed the other. As a result, Firestone and Ford were savaged by the press, public opinion, the government, and a host of salivating lawyers. Massive tire recalls destroyed the bottom line and even endangered the viability of Bridgestone/Firestone; sales of the Ford Explorer, the world's best-selling sport-utility vehicle (SUV), plummeted 22 percent in April 2001 from the year before, even as domestic sales of SUVs overall climbed 9 percent.

A HORROR SCENARIO

Firestone tires mounted on Ford Explorers were linked to more than 200 deaths from rollovers in the United States, as well as more than 60 in Venezuela and a reported 14 in Saudi Arabia and neighboring countries. A widely publicized lawsuit took place in Texas in the summer of 2001. It was expected that the jury would determine who was most to blame for the deaths and injuries from Explorers outfitted with Firestone tires.

Ford settled its portion of the suit for $6 million one month before the trial began. While Firestone now became the sole defendant, the jurors were also asked to assess Ford's responsibility for the accident.

The lawsuit was brought by the family of Marisa Rodriguez, a mother of three who was left brain-damaged and paralyzed after the steel belts and treads of a

Firestone tire tore apart during a trip to Mexico in March 2000. As a result, the Explorer rolled over three times, crushing the roof above Mrs. Rodriguez in the rear seat; her husband, Joel, who was asleep in the front passenger seat, was also injured. The live pictures of Mrs. Rodriguez in a wheelchair received wide TV coverage.

After the federal court jury in the Texas border town of McAllen had been deadlocked for four days, a settlement was reached with Bridgestone/Firestone for $7.85 million. (The plantiffs originally had asked for $1 billion.)

The out-of-court settlements with Ford and Firestone did not resolve the issue of who was most to blame for this and the hundreds of other injuries and deaths. But a lawyer for the Rodriguez family predicted that sooner or later a verdict would emerge: "There's going to be trials and there's going to be verdicts. We've got Marisa Rodriguezes all over the country."[1]

ANATOMY OF THE PROBLEM

The Ford/Firestone Relationship

Ford and Firestone had a long, intimate history. In 1895, Harvey Firestone sold tires to Henry Ford for his first automobile. In 1906, the Firestone Tire & Rubber Company won its first contract for Ford Motor Company's mass-produced vehicles, a commitment that continued through the decades.

Henry Ford and Harvey Firestone became business confederates and best friends who went on annual summer camping trips, riding around in Model T's along with Thomas Edison and naturalist John Burroughs. Further cementing the relationship, in 1947 Firestone's granddaughter, Martha, married Ford's grandson, William Clay Ford, in a dazzling ceremony in Akron, Ohio, that attracted a Who's Who of dignitaries and celebrities. Their son, William Clay Ford Jr., was to become Ford's chairman.

In 1988, Tokyo-based Bridgestone Corporation bought Firestone, 20 years after the Japanese company sold its first tires in the United States under the Bridgestone name. In 1990, Ford introduced the Explorer SUV to replace the Bronco II in the 1991 model year. It became the nation's top-selling SUV, and the Explorer generated huge profits for more than a decade. Bridgestone/Firestone was the sole supplier of the Explorer's tires.

The Relationship Worsens

The first intimation of trouble came in 1999, when, after 14 fatalities occurred, Ford began replacing the tires of Explorers in Saudi Arabia and nearby countries. The tire failures were blamed on hot weather and under-inflation. At the time, overseas fatalities did not have to be reported to U.S. regulators, so the accidents received scant attention in the media.

---

[1] "Firestone Agrees to Pay $7.5 Million in Tire Suit," *Cleveland Plain Dealer*, August 25, 2001, pp. A1 and A13; Milo Geyelin and Timothy Aeppel, "For Firestone, Tire Trial Is Mixed Victory," *Wall Street Journal*, August 27, 2001, pp. A3 and A4.

The media caught the scent in early 2000 when television reports in Houston revealed instances of tread separation on Firestone's ATX tires, and the National Highway Traffic Safety Administration (NHTSA) started an investigation. By May, four fatalities had been reported, and NHTSA expanded the investigation to 47 million ATX, ATXII, and Wilderness tires.

In August 2000, as mounting deaths led to increasing pressure from consumers and multiple lawsuits, Firestone voluntarily recalled 14.4 million 15-inch radial tires because of tread separation. The plant in Decatur, Illinois, was implicated in most of these accidents. Ford and Firestone agreed to replace the tires, but estimated that 6.5 million were still on the road. Consumer groups sought a still wider recall, charging that Explorers with other Firestone tire models were also prone to separation leading to rollovers.

In December 2000, Firestone issued a report blaming Ford for the problems, claiming that the Explorer's design caused rollovers with any tread separations. On April 20, 2001, Ford gave NHTSA a report blaming Firestone for flawed manufacturing.

In May 2001, Ford announced that it was replacing all 13 million Firestone Wilderness AT tires remaining on its vehicles, saying that the move was necessary because it had no confidence in the tires' safety. "We feel it's our responsibility to act immediately," said Ford CEO Jacques Nasser. Ford claimed that the move would cost the automaker $2.1 billion, although it hoped to get this money back from Firestone.

Firestone Chairman and CEO John Lampe defended his tires, saying "no one cares more about the safety of the people who travel on our tires than we do. When we have a problem, we admit it and we fix it."[2]

The Last Days

It is lamentable when a long-lasting close relationship is severed. But on May 21, 2001, Lampe abruptly ended the 95-year association, accusing Ford of refusing to acknowledge safety problems with its vehicles, thus putting all the blame on Firestone.

The crisis had been brewing for months. Many Firestone executives did not trust Ford. Even simple exchanges of documents were rancorous, and there were major disagreements in interpreting the data. Firestone argued that tread-separation claims occurred ten times more frequently on Ford Explorers than on Ranger pickups with the same tires, thus supporting its contention that the Explorer was mostly at fault. Ford rejected Firestone's charges about the Explorer, saying that for ten years the model "has ranked at or near the top in terms of safety among the 12 SUVs in its class." It stated that 2.9 million Goodyear tires mounted on more than 500,000 Explorers had "performed with industry-leading safety."[3]

The climax came at a May 21 meeting attended by Lampe and a contingent of Ford officials. Each side maintained that the other was to blame. Discussions broke

[2] Ed Garsten, Associated Press, as reported in "Ford Tire Tab $2.1 Billion," *Cleveland Plain Dealer*, May 23, 2001, pp. 1-C and 4-C.
[3] Timothy Aeppel, Joseph B. White, and Stephen Power, "Firestone Quits as Tire Supplier to Ford," *Wall Street Journal*, May 22, 2001, pp. A3 and A12.

down regarding the possibility of working together to examine Explorer's role in the accidents. At that point, Lampe ended their relationship. Each party was left to defend itself before Congress and the court of public opinion, and ultimately a siege of lawsuits. See the Information Box: How Emotion Influences Company Reputation for a discussion of how emotion drives consumers' perceptions, good and bad, of companies.

INFORMATION BOX

HOW EMOTION INFLUENCES COMPANY REPUTATION

The second annual corporate-reputation survey conducted by the Harris market-research firm and the Reputation Institute, involving 26,011 respondents, found that Emotional Appeal—trust, admiration and respect, and generally good feelings toward the firm—was the driving force in how people rated companies. The survey found that advertising did not necessarily change opinions. For example, despite a $100 million advertising campaign about what a good citizen Philip Morris Company was in feeding the hungry and helping victims of domestic violence, the company still received low marks on trust, respect, and admiration. But the most recent poll showed that Philip Morris no longer had the worst reputation in America. This distinction went to Bridgestone/Firestone, with Ford receiving the lowest reputation rating among auto companies.[4]

Once lost, a company's reputation or public image is usually difficult to regain. For example, Exxon Mobil's reputation for environmental responsibility was still given low grades more than a decade after the destructive Alaskan oil spill involving the tanker *Exxon Valdez*.

Do you think Firestone's quest to improve its reputation should face the same problems as were caused by the *Exxon Valdez* accident? Why or why not?

Advantage to Competitors

Major competitors Goodyear and Michelin, as well as smaller competitors and private-label tire makers, predictably raised tire prices 3 to 5 percent. Goodyear then tried to increase production robustly to replace the millions of Firestone tires recalled or soon to be, but it was trying to avoid overtime pay to bolster profits. In a written statement, Goodyear said, "We are working very closely with Ford to jointly develop an aggressive plan to address consumers' needs as quickly as possible."[5]

The decrease in auto sales in the slowing economy that began in 2000 had led Goodyear to production cutbacks, including cutting 7,200 workers worldwide as it

---

[4] Ronald Alsop, "Survey: Emotion Drives Public Perception of Companies," *Wall Street Journal*, February 11, 2001, p. 5-H.

[5] Thomas W. Gerdel, "Goodyear, Michelin Raising Consumer Tire Prices," *Cleveland Plain Dealer*, May 23, 2001, pp. 1-C and 4-C.

posted an 83 percent decline in profits in 2000. Now it was challenged to gear up to handle the windfall of the ending of the Ford/Firestone relationship.

WHERE LIES THE BLAME?

In years to come, courts and lawyers will sort out the culpability controversy. The outcome is in doubt, and the finger of blame points to a number of sources, though the weighting is uncertain. While Ford and Firestone should share major responsibility, NHTSA and the motoring public were hardly blameless.

Ford

The question of whether the design of Ford's Explorer made it more prone to rollover than other SUVs would be decided in the courtroom. One thing seemed clear: Ford recommended a low inflation level for its Firestone-equipped tires, and this subjected them to more flex in the sidewall and greater heat buildup. With high-speed driving in hot weather, a vehicle like the Explorer, with its high profile, would be more prone to roll over with any tire trouble, especially with inexperienced drivers. For example, Ford's recommended tire pressure was 26 pounds, and this would bring the car's center of gravity lower to the ground. This seems good, but only at first look. Required by the government, the Uniform Tire Quality Grade (UTQG) provides comparative manufacturer information. Tires are subjected to a series of government-mandated tests that measure performance in tread wear, traction, and temperature resistance. All testing is done by the tire manufacturer. Ford was alone among SUV makers in equipping the Explorer with grade C tires rather than the more heat-resistant B tires that were the near-universal standard on most sport utility vehicles. To make the C grade, tires had to withstand only two hours at 50 mph when properly inflated and loaded, plus another 90 minutes at speeds up to 85 mph. This standard dated back to 1968, when sustained highway speeds were much lower than today. Now, people drive hour after hour at speeds well above 70 mph.

The C-rated Firestones were used on millions of Ford pickup trucks without problems. However, in contrast with SUVs, most pickup trucks are not taken on long-haul, high-speed road trips filled with family and luggage.

Ford CEO Jacques Nasser justified replacing 13 million tires by claiming that the Firestones were failing at a rate higher than the Goodyears mounted on 2 million Explorers in the mid-1990s. But the Goodyears carried the B rating. The dangerous effect of heat buildup was shown by the fact that most Explorer accidents took place in hot Southern states and in hot-climate countries with high speed limits.

Ford engineers should have been aware of these dangers, if not immediately, then certainly after a few years—and should have adapted the Explorer to customers who drive fast, pay little attention to tire maintenance, and are prone to panic with a blowout and flip the car. Unfortunately, the American legal environment and the tort system make the manufacturer vulnerable to lawsuits and massive damage claims should it acknowledge in retrospect that it had made a bad mistake in its tire selection and pressure recommendation. So the temptation was to blame the tiremaker, and spend millions turning it into a media monster.

Bridgestone/Firestone

Firestone tires were far from blameless. Early on, investigations of deadly vehicle accidents linked the causes to tire failure, notably due to shoddy manufacturing practices at Firestone's Decatur plant; the 6.5 million tire recall by Firestone was of the 15-inch radial ATX and ATX11 tires and Wilderness AT tires made in this plant. In June 27, 2001, the company announced that the plant would be closed. But Firestone's poorly controlled manufacturing process proved not to be limited to this single operation. See the Information Box: A Whistleblower "Hero" about the whistleblower who exposed another plant's careless disregard of safe tire production.

INFORMATION BOX

A WHISTLEBLOWER "HERO"

Alan Hogan was honored in June 2001 by the Civil Justice Foundation for exposing how employees at a Bridgestone/Firestone plant in North Carolina routinely made defective tires. This consumer advocacy group, founded by the Association of Trial Lawyers of America, bestowed similar "community champion" awards on tobacco whistle-blower Jeffrey Wigand and on Erin Brockovich, who exposed hazardous waste dangers and was the subject of a popular movie.

With his insider's knowledge of shoddy tire-building practices, Hogan was widely credited with bringing about the first recall. He testified at a wrongful-death lawsuit in 1999 that he had witnessed the crafting of countless bad tires built from dried-out rubber with wood bits, cigarette butts, screws, and other foreign materials mixed in. Hogan, who had quit the company and opened an auto-body shop in his hometown, became a pariah among many people for his revelations about the community's major employer, and company attorneys looked into his work and family life for anything they could use to discredit him. They tried to portray him as a disgruntled former employee. An anonymous fax accused him of spreading "vicious, malicious allegations" about the company. Employees were warned not to do business with car dealerships that dealt with his body shop.

But Hogan persevered, and eventually won recognition and accolades. "I'm surprised it took this long," he said. "Maybe now people will see this is the way it's been since 1994, 1995, when they started covering this up." His whistle-blowing credentials were now in high demand as an expert witness in other lawsuits.[6]

Do you see any reasons why Hogan may not have been completely objective in his whistle-blowing efforts?

---

[6] Dan Chapman, Cox News, as reported in "Firestone Ex-Worker Called Hero in Recall," *Cleveland Plain Dealer*, May 29, 2001, p. 1-C.

Still, there were contrary indications that the fault was not all Bridgestone/Firestone's, and that Ford shared the blame. General Motors had detected no problems with the Firestones it used as standard equipment in 14 of its models. In fact, in July 2001 GM named Firestone as its supplier of the year for the sixth consecutive time. Honda of America was also loyal to Firestones, which it used on best-selling Civics and Odysseys.[7]

On September 14, 2001, months after all Firestones had been recalled from Ford Explorers, an apparently skilled driver, a deputy bailiff driving home from court, was killed when he lost control of his Explorer and it flipped over a guardrail, slid down an embankment, and rolled over several times.[8]

Government

Public Citizen and other consumer groups were critical of the government, maintaining that it was too slow in completing its initial Firestone investigation and had dragged its feet about investigating the Explorer. A Public Citizen study saw the use of the specific Firestone tires as coming from cost- and weight-saving miscalculations and gambles by Ford, "making what was already a bad problem into a lethal one." It was not just the companies that were at fault; federal regulators were lax in not toughening standards on SUVs to prevent roofs from collapsing in rollover crashes. "The human damage caused is barbaric and unnecessary," the study concluded.[9]

The Driver

There is no doubt that the Explorer drivers contributed to the accidents. They did so by neglecting tire pressure so that it was often below even Ford's low recommendations, by heavily loading their vehicles, and by driving too fast over long periods so that heat could build up to danger levels. Added to this, the lack of driving expertise to handle emergency blowouts was often the fatal blow. Yet, could a carmaker, tiremaker, or government agency really expect the average consumer to act with strict prudence? Precautions, be they car standards or tire standards, needed to be imposed with the worst consumer-behavior scenarios in mind.

CONSEQUENCES

Each company maneuvered to cast blame primarily on the other. Ford announced in May 2001 that it would triple the size of the Firestone recall—a $2.8 billion prospect, a cost Ford wanted to shift to the tire maker. Firestone, at that point, severed its long relationship with Ford by refusing to supply the company with more tires.

---

[7] Garsten, "Ford Tire Tab," pp, C1 and C4; Alison Grant, "Bridgestone/Firestone Faces Struggle to Survive," *Cleveland Plain Dealer*, August 5, 2001, pp. H1 and H5.
[8] "SUV Flips, Killing Deputy Bailiff, 24," *Cleveland Plain Dealer*, September 15, 2001, p. B5.
[9] Alison Grant, "Government, Goodyear Still Navigating a Bumpy Road," *Cleveland Plain Dealer*, August 5, 2001, p. H5.

CEO Lampe maintained that Ford was trying to divert scrutiny of the rollover-prone Explorer by casting doubt on the safety of Firestone tires.

Both parties suffered in this name-calling and buck-passing. By the fall of 2001, sales of Explorers were off sharply, as consumers wondered whether the hundreds of Explorer crashes were due to the SUV's design, or Firestone tires, or both. Ford lost market share to Toyota and other foreign rivals in the SUV market. In July 2001, it reported its first loss from operations since 1992. It also faced 200 product-liability lawsuits involving Explorer rollovers. Still, Ford was big enough to absorb problems with one of its models.

Smaller Bridgestone/Firestone faced a more dangerous situation. In 2000, its earnings dropped 80 percent, reflecting the cost of recalling millions of tires as well as a special charge to cover legal expenses. The Firestone unit, which accounted for 40 percent of the parent company's revenue, posted a net loss of $510 million after it took a $750 million charge for legal expenses. Sales were forecast to plunge 20 percent in 2001, and the cost of lawsuits could eventually reach billions of dollars, to the point where some analysts doubted that Firestone could survive as a brand.[10]

Options Firestone Faced

The esteemed Firestone brand, launched more than a century before, had been the exclusive tire supplier to the Indy 500. Now its future was in doubt, despite decades of brand loyalty. The brand faced three options:

Option 1. Some thought the company should try to deemphasize Firestone and push business to the Bridgestone label. This would likely result in some loss of market segmentation and the flexibility of having distinct low-end, mid-level, and premium tires. Others thought that such a halfhearted approach would simply prolong the agony of hanging on to a besmirched brand.

Option 2. Obliterate the Firestone name, since it was irretrievable. "Firestone should just give up," said one public relations analyst. "They've damaged themselves so severely." A University of Michigan Business School professor called the brand dead: "Can you imagine any jury claiming that somebody who's suspected of building bad tires is innocent?"[11]

Option 3. Try to salvage the brand. Some questioned the wisdom of abandoning the century-old Firestone name, with its rich tradition and millions of cumulative advertising dollars. They thought that with money, time, and creative advertising, Bridgestone/Firestone should be able to restore its image. But to do so, Roger Blackwell of Ohio State University argued, the company needed to make an admission of regret: "The lawyers will tell them not to admit blame... But they need to do what Johnson & Johnson did when someone was killed by their product [cyanide-tainted Tylenol]. A credible spokesman got on TV and had tears in his eyes when he spoke." An independent tire dealer who

---

[10] Akiko Kashiwagi, "Recalls Cost Bridgestone Dearly; Firestone's Parent's Profit Drops 80%," *Washington Post*, Feb. 23, 2001, p. E03.
[11] Grant, "Struggle to Survive," p. H5.

lost $100,000 in sales in 2000, but was confident of a rebound, supported this option: "The American public is quick to forget," he said.[12]

POSTMORTEM

Buyers of Ford Explorers with Firestone tires had for years faced a far higher risk of death and injury, both in the United States and abroad, than they would have from other models. The *New York Times* reported that the tire defects, and their contribution to accidents, were known in 1996.[13] Not until August 1999 did Ford begin replacing tires on Explorers in Saudi Arabia, calling the step a "customer notification enhancement program." Fourteen fatalities had already been reported. Not until March 2000, after television reports of problems, did federal regulators and the two manufacturers take all this seriously.

Ford, in its concern with the bottom line, stubbornly refused to admit that anything was wrong with its SUV; meanwhile, Firestone couldn't seem to clean up its act in the Decatur plant and in some other plants where carelessness and lack of customer concern prevailed. Minor ethical abuses became major when lives were lost, but the foot-dragging continued until lawyers came on the scene. Then the two companies tried to cover their mistakes with finger-pointing, while a vulnerable public continued to be in jeopardy. Throughout this whole time, saving lives did not apparently have a very high priority. Eventually the consequences came back to haunt the companies, with hundreds of lawsuits, millions of tire recalls, and denigration of their public images.

How could this have been permitted to happen? After all, those in top management were not deliberately vicious men. They were well intentioned, albeit badly misguided. Perhaps their worst sin was first to ignore the increasingly apparent serious risk factors and then refuse to admit anything was wrong and try to cover it up.

Part of the problem was the stubborn mindset of top executives that nothing was wrong: a few accidents, in their view, reflected driver carelessness, not a defective product. Neither company would assume the worst scenario: that this was a dangerous product used on a dangerous product that was killing people, and neither Ford nor Firestone could escape blame.

Forty years before, a somewhat similar situation occurred with the GM Corvair, a rear-engine car that exhibited instability under extreme cornering conditions causing it to flip over. Ralph Nader's reputation as a consumer advocate came from his condemnation of this "unsafe" car with a best-selling book, *Unsafe at Any Speed*. But GM executives refused to admit there was any problem—until eventually the evidence was overwhelming, lawsuits flourished, and the federal government stepped in with the National Traffic and Motor Vehicle Safety Act of 1966. Among other things, the act required manufacturers to notify customers of any defects or flaws later discovered in their vehicles.

[12] *Ibid.*

[13] Keith Bradsher, "SUV Tire Defects Were Known in '96 But Not Reported; 190 Died in Next 4 years," *New York Times*, June 24, 2001, p. 1 N.

The GM executives, like those of Ford and Firestone 40 years later, were honorable men. Yet, something seems to happen to the conscience and the moral sensitivity of top executives. They commission actions in their corporate personas that they would hardly dream of doing in their private lives. John DeLorean, former GM executive, was one of the first to note this dichotomy:

> These were not immoral men who were bringing out this car the Corvair. These were warm, breathing men with families and children who as private individuals would never have approved [this project] for a minute if they were told, "You are going to kill and injure people with this car." But these same men, in a business atmosphere, where everything is reduced to terms of costs, corporate goals, and production deadlines, were able to approve a product most of them wouldn't have considered approving as individuals.[14]

We have to ask: Why this lockstep obsession with sales and profits at all costs? See the Information Box: The "Groupthink" Influence on Unethical Behavior for a discussion of this issue.

INFORMATION BOX

THE "GROUPTHINK" INFLUENCE ON UNETHICAL BEHAVIOR

The callousness about "killer" cars would, as John DeLorean theorized, probably never have prevailed if an individual was making the decision outside the corporate environment. But bring in *groupthink*, which is decision by committee, and add to it a high degree of organizational loyalty (versus loyalty to the public interest), and such callousness can manifest itself. Why are the moral standards of groupthink often so much lower than individual moral standards?

Perhaps the answer lies in the "pack mentality" that characterizes certain committees or groups highly committed to organizational goals. All else then becomes subordinated to these goals, making for a single-minded perspective. In any committee, individual responsibility is diluted because decisions are made by the whole membership. Furthermore, without the contrary arguments of a strong devil's advocate to present the opposing viewpoint, sometimes simply to be sure that all sides of an issue are considered, a follow-the-leader syndrome can take place, with no one willing to oppose the majority view.

But there is more to it than that. Chester Barnard, a business executive, scholar, and philosopher, noted the paradox: We all have a number of private moral codes that affect our behaviour in different situations, and these codes are not always compatible. Codes for private life, regarding family and religion, may be far different from codes for business life. Throughout the history of business, it has not been unusual to find that the scrupulous and God-fearing churchgoer is far different when conducting business during

---

[14] J. Patrick Wright, *On a Clear Day You Can See General Motors*, Grosse Point, Mich.: Wright Enterprises, 1979, pp. 5–6.

the week: A far lower ethical standard prevails during the week than on the Sabbath. Nor has it been unusual to find that people can be paragons of love, understanding, and empathy with their families but be totally lacking in such qualities with employees or customers.[15] We might add that even tyrants guilty of the most extreme atrocities, such as Hitler and Saddam Hussein, have been known to exude great tenderness and consideration for their intimates.

What does it take for a person to resist and not accept the majority viewpoint? What do you think would be the characteristics of such a person? Do you see yourself as such a rebel?

LATER DEVELOPMENTS

On October 30, 2001, Ford Motor Company announced that Jacques Nasser would be replaced as CEO by William Clay Ford Jr.—the first Ford family member to be in charge since 1979. Ford is the son of William Clay Ford Sr., who is the grandson of founder Henry Ford and brother of Henry Ford II. Nasser had been under pressure for months because of Ford's loss of market share and tumbling profitability and the adverse publicity of the Explorer.

In December 2001, the newly designed 2002 Ford Explorer received a top score in a crash test by the Insurance Institute for Highway Safety. Changes in the 2002 Explorer to improve passenger protection were part of the automaker's "commitment to continuous improvements," a Ford spokesperson said.[16]

Firestone also bounced back, despite dire predictions of the brand's demise as its U.S. operations suffered a $1.7 billion loss in 2001 on top of a $510 million loss in 2000. Some called this "the most unlikely brand resurrection in marketing history." Much of the credit for the company's survival was credited to Firestone CEO John Lampe, who crisscrossed the country giving pep talks to hundreds of Firestone's 10,000 dealers. These dealers became fiercely loyal at a time when 75 percent of tire buyers were influenced by dealer recommendations, according to industry estimates. Several splashy new tires were brought out, including the Firehawk Indy 500, which became a hit with racing fans. "We are selling as many Firestone tires as we've ever sold," one large dealer noted.

With communication improving between the two companies, Lampe could see signs that the rift with Ford was ending, and William Clay Ford even mentioned his great-grandfather Harvey Firestone in a Ford commercial. "It was a very honest thing to do. He didn't have to do that," Lampe observed.[17]

---

[15] Chester I. Barnard, *The Functions of the Executive*, Cambridge, Mass.: Harvard University Press, 1938, p. 263.

[16] Christopher Jensen, *Cleveland Plain Dealer*, December 12, 2001, pp. C1 and C4.

[17] Todd Zaun, "Defying Expectations, Bridgestone Embarks on a Turnaround," *Wall Street Journal*, March 12, 2002, p. A21; Jonathan Fahey, "Flats Fixed," *Forbes*, May 27, 2002, pp. 40–41.

✧ ✧ ✧

Invitation to Make Your Own Analysis and Conclusions

Design a program for pursuing a better relationship between Ford and Firestone executives during the crisis. How would you sell your program to the executives? What do you think would be the likely result? Are there any worthwhile learning experiences that could come from this?

✧ ✧ ✧

WHAT CAN BE LEARNED?

A firm today must zealously guard against product-liability suits.— Any responsible executive needs to recognize that product-liability suits, in today's litigious environment, can bankrupt a firm. The business arena has become more risky, more fraught with peril for the unwary or the naively unconcerned. Consequently, firms need to do careful and objective testing of any product that can affect customer health and safety. Sometimes testing may require that production be delayed, even if the competition gains some advantage from the delay. The risks of putting an unsafe product on the market outweigh competitive concerns.

Suspicions and complaints about product safety must be thoroughly investigated.— We should learn from this case that immediate and thorough investigation of any suspicions or complaints is essential, regardless of the confidence management may have in the product or of the glowing recommendations of persons whose objectivity could be suspect. To procrastinate or ignore complaints poses risks that should be unacceptable.

Sometimes the root of the problem is not obvious, or is more complex than first thought. In the Ford/Firestone case, objective research should have focused on both the Explorer and the Firestone tires, and on how the situation could be remedied to minimize rollovers and save lives.

Health and safety of customers are entirely compatible with a firm's well-being.— It is a lose/lose situation if this is ignored: The customer is jeopardized, but eventually the firm is too, as lawsuits grow and damages increase. Why, then, the corporate mindset of "us versus them"? There should be no conflicting goals. Both win when customer welfare is maximized.

In the worst scenario, go for a conciliatory salvage strategy.—Ford and Firestone faced a crossroads by late 1999 and early 2000. Reports of fatalities linked to Ford Explorers and Firestone tires were trickling in, the first occurring in the hot climate of Saudi Arabia, and in a matter of months these were to become a flood. How should a company react?

A salvage strategy can attempt to tough it out, trying to combat the bad press, denying culpability, blaming someone else, and resorting to the strongest possible legal defense. This essentially is what Ford opted to do—it blamed Firestone for everything and spent millions advertising to promote this contention.

Firestone was more vulnerable because its shredded tires could hardly be denied, and it was forced to recall millions of tires, although it stoutly maintained that the cause of the shredding was underinflation and selection of tires of the wrong quality, as well as the Explorer itself. At stake were two companies' reputations and economic positions, viability for Firestone, and, most important, the lives of hundreds of users.

Conciliation usually is the better salvage strategy. This calls for recognition and full admission of the problem and removal of the risk, even if it entails a full-market withdrawal until the source of the problem can be identified and correction made. Expensive, yes, but far less risky for the viability of the company and certainly for the health of the customers involved.

Neither strategy is without substantial costs. But the first course of action puts major cost consequences in the future, where they may turn out to be vastly greater as legal expenses and damage awards skyrocket. The second course of action poses an immediate impact on profitability, and will not avoid legal expenses, but may save the company and its reputation and return it to profitability in the near future.

Where blame is most likely shared, the solution of the problem lies not in confrontation but in cooperation.—This is the most grievous component of the violations of the public trust by Ford and Firestone: denial and confrontation, rather than both parties working together to solve the problem of product safety. But accepting this is so hard for proud executives (and also scared ones) who fear admitting that they may be culpable.

CONSIDER

Can you think of additional learning insights?

QUESTIONS

1. Can a firm guarantee complete product safety? Discuss.

2. Based on the information presented, which company do you think was most to blame for the deaths and injuries? What led you to your conclusion?

3. "If an Explorer driver never checks the tire pressure and drives well above the speed limit, he has no one to blame but himself in an accident—not the vehicle and not the tires." Discuss.

4. Do you think the government should be blamed in the Explorer deaths and injuries? Why or why not?

5. Would you give credence to the "community champion" awards bestowed by a consumer advocacy group founded by the Association of Trial Lawyers, and given to Alan Hogan in June 2001 for exposing careless tire production? Why or why not?

6. "Admittedly the groupthink mindset may be responsible for a few unethical and bad decisions, but isn't this mindset more likely to consider the

consequences to the company of delivering unsafe products, and thus to support aggressive corrective action?" Evaluate this statement.

7. Have you had any experience with a Ford Explorer? If so, what is your perception of its performance and safety?

8. Have you had any experience with Firestone tires? What is your perception of their performance and safety?

HANDS-ON EXERCISES

1. Put yourself in the position of John Lampe, CEO of Firestone, as the crisis worsens and accusations mount. Discuss how you would try to change the climate with Jacques Nasser of Ford from confrontational to cooperative. Be as specific as you can. Do you think you would be successful?

2. Firestone is on its knees after massive tire recalls and monstrous damage suits. You are a consultant brought in to help the firm recover. Be as specific as you can in recommending a course of action and in prioritizing things to do. Make any assumptions you need to, but keep them reasonable. Defend your recommendations. (Do not be swayed by what actually happened. Maybe things could have been done better.)

3. You are a trusted aide of Nasser. Support his confrontational stance with Firestone before the Ford board of directors.

4. *Be a Devil's Advocate.* In a staff meeting the topic comes up that your SUVs have been involved in a number of deaths. The group passes this off as due to reckless drivers. Argue persuasively a contrary position.

TEAM DEBATE EXERCISES

1. Debate the issue of dropping or keeping the Firestone name. Defend your position and attack the other side.

2. Debate the issue of whether to stand by Nasser at the height of the confrontation or to remove him. Be as persuasive as you can.

INVITATION TO RESEARCH

Can you find statistics about how competing tire companies, particularly Goodyear and Michelin, fared during and after the Firestone recall? Are Ford and Firestone friends again? Is the Ford Explorer still the top SUV?

PART TWO

GREAT COMEBACKS

CHAPTER FIVE

Continental Airlines: Salvaging from the Ashes

Massive marketing and management blunders almost destroyed Continental Airlines, but in only a few years, with a remarkable turnaround by new management, Continental became a star of the airline industry. The changemaker, CEO Gordon Bethune, wrote a best-selling book on how he turned around the moribund company, titled *From Worst to First*. In this chapter we will look at the scenario leading to Continental's difficulties, and then examine the ingredients of the great comeback.

THE FRANK LORENZO ERA

Frank Lorenzo was a consummate manipulator, parlaying borrowed funds and little of his own money to build an airline empire. By the end of 1986, he controlled the largest airline network in the non-Communist world: only Aeroflot, the Soviet airline, was larger. Lorenzo's network was a leveraged amalgam of Continental, People Express, Frontier, and Eastern, with $8.6 billion in sales—all this from a small investment in Texas International Airlines in 1971. In the process of building his network, Lorenzo defeated unions and shrewdly used the bankruptcy courts to further his ends. When he eventually departed, his empire was swimming in red ink, had a terrible reputation, and was burdened with colossal debt and aging planes.

The Start

After getting an MBA from Harvard, Lorenzo's first job was as a financial analyst at Trans World Airlines. In 1966, he and Robert Carney, a buddy from Harvard, formed an airline consulting firm, and in 1969, the two put together $35,000 to form an investment firm, Jet Capital. Through a public stock offering they were able to raise an additional $1.15 million. In 1971, Jet Capital was called in to fix ailing Texas

International and wound up buying it for $1.5 million, and Lorenzo became CEO. He restructured the debt as well as the airline's routes, found funds to upgrade the almost obsolete planes, and brought Texas International to profitability.

In 1978, acquisition-minded Lorenzo lost out to Pan Am in a bidding war for National Airlines, but he made $40 million on the National stock he had acquired. In 1980, he created nonunion New York Air and formed Texas Air as a holding company. In 1982 Texas Air bought Continental for $154 million.

Lorenzo's Treatment of Continental

In 1983, Lorenzo took Continental into bankruptcy court, filing for Chapter 11. This permitted the corporation to continue operating but spared its obligation to meet heavy interest payments and certain other contracts while it reorganized as a more viable enterprise. The process nullified the previous union contracts, and this prompted a walkout by many union workers.

Lorenzo earned the lasting enmity of organized labor as a union-buster by replacing strikers with nonunion workers at much lower wages. (A few years later, he reinforced this reputation when he used the same tactics with Eastern Airlines.)

In a 1986 acquisition achievement that was to backfire a few years later, Lorenzo struck deals to acquire a weak Eastern Airlines and a failing People Express/Frontier Airlines. That same year Continental emerged out of bankruptcy. Now Continental, with its nonunion workforce making it a low-cost operator, was Lorenzo's shining jewel. The low bid accepted for Eastern reinforced Lorenzo's reputation as a visionary builder.

What kind of executive was Lorenzo? Although he was variously described as a master financier and visionary, his handling of day-to-day problems bordered on the inept.[1] One former executive was quoted as saying, "If he agreed with one thing at 12:15, it would be different by the afternoon.[2] Inconsistent planning and poor execution characterized his lack of good operational strength. Furthermore, his domineering and erratic style alienated talented executives. From 1983 to 1993, nine presidents left Continental.

But Lorenzo's treatment of his unions brought the most controversy. He became the central figure of confrontational labor-management relations to a degree perhaps unmatched by any other person in recent years. Although he won the battle with Continental's unions and later with Eastern's, he was burdened with costly strikes and a residue of ill feeling that impeded any profitable recovery during his time at the helm.

The Demise of Eastern Airlines

In an environment of heavy losses and its own militant unions, Eastern in 1986, accepted Lorenzo's low offer. With tough contract demands and the stockpiling

---

[1] See, for example, Todd Vogel, Gail DeGeorge, Pete Engardio, and Aaron Bernstein, "Texas Air Empire in Jeopardy," *Business Week*, March 27, 1989, p. 30.

[2] Mark Ivey and Gail DeGeorge, "Lorenzo May Land a Little Short of the Runway," *Business Week*, February 5, 1990, p. 48.

of $1 billion in cash as strike insurance, Lorenzo seemed eager to precipitate and then crush a strike. He instituted a program of severe downsizing, and in 1989, after 15 months of fruitless talks, some 8,500 machinists and 3,800 pilots went on strike. Lorenzo countered the strike at Eastern by filing for Chapter 11 bankruptcy, and replaced many of the striking pilots and machinists within months.

At first Eastern appeared to be successfully weathering the strike, while Continental benefited with increased business. But soon revenue dropped drastically, with Eastern planes flying less than half full amid rising fuel costs. Fares were slashed in order to regain business, and a liquidity crisis loomed. Then, on January 16, 1990, an Eastern jet sheared the top off a private plane in Atlanta. Even though the accident was attributed to air controller error, Eastern's name received the publicity.

Eastern creditors, now despairing of Lorenzo's ability to pay them back in full, pushed for a merger with Continental, which would expose it to the bankruptcy process. On December 3, 1990, Continental again tumbled into bankruptcy, burdened with overwhelming debt. In January 1991, Eastern finally went out of business.

CONTINENTAL'S EMERGENCE FROM BANKRUPTCY, AGAIN

Lorenzo was gone. The legacy of Eastern remained, however. Creditors claimed more than $400 million in asset transfers between Eastern and Continental, and Eastern still had $680 million in unfunded pension liabilities. The board brought in Robert Ferguson, veteran of Braniff and Eastern bankruptcies, to make changes. On April 16, 1993, the court approved a reorganization plan for Continental to emerge from bankruptcy, the first airline to have survived two bankruptcies. However, creditors got only pennies on the dollar.[3]

Despite its long history of travail and a terrible profit picture, Continental in 1992 was still the nation's fifth-largest airline, behind American, United, Delta, and Northwest, and it served 193 airports. Table 5.1 shows the revenues and net profits (or losses) of Continental and its major competitors from 1987 through 1991.

Lorenzo's Legacy

Continental was savaged in its long tenure as a pawn in Lorenzo's dynasty-building efforts. He had saddled it with huge debts, brought it into bankruptcy twice, left it with aging equipment. Perhaps a greater detriment was the ravished corporate culture. The following Information Box discusses corporate culture and its relationship to public image or reputation.

---

[3] Bridget O'Brian, "Judge Backs Continental Airlines Plan to Regroup, Emerge from Chapter 11," *Wall Street Journal*, April 19, 1993, p. A4.

TABLE 5.1. Performance Statistics, Major Airlines, 1987–1991

	1987	1988	1989	1990	1991	Percent 5-Year Gain
Revenues: (millions $)						
American	6,368	7,548	8,670	9,203	9,309	46.0
Delta	5,638	6,684	7,780	7,697	8,268	46.6
United	6,500	7,006	7,463	7,946	7,850	20.8
Northwest	3,328	3,395	3,944	4,298	4,330	30.1
Continental	3,404	3,682	3,896	4,036	4,031	18.4
Income (millions $)						
American	225	450	412	(40)	(253)	
Delta	201	286	467	(119)	(216)	
United	22	426	246	73	(175)	
Continental	(304)	(310)	(56)	(1,218)	(1,550)	

Source: Company annual reports.

Commentary: Note the operating performance of Continental relative to its major competitors during this period. It ranks last in sales gain. It far and away has the worst profit performance, having had massive losses in each of the years in contrast to its competitors, who, while incurring some losses, had neither the constancy nor the magnitude of losses of Continental. And the relative losses of Continental are even worse than they at first appear: Continental is the smallest of these major airlines.

INFORMATION BOX

IMPORTANCE OF CORPORATE CULTURE

A corporate or organizational culture can be defined as the system of shared beliefs and values that develops within an organization and guides the behavior of its members.[4] Such a culture can be a powerful influence on performance and customer satisfaction:

> If employees know what their company stands for, if they know what standards they are to uphold, then they are much more likely to make decisions that will support those standards. They are also more likely to feel as if they are an important part of the organization. They are motivated because life in the company has meaning for them.[5]

Lorenzo had destroyed the former organizational climate as he beat down the unions. Replacement employees had little reason to develop a positive culture or esprit de corps given the many top-management changes, the low pay relative to other airline

---

[4] Edgar H. Schein, "Organizational Culture," *American Psychologist*, vol. 45, (1990), pp. 109–119.
[5] Terrence E. Deal and Alan A. Kennedy, *Corporate Cultures: The Rites and Rituals of Corporate Life*, Reading, MA: Addison-Wesley, 1982, p. 22.

employees, and the continuous possibility of corporate bankruptcy. Employees had little to be proud of, and this impacted on the service the airline gave and its consequent reputation among the traveling public.

But this was to change abruptly under new management.

Can a corporate climate be too upbeat? Discuss.

A devastated reputation proved to be a major impediment. The reputation of a surly labor force had repercussions far beyond the organization itself. For years Continental had a problem wooing the better-paying business travelers. Being on expense accounts, they wanted quality service rather than cut-rate prices. A reputation for good service is not easily or quickly achieved, especially when the opposite reputation is well entrenched.

On another dimension, Continental's reputation also hindered competitive parity. Surviving two bankruptcies does not engender confidence among investors, creditors, or even travel agents.

A Sick Airline Industry

Domestic airlines lost a staggering $8 billion in the years 1990 through 1992. Fare wars and excess planes proved to be albatrosses. Even when planes were filled, discount prices often did not cover overhead.

A lengthy recession drove both firms and individuals to fly more sparingly. Business firms found teleconferencing a viable substitute for business travel, and consumers, facing diminished discretionary income as well as the threat of eventual layoffs or forced retirements, were hardly optimistic. The airlines suffered.

Part of the blame for the red ink lay directly with the airlines—and especially their reckless expansion efforts—yet they did not deserve total blame. In the late 1980s, passenger traffic climbed 10 percent per year, and in response the airlines ordered hundreds of jetliners.[6] The recession arrived just as the new planes were being delivered. The airlines greatly increased their debt in these expansion efforts: the big three, for example—American, United, and Delta—doubled their leverage in the four years after 1989, with debt at 80 percent of capitalization by 1993.[7]

In such a climate, cost-cutting efforts prevailed. But how much can be cut without jeopardizing service and even safety? Some airlines found that hubs, heralded as the great strategy of the 1980s, were not as cost-effective as expected. With hub cities, passengers were gathered from outlying "spokes" and then flown to final destinations. Maintaining too many hubs, however, brought costly overheads. While the concept was good, some retrenchment seemed necessary to be cost-effective.

[6] Andrea Rothman, "Airlines: Still No Wind at Their Backs," *Business Week*, January 11, 1993, p. 96.
[7] *Ibid.*

Airlines such as Continental with heavy debt and limited liquidity had two major concerns: first, how fast the country could emerge from recession; second, the risk of fuel-price escalation in the coming years. Despite Continental's low operating costs, external conditions impossible to predict or control could affect viability.

THE GREAT COMEBACK UNDER GORDON BETHUNE

In February 1994, Gordon Bethune left Boeing and took the job of president and chief operating officer of Continental. He faced a daunting challenge. While it was the fifth largest airline, Continental was by far the worst among the nation's ten biggest according to these quality indicators by the Department of Transportation:

- On-time percentage (the percentage of flights that land within 15 minutes of their scheduled arrival).
- Number of mishandled-baggage reports filed per 1,000 passengers.
- Number of complaints per 100,000 passengers.
- Involuntarily denied boarding, i.e., passengers with tickets who are not allowed to board because of overbooking or other problems.[8]

In late October Bethune became chief executive officer. Now he was sitting in the pilot's seat.

He made dramatic changes. In 1995, through a "renewed focus on flight schedules and incentive pay," he greatly improved on-time performance, along with lost-baggage claims and customer complaints. Now, instead of being dead-last in these quality indicators of the Department of Transportation, Continental by 1996 was third-best or better in all four categories.

Customers began returning, especially the higher-fare business travelers, climbing from 32.2 percent in 1994 to 42.8 percent of all customers by 1996. In May 1996, based on customer surveys, Continental was awarded the J. D. Power Award as the best airline for customer satisfaction on flights of 500 miles or more. It also received the award in 1997, the first airline to win two years in a row. Other honors followed. In January 1997, it was named "Airline of the Year" by *Air Transport World*, the leading industry monthly. In January 1997, *Business Week* magazine named Bethune one of its top managers of 1996.

Bethune had transformed the workforce into a happy one, as measured by these statistics:

- Wages up an average of 25 percent.
- Sick leave down more than 29 percent.
- Personnel turnover down 45 percent.
- Workers compensation claims down 51 percent.
- On-the-job injuries down 54 percent.[9]

---

[8] Gordon Bethune, *From Worst to First*, New York: Wiley, 1998, p. 4.
[9] *Ibid.*, pp. 7–8.

TABLE 5.2. **Continental Sales and Profits, Before and After Bethune, 1992–1997**

	Before Bethune			After Bethune		
	1992	1993	1994	1995	1996	1997
Revenues (millions $)	5,494	3,907	5,670	5,825	6,360	7,213
Net income (millions $)	−110	−39	−612	224	325	389
Earnings per share ($)		−1.17	−11.88	3.60	4.25	5.03

Source: Company annual reports.

Commentary: While the revenue statistics do not show a striking improvement, the net income certainly does. Most important to investors, the earnings per share show a major improvement.

These statistics suggest the fallacy of a low-price strategy at the expense of profitability in the 1992–1994 era. At the same time, we have to realize that the early 1990s were recession years, particularly for the airline industry.

Perhaps nothing illustrates the improvement in employee morale as much as this: In 1995, not all that long after he became top executive, employees were so happy with their new boss's performance that they chipped in to buy him a $22,000 Harley-Davidson.[10]

Naturally these improvements in employee relations and customer service had a major impact on revenues and profitability. See Table 5.2 for the three years before and after Bethune.

Gordon Bethune

Bethune's father was a crop duster, and as a teenager Gordon helped him one summer and learned first hand the challenges of responsibility: in this case, preparing a crude landing strip for nighttime landings, with any negligence disastrous. He joined the Navy at 17, before finishing high school. He graduated second in his class at the Naval Technical School to become an aviation electronics technician, and over 19 years worked his way up to lieutenant. After leaving the Navy he joined Braniff, then Western, and later Piedmont Airlines as senior vice president of operations. He finally left Piedmont for Boeing as VP/general manager of customer service. There he became licensed as a 757 and 767 pilot: "An amazing thing happened. All the Boeing pilots suddenly thought I was a great guy," he writes. "I hope I hadn't given them any reason to think otherwise of me before that, but this really got their attention."[11]

HOW DID HE DO IT?

Bethune stressed the human element in guiding the comeback of a lethargic, even bitter, organization by doing the simple things: "On October 24, 1994, I did a very

[10] *Ibid.*, frontispiece.
[11] *Ibid.*, p. 268.

significant thing in the executive suite of Continental Airlines . . . I opened the doors . . . [Before this] The doors to the executive suite were locked, and you needed an ID to get through. Security cameras added to the feeling of relaxed charm . . . So the day I began running the company, I opened the doors. I wasn't afraid of my employees, and I wanted everybody to know it."[12] Still, he had to entice employees to the twentieth floor of headquarters, and he did this with open houses, supplying food and drink, and personal tours and chat sessions. "I'd take a group of employees into my office, open up the closet, and say, 'You see? Frank's not here.' Frank Lorenzo had left Continental years before; the legacy of cost cutting and infighting of that era was finally gone, and I wanted them to know it."[13]

Of course, the improvement in employee relations needed tangible elements to cement and sustain it, and to improve morale. Bethune worked hard to instill a spirit of teamwork. He did this by giving on-time bonuses to all employees, not just pilots. He burned the procedure manual that bound employees to rigid policies instead of being able to use their best judgment. He even gave the planes a new paint job to provide tangible evidence of a disavowal of the old and an embracing of new policies and practices. The new image impressed both employees and customers.

Better communications was also a key element in improving employee relationships and the spirit of teamwork. Information was shared with employees through newsletters, updates on bulletin boards, e-mail, voice-mail, and electronic signs over worldwide workplaces. To Bethune it was a cardinal sin for any organization if employees first heard about something that affected them through the newspaper or other media. The following Information Box contrasts the classic idea of Theory X and Theory Y managers. Bethune was certainly a Theory Y manager, and Lorenzo Theory X.

INFORMATION BOX

THEORY X AND THEORY Y MANAGERS

Douglas McGregor, in his famous book, *The Human Side of Enterprise*, advanced the thesis that there are two different types of managers, the traditional Theory X manager with a rather low opinion of subordinates, and the new Theory Y manager, whom we might call a human-relations type of manager.

Schermerhorn contrasts the two styles as follows:[14]

Theory X views subordinates as:

Disliking work

Lacking in ambition

---

[12] *Ibid.*, p. 14.
[13] *Ibid.*, p. 32.
[14] Douglas McGregor, *The Human Side of Enterprise*, New York: McGraw-Hill, 1960; John R. Schermerhorn, Jr., *Management*, 6th ed., New York: Wiley 1999, p. 79.

Irresponsible

Resistant to change

Preferring to be led rather than to lead

Theory Y sees subordinates this way:

Willing to work

Willing to accept responsibility

Capable of self-direction

Capable of self-control

Capable of imagination, ingenuity, creativity

Which is better? With the success of Bethune in motivating his employees for strong positive change in the organization, one would think Theory Y is the only way to go. McGregor certainly thought so and predicted that giving workers more participation, freedom, and responsibility would result in high productivity.

Is there any room for a Theory X manager today? If so, under what circumstances?

Now Continental had to win back customers. Instead of the company's old focus on cost savings, efforts were directed to putting out a better product through better service. This meant emphasis on on-time flights, better baggage handling, and the like. By giving employees bonuses for meeting these standards, the incentive was created.

Bethune sought to do a better job of designing routes with good demand, to "fly places people wanted to go." This meant, for example, cutting back on the six flights a day between Greensboro, North Carolina, and Greenville, South Carolina. It meant not trying to compete with Southwest's Friends Fly Free Fares, which "essentially allowed passengers to fly anywhere within the state of Florida for $24.50.[15] The frequent flyer program was reinstated. Going a step further, the company apologized to travel agents, business partners, and customers and showed them how it planned to do better and earn their business back.

Continental queried travel agents about their biggest clients, the major firms that did the most traveling, asking how could it better serve these customers. As a result, more first-class seats were added, certain destinations were given more attention, volume discounts were instituted. Travel agents were made members of the team and given special incentives beyond normal airline commissions.

This still left financial considerations. Bethune was aggressive in renegotiating loans and poor airplane lease agreements, and in getting supplier financial cooperation. Controls were set up to monitor cash flow and stop waste. Tables 5.3 and 5.4 show the results of Bethune's efforts from the dark days of 1992–94, and how the competitive position of Continental changed. Remember, Bethune joined the firm in February 1994 and did not become the top executive until late October of that year.

---

[15] *Ibid.*, pp. 51–52.

TABLE 5.3. **Competitive Position of Continental before and After Bethune, 1992–1997**

	Before Bethune			After Bethune		
	1992	1993	1994	1995	1996	1997
Revenues (millions $):						
AMR (American)	14,396	15,701	16,137	16,910	17,753	18,570
UAR (United)	12,890	14,511	13,950	14,943	16,362	17,378
Delta	10,837	11,997	12,359	12,194	12,455	13,590
Northwest	NA	8,649	9,143	9,085	9,881	10,226
Continental	5,494	3,907	5,670	5,825	6,360	7,213
Continental's Market Share (percent of total sales of Big Five Airlines):		7.1%	9.9%	9.9%	10.1%	10.8%

Sources: Company annual reports.

NA = Information not available.

Commentary: Most significant is the gradual increase in Continental's market share over its four major rivals. This is an improving competitive position.

TABLE 5.4. **Profitability Comparison of Big Five Airlines, 1992–1997**

	Before Bethune			After Bethune		
	1992	1993	1994	1995	1996	1997
Net Income (millions $):						
AMR	−474	−96	228	196	1,105	985
UAL	−416	−31	77	378	600	958
Delta	−505	−414	−408	294	156	854
Northwest	NA	−114	296	342	536	606
Continental	−110	−39	−696	224	325	389

Source: Company annual reports. NA = Information not available.

Commentary: Of interest is how the good and bad times for the airlines seem to move in lockstep. Still, the smallest of the Big Five, Continental, incurred the biggest loss of any airline in 1994. Under Bethune, it has seen a steady increase in profitability, but so have the other airlines, although AMR and Delta have been more erratic.

UPDATE

As the airline industry moved into the new millennium, external circumstances impacted negatively on the whole industry. The 9/11 disaster of 2001 had a profound effect, all the more because passenger planes were the instruments of destruction

TABLE 5.5. Comparison of Continental with Its Two Major Competitors Not in Bankruptcy, 2002–2005 (millions of $)

	2002	2003	2004	2005
Revenues:				
AMR (American)	17,299	17,440	18,645	20,712
Southwest	5,522	5,937	6,530	7,584
Continental	8,402	8,870	9,744	11,208
Continental's market share (Continental's sales divided by total sales of these three airlines)	26.9%	27.5%	27.9%	28.4%
Net Income:				
AMR	−2,523	−1,228	−761	−861
Southwest	241	442	313	548
Continental	−451	38	−363	−68

Source: Company annual reports.

Commentary: Of particular interest is how Continental has improved its market share relative to these two competitors each year since 2002. Of course, it had other competitors—Northwest, United, Delta, and US Air—who were in bankruptcy with operating statistics not available. In the income comparisons, AMR shows up by far the worst, while Southwest alone of all the airlines was profitable every year. Continental's three years of losses, while erratic, show an improving picture.

by the terrorists. Passenger traffic was down, restrictions and inconveniences were the order of the day. Then surging oil prices were the double whammy. U.S. airlines posted losses of some $8 billion in 2002, after 2001's record loss of $7.7 billion. The loss in the more profitable business travel was particularly acute. High-cost airlines faced enormous pressure from low-fare carriers, most notably Southwest and JetBlue Airways. United Airlines and US Airways fell into bankruptcy in late 2002, and were joined by Northwest and Delta in 2005, leaving only AMR and Continental of the six major carriers to escape bankruptcy. Airlines needed to slash billions in operating costs, notably through labor givebacks of extravagant union contracts, and restructuring was the order of the day. In this climate, Continental's revenue rose, although red ink prevailed most years. Table 5.5 compares Continental's operating results for 2002 through 2005 with those of American Airlines (now AMR) and Southwest Airlines, the only carrier to make a profit every year.

Gordon Bethune retired at the end of 2004 after a distinguished career. He joined the lecture circuit, and his speaker's fees ranged from $30,000 to $50,000. In 2006, he became CEO of Aloha Airlines.

Bethune's Legacy

While Bethune was gone by mid-decade, his fine-tuning of Continental lived on. In 2006, awards continued to be showered on the airline. A survey of business travelers by *Conde Nast Traveler* found Continental running the best business class of any U.S. airline on foreign routes, and the best premium service on domestic routes. Earlier in the year, it was ranked first in a poll by J. D. Power & Associates. While only the fourth-largest U.S. carrier, Continental flew to more international destinations than any other U.S. airline. It catered to business travelers, who paid the highest fares and flew most frequently, with more comfortable seats, special waiting areas, and bags tagged for first unloading. At a time when most airlines were drastically cutting back on amenities in coach, Continental still provided free blankets, pillows, and hot meals.

Continuing with the Bethune legacy, the airline valued its employees. After the 9/11 attacks hurt air travel, Continental's executives gave up their pay for the rest of the year. They later squeezed more than $1 billion out of operations before turning to employees for $500 million in pay cuts when fuel costs soared. The result was peaceful labor relations, higher morale, and better service.[16]

◦ ◦ ◦

Invitation to Make Your Own Analysis and Conclusions

Gordon Bethune's approach to salvaging Continental seems almost too good to be true. Surely he must have shown some management flaws or missteps. What could he have done better? Your recommendations, please.

◦ ◦ ◦

WHAT CAN BE LEARNED?

It is possible to quickly turn around an organization.—This idea flies in the face of conventional wisdom. How can a firm's bad reputation with employees, customers, creditors, stockholders, and suppliers be overcome without years of trying to prove that it has changed for the better? This conventional wisdom is usually correct: a great comeback does not often occur easily or quickly. But it sometimes does, with a streetwise leader, and a bit of luck perhaps. Gordon Bethune is proof that negative attitudes can be turned around quickly.

The possibility of a quick turnaround should be inspiring to other organizations mired in adversity.

Still, reputation should be carefully guarded. In most cases, a poor image is difficult to overcome, with trust built up only over time. The prudent firm is careful to safeguard its reputation.

Give employees a sense of pride and a caring management.—Bethune proved a master at changing employees' attitudes and their sense of pride. Few top executives ever faced such a negative workforce, reflecting the Lorenzo

---

[16] Jane Engle, "Continental Could Be the Airline of the Future," *Los Angeles Times*, as reported in *Cleveland Plain Dealer*, October 22, 2006, p. G1.

years. But Bethune changed all this, and in such a short time. His open-door policy and open houses to encourage employees to interact with him and other top executives was a simple gesture, but so effective, as was his opening wide the channels of communication about company plans. The incentive plans for improving performance, and the freeing up of employee initiatives by abolishing the rigidity of formal policies, were further positives. He engendered an atmosphere of teamwork and a personal image of an appreciative CEO. What is truly remarkable is how quickly such simple actions could turn around the attitudes of a workforce from adversarial, with morale in the pits, to pride and an eagerness to build an airline.

Contradictory and inconsistent strategies are vulnerable.—Lorenzo was often described as mercurial and subject to knee-jerk planning, and poor execution.[17] Clearly focused objectives and strategies mark effective firms. They bring stability to an organization and give customers, employees, and investors confidence in undeviating commitments. Admittedly, some objectives and strategies may occasionally have to be modified to meet changing environmental and competitive conditions, but the spirit of the organization should be resolute, provided it is a positive influence and not a negative one.

Try to avoid an adversarial approach to employee relations.—Lorenzo used a confrontational and adversarial approach to his organization and the unions. He was seemingly successful in destroying the unions and hiring nonunion replacements at lower pay scales. This resulted in Continental's becoming the lowest-cost operator of the major carriers, but there were negatives: service problems, questionable morale, diminished reputation, and devastated profitability.

Bethune took the opposite tack. It is hard to argue against nurturing and supporting an existing organization, thereby avoiding the adversarial mindset of "them or us." Admittedly this may sometimes be difficult—sometimes impossible, at least in the short run—but it is worth trying. It should result in better morale, motivation, and commitment to the company's best interests.

The dangers of competing mostly on low price.—Bethune inherited one of the lowest-cost air carriers, and it was doing badly. He says, "You can make an airline so cheap nobody wants to fly it, [just as] you can make a pizza so cheap nobody wants to eat it. Trust me on this—we did it... In fact, it was making us lousy, and people didn't want to buy what we offered."[18]

We might add here that competing strictly on a price basis usually leaves a firm vulnerable. Low prices can often (though not always) be matched or countered by a competitor if they are attracting enough customers. On the other hand, competition based on nonprice factors like better service, quality of product, and a good public image or reputation are not so easily matched, and can be more attractive to many customers.

In four other cases in this book we see firms competing successfully with a low-price strategy. Vanguard, Dell, Southwest Air, and Wal-Mart have for decades

---

[17] For example, Ivey and DeGeorge, p. 48.
[18] Bethune, p. 50.

had operational efficiencies unmatched in their industries, but Dell and Southwest are now seeing their advantage eroding somewhat, and Wal-Mart is experimenting with some higher-priced goods.

CONSIDER

Can you add any other learning insights?

QUESTIONS

1. Could Lorenzo's confrontation with Continental's unions have been more constructively handled? How?

2. Compare Bethune's handling of employees with Kelleher's at Southwest Airlines in Chapter 17. Are there commonalities? Contrasts?

3. Compare Bethune's management style with Lorenzo's. What conclusions can you draw?

4. Bethune gave great credit to his open-door policy when he became CEO. Do you think this was a major factor in the turnaround? How about changing the color of the planes?

5. How do you motivate employees to give a high priority to customer service?

6. Evaluate the causes and the consequences of frequent top-executive changes such as Continental experienced in the days of Lorenzo?

7. How can replacement workers—in this case, pilots and skilled maintenance people hired at substantially lower salaries than their unionized peers at other airlines—be sufficiently motivated to provide top-notch service and a constructive esprit de corps?

HANDS-ON EXERCISES

1. It is 1994 and Bethune has just taken over. He has asked you as his staff adviser to prepare a report on improving customer service as quickly as possible. He has also asked you to design a program to inform potential business and nonbusiness customers of this new commitment. Be as specific as possible in your recommendations.

2. You are the leader of the machinists' union at Eastern. It is 1986 and Lorenzo has just acquired your airline. You know full well how he broke the union at Continental, and rumors are flying that he has similar plans for Eastern. Describe your tactics under two scenarios:

    a. You decide to take a conciliatory stance.
    b. You plan to fight him every step of the way.

    How successful do you think you will be in saving your union?

YOUR PROGNOSIS FROM LATEST DEVELOPMENTS

What is your prognosis from the latest developments for Continental?

TEAM DEBATE EXERCISES

1. Bethune was quoted as saying, "You can make an airline so cheap nobody wants to fly it."
2. Debate this issue, and the related issue of how an airline can make itself so unique that it can command higher prices than its competitors.

INVITATION TO RESEARCH

What is Continental's current situation? Have all the major airlines emerged from bankruptcy? Is the U.S. airline industry healthy now? Whatever happened to Lorenzo? How is Bethune doing with Aloha Airlines?

CHAPTER SIX

Harley-Davidson: A Long-Overdue Revival

*H*arley-Davidson, a century-old firm, has exhibited stark contrasts in its history. In its first 60 years it destroyed all of its U.S. competitors and had a solid 70 percent of the motorcycle market. Then, in the early 1960s, its staid and unexciting market was shaken up, rocked to its core by the most unlikely invader. The intruder was a smallish Japanese firm that had risen out of the ashes of World War II and was now trying to encroach on U.S. territory.

Almost inconceivably, in half a decade Harley-Davidson's market share was to fall to 5 percent, even as the total market expanded many times over what it had been for decades. The foreign invader had furnished a textbook example of the awesome effectiveness of a carefully crafted strategy. In the process, the confrontation between Honda and Harley-Davidson was a harbinger of the Japanese invasion of the auto industry.

Eventually, by the late 1980s, Harley began to make a comeback. But only after more than two decades of travail and mediocrity. As it surged forward in the last of the old century, it had somehow built up a mystique, a cult following, for its big bikes. In January 7, 2002, *Forbes* declared Harley to be its "Company of the Year," a truly prestigious honor. But let us go back first to the dire days of the Japanese invasion.

THE INVASION

Sales of motorcycles in the United States were around 50,000 per year in the 1950s, with Harley-Davidson, Britain's Norton and Triumph, and Germany's BMW accounting for most of the market. By the turn of the decade, Honda began to penetrate the U.S. market. In 1960 fewer than 400,000 motorcycles were registered in the United States. While this was an increase of almost 200,000 from the end of World War II 15 years before, it was far below the increase in other motor vehicles. But by 1964, only four years later, the number had risen to 960,000; two years later it was 1.4 million; and by 1971 it was almost 4 million.

In expanding the demand for motorcycles, Honda instituted a distinctly different strategy. The major elements of this strategy were lightweight cycles and an advertising approach directed toward a new customer. Few firms have ever experienced such a shattering of market share as did Harley-Davidson in the 1960s. (Although its competitive position declined drastically, its total sales remained nearly constant, indicating that it was getting none of the new customers for motorcycles.)

Reaction of Harley-Davidson to the Honda Threat

Faced with an invasion of its static U.S. market, how did Harley react to the intruder? It did not react! At least not until far too late. Harley-Davidson considered itself the leader in full-size motorcycles. While the company might shudder at the image tied in with its product's usage by the leather-jacket types, it took solace in the fact that almost every U.S. police department used its machines. Perhaps this is what led Harley to stand aside and complacently watch Honda make deep inroads into the American motorcycle market. The management saw no threat in Honda's thrust into the market with lightweight machines. The attitude was exemplified in this statement by William H. Davidson, the president of the company and son of the founder:

> Basically, we don't believe in the lightweight market. We believe that motorcycles are sport vehicles, not transportation vehicles. Even if a man says he bought a motorcycle for transportation, it's generally for leisure-time use. The lightweight motorcycle is only supplemental. Back around World War I, a number of companies came out with lightweight bikes. We came out with one ourselves. They never got anywhere. We've seen what happens to these small sizes.[1]

Eventually Harley recognized that the Honda phenomenon was not an aberration, and that there was a new factor in the market. The company attempted to fight back by offering an Italian-made lightweight in the mid-1960s. But it was far too late; Honda was firmly entrenched. The Italian bikes were regarded in the industry as of lower quality than the Japanese. Honda, and toward the end of the 1960s other Japanese manufacturers, continued to dominate what had become a much larger market than ever dreamed.

AFTERMATH OF THE HONDA INVASION: 1965–1981

In 1965, Harley-Davidson made its first public stock offering. Soon after, it faced a struggle for control. The contest was primarily between Bangor Punta, an Asian company, and AMF, an American company with strong interests in recreational equipment including bowling. In a bidding war, Harley-Davidson's stockholders chose AMF over Bangor Punta, even though the bid was $1 less than Bangor's $23 a share offer. Stockholders were leery of Bangor's reputation for taking over a company,

---

[1] Tom Rowan, "Harley Sets New Drive to Boost Market Share," *Advertising Age*, January 29, 1973, pp. 34–35.

squeezing it dry, and then scrapping it for the remaining assets. AMF's plans for expansion of Harley-Davidson seemed more compatible.

But the marriage was troubled: Harley-Davidson's old equipment was not capable of the expansion envisioned by AMF. At the very time that Japanese manufacturers—Honda and others—were flooding the market with high-quality motorcycles, Harley was falling down on quality. One company official noted that "quality was going down just as fast as production was going up."[2] Indicative of the depth of the problem at a demoralized Harley-Davidson, quality-control inspections failed 50–60 percent of the motorcycles produced. This compared to the 5 percent of Japanese motorcycles failing their quality-control checks.

AMF put up with an average $4.8 million operating loss for 11 years. Finally, AMF called it quits and put the division up for sale in 1981. Vaughan Beals, vice president of motorcycle sales, still had faith in the company. He led a team that used $81.5 million in financing from Citicorp to complete a leveraged buyout. All ties with AMF were severed.

VAUGHAN BEALS

Beals was a middle-aged Ivy Leaguer, a far cry from the usual image of a heavy-motorcycle aficionado. He had graduated from MIT's Aeronautical Engineering School, and was considered a production specialist.[3] But he was far more than that. He had a true commitment to motorcycles, personally as well as professionally. Deeply concerned with AMF's declining attention to quality, he achieved the buyout from AMF.

The prognosis for the company was bleak. Its market share, which had dominated the industry before the Honda invasion, was now 3 percent. In 1983, Harley-Davidson would celebrate its 80th birthday; some doubted it would still be around by then. Tariff protection seemed Harley's only hope. And massive lobbying paid off. In 1983, Congress passed a huge tariff increase on Japanese motorcycles. Instead of a 4 percent tariff, now Japanese motorcycles would be subject to a 45 percent tariff for the coming five years.

The tariff gave the company new hope, and it slowly began to rebuild market share. Key to this was restoring confidence in the quality of its products. And Beals took a leading role in this. He drove Harley-Davidsons to rallies where he met Harley owners. There he learned of their concerns and their complaints, and he promised changes. At these rallies a core of loyal Harley-Davidson users, called HOGs (for Harley Owners Group), were to be trailblazers for the successful growth and mystique to come.

Beals had company on his odyssey: Willie G. Davidson, grandson of the company's founder, and vice president of design. Willie was an interesting contrast to the more urbane Beals. His was the image of a middle-age hippie. He wore a Viking helmet over

[2] Peter C. Reid, *Well Made in America: Lessons from Harley Davidson on Being the Best*, New York: McGraw-Hill, 1990, p. 10.
[3] Rod Willis, "Harley-Davidson Comes Roaring Back," *Management Review*, March 1986, pp. 20–27.

long, unkempt hair, while a straggly beard hid some of his wind-burned face. An aged leather jacket was compatible. Beals and Davidson fit in nicely at the HOG rallies.

THE STRUGGLE BACK

In December 1986, Harley-Davidson asked Congress to remove the tariff barriers, more than a year earlier than originally planned. The company's confidence had been restored, and it believed it could now compete with the Japanese head to head.[4]

Production Improvements

Shortly after the buyout, Beals and other managers visited plants in Japan and Honda's assembly plant in Marysville, Ohio. They were impressed by the discovery that they were being beaten not by "robotics, or culture, or morning calisthenics and company songs, [but by] professional managers who understood their business and paid attention to detail."[5] As a result, Japanese production costs were as much as 30 percent lower than Harley's.

Beals and his managers tried to implement some of the Japanese managerial techniques. Each plant was divided into profit centers, with managers given total responsibility within their assigned areas. Just-in-time (JIT) inventory and a materials-as-needed (MAN) system sought to control and minimize all inventories both inside and outside the plants. Quality circles (QCs) were formed to increase employee involvement in quality goals and to improve communication between management and workers. See the following Quality Circles Information Box for further discussion. Another new program called statistical operator control (SOC) gave employees the responsibility for checking the quality of their own work and making corrective adjustments. Efforts were made to improve labor relations by more sensitivity to employees and their problems as well as better employee assistance and benefits. Certain product improvements were also introduced, notably a new engine and mountings on rubber to reduce vibration. A well-accepted equipment innovation entailed motorcycle helmets with built-in stereo systems and intercoms.

The production changes between 1981 and 1988 resulted in:[6]

Inventory reduced by 67 percent
Productivity up by 50 percent
Scrap and rework down two-thirds
Defects per unit down 70 percent

In the 1970s, the joke among industry experts was, "If you're buying a Harley, you'd better buy two—one for spare parts."[7] Now this had obviously changed, but the change still had to be communicated to consumers, and believed.

---

[4] "Harley Back in High Gear," *Forbes*, April 20, 1987, p. 8.
[5] Dexter Hutchins, "Having a Hard Time with Just-in-Time," *Fortune*, June 19, 1986, p. 65.
[6] Hutchins, p. 66.
[7] *Ibid.*

INFORMATION BOX

QUALITY CIRCLES

Quality circles were adopted by Japan in an effort to rid its industries of poor quality and junkiness after World War II. Quality circles are worker-management committees that meet, usually weekly, to talk about production problems, plan ways to improve productivity and quality, and resolve job-related gripes on both sides.

At the height of their popularity they were described as "the single most significant reason for the truly outstanding quality of goods and services produced in Japan."[8] At one time Mazda had 2,147 circles with more than 16,000 employees involved. The circles usually consisted of seven or eight volunteers who met on their own time to discuss and solve the issues they were concerned with. In addition to making major contributions to increased productivity and quality, quality circles gave employees an opportunity to participate and gain a sense of accomplishment.[9]

The idea of quality circles—like so many ideas adopted by the Japanese—did not originate with them; it came from two American personnel consultants. But the Japanese refined the idea and ran with it. In the 1980s, American industry, unable to match the quality of Japanese imports, saw quality circles as the elixir in quality enhancement. Firms also found them a desirable way to promote teamwork and good feelings, and to avoid some of the adversarial relations stemming from collective bargaining and union grievances.

Despite the glowing endorsements for quality circles, in the United States they were more a fad that quickly faded. Workers claimed that they smacked of "tokenism," and were an impractical facade, with no lasting benefits once the novelty had worn off. Others saw them as time wasted, and, unlike their Japanese counterparts, few American workers accepted the idea of participating in quality circles on their own time.

How would you feel about devoting an hour or more to quality-circle meetings every week or so on your own time? If your answer is "No way," do you think this is a fair attitude on your part? Why or why not?

Invitation to Research: Can you find any U.S. firms that are still using quality circles?

Marketing Moves

Despite its bad times and its poor quality, Harley had an almost unparalleled cadre of loyal customers. Company research maintained that 92 percent of its customers remained with Harley.[10] Despite these hard-core loyalists, the company had always had a serious public-image problem. It was linked to the image of the pot-smoking, beer-drinking, woman-chasing, tattoo-covered, leather-clad biker: "When your company's logo is the number one requested in tattoo parlors, it's time

---

[8] "A Partnership to Build the New Workplace," *Business Week*, June 30, 1980, p. 101.
[9] As described in a Mazda ad in *Forbes*, May 24, 1982, p. 5.
[10] Mark Marvel, "The Gentrified HOG," *Esquire*, July 1989, p. 25.

to get a licensing program that will return your reputation to the ranks of baseball, hot dogs, and apple pie."[11]

Part of Harley's problem had been with bootleggers ruining the name by placing it on unlicensed goods of poor quality. Now the company began to use warrants and federal marshals to crack down on unauthorized uses of its logo at motorcycle conventions. And it began licensing its name and logo on a wide variety of products, from leather jackets to cologne and jewelry—even to pajamas, sheets, and towels. Suddenly retailers realized that these licensed goods were popular, and were even being bought by a new type of customer, undreamed of until now: bankers, doctors, lawyers, and entertainers. This new breed soon expanded their horizons to include the Harley-Davidson bikes themselves. They joined the HOGs, only now they became known as Rubbies—rich urban bikers. And high prices for bikes did not bother them in the least.

Beals was quick to capitalize on this new market by expanding the product line with expensive heavyweights. In 1989 the largest motorcycle was introduced, the Fat Boy, with 80 cubic inches of V-twin engine and capable of a top speed of 150 mph. By 1991, Harley had 20 models, ranging in price from $4,500 to $15,000.

The Rubbies brought Harley back to a leading position in the industry by 1989, with almost 60 percent of the super-heavyweight motorcycle market; by the first quarter of 1993, this had become 63 percent. The importance of this customer to Harley could be seen in the demographic statistics supplied by the *Wall Street Journal* in 1990: "One in three of today's Harley-Davidson buyers are professionals or managers. About 60 percent have attended college, up from only 45 percent in 1984. Their median age is 35, and their median household income has risen sharply to $45,000 from $36,000 five years earlier."[12]

In 1989, Beals stepped down as CEO, turning the company over to Richard Teerlink, the chief operating officer of the Motorcycle Division. Beals, however, retained his position as chairman of the board. The legacy of Beals in the renaissance of Harley led management writer John Schermerhorn to call him a visionary leader. The following Information Box discusses visionary leadership.

INFORMATION BOX

VISIONARY LEADERSHIP

Vision has been identified as an essential ingredient of effective leadership. Having vision characterizes someone who has a clear sense of the company's future environment and the actions needed to thrive in it.

---

[11] "Thunder Road," *Forbes*, July 18, 1983, p. 32.
[12] Robert L. Rose, "Vrooming Back," *Wall Street Journal*, August 31, 1990, p. 1.

Undoubtedly, a visionary leader is an asset in a dynamic environment. Such a leader can help a firm grasp opportunities ahead of competitors, revitalize itself, pull itself up from adversity. Schermerhorn states that a visionary begins with a clear vision, communicates it to all concerned, and motivates and inspires them in pursuit of the vision. He proposes these five ingredients of visionary leadership:

1. **Challenge the process**. Be a pioneer—encourage innovation and people with ideas.
2. **Be enthusiastic**. Inspire others through personal example to share in a common vision.
3. **Help others to act**. Be a team player, and support the efforts and talents of others.
4. **Set the example**. Provide a consistent model of how others should act.
5. **Celebrate achievements**. Bring emotion into the workplace and rally "hearts" as well as "minds."[13]

Can you name any visionary leaders? What makes you think they were visionary? Could some supposedly visionary leaders have been merely lucky rather than prophetic?

SUCCESS

By 1993, Harley-Davidson had a new problem, one born of success. Now it could not even come close to meeting demand. Customers faced empty showrooms, except perhaps for rusty trade-ins or antiques. Waiting time for a new bike could be six months or longer, unless the customer was willing to pay a 10 percent or higher premium to some gray marketer advertising in biker magazines.

Some of the 600 independent dealers in the United States worried that empty showrooms and long waiting lists would induce customers to turn to foreign imports, much as they had several decades before. But other dealers recognized that somehow Beals and company had engendered a brand loyalty unique in this industry, and perhaps in all industries. Assuaging the lack of big bike business, dealers were finding other sources of revenue. Harley's branded line of merchandise, available only at Harley dealers and promoted through glossy catalogs, had really taken off. Harley black leather jackets were bought eagerly at $500; fringed leather bras went for $65; even shot glasses brought $12—all it seemed to take was the Harley name and logo. So substantial was this ancillary business that in 1992 non-cycle business generated $155.7 million in sales, up from $130.3 million in 1991.

---

[13] John R. Schermerhorn, Jr., *Management*, 6th ed. New York, Wiley, 1999, pp. 262–263.

Production

In one sense, Harley's production situation was enviable, for it had far more demand than production capability. More than this, it had so loyal a body of customers that delays in product gratification were not likely to turn many away to competitors. The problem, of course, was that full potential was not being realized.

Richard Teerlink, the successor to Beals, expressed the corporate philosophy on expanding quantity to meet the demand: "Quantity isn't the issue, quality is the issue. We learned in the early 1980s you do not solve problems by throwing money at them."[14]

The company increased output slowly. In early 1992 it was making 280 bikes a day; by 1993, this had risen to 345 a day. With increased capital spending, the goal was to produce 420 bikes a day, but not until 1996.

Export Potential

Some contrary concerns about Teerlink's conservative expansion plans surfaced in regard to international operations. The European export market beckoned. Harleys had become very popular in Europe. But the company had promised its domestic dealers that exports would not go beyond 30 percent of total production until the North American market was fully satisfied. Suddenly the European big-bike market grew by an astounding 33 percent between 1990 and 1992. Yet, because of its production constraints, Harley could only maintain a 9 to 10 percent share of this market. In other words, it was giving away business to foreign competitors.

To enhance its presence in Europe, Harley opened a branch office of its HOG club in Frankfurt, Germany, for its European fans.

Specifics of the Resurgence of Harley-Davidson

Table 6.1 shows the trend of Harley's revenues and net income from 1982 through 1994. The growth in sales and profits did not go unnoticed by the investment community. In 1990, Harley-Davidson stock sold for $7; in January of 1993, it hit $39. Its market share of heavyweight motorcycles (751 cubic centimeters displacement and larger) had soared from 12.5 percent in 1983 to 63 percent by 1993. Let the Japanese have the lightweight bike market! Harley would dominate the heavyweights.

Harley acquired Holiday Rambler in 1986. As a wholly owned subsidiary, this manufacturer of recreational and commercial vehicles was judged by Harley's management to be compatible with the existing motorcycle business and, in addition, would moderate some of the seasonality of the motorcycle business. The diversification proved rather mediocre. In 1992, it accounted for 26 percent of total corporate sales, but only 2 percent of profits.[15]

---

[14] Gary Slutsker, "Hog Wild," *Forbes*, May 24, 1993, p. 46.
[15] Company annual reports.

TABLE 6.1. Harley-Davidson's Growth in Revenue and Income, 1982–1994 (Millions of dollars)

Year	Revenue	Net Income
1982	$ 210	def. $25.1
1983	254	1.0
1984	294	2.9
1985	287	2.6
1986	295	4.3
1987	685	17.7
1988	757	27.2
1989	791	32.6
1990	865	38.3
1991	940	37.0
1992	1,100	54.0
1993	1,210	68.0
1994	1,537	83.0

Source: Company annual reports.

Commentary: The steady climb in sales and profits, except for a pause in 1985, is noteworthy. The total gain in revenues over these years was 631.9%, while income rose more than eighty-fold since 1983.

Big motorcycles, made in America by the only U.S. manufacturer, continued to be the rage. Harley's 90th anniversary was celebrated in Milwaukee on June 12, 1993. As many as 100,000 people, including 18,000 HOGS, were there to celebrate. Hotel rooms were sold out for a 60-mile radius. Harley-Davidson was up and doing real well.

More Recent Developments

The 1990s continued to be kind to Harley. Demand grew, with the mystique as strong as ever. The company significantly increased its motorcycle-production capacity with a new engine plant in Milwaukee completed in 1997 and a new assembly plant in Kansas City in 1998. It expected that demand in the United States would still exceed the supply of Harley bikes.

The following numbers show how motorcycle shipments (domestic and export) increased from 1993 to 1997 (in thousands of units):

	U.S.	Exports
1997	96.2	36.1
1993	57.2	24.5

Despite continuous increases in production, U.S. consumers still had to wait to purchase a new Harley-Davidson bike, but the wait only added to the mystique.

The following shows the growth in revenues and income from 1993 to 1997:

	Revenues ($M)	Net Income ($M)
1997	1,763	174.0
1993	1,217	18.4

As an indication of the popularity of the Harley-Davidson logo, Wolverine World Wide, original maker of Hush Puppies but now the largest manufacturer of footwear in the United States, entered into a licensing agreement with Harley to use its "sexy" name for a line of boots and fashion shoes to come out in late 1998.[16]

In its January 7, 2002 issue, *Forbes* declared Harley to be its "Company of the Year," a truly prestigious honor. In supporting its decision, *Forbes* noted that:

> In a disastrous year for hundreds of companies, Harley's estimated 2001 sales grew 15 percent to $3.3 billion and earnings grew 26 percent to $435 million. Its shares were up 40 percent in 2001, while the S&P stock averages dropped 15 percent. Since Harley went public in 1986, its shares have risen an incredible 15,000 percent. Since 1986, GE, generally considered the paragon of American business, had risen only 1,050 percent.

Jeffrey Bleustein, a 26-year company veteran and the current Harley CEO, was diversifying into small, cheaper bikes to attract younger riders as well as women who had shunned the big lumbering machines and who represented only 9 percent of Harley riders. The cult image was stronger than ever. Half of the company's 8,000 employees rode Harleys, and many of them appeared at rallies around the country for pleasure and to promote the company. In 2002, there were 640,000 owners, the parts-and-accessories catalog numbered 720 pages, and the Harley-Davidson name was on everything from blue jeans to pickup trucks. Harley would celebrate its 100th birthday in 2002, and some 250,000 riders were expected at the rally in Milwaukee.[17]

By 2005, a rental program, which had started in 1999 as a tool for Harley-Davidson to hook customers on riding and thereby entice them to buy, had ballooned from six participating dealers to 250, including 52 in Canada, Mexico, Costa Rica, Australia, France, and Italy. The number of days the motorcycles were rented zoomed from 401 in 1999 to 224,134 in 2004. Harley found that 32 percent of rental customers bought a bike after renting, and another 37 percent planned to buy one within a year. About half of the renters spent more than $100 on Harley accessories such as T-shirts and gloves.[18]

By 2006, the popularity of Rallies and the eagerness of many communities to welcome bikers seemed insatiable. The following Information Box describes this phenomenon.

---

[16] Carleen Hawn, "What's in a Name? Whatever You Make It," *Forbes*, July 27, 1998, p. 88.

[17] Jonathan Fahey, "Love into Money," *Forbes*, January 7, 2002, pp. 60–65.

[18] Ryan Nakashima, *Associated Press*, as published in "Harley Rents Bikes to Boost Sales," *Cleveland Plain Dealer*, July 5, 2005, p. C2.

INFORMATION BOX

THE BOOM IN HARLEY RALLIES

Imagine this: It is an early week in August 2006, and your town of Sturgis, with all of 6,500 people, situated on the rolling Dakota plains nestled against the Black Hills, is playing host to half a million bikers from around the world for the 66th Sturgis Motorcycle Rally. For weeks motorcycles have been roaring around Sturgis, clogging the main streets and nearly doubling the state's population. The blaring of classic rock and country music almost drowns out the sounds of the revving engines. All available rooms have long been filled and biker tents are pitched on every available space, while shops and saloons are open from dawn to midnight and beyond. Still, you wonder how the town can accommodate such a horde.

Your neighbors couldn't be happier. "We do like to see them come. They're fun, good people," says the executive director of the chamber of commerce.

Why? You wonder. But then you know. These rallies are great for business. With the average Harley owner making about $75,000 a year, they are free spenders "and good tippers." A one-week event can bring several hundred million dollars to the local economy, and to the state in sales taxes.

Sturgis is not alone in attracting bikers. Laconia, New Hampshire, and Daytona Beach, Florida, also host hundreds of thousands of bikers, while hundreds of smaller events appear across the country every year. Johnstown, Pennsylvania, is one of the fastest-growing rallies, starting in 1998 with 3,500 bikers, and by 2006 drawing 200,000. The social calendar for motorcyclists has been rapidly filling up in recent years, as communities offer such popular activities as vintage bike shows, parades, stunt shows, races, scenic rides, and live music. "The residents come down, bring their kids. You'll see people here who don't even own motorcycles dressed like bikers." The old Viking and Hells Angel image of outlaws, barbarians, and wild men seems no more.[19]

How do you personally feel about motorcycles? Do you have one? Would you rent one? Would a rally attract you?

ANALYSIS

One of Vaughan Beals's first moves after the 1981 leveraged buyout was to improve production efficiency and quality control. This became the foundation for the strategic-regeneration moves to come. In this quest, he borrowed heavily from the Japanese, in particular by cultivating employee involvement.

The cultivation of a new customer segment for the big bikes had to be a major factor in the company's resurgence. To some, discovering that more affluent consumers embraced the big, flashy Harley motorcycles was a surprise of no small moment. After all, how could you have two more incompatible groups than the

[19] Peter Schroeder, "Their Economic Engines Are Harleys," *Wall Street Journal*, August 24, 2006, p. D8.

stereotyped black-jacketed cyclists and the Rubbies? Perhaps the change was due in part to the participation of high-profile people like Beals and some of his executives at motorcycle rallies and charity rides. Technological and comfort improvements in motorcycles and their equipment added to the new attractiveness. Dealers were coaxed to make their stores more inviting.

Along with this, expanding the product mix not only made Harley-branded merchandise a windfall for company and dealers alike, but also piqued the interest of upscale customers in motorcycles. The company was commendably aggressive in running with the growing popularity of the ancillary merchandise and making this well over a $100 million revenue booster.

Some questions remained. How durable was the popularity of the big bikes and the complementary merchandise with this affluent customer segment? Would it prove to be only a passing fad? If so, then Harley needed to seek diversifications as quickly as possible, even though the Holiday Rambler Corporation had brought no notable success by 1992. Diversifications often bring disappointed earnings compared with a firm's core business.

Another question concerned Harley's slowness in expanding production capability. Faced with a burgeoning demand, was it better to go slowly, be carefully protective of quality, and refrain from heavy debt commitments? This had been Harley's most recent strategy, but it raised the risk of permitting competitors to gain market share in the United States and especially in Europe. The following Issue Box discusses aggressive versus conservative planning.

ISSUE BOX

SHOULD WE BE AGGRESSIVE OR CONSERVATIVE IN OUR PLANNING?

The sales forecast—the estimate of sales for the periods ahead—serves a crucial role because it is the starting point for all detailed planning and budgeting. A volatile situation presents some high-risk alternatives: Should we be optimistic or conservative?

On one hand, with conservative planning in a growing market, a firm risks underestimating demand and being unable to expand its resources sufficiently to handle the potential. It may lack the manufacturing capability and sales staff to handle growth potential, and it may have to abdicate a good share of the growing business to competitors who are willing and able to expand their capability to meet the demands of the market.

On the other hand, a firm facing burgeoning demand should consider whether the growth is likely to be a short-term fad or a more permanent situation. A firm can easily become overextended in the buoyancy of booming business, only to see the collapse of such business jeopardizing its viability.

Harley's conservative decision was undoubtedly influenced by concerns about expanding beyond the limits of good quality control. The decision was probably also influenced by management's belief that Harley-Davidson had a loyal body of customers who would not switch despite the wait.

Do you think Harley-Davidson made the right decision by expanding conservatively? Why or why not? Defend your position.

❀ ❀ ❀

Invitation to Make Your Own Analysis and Conclusions

Do you think Beal's rejuvenation efforts could have been better handled? Support your conclusions.

❀ ❀ ❀

WHAT CAN BE LEARNED?

Again, a firm can come back from adversity.—The resurrection of Harley-Davidson almost from the point of extinction proves that adversity can be overcome. It need not be fatal or forever. This should be encouraging to all firms facing difficulties, and to their investors. Harley, however, is noteworthy in the time it took to grasp opportunities and counter competitors—it was decades before a Vaughan Beals came on the scene as change maker.

What does a turnaround require? Above all, it takes a leader who has the vision and confidence that things can be changed for the better. The change may not necessitate anything particularly innovative. It may involve only a rededication to basics, such as better quality control or an improved commitment to customer service brought about by a new, positive attitude among employees. But such a return to basics requires that a demoralized or apathetic organization be rejuvenated and remotivated. This calls for leadership of a high order. If the core business has been maintained, it at least provides a base to work from.

Preserve the core business at all costs.—Every viable firm has a basic core or distinctive position—sometimes called an *ecological niche*—in its business environment. This unique position may be due to its location or to a certain product. It may come from somewhat different operating methods, from the customers served, or from whatever makes the firm better than its competitors. This stronghold is the basic core of the company's survival. Though it may diversify and expand far beyond this area, the firm should not abandon its main bastion of strength.

Harley almost did this. Its core and, indeed, only business was its heavyweight bikes sold to a limited and loyal, though not at the time particularly savory, customer segment. Harley almost lost this core business by abandoning reasonable quality control to the point that its motorcycles became the butt of jokes. To his credit, upon assuming leadership Beals acted quickly to correct the production and employee-motivation problems. By preserving the core, Beals was able to pursue other avenues of expansion.

The power of a mystique.—Few products have been able to gain a mystique or cult following. Coors beer did for a few years in the 1960s and early 1970s, when it became the brew of celebrities and the emblem of the purity and freshness of the West. In the cigarette industry, Marlboro rose to become the top seller from a somewhat similar advertising and image thrust: the Marlboro man. The Ford Mustang had a mystique at one time. Somehow the big bikes of Harley-Davidson developed a more enduring mystique as they appealed to two disparate customer segments: the HOGS and the Rubbies. Different they might be, but both were loyal to their Harleys. The mystique led to "logo magic": Simply put the Harley-Davidson name and logo on all kinds of merchandise, and watch the sales take off.

How does a firm develop (or acquire) a mystique? There is no simple answer, no guarantee. Certainly a product has to be unique, but though most firms strive for this differentiation, few achieve a mystique. Image-building advertising, focusing on the target buyer, may help. Perhaps even better is image-building advertising that highlights the people customers might wish to emulate. But what about the black-leather-jacketed, perhaps bearded, cyclist?

Perhaps, in the final analysis, acquiring a mystique is more accidental and fortuitous than something that can be deliberately orchestrated. Two lessons, however, can be learned about mystiques: First, they do not last forever. Second, firms should run with them as long as possible and try to expand the reach of the name or logo to other goods, even unrelated ones, through licensing.

CONSIDER

What additional learning insights can you see coming from the Harley-Davidson resurgence?

QUESTIONS

1. Do you see any limitations to the viability and growth of Harley in the future? Discuss how these might be countered.

2. How durable do you think the Rubbies' infatuation with the heavyweight Harleys will be? What leads you to this conclusion?

3. A Harley-Davidson stockholder criticizes present management: "It is a mistake of the greatest magnitude that we abdicate a decent share of the European motorcycle market to foreign competitors, simply because we do not gear up our production to meet the demand." Discuss.

4. Given the resurgence of Harley-Davidson in the 1990s, would you invest money now in the company? Discuss, considering as many factors bearing on this decision as you can.

5. "Harley-Davidson's resurgence is only the purest luck. Who could have predicted, or influenced, the new popularity of big bikes with the affluent?" Discuss.

6. "The tariff increase on Japanese motorcycles in 1983 gave Harley-Davidson badly needed breathing room. In the final analysis, politics is more important than management in competing with foreign firms." What are your thoughts?

HANDS-ON EXERCISES

1. *Be a Devil's Advocate* (One who opposes a position to establish its merits and validity). Your mutual fund has a major investment in Harley-Davidson, and you are concerned with Vaughn Beals's presence at motorcycle rallies hobnobbing with black-jacketed motorcycle gangs. He maintains that this is the way to cultivate a loyal core of customers. Argue against Beals.

2. As a vice president at Harley-Davidson in the 1990s, you believe the recovery efforts should have gone well beyond the heavyweight bikes into lightweights. What arguments would you present for this change in strategy, and what specific recommendations would you make for the new course of action? What contrary arguments would you expect? How would you counter them?

3. As a staff assistant to Vaughan Beals when he first took over, you have been charged to design a strategy to bring a mystique to the Harley-Davidson name. How would you propose to do this? Be as specific as you can, and defend your reasoning.

YOUR PROGNOSIS FROM THE LATEST DEVELOPMENTS

Do you think the public's willingness to promote biker rallies is reaching a saturation point? Why or why not? How does your prediction impact on Harley?

TEAM DEBATE EXERCISE

A major schism has developed in the executive ranks of Harley-Davidson. Many executives believe it is a monumental mistake not to gear up production to meet the burgeoning worldwide demand for Harleys. Others see the present go-slow approach to increasing production as more prudent. Persuasively support your position and attack the other side.

INVITATION TO RESEARCH

What is the situation with Harley-Davidson today? Has the cult following remained as strong as ever? How are the new lightweight bikes faring? Are many women being attracted to Harleys? Have any new competitors emerged? Has Harley diversified beyond bikes? Are rallies still drawing hundreds of thousands of bikers?

CHAPTER SEVEN

IBM: A Fading Giant Rejuvenates

*L*ike Continental Air, IBM seemed to be on a roller-coaster, with the major difference that it was so much bigger and had so many years of industry domination. The common notion is that the bigger the firm, the more difficult to turn it around, just as a giant ocean liner needs far more room to maneuver to avoid catastrophe than a smaller vessel.

THE REALITY AND THE FLAWED ILLUSION

On January 19, 1993, International Business Machines Corporation reported a record $5.46 billion loss for the fourth quarter of 1992, and a deficit for the entire year of $4.97 billion, the biggest annual loss in American corporate history. (General Motors recorded a 1991 loss of $4.45 billion, after huge charges for cutbacks and plant closings. And Ford Motor Company reported a net loss of more than $6 billion for 1992, but that was a non-cash charge to account for the future costs of retiree benefits.) The human cost, as far as employment was concerned, was also consequential; some 42,900 had been laid off in 1992, with an additional 25,000 planned to go in 1993. In its fifth restructuring since 1985, seemingly endless rounds of job cuts and firings had eliminated 100,000 jobs in less than a decade. Not surprisingly, IBM's share price, which was above $100 in the summer of 1992, closed at an 11-year low of $48.375. Yet IBM had long been the ultimate blue-chip company, reigning supreme in the computer industry. How could its problems have surfaced so suddenly and so violently?

THE ROAD TO INDUSTRY DOMINANCE

"They hired my father to make a go of this company in 1914, the year I was born," said Thomas J. Watson Jr. "To some degree I've been a part of IBM ever since."[1] Watson

---

[1] Michael W. Miller, "IBM's Watson Offers Personal View of the Company's Recent Difficulties," *Wall Street Journal*, December 21, 1992, p. A3.

89

took over his father's medium-sized company in 1956 and built it into a technological giant. Retired for almost 19 years by 1992, he now was witnessing the company in the throes of its greatest adversity.

IBM had become the largest computer maker in the world. With its revenues steadily growing since 1946, it had become the bluest of blue-chip companies. It had 350,000 employees worldwide and was one of the largest U.S.-based employers. Its 1991 revenues had approached $67 billion, and while profits had dropped some from the peak of $6.5 billion in 1984, its common stock still commanded a price-earnings ratio of over 100, making it a darling of investors. In 1989, it ranked first among all U.S. firms in market value (the total capitalization of common stock, based on the stock price and the number of shares outstanding), fourth in total sales, and fourth in net profits.[2]

In Watson's day, IBM was known for its centralized decision making. Decisions affecting product lines were made at the highest levels of management. Even IBM's culture was centralized and standardized, with strict behavioral and dress codes. For example, a blue suit, white shirt, and dark tie were the public uniform, and IBM became widely known as "Big Blue."

One of IBM's greatest assets was its research labs, by far the largest and costliest of their kind in the world, with staffs that included three Nobel Prize winners. IBM treated its research and development function with tender, loving care, regularly budgeting 10 percent of sales for this forward-looking activity. In 1991, for example, the R & D budget was $6.6 billion.

The past success of IBM and future expectations based on its seeming stranglehold over the technology of the future made it a darling of consultants, analysts, and market researchers. Management theorists, all the way from Peter Drucker to Tom Peters (of *In Search of Excellence* fame), lined up to analyze what made IBM so good. And the business press regularly produced articles of praise and awe of IBM.

Alas, the adulation was to change abruptly by 1992. Somehow, insidiously, IBM had gotten fat and complacent over the years. IBM's problems, however, went deeper, as we will explore in the next section.

CHANGING FORTUNES

The great IBM debacle of 1992 began in the early 1980s with a questionable management decision. Perhaps the problems were more deep-rooted than any single decision; perhaps they were more a consequence of the bureaucracy that often typifies behemoth organizations (Sears and General Motors faced somewhat similar worsening problems), growing layers of policies, and entrenched interests.

In the early 1980s, two little firms, Intel and Microsoft, were upstarts, just emerging in the industry dominated by IBM. Their success by the 1990s can be largely attributed to their nurturing by IBM. Each got a major break when it was "anointed" as a key supplier for IBM's new personal computer (PC). Intel was

---

[2] "Ranking the Forbes 500s," *Forbes*, April 30, 1990, p. 306.

signed on to make the chips, and Microsoft, the software. The aggressive youngsters proceeded to set standards for successive PC generations, and in the process wrested control over the PC's future from IBM. And the PC was to become the product of the future, shouldering aside the giant mainframe that was IBM's strength.

As IBM began losing ground in one market after another, Intel and Microsoft were gaining dominance. Ten years before, in 1982, the market value of the stock of Intel and Microsoft combined amounted to about a tenth of IBM's. By October 1992, their combined stock value surpassed IBM's; by the end of the year, they topped IBM's market value by almost 50 percent. See Table 7.1 for comparative operating statistics of IBM, Intel, and Microsoft. Table 7.2 shows the market valuations of IBM, Intel, and Microsoft from 1989 to 1992, the years before and during the collapse of investor esteem.

Defensive Reactions of IBM

As the problems of IBM became more visible to the entire investment community, Chairman John Akers sought to institute reforms to turn the behemoth around. His problem—and need—was to uproot a corporate structure and culture that had developed when IBM had no serious competition.

A cumbersome bureaucracy stymied the company from being innovative in a fast-moving industry. Major commitments still went to high-margin mainframes, but these were no longer necessary in many situations, given the computing power of

TABLE 7.1. Growth of IBM and the Upstarts, Microsoft and Intel, 1983–1992 ($ million)

	1983	1985	1987	1989	1991	1992
IBM:						
Revenues	$40,180	50,056	$54,217	$62,710	$64,792	$67,045
Net Income	5,485	6,555	5,258	3,758	(2,827)	(2,784)
% of Revenue	13.6%	13.1%	9.7%	6.0%	—	—
Microsoft:						
Revenues	$50	$140	$346	$804	$1,843	$2,759
Net Income	6	24	72	171	463	708
% of Revenue	12.0%	17.1%	20.8%	21.3%	25.1%	25.7%
Intel:						
Revenues	$1,122	$1,365	$1,907	$3,127	$4,779	$5,192
Net Income	116	2	176	391	819	827
% of Revenue	10.3%	0.1%	9.2%	12.5%	17.1%	15.9%

Source: Company annual statements; 1992 figures are estimates from *Forbes,* "Annual Report of American Industry." January 4, 1993, pp. 115–116.

Commentary: Note the great growth of the upstarts in recent years, both in revenues and in profits, compared with IBM. Also note the great performance of Microsoft and Intel in profit as a percent of revenues.

TABLE 7.2.   Market Value and Rank Among All U.S. Companies of IBM
and the Upstarts, Microsoft and Intel, 1989 and 1992

	Rank		Market Value ($mil)	
	1989	1992	1989	1992
IBM	1	13	$60,345	$30,715
Microsoft	92	25	6,018	23,608
Intel	65	22	7,842	24,735

Source: Forbes Annual Directory Issue, "The Forbes Market Value 500," April 13, 1990, pp. 258–259, and April 26, 1993, p. 242. The market value is the per share price multiplied by the number of shares outstanding for all classes of common stock.

Commentary: The market valuation reflects the stature of the firms in the eyes of investors. Obviously, IBM has lost badly during this period, while Microsoft and Intel have more than tripled their market valuation, almost approaching that of IBM. Yet IBM's sales were $65.5 billion in 1992, against sales of Microsoft of $3.3 and Intel of $5.8.

desktop PCs. IBM had problems getting to market quickly with the technological innovations that were revolutionizing the industry. In 1991, Akers warned an unbelieving group of IBM managers of the coming difficulties. "The business is in crisis."[3]

He attempted to push power downward, to decentralize some of the decision-making that for decades had resided at the top. His more radical proposal was to break up IBM, dividing it into 13 divisions and giving each more autonomy. He sought to expand the services business and make the company more responsive to customer needs. Perhaps most important, he saw a crucial need to pare costs by cutting the fat from the organization.

The need for cost-cutting was evident to all but the entrenched bureaucracy. IBM's total costs grew 12 percent a year in the mid-1980s, while revenues were not keeping up with this growth.[4] Part of the plan for reducing costs involved cutting employees, which violated a cherished tradition dating back to Thomas Watson's father and the beginning of IBM: a promise never to lay off IBM workers for economic reasons.[5] Most of the downsizing was indeed accomplished by voluntary retirements and attractive severance packages, but eventually outright layoffs became necessary.

The changes decreed by Akers would leave the unified sales division untouched, but each of the new product group divisions would act as a separate operating unit, with financial reports broken down accordingly. Particularly troubling to Akers was the recent performance of the personal computer business. At a time when demand, as well as competition, was burgeoning for PCs, this division was languishing. Early in 1992 Akers tapped James Cannavino to head the $11 billion Personal Systems Division, which also included workstations and software.

[3] David Kirkpatrick, "Breaking up IBM," *Fortune*, July 27, 1992, p. 44.
[4] *Ibid.*, p. 53.
[5] Miller, p. A4.

IBM PC

PCs had been the rising star of the company, despite the fact that mainframes still accounted for about $20 billion in revenues. But in 1990, market share dropped drastically as new competitors offered PCs at much lower prices than IBM; many experts claimed that these clones were at least equal to IBM's PCs in quality. Throughout 1992, IBM had been losing market share in an industry price war. Even after it attempted to counter Compaq's price cuts in June, IBM's prices still remained as much as one-third higher than its competitors' prices. Even worse, IBM had announced new fall models, and this development curbed sales of current models. At the upper end of the PC market, Sun Microsystems and Hewlett-Packard were bringing out more powerful workstations that tied PCs together with mini- and mainframe computers. James Cannavino faced a major challenge in reviving the PC.

Cannavino planned to streamline operations by slicing off a new unit to focus exclusively on developing and manufacturing PC hardware. By so doing, he would cut PCs loose from the rest of Personal Systems and the workstations and software. This, he believed, would create a streamlined organization that could cut prices often, roll out new products several times a year, sell through any kind of store, and provide customers with whatever software they wanted, even if it was not IBM's.[6] Autonomy in these areas was deemed necessary in order to respond quickly to competitors and opportunities, without having to deal with the IBM bureaucracy.

THE CRISIS

On January 25, 1993, John Akers announced that he was stepping down as IBM's chairman and chief executive. He had lost the confidence of the board of directors. Until mid-January, Akers had been determined to see IBM through its crisis, at least until he reached IBM's customary retirement age of 60, which would be December 1994. But the horrendous $4.97 billion loss in 1992 changed that, and investor and public pressure mounted for a top management change. The fourth quarter of 1992 was especially shocking, brought on by weak European sales and a steep decline in sales of minicomputers and mainframes. Now IBM's stock sank to a 17-year low, below 46.

Other aspects of the operation also accentuated IBM's fall from grace: most notably, the jewel of its operation, its mainframe processors and storage systems.

For 25 years IBM had dominated the $50 billion worldwide mainframe industry. In 1992, overall sales of such equipment grew at only 2 percent, but IBM experienced a 10 to 15 percent drop in revenue. At the same time, its major mainframe rivals, Amdahl Corp. and Unisys Corp., had respective sales gains of 48 percent and 10 percent.[7]

---

[6] "Stand Back, Big Blue—And Wish Me Luck," *Business Week*, August 17, 1992, p. 99.
[7] John Verity, "Guess What: IBM Is Losing Out in Mainframes, Too," *Business Week*, February 8, 1993, p. 106.

IBM was clearly lagging in developing new computers that could out-perform the old ones, such as IBM's System/390. Competitors' models exceeded IBM's old computers not only in absolute power but in prices, selling at prices of a tenth or less of IBM's price per unit of computing. For example, with IBM's mainframe computers, customers paid approximately $100,000 for each MIPS, or the capacity to execute 1 million instructions per second, this being the rough gauge of computing power. Hewlett-Packard offered similar capability at a cost of only $12,000 per MIPS, and AT&T's NCR unit could sell a machine for $12.5 million that outperformed IBM's $20 million ES/9000 processor complex.[8]

In a series of full-page advertisements appearing in the *Wall Street Journal* and other business publications, IBM defended the mainframe and attacked the focus on MIPS:

> One issue surrounding mainframes is their cost. It's often compared using dollars per MIPS with the cost of microprocessor systems, and on that basis mainframes lose. But ... dollars per MIPS alone is a superficial measurement. The real issue is function. Today's appetite for information demands serious network and systems management, around-the-clock availability, efficient mass storage and genuine data security. MIPS alone provides none of these, but IBM mainframes have them built in, and more fully developed than anything available on microprocessors.[9]

On March 24, 1993, 51-year-old Louis V. Gerstner Jr. was named the new chief executive of IBM. The two-month search for a replacement for Akers had captivated the media, with speculation ranging widely. The choice of an outsider caught many by surprise. Gerstner was chairman and CEO of RJR Nabisco, a food and tobacco giant, but Nabisco was a far cry from a computer company. And IBM had always prided itself on promoting from within—most IBM executives, including John Akers, were life-long IBM employees. Not all analysts supported the selection of Gerstner. While most did not criticize the board for going outside IBM to find a replacement for Akers, some questioned going outside the computer industry or other high-tech industries. Geoff Lewis, senior editor of *Business Week*, fully supported the choice. He had suggested the desirability of bringing in some outside managers to Akers in 1988:

> Akers seemed shocked—maybe even offended—by my question. After a moment, he answered "IBM has the best recruitment system anywhere and spends more than anybody on training. Sometimes it might help to seek outsiders with unusual skills, but the company already had the best people in the world."[10]

See the Issue Box: Should We Promote from Within? for a discussion of this.

---

[8] *Ibid.*

[9] Taken from advertisement, *Wall Street Journal*, March 5, 1993, p. B8.

[10] Geoff Lewis, "One Fresh Face at IBM May Not Be Enough," *Business Week*, April 12, 1993, p. 33

ISSUE BOX

SHOULD WE PROMOTE FROM WITHIN?

A heavy commitment to promoting from within, as long characterized IBM, is sometimes derisively called "inbreeding." The traditional argument against this practice maintains that an organization with such a policy is not alert to needed changes and it is enamored with the status quo, "the way we have always done it." Proponents of promotion from within talk about the motivation and great loyalty it engenders, with every employee knowing that he or she has a chance of becoming a high-level executive.

The opposite course of action—that is, heavy commitment to placing outsiders in important executive positions—plays havoc with the morale of trainees and lower-level executives and destroys the sense of continuity and loyalty. A middle ground seems preferable: filling many executive positions from within, promoting this idea to encourage both the achievement of current executives and the recruiting of trainees, and at the same time bringing the strengths and experiences of outsiders into the organization.

Do you think there are circumstances in which one extreme or the other regarding promotion policy might be best? Discuss.

Later in this chapter we will describe and comment on the great comeback engineered by Gerstner. But for now, let us examine the factors leading to the decline in IBM's fortunes.

ANALYSIS

In examining the major contributors to IBM's fall from grace, we will analyze the predisposing or underlying factors, resultants, and controversies.

Predisposing Factors

Cumbersome Organization

As IBM grew with its success, it became more and more bureaucratic. One author described it as big and bloated. Another said it had an "inward-looking culture that kept them from waking up on time."[11] Regardless of phraseology, by the late 1980s IBM could not bring new machines quickly into the market, nor was it able to make the fast pricing and other strategic decisions of its smaller competitors. Too many layers of management, too many vested interests, a tradition-ridden mentality, and a gradually emerging contentment with the status quo shackled it—this in an industry

---

[11] Jennifer Reese, "The Big and the Bloated: It's Tough Being No. 1," *Fortune*, July 27, 1992, p. 49.

that some thought to be mature, but which in reality was gripped by burgeoning change. The cumbersome IBM found itself at a competitive disadvantage compared with smaller, hungrier, more aggressive, and above all, more nimble firms. Impeding every effort to make major changes effective was the typical burden facing all large and mature organizations: resistance to change. The Information Box: Resistance to Change discusses this phenomenon.

INFORMATION BOX

RESISTANCE TO CHANGE

People and organizations have a natural reluctance to embrace change. Change is disruptive. It can destroy accepted ways of doing things and familiar authority-responsibility relationships. It makes people uneasy because their routines will likely be disrupted; their interpersonal relationships with subordinates, co-workers, and superiors may well be modified. Positions that were deemed important before the change may be downgraded. And those who view themselves as highly competent in a particular job may be forced to assume unfamiliar duties.

Resistance to change can be combated by good communication with participants about forthcoming changes. Without such communication, rumors and fears can assume monumental proportions. Acceptance of change can be facilitated if managers involve employees as fully as possible in planning the changes, solicit and welcome their participation, and assure them that their positions will not be impaired, only changed. Gradual rather than abrupt changes also make a transition smoother, as participants can be initially exposed to the changes without drastic upheavals.

In the final analysis, however, needed changes should not be delayed or canceled because of their possible negative repercussions on the organization. If change is necessary, it should be initiated. Individuals and organizations can adapt to change—although it may take some time.

The worst change an employee may face is layoff. And when no one knows when the next layoff will occur or who will be affected, morale and productivity may both be devastated. Discuss how managers might best handle the necessity of upcoming layoffs.

Overly Centralized Management Structure

Often related to a cumbersome bureaucratic organization is rigid centralization of authority and decision making. Certain negative consequences may result when all major decisions have to be made at corporate headquarters rather than down the line. Decision making is necessarily slowed, since executives feel they must fully investigate all aspects, and, not being personally involved with the recommendation, they may be not only skeptical but critical of new projects and initiatives. More than this, the enthusiasm and creativity of lower-level executives may be curbed by the typical conservatism of a higher-management team divorced from the intimacy of the problem or the opportunity. The motivation and morale needed for a climate of innovation and creativity is stifled under the twin bureaucratic attitudes "Don't take a chance" and "Don't rock the boat."

The Three Cs Mindset of Vulnerability

Firms that are well entrenched in their industry and have dominated it for years tend to fall into a mindset that leaves them vulnerable to aggressive and innovative competitors. (We will encounter this syndrome again in Chapter 12 with Boeing. But it bears repeating.)

The "three Cs" that are detrimental to a front-runner's continued success are:

Complacency
Conservatism
Conceit

Complacency is smugness—a complacent firm is self-satisfied, content with the status quo, no longer hungry and eager for growth. *Conservatism*, when excessive, characterizes a management that is wedded to the past, to the traditional, to the way things have always been done. Conservative managers see no need to change because they believe nothing is different today (e.g., "Mainframe computers are the models of the industry and always will be"). Finally, *conceit* reinforces the myopia of the mindset: conceit for present and potential competitors. The beliefs that "we are the best" and "no one else can touch us" can easily permeate an organization that has enjoyed success for years.

The three Cs mindset leave no incentive to undertake aggressive and innovative actions, and contributes to growing disinterest in such important facets of the business as customer relations, service, and even quality control. Furthermore, it inhibits interest in developing innovative new products that may *cannibalize*—that is, take business away from—existing products or disrupt entrenched interests. (We will discuss cannibalization in more detail shortly.)

Resultants

Over-Dependence on High-Margin Mainframes

The mainframe computers had long been the greatest source of market power and profits for IBM. But its conservative and tradition-minded bureaucracy could not accept the reality that computer power was becoming a desktop commodity. Although a market still existed for the massive mainframes, it was limited and had little growth potential; the future belonged to desktop computers and workstations. And here IBM, in a lapse of monumental proportions, relinquished its dominance. First there were the minicomputers, and these opened up a whole new industry, one with scores of hungry competitors. But the cycle of industry creation and decline started anew by the early 1980s as personal computers began to replace minicomputers in defining new markets and fostering new competitors. While the mainframe was not replaced, its markets became more limited, and cannibalization became the fear. See the Information Box: Cannibalization.

INFORMATION BOX

CANNIBALIZATION

Cannibalization occurs when a company's new product takes some business away from an existing product. The new product's success consequently does not contribute its full measure to company revenues, because some sales will be switched from older products. The amount of cannibalization can range from virtually none to almost total. In this latter case, then, the new product simply replaces the older product, with no real sales gain achieved. If the new product is less profitable than the older one, the impact and the fear of cannibalization becomes all the greater.

For IBM, PCs and the other equipment smaller than mainframes would not come close to replacing the bigger units. Still, some cannibalizing was likely. And the profits on the lower-price computers were many times less than those of mainframes.

The argument can justifiably be made that if a company does not bring out new products, then its competitors will, and that it is better to compete with one's own products. Still, the threat of cannibalization can cause a hesitation, a blink, in a full-scale effort to rush to market with an internally competing product. This reluctance and hesitation needs to be guarded against, lest the firm find itself no longer in the vanguard of innovation.

Assume the role of a vocal stockholder at the annual meeting. What arguments would you make for a crash program to rush the PC to market despite possible cannibalization? What contrary arguments would you expect, and how would you counter them?

Neglect of Software and Service

At a time when software and service had become ever more important, IBM still had a fixation on hardware. In 1992, services made up only 9 percent of IBM's revenue. Criticism flowed:

> Technology is becoming a commodity, and the difference between winning and losing comes in how you deliver that technology. Service will be the differentiator. As a customer, I want a supplier who's going to make all my stuff work together. The job is to understand the customer's needs in detail.[12]

In the process of losing touch with customers, the sales force had become reluctant to sell low-margin open systems if it could push proprietary mainframes or minicomputers.

Bloated Costs

As indications of the fat that had insidiously grown in the organization, some 42,900 jobs were cut in 1992, thankfully all through early-retirement programs. An additional 25,000 people were expected to be laid off in 1993, some without

---

[12] Kirkpatrick, pp. 49,52.

the benefit of early-retirement packages. Health benefits for employees were also scaled down. Manufacturing capacity was reduced 25 percent, and two of three mainframe-development labs were closed. But perhaps the greatest bloat was R & D.

Diminishing Payoff of Massive R & D Expenditures

As noted earlier, IBM spent heavily on research and development, often as much as 10 percent of sales (see Table 7.3). Its research labs were by far the largest and costliest of their kind in the world.

IBM labs were capable of inventing amazing things. For example, they developed the world's smallest transistor, 1 / 75,000th the width of a human hair. Somehow, with all these R & D resources and expenditures, IBM lagged in transferring its innovation to the marketplace. The organization lacked the ability to quickly translate laboratory prototypes into commercial triumphs. Commercial R & D is wasted without this.

Controversies

Questionable Decisions

No executive has a perfect batting average of good decisions. Indeed, most executives are doing well if they bat more than 500—in other words, make more good decisions than bad decisions. But, alas, decisions are all relative. Much depends on the importance, the consequences, of these decisions.

IBM made a decision of monumental long-term consequences in the early 1980s. At that time, IBM designated two upstart West Coast companies to be the key suppliers for its new personal computer. In doing so, it gave away its chances to control the personal computer industry. Over the next ten years, each of these two firms would develop a near-monopoly—Intel in microprocessors, and Microsoft in operating-systems software. Instead of keeping such developments proprietary (i.e., within its own organization), IBM, in an urge to save developmental time, gave these two small firms a golden opportunity, which both grasped to the fullest. By 1992, Intel and Microsoft had emerged as the computer industry's dominant firms.

The decision still is controversial. It saved IBM badly needed time in bringing its PC to market, and as computer technology became ever more complex, not even an

TABLE 7.3.   IBM Research and Development Expenditures as a Percent of Revenues, 1987–1991

	1987	1988	1989	1990	1991
Revenues ($ million)	$54,217	$59,681	$62,710	$64,792	$67,045
Research, development, and engineering costs	5,434	5,925	6,827	6,554	6,644
Percent of revenues	10.0%	9.9%	10.9%	10.1%	9.9%

Source: Company annual reports.

Commentary: Where is the significant contribution from about 10 percent of sales budgeted for R&D?

IBM could be expected to have the ability and resources to go it alone. Linking up with competitors offers better products and services and a faster flow of technology today, and seems the wave of the future.

Former IBM CEO Thomas Watson Jr. has criticized his successors Frank Cary and John Opel for phasing out rentals and selling the massive mainframe computer outright. Originally, purchasers could only lease the machines, thus giving IBM a dependable cushion of cash each year ("my golden goose," Watson called it.)[13] Doing away with renting left IBM a newly volatile business just as the industry position began worsening. John Akers, newly installed as CEO, was thus left with a hostile environment without the cushion or support of steady revenues coming from rentals, according to Watson's argument. But the counter-position holds that selling brought needed cash quickly into company coffers. Furthermore, it was unlikely, given the more competitive climate that was emerging in the 1980s, that big customers would continue to tolerate the leasing arrangement when they could buy their machines, if not from IBM, then from another supplier whose machines were just as good or better.

Breaking Up IBM

The general consensus of management experts favored Akers's reforms, which broke up Big Blue into 13 divisions and gave them increasing autonomy—even to the point that shares of some of the new Baby Blues might be distributed to stockholders. The idea was not unlike Japan's *keiretsu*, in which alliances of substantially independent companies with common objectives seek and develop business individually.

The assumption in favor of such breaking up is that the sum of the parts is greater than the whole, so that autonomy and motivation will bring more total revenues and profits. But these hypothesized benefits are not assured. At issue is whether the good of the whole would be better served by sub-optimizing some business units—that is, by reducing the profit maximizing of some units in order to have the highest degree of coordination and cooperation. Asking disparate units of an organization to pursue their own individual profit maximization plants the seeds of intense intramural competition, with cannibalization and infighting likely. Is the whole better served by a less intensely competitive internal environment?

THE COMEBACK UNDER GERSTNER

Louis Gerstner took command in March 1993. The company, as we have seen, was reeling. In a reversal of major proportions, he brought IBM back to record profitability. Table 7.4 shows the statistics of what seemed to be a sensational turnaround. In 1994, the company earned $3 billion, its first profitable year since 1990. Perhaps of greater significance, compared with the previous year this represented a profit swing of $11 billion. And revenues grew for the first time since 1990. Annual expenses were reduced by $3.5 billion, some 15 percent. Equally important, 1994 finished with

[13] Miller, p. A4

Table 7.4.   IBM's Resurgence under Gerstner, 1993–1995

	1993	1994	1995
	(millions of dollars)		
Revenue	$62,716	64,052	$71,940
Net Earnings (loss)	(8,101)	3,021	4,178
Net Earnings (loss) per Share of Common Stock	(14.22)	5.02	7.23
Working Capital	6,052	12,112	9,043
Total Debt	27,342	22,118	21,629
Number of Employees	256,207	219,839	225,347

Source: Company annual reports.

Commentary: In virtually all measures of performance, IBM made a significant turnaround from 1993 to 1995. Note in particular the decrease in debt and the great profit turnaround.

financial strength: IBM had more than $10 billion in cash, and basic debt was reduced by $3.3 billion. Of greater importance to stockholders, IBM stock nearly tripled in price, racing from a 1993 low of 40 to a high of 114 on August 17, 1995.

By all such performance statistics, Gerstner had done an outstanding job of turning the behemoth around. At first there had been doubters. For the most part, their skepticism was rooted in the notion that Gerstner was not aggressive enough, that he did not tamper mightily with the organizational structure of IBM. For example, a 1994 *Fortune* article questioned: "Is He Too Cautious to Save IBM?" The article went on to say, "After running IBM for more than a year and a half, CEO Lou Gerstner has revealed himself to be something other than the revolutionary whom the directors of this battered and demoralized enterprise once seemed to want ... he seems to be attempting a conventional turnaround: deep-cleaning and redecorating the house rather than gutting and renovating it."[14] The article acknowledged the "surprisingly good" results, but attributed them to luck: "Unexpectedly high demand for mainframe computers has given the company temporary respite from the inevitable shift to less lucrative products."[15]

Before Gerstner took over, IBM was moving toward a breakup into 13 independent units: one for mainframes, one for PCs, one for disk drives, and so on. But he saw IBM's competitive advantage as lying in its ability to offer customers a complete package, a one-stop shopping for everyone seeking help in solving technological problems: a unified IBM—somehow, an IBM with a single, efficient team.

The Quiet Revolution

Critics inclined toward revolutionary measures were disappointed. "Transforming IBM is not something we can do in one or two years," Gerstner stated. "The better we are at fixing some of the short-term things, the more time we have to deal with the

[14] Allison Rogers, "Is He Too Cautious to Save IBM?" *Fortune*, October 3, 1994, p. 78.
[15] *Ibid.*

long-term issues."[16] His efforts were contrasted with those of Albert Dunlap, who was overhauling Scott Paper at about the same time. Dunlap replaced 9 of the 11 top executives in the first few days and laid off one-third of the total workforce. Gerstner brought in only eight top executives from outside IBM to sit on the 37-person Worldwide Management Council.

A non-technical man, Gerstner's strengths were in selling: cookies and cigarettes at RJR, travel services during an 11-year career at American Express Company. Weeks after taking over, he talked to IBM's top 100 customers at a retreat in Chantilly, Virginia. He asked them what IBM was doing right and wrong. They were surprised and delighted. This was the first time the chairman of the 72-year-old company had ever polled its customers. The input was revealing:

> The customers told him IBM was difficult to work with and unresponsive to customers' needs. For example, customers who needed IBM's famed mainframe computers were being told that the machines were dinosaurs and that the company would have to consider getting out of the business.[17]

Gerstner told these customers that IBM was in mainframes to stay, and would aggressively cut prices and focus on helping them set up, manage, and link the systems.

Perhaps the most obvious change Gerstner instituted was the elimination of a dress code that once kept IBM salespeople in blue suits and white shirts.

By the spring of 1997, *Fortune* highlighted Gerstner on its cover with the feature article, "The Holy Terror Who's Saving IBM."[18] The growth continued. Revenues in 1997 were over $78 billion and net income over $6 billion. For 1998, IBM shares were one of the leading gainers among the companies that make up the Dow Jones Industrial Average.

Gerstner's turnaround was no fluke.

UPDATE

Louis Gerstner, age 60, stepped down from the chairmanship of IBM at the end of 2002 to become chairman of the Carlyle Group investment firm. He succeeded former U.S. Defense Secretary Frank Carlucci, 72 years old, who had been chairman for a decade. Carlyle was overseeing $13.5 billion in investments for institutions and wealthy clients, and had long been politically connected with such notables as former President George H.W. Bush, ex-Secretary of State James Baker, and former British Prime Minister John Major. The founding partner of Carlyle said that Gerstner could help Carlyle unify its culture and strategy: "That's exactly what he did at IBM and it's directly applicable here."[19] Thus, **managerial skills are often transferable**.

---

[16] *Ibid.*, p.78.
[17] "IBM Focuses on Sales," *Cleveland Plain Dealer*, September 10, 1996, p. 6 C.
[18] Betsy Morris, "He's Saving Big Blue," *Fortune*, April 14, 1997, pp. 68–81.
[19] Kara Scannell and William M. Bulkeley, "IBM's Gerstner to Join Carlyle as Chairman," *Wall Street Journal*, November 22, 2002, p. A5.

Samuel J. Palmisano, having led IBM's Global Services, replaced Gerstner on January 29, 2002. By 2005, IBM's revenues were $91 billion, and services and consulting (Global Service) revenues were larger than those from manufacturing (Hardware). The company has been steadily increasing its workforce in developing countries (notably, India), and retrenching in the United States and Europe. In May 2005, IBM got out of the PC business, selling to Chinese computer maker Lenovo, in which it would still have a 19 percent stake.[20]

○ ○ ○

Invitation to Make Your Own Analysis and Conclusion

To what do *you* ascribe Gerstner's success?

Do you agree with everything he did?

Do you agree with the more recent sale of the PC business to a Chinese firm? Why or why not?

○ ○ ○

WHAT CAN BE LEARNED?

Beware of the cannibalization phobia.—We have just set the parameters of the issue of cannibalization—the question of how far a firm should go in developing products and encouraging intramural competition that will take away sales from its other products and units. The issue is particularly troubling when the part of the business that is likely to suffer is the most profitable in the company. Yet cannibalization should not even be an issue. At stake is the forward-leaning of the company, its embracing of innovation and improved technology, as well as its competitive stance. Unless a firm has an assured monopoly position, it can expect competitors to introduce advances in technology and/or new efficiencies of productivity and customer service.

In general, no firm should rest on its laurels. Businesses must introduce improvements and change as soon as possible, hopefully ahead of the competition—all this without regard to any possible impairment of sales and profits of existing products and units.

Need to be "lean and mean" (sometimes called "acting small").—The marketplace is uncertain. Especially is this true in high-tech industries. In such environments, a larger firm needs to keep the responsiveness and flexibility of smaller firms. It must avoid layers of management, delimiting policies, and a tradition-bound mindset. Otherwise our big firm is like the behemoth vessel, unable to stop or change course without losing precious time and distance. But how can a big firm keep the maneuverability and innovative-mindedness of a smaller firm? How can it remain "lean and mean" with increasing size?

---

[20] Company annual reports.

We can identify certain conditions or factors of lean and mean firms:

1. They have simple organizations. Typically, they are decentralized, with decision-making moved lower in the organization. This discourages the buildup of cumbersome bureaucracy and staff, which tends to add both increasing overhead expenses and the red tape that stultifies fast reaction time.

   With a simple organization comes a relatively flat one, with less levels of management than comparable firms. This also has certain desirable consequences. Overhead is greatly reduced because there are fewer executives and their expensive staffs. But communication is also improved, since higher executives are more accessible, and directions and feedback are less distorted because of more direct communication channels. Even morale is improved because of the better accessibility to leaders of the organization.

2. Receptivity and encouragement of new ideas. A major factor in the inertia of large firms consists of the vested interests who see their power threatened by new ideas and innovative directions. Consequently, real creativity is stymied by not being appreciated; often it is even discouraged.

   A firm that wishes to be lean and mean must seek new ideas. This implies rewards and recognition for creativity, but, even more, acting upon worthwhile ideas. Few things are more thwarting to organizational creativity than pigeon-holing the good ideas of eager employees.

3. Participation in planning should be moved as low in the organization as possible. Important employees and lower-level managers should be involved in decisions concerning their responsibilities, with their ideas receiving reasonable weight in final decisions. Performance goals—and rewards—should be moved as low in the organization as possible. Such an organizational climate encourages innovation, improves motivation and morale, and can lead to the fast reaction time that characterizes small organizations and so seldom the large.

4. The philosophy of minimum frills, even austerity, at the corporate level is a final factor that characterizes some highly successful proactive larger organizations. Two of the most successful firms today, Wal-Mart and Southwest Airlines (described in later cases in this book), evince this philosophy to the furthest degree. A no-frills orientation by top management is the greatest corporate model for curbing frivolous costs throughout an organization.

Beware the "king of the hill" three Cs mindset.—As a firm gains dominance and maturity, a natural mindset evolution can occur, and must be guarded against. Conservatism, complacency, and conceit insidiously move in. Usually this happens at the highest levels, and readily filters down to the rest of the organization. As discussed earlier, this mindset leaves a firm highly vulnerable to competitors who are smaller and hungrier. And so the king of the hill is toppled.

Top management usually initiates such a mindset, but can also lead in inhibiting it. The lean-and-mean organization is anathema to the three Cs mindset. If we can curb bureaucratic buildup, then the seeds are thwarted. The most important way to prevent this mindset is to encourage innovative thinking throughout the organization, as well as to bring in fresh blood from outside the organization to fill some positions. A strict adherence to promotion from within is inhibiting.

The power of greater commitment to customers.—One of Gerstner's bigger contributions to the turnaround of IBM was his customer focus: putting the needs of customers first, asking—not merely talking. He found out what customers wanted, saw what could be done to best meet their needs as quickly as possible, and at the same time toned down the arrogance of an "elite" staff of sales representatives. The style change from blue suits and white shirts was the visible sign of a change in culture and attitudes.

Many firms profess a great commitment to customers and service. So common are such statements that one wonders how much is mere lip service. It is so easy to say this, and then not really follow up. In so doing, the opportunity to develop a trusting relationship is lost.

We can overcome adversity!—We saw this with Continental Airlines and now with IBM. Such examples should be motivating and inspiring for all organizations and the executives trying to turn them around. Adversity need not be forever. Firms and their managers should be capable of learning from mistakes. As such, mistakes can be valuable learning experiences, leading the way to better performance and future decisions.

CONSIDER

What additional learning insights do you see emerging from the IBM case?

QUESTIONS

1. Assess the pro and con arguments for the 1982 decision to delegate to Microsoft and Intel a foothold in software and operating systems. (Keep your perspective to that of the early 1980s; don't be biased with the benefit of hindsight.)

2. Do you see any way that IBM could have maintained its nimbleness and technological edge as it grew to a $60 billion company? Reflect on this, and be as creative as you can.

3. "Tradition has no place in corporate thinking today." Discuss this statement.

4. Can you defend the position that the problems besetting IBM were not its fault, that they were beyond its control?

5. Would you say that the major problems confronting IBM were marketing rather than organizational? Why or why not?

6. Which of the three Cs do you think was most to blame for IBM's problems? Why?

HANDS-ON EXERCISES

1. *Be a Devil's Advocate* (one who argues a contrary position to test the decision). It is early 1993, and Louis Gerstner, an outsider and not even a computer man, but the chief executive of Nabisco, a food and tobacco firm, is on the verge of being selected for chief executive of IBM. You have been asked to argue against this choice. Array all the negative arguments you can for this appointment, and be as persuasive as you can. (Do not be swayed by what actually happened; place yourself in 1993.)

2. As the new CEO brought in to turn IBM around in 1993, what would you propose to do? (State any assumptions you find necessary, but keep them reasonable. And don't be influenced by what actually happened. Perhaps better actions could have been taken.) Be as specific as you can, and discuss the constraints likely to face your turnaround program.

3. You are a consultant reporting to the CEO in the late 1980s. IBM is still racking up revenue and profit gains. But you detect serious emerging weaknesses. What would you advise management at this time? (Make any assumptions you feel necessary, but state them clearly.) Persuasively explain your rationale.

TEAM DEBATE EXERCISE

At issue: Whether to break up the company into 10 to 15 semiautonomous units, or to keep basically the same organization. Debate the opposing views as persuasively as possible.

INVITATION TO RESEARCH

Research IBM's rationale for selling its PC business to a Chinese firm. Do you see any major flaws in this decision?

PART THREE

MERGER PITFALLS

CHAPTER EIGHT

Snapple: Quaker's Reckless Acquisition

*I*n late 1994, Quaker Oats CEO William D. Smithburg bought Snapple Beverage Company for $1.7 billion. Many thought he had paid too much for this maker of non-carbonated fruit-flavored drinks and iced teas. But in a similar acquisition 11 years before, he had outbid Pillsbury to buy Stokely–Van Camp, largely for its Gatorade, then a $90 million sports drink. Despite criticisms of that purchase, Gatorade went on to become a billion-dollar brand, and Smithburg was a hero. He was not to be a hero with Snapple.

THE COMPANY, QUAKER OATS

Quaker Oats had nearly $6.4 billion in fiscal 1995 sales, of which $1.7 billion was from foreign operations. Its brands were generally strong in certain grocery products and beverage areas. In hot cereals, generations had used Quaker oatmeal, and it was still the number-three selling brand in the overall cereal category. Quaker's ready-to-eat cereals included Cap'n Crunch and Life brands. The firm was a leading competitor in the fast-growing rice cake and granola bar categories, and also in rice and pasta with its Rice-A-Roni, Pasta Roni, and Near East brands. Other products included Aunt Jemima frozen French toast, pancake mixes, and syrups; Celeste frozen pizza; as well as grits, tortilla flour, and corn meal.

With the purchase of Snapple, sales of its beverage operation would approach $2 billion, or about one-third of total corporate sales. Gatorade alone accounted for $1.3 billion worldwide in fiscal 1995, and growth continued, with sales in the United States increasing 7 percent over the previous year, while overseas the gain was a whopping 51 percent. In order to help pay for the Snapple acquisition, several mature but still moneymaking units were divested, including pet foods and chocolates.

THE SNAPPLE ACQUISITION

Snapple had a modest beginning in 1972 in Brooklyn, New York, and its beverages were initially sold to health-food stores. As the healthy lifestyle became popular among certain segments of the general public, Snapple's sales for a time increased as much as 60–70 percent a year, especially in the Northeast and on the West Coast. In 1992, it was purchased for $27.9 million by Boston-based Thomas H. Lee Co., which took the now-trendy brand public and built it up to almost $700 million in sales.

Unlike Gatorade, however, Snapple faced formidable competitors, including Coke's Fruitopia and Pepsi's joint venture with Lipton, which used low prices to capture 31 percent of the iced-tea market. Snapple's growth rate had turned to declines by December 1994 when, in an outpouring of supreme confidence in his own judgment, Smithburg bought Snapple for $1.7 billion. Before long, many said that he had paid about $1 billion too much. Table 8.1 shows the quarterly sales results of Snapple before and after the acquisition.

William Smithburg

At the time of the purchase, Smithburg was 56 years old, but looked younger. He liked to wear suspenders stretched tightly over muscular shoulders that he had developed from years of tournament handball. He had been CEO at Quaker Oats since 1981 and had evolved from a flashy boy wonder to a seasoned executive. He was also a fitness buff, and perhaps this colored his zeal for products like Gatorade and Snapple.

His interest in fitness developed as a result of a childhood bout with polio. While he recovered with no permanent damage, the experience shaped his life: "As soon as I started to walk and run again, I said, 'I have to stay healthy,' and it just became part of my life."[1] In his long tenure as CEO, this passion also shaped Quaker. The company developed extensive fitness programs, including a heavily subsidized health

TABLE 8.1. Snapple's Sales Growth, 1993–1996

	Sales Growth (millions of dollars)							
	1993	%	1994	%	1995	%	1996	%
1st quarter			$134		$112	− 12%		
2nd quarter	$130		243	+ 87%	200	− 18%	180	− 10%
3rd quarter	203		191	− 6%				− 20%
4th quarter	118		105	− 11%				

Note: While we do not have complete information for all the quarters, the negative sales since the second quarter of 1994—before the Snapple acquisition—can be readily seen: Every quarter since then saw losses from the same quarter the preceding year.

Source: 1995 *Quaker Annual Report*, and various 1996 updates.

[1] Greg Burns, "Crunch Time at Quaker Oats," *Business Week*, September 23, 1996, p. 72.

club at headquarters. Quaker's product line increasingly emphasized low-fat foods compatible with a healthy lifestyle.

Indicative of Smithburg's personality, after graduating from DePaul University in 1960 with a BS in economics and marketing, he defied his father by quitting his first job only three days later. He decided to enroll in Northwestern's business school.

With an MBA in hand he joined the Leo Burnett ad agency, and later, McCann Erickson. After five years of ad agency experience, he went to Quaker as brand manager for frozen waffles in 1966. There it took him ten years to become executive vice-president of U.S. grocery products, Quaker's biggest division. Five years later, in 1981, he became CEO, and he was named chairman two years after that.

The same year he became chairman, Smithburg acquired Stokely-Van Camp, overbidding Pillsbury's $62-per-share bid with a $77 offer, which carried a price tag of $238 million. His own investment banker considered this too steep, and critics in the business press abounded. But Smithburg had done his homework, and his intuition was prescient. He recognized the potential in Stokely's Gatorade, a sport drink meant to replenish salts and fluids lost by athletes. "I'd been drinking Gatorade myself, and I knew the product worked."[2] A $90 million brand in 1983, by 1996 Gatorade was a $1.3 billion-dollar brand and held 80 percent of the growing sport-drink market.

Somehow, Smithburg did not do his homework well with Snapple, despite its seeming similarity to Gatorade.

Rationale for the Snapple Purchase

Snapple was the largest acquisition in Quaker's history. The *Quaker Oats 1995 Annual Report* discussed the rationale for this purchase and the "growth opportunity it offers to shareholders":

> Snapple appeals to all ages with its incomparable flavor variety in premium iced teas and juice drinks. Current sales are concentrated in the Northeast and West Coast. So, the rest of the country presents fertile territory for developing the brand. Because of its excellent cold-channel distribution, the Snapple brand has taught us a great deal about reaching consumers outside our traditional grocery channels. We can apply this knowledge to Gatorade thirst quencher, thereby enhancing its availability as well.[3]

Smithburg saw a great opportunity to expand distribution of Snapple geographically from its present regional concentration. He thought that it had wide appeal and could enhance sales of the already highly successful Gatorade.

Snapple beverages held good regional market positions in both the premium ready-to-drink tea and single-serve juice-drink categories. It was seemingly well positioned if consumer preferences continued to shift to all-natural beverages—and away from highly carbonated, artificially flavored, chemically preserved soft drinks.

Apparently, not the least of the reasons for Smithburg's infatuation with Snapple was that it had a "sexy aura," even though problems were already emerging when he bought it. He liked to contrast it with Quaker's pet food: "a dead, flat business with

[2] *Ibid.*, p. 74.
[3] *Quaker Oats 1995 Annual Report*, p. 6.

five or six big companies beating their brains out in it."[4] It was not surprising that just a few months after he acquired Snapple he sold Quaker's pet food business, which had been acquired less than nine years earlier.

Speculation abounded as to why Smithburg chased Snapple, besides misreading its growth potential. Some thought that he wanted to make Quaker, at the time a hotly rumored acquisition candidate, less vulnerable to a takeover. Others suggested that he had become bored with Quaker and sought the excitement of a splashy deal.[5]

PROBLEMS

One would think that Snapple's resemblance to Gatorade would bring instant compatibility and efficiencies in marketing the two brands. After all, with the proven success of Gatorade, Quaker had become the third-largest beverage company, after only Coca-Cola and Pepsi. And like Gatorade, Snapple was a flavored, noncarbonated drink. Surely this was a compatible marriage.

But this was not the case. Only after it bought Snapple did Quaker fully realize that Snapple's production and distribution systems were completely different from Gatorade's.

Quaker's production and distribution of Gatorade was state of the art. Its computers were closely integrated with those of its largest distributors and automatically kept them well stocked, but not overstocked, with Gatorade.

The advertising of Gatorade was also markedly different. Several hundred million dollars a year was spent for Gatorade, with highly successful ads featuring Chicago Bulls star Michael Jordan (a personal friend of Smithburg's). Snapple's advertising, on the other hand, had run out of steam and was notably ineffective.

The production, distribution, and marketing efforts of Snapple at the time of the purchase were haphazard. Bottling was contracted to outsiders, and this resulted in expensive contracts for excess capacity when demand slowed. Snapple's 300 distributors delivered directly to stores; Gatorade's distributors delivered to warehouses. Quaker's efforts to consolidate the two distribution systems only created havoc. It tried to take the supermarket accounts away from Snapple distributors and give them to Gatorade, directing the Snapple people to concentrate on convenience stores and mom-and-pop retailers. Not surprising, Snapple distributors refused this downsizing of their operations. Eventually, Quaker backed down. But efforts at creating coordination and distribution efficiencies for 1995 were seriously delayed.

At the same time, Quaker failed to come up with a new business plan for Snapple in time for the peak 1995 season, which began in April. Tim Healy, president of a Snapple distributor in Chicago, noted: "There was no marketing plan, no initiatives, and no one to talk to [at Quaker]."[6]

The result was that Snapple's 1995 sales fell 9 percent, and there was a $100 million loss.

---

[4] Burns, p. 74.
[5] *Ibid.*
[6] Scott McMurray, "Drumming Up New Business: Quaker Marches Double Time to Put Snap Back in Its Snapple Drink Line," *U. S. News & World Report*, April 22, 1996, p. 59.

CORRECTIVE EFFORTS, 1996

As the dismal results of 1995 became widely publicized, Quaker faced the urgent need to vindicate the purchase of Snapple and somehow resurrect its failing fortunes. To aid the distributors, the company streamlined operations to reduce from two weeks to three days the time it took to get orders from bottlers to distributors. To do so, it coordinated its computers with the top 50 distributors, representing 80 percent of Snapple's sales, so that it could replenish their inventory automatically, the way it was doing with Gatorade.

The company also introduced some packaging and product changes that it hoped would be more appealing both to dealers and to customers. It brought out 32- and 64-ounce plastic bottles of Snapple for families, along with 12-packs and 4-packs in glass bottles. It reduced the number of flavors from 50 to 35 and made taste improvements in some of the retained flavors. At the same time, seasonal products were introduced, such as cider tea for Halloween.

To develop distributor enthusiasm, a two-day meeting was held in San Diego. Quaker brought in comedian Bill Cosby to entertain and General Norman Schwarzkopf to motivate with a stirring speech on leadership. Then distributors were told that highly visible Snapple coolers would be placed in supermarkets, convenience stores, and schools—just like Coke and Pepsi.[7]

The weakness in the 1995 advertising also received what was hoped would be corrective action. Quaker enlisted the creativity of Spike Lee, who had designed hyperkinetic TV commercials for Nike. While the campaign kept Snapple's "Made from the best stuff on earth," the new ads focused on Snapple's hope to become America's third choice in soft drinks, behind Coke and Pepsi, with such slogans as "We want to be No. 3," and "Threedom = freedom." The goal of the advertising campaign, Smithburg explained, was to maintain Snapple's "funky" image while broadening its appeal beyond the East and West Coast markets.[8]

Still, sales languished. In late July, a huge nationwide sampling campaign was undertaken. In a $40 million effort, millions of bottles of the fruit-juice and ice-tea lines were given away at the height of the selling season, hopefully to spur consumer interest regardless of cost.

RESULTS OF 1996 EFFORTS

Unfortunately, the results of the summer giveaways were dismal. Instead of gaining market share during the important summer selling months, Snapple lost ground. Snapple tea sales fell 14 percent, and juice sales fell 15 percent. This compared poorly with industry tea sales, which also dropped but only 4 percent, and industry juice sales, which fell 5 percent during an unusually cool summer in the Northeast.[9]

[7] Zina Moukheiber, "He Who Laughs Last," *Forbes*, January 1, 1996, p. 42.
[8] *Ibid.*, p. 60.
[9] "Snapple Continues to Lose Market Share Despite Big Giveaway," *Wall Street Journal*, October 8, 1996, p. B9.

Relentless media scrutiny even found fault with the way in which Snapple was being given away. One critic observed the sampling at a New Jersey concert in which 16-ounce cans were handed out only 20 feet from the entrance in front of signs prohibiting food or drink beyond the gate. Most people barely had time to taste the drink before throwing it away. Furthermore, "for its brand undermining efforts, Quaker gets no consumer research either. Solution: In exchange for the self-serve sample, ask a few short . . . questions."[10]

Smithburg's reputation was being eroded, his early success with Gatorade not enough to weather much more adversity. Online, cyber-critics assailed him. In conference calls with financial analysts, he was peppered with barbed questions about this $600 million beverage for which he had paid $1.7 billion. "Even my dad," Smithburg laughed, "He says, 'What are you doing with Snapple?'"[11]

Under pressure, Smithburg cast off president and chief operating officer Philip Marineau, whom he had been grooming as heir apparent for many years. This departure was widely interpreted to be the result of Snapple's failure to justify its premium pricing, with Marineau the scapegoat. Nine months later, Donald Uzzi was replaced as president of Quaker's North America beverages unit. His successor was Michael Schott, former vice president of sales of Nantucket Nectars, a small, privately held drink maker.

Some critics assumed that Smithburg's job was in jeopardy, that he could not escape personal blame for the acquisition snafu. His past success with Gatorade, however, continued to sustain him. The board of directors remained supportive, although they denied him a bonus for 1995. What made the continued loyalty of the board more uncertain was Quaker's stock price, which had fallen 10 percent since just before the acquisition, even as the Standard & Poor's 500-stock index had climbed to new highs.

If Snapple could not be revitalized, Smithburg had several options. All of these, of course, would be admissions of defeat and of having made a major mistake in acquiring Snapple. Any one of them might cost Smithburg his job.

One option would be to spin off the ailing Snapple to shareholders, perhaps under the wing of the booming Gatorade. Smithburg was no stranger to such maneuverings, since he had divested retail, toy, and pet-food operations in his years as CEO. An outright sale could probably only be made at bargain-basement prices and would certainly underscore the billion-dollar mistake of Smithburg's purchase. A less extreme option would be to draw back from attempts to make Snapple a national brand, and keep it as a regional brand in the Northeast and on the West Coast, where it was well entrenched.

Perseverance

By early 1997, Smithburg still had not given up on Snapple. Quaker Oats announced that it was pumping $15 million into a major 4-month sweepstakes promotion for Snapple's diet drinks, this to start right after the new year when consumers might

---

[10] Gabe Lowry, "They Can't Even Give Snapple Away Right," *Brandweek*, September 30, 1996, p. 16.
[11] Burns, p. 71.

be more concerned with undoing the excesses of the holiday season, and when competitors would be less likely to advertise chilled drinks in cold weather. The theme was to be "Escape with Taste," and the 50 top winners would be awarded grand-prize trips to the refurbished Doral Resort and Spa in Miami. If the campaign developed any momentum, it should carry over to a retooled image campaign planned to begin immediately afterwards in the spring.

This promotion was the first from new president Michael Schott, and it built on a product category that had managed to grow 16 percent in convenience stores during the previous summer, even as core juices and teas slid drastically. The promotion plan was well received by distributors: "This one [promotion] is wonderfully thought out," one distributor said. "Diet drinks in the first quarter? It's a no-brainer."[12]

Since being named the brand's president late in the year, Schott had been visiting distributors to build up relations, offer greater support, and dispel rumors that Snapple was going to retrench to a regional brand. Still, Snapple's sales and profits showed no rebound.

On March 27, 1997, Smithburg finally threw in the towel. He sold the ailing Snapple to Nelson Peltz, chief executive of the smallish Triarc Cos., owner of RC Cola and Arby's restaurants. The price was shockingly low, only $300 million, or just over half of Snapple's $550 million in sales. Only three years before, Smithburg had paid $1.7 billion for the brand. The founder of Snapple, Leonard Marsh, who had previously sold his controlling interest, said that "they stole the company."[13]

Undoubtedly, Quaker was desperate to sell the money-draining Snapple, but at such a fire-sale price? As it turned out, the company had few options. Major suitors, such as PepsiCo, Coca-Cola, and Procter & Gamble, only wanted to consider a Snapple purchase along with Gatorade, Smithburg's crown jewel and most profitable brand.

On April 24, 1997, the *Wall Street Journal* reported that Quaker Oats had posted a $1.11 billion quarterly loss reflecting the final resolution of the Snapple affair, and that William Smithburg was stepping down. "Many investors have been asking for a long time why he hasn't stepped aside sooner," said one food-industry analyst.[14]

LATER DEVELOPMENTS

Quaker's Gatorade remained a great strength of the company, having an estimated 78 percent of the sport-drink market. This made Quaker an attractive acquisition. In 2000, Coca-Cola expressed interest in buying Quaker, but faced a sticker price of $16 billion that its board of directors, among them Warren Buffett, one of the country's most astute investors, decided to reject.

Just a few months later, PepsiCo bid $14.02 billion, which Quaker accepted. The deal was expected to close by the end of June 2001, but federal antitrust enforcers

[12] Gerry Khermouch, "Snapple Diet Line Gets $15 mil Push," *Brandweek*, November 4, 1996, p. 1.
[13] I. Jeanne Dugan, "Will Triarc Make Snapple Crackle?" *Business Week*, April 28, 1997, p. 64.
[14] Michael J. McCarthy, "Quaker Oats Posts $1.11 Billion Quarterly Loss," *Wall Street Journal*, April 24, 1997, pp. A3 and A12.

continued to raise objections. The Federal Trade Commission was concerned that the merger would give Quaker's Gatorade brand even greater dominance once it became part of Pepsi's powerful distribution network. Coca-Cola's Powerade brand had only a 15 percent share of the sport-drink market, while Pepsi's All-Sport, which the company agreed to sell, was a distant third. Opponents of the deal argued that it would enable Pepsi to gain too much clout with retailers, particularly convenience stores where Gatorade and other Pepsi products such as Mountain Dew were already strong. FTC approval was difficult to obtain, although the deal had already been approved by several foreign regulators, including the European Union's antitrust authority. Then, on August 2, 2001, in a rare deadlocked 2–2 vote, the FTC let PepsiCo proceed with the now $13.8 billion buyout of Quaker Oats Co.[15]

ANALYSIS

Beyond doubt the price paid for Snapple was wildly extravagant. Demand was slumping, distribution inefficiencies had surfaced, and the advertising had run out of steam. We can understand Smithburg's reasoning that he had bought Gatorade at a high price and turned it into a winner, so why not do the same thing with Snapple? The price paid for Gatorade, $238 million for sales of $90 million at the time, was roughly comparable to the $1.7 billion for Snapple with sales of almost $700 million.

But we can surely fault Smithburg for not demanding that his subordinates analyze more thoroughly the compatibility of the two operations. It should not have come as a surprise after the sale that the distribution systems of Gatorade and Snapple were not compatible and maybe could not be made so. Furthermore, for a purchase of this magnitude, it seems only reasonable to expect that research and planning would also have been done concerning whether Snapple's promotional efforts were adequate for the coming year or whether changes needed to be made, and if so, what changes. Should not stockholders have expected that rather solid business plans would be in place before Quaker finalized the acquisition? Without them, the decision to let go of $1.7 billion seems rather like decision-making by hunch and intuition. Perhaps it was.

The spinning of wheels in 1996, after the disastrous 1995, suggests that Smithburg had fallen prey to the decision-making error called *escalating commitment*. This is a resolve to increase efforts and resources to pursue a course of action that is *not* working, to be unable to "call it quits."[16]

See the following Information Box for advice by John Schermerhorn on not being trapped in an escalation commitment.

---

[15] John R. Wilke and Betsy McKay, "PepsiCo Cites FTC for Further Delay of Quaker Deal," *Wall Street Journal*, June 11, 2001, p. B6; "FTC Allows PepsiCo to Buy Quaker Oats Despite Concerns," Associated Press, as reported in *Cleveland Plain Dealer*, August 2, 2001, p. C5.

[16] Peter F. Drucker, "The Global Economy and the Nation-State," *Foreign Affairs*, vol. 76, September–October 1997, pp. 159–171.

INFORMATION BOX

HOW TO AVOID THE ESCALATION TRAP

When should we call it quits, admit the mistake, and leave the scene as gracefully as possible, amid the cries of critics, the debris of sunk costs in a hopeless cause, and even embarrassment and shame and possible ouster by a board of directors tormented by irate investors? John Schermerhorn offers these guidelines to avoid staying in a lost cause too long:

1. Set advance limits on your involvement in any given course of action, and stick to it.

2. Make your own decisions; others may also be prone to escalation.

3. Carefully consider why you want to continue this course of action; unless there are sufficient reasons to continue, don't.

4. Consider the costs of continuing, and the savings in costs as a reason to discontinue.

5. Be on guard for escalation tendencies, especially where a big commitment has already been made.[17]

Do you think Drucker's idea of an escalating commitment and Schermerhorn's suggestions for avoiding it have any downsides? In other words, when do you call it quits?

It is easy to imagine how the big commitment already made by Snapple would have stimulated the escalating commitment to the fullest: "We have too much invested for this to fail."

If the product life cycle of Snapple had peaked before the Quaker's purchase, this would account for the inability of Quaker's management to reverse the downward trend of sales and profits. But such a possibility should surely have been considered before the acquisition decision. (See the following Information Box for a discussion of the product life cycle.)

One would think that the best minds in a major corporation, and any outside consultants they used, should have been able to bring Snapple to more healthy national and international sales, or at least to a more profitable situation, even if the product life cycle had become less favorable. But in high-stakes, near-crisis situations, prudent judgment may be abandoned as money is flung about in a desperate effort to turn things around. Often this merely aggravates the situation, as was the case with the expensive and poorly planned $40 million sampling effort and the $15 million sweepstakes program.

---

[17] John R. Schermerhorn Jr., *Management*, 6th ed., New York: John Wiley, 1999, p. 67.

INFORMATION BOX

THE PRODUCT LIFE CYCLE

Just like people and animals, products go through stages of growth and maturity—that is, life cycles. They are affected by different competitive conditions at each stage, often ranging from no competition in the early stages to intense competition later on. We can recognize four stages in a product's life cycle: introduction, growth, maturity, and decline.

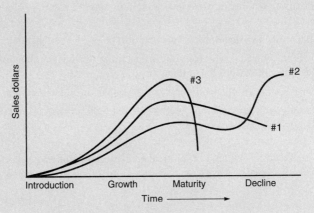

Figure 8.1. The Product Life Cycle.

Figure 8.1 depicts three different product life cycles. Number 1 is that of a standard item in which sales take some time to develop and then eventually begin a slow decline. Number 2 shows a life cycle for a product in which a modification of the product or else the uncovering of a new market rejuvenates the product so that it takes off on a new cycle of growth (the classic examples are Listerine, originally sold as a mild external antiseptic, and Arm & Hammer Baking Soda, which was repositioned as a deodorizer). Number 3 shows the life cycle for a fad item or one experiencing rapid technological change and intense competition. Note its sharp rise in sales and the abrupt downturn.

Which life cycle most closely represents Snapple at the time of the acquisition? Snapple was definitely on a downward trend, which began the summer before Quaker purchased it, and the downward trend continued and even accelerated through 1995 and 1996 (see Table 8.1). This suggests that Snapple had reached the maturity stage of its life cycle. As an admittedly trendy product, its curve in the worst scenario would resemble Number 3, the fad. An optimistic scenario would see a Number 2 curve, with strong efforts in 1997 bringing a rejuvenation. Perhaps the more likely life cycle is something akin to Number 1, with a slow downturn continuing for a lengthy period while aggressive efforts fail to stem the decline in an environment of more intense competition and less eager demand.

Do you agree with this prognosis? Why or why not?

Finally, it is worth emphasizing again that extensive homework is necessary in the acquisition quest. These are major, major decisions. Hundreds of millions of dollars, even billions, are at stake if an unwise acquisition has to be divested a few years later. In addition, there is the management time taken up with a poorly performing product line at the expense of other responsibilities.

❖ ❖ ❖

Invitation to Make Your Own Analysis and Conclusions

What do you see as the major blunder in the Snapple acquisition?
How might this have been better handled?

❖ ❖ ❖

WHAT CAN BE LEARNED?

The illusion of compatibility.—Bad acquisition decisions, in which the merger or acquisition turns out to be a mistake, often result from miscalculating the mutual compatibility of the two operations. Expectations are that consolidating various operations will result in significant cost savings. For example, two headquarters' staffs can be reduced perhaps to a beefed-up single one. Sometimes certain aspects of production can be combined, allowing some facilities to be closed for greater cost efficiencies. Computer operations, sales forces, and distribution channels might be combined. But for these combinations and consolidations to be feasible, the two operations essentially should be compatible.

As we saw in the case, the distribution channels of Snapple and Gatorade were not compatible, and efforts to consolidate brought serious rancor among those who would be affected. Quaker had failed to do its homework and probe deeply enough to determine the real depth of compatibility; it should not have merely assumed compatibility because of product similarities.

Certainly we see many acquisitions and mergers of dissimilar operations: These are called *diversifications*. Some of them have little or no compatibility, and may not provide significant opportunities for reducing costs. Instead, they may take place because of perceived growth opportunities, to lessen dependence on mature products, to smooth out seasonality, and so on. Unfortunately, many of these dissimilar diversifications prove to be disappointing, and are candidates for divestiture some years later.

The acquisition contest.—Once an acquisition candidate is identified, negotiations sometimes become akin to an athletic contest: Who will win? Not infrequently, several firms may be drawn to what they see as an attractive would-be acquisition, and a bidding war commences. Sometimes the management of the takeover firm strongly resists. The whole situation evolves into a contest, almost a game. And aggressive executives get caught up in the game, sometimes overreaching themselves in their struggle to win. No matter how attractive a takeover firm might be, if you pay way too much, it was a bad buy.

The paradox of perseverance—when do we give up?—We admire people who persevere despite great odds: the student who continues with school even though family and work commitments may drag it out for ten years or more; the athlete who never gives up; the author who has a hundred rejection slips but still keeps trying. How long should we persevere in what seems to be a totally losing cause? Isn't there such a thing as futility and unrealistic dreams, so that constructive efforts should be directed elsewhere? The enigma of futility has been captured in classic literature with Don Quixote, the "Man from LaMancha," tilting his lance at windmills.

The line is blurred between perseverance and futile stubbornness, the escalating commitment of Peter Drucker. Circumstances vary too much to formulate guidelines. Still, if a direct assault continues to fail, perhaps it is time to make an end run.

When should a weak product be axed?—Weak products tend to take up too much management, sales force, and advertising attention—efforts that could be better spent improving healthy products and/or developing replacements. Publicity about such products may even cause customer misgivings and tarnish the company's image. This suggests that weak and/or unprofitable products or divisions ought to be gotten rid of, provided that the problems are enduring and not a temporary aberration.

Not all weak products should be pruned, however, because there is sometimes a strong rationale for keeping them. In particular, the weak products may be necessary to complete a line to benefit sales of other products. They may be desirable for customer goodwill. Some weak products may enhance a company's image or prestige. Although weak products make no money in themselves, their intrinsic value to the firm may be substantial. Other weak products may merely be unproven, too new in their product life cycle to have become profitable; in their growth and maturity stage they may contribute satisfactory profits. Finally, perhaps a new business strategy will rejuvenate the weak product. That is the hope, and the proffered justification, for keeping a weak product when its demise is overdue.

Where does Snapple fit in this theoretical discussion? The only justification for procrastination would seem to be that the company had not exhausted its business strategy alternatives to turn around the brand. In the meantime, the image of Quaker Oats in the eyes of investors, and the reflection of this in stock prices, was being savaged.

Be cautious with possible fad-product life cycles—With hindsight, we can classify Snapple's popularity as a short-term phenomenon. But it was heady and contagious while it lasted. Snapple transformed iced tea into a new-age product by avoiding preservatives, adding fruit flavors, and introducing innovative wide-mouth, 16-ounce bottles. It also used Howard Stern, with his cult following, as its spokesman.

The public offering of stock in 1993 was sensational. The original offering price was to be $14, but was raised to $20; in the first day of trading the stock closed at $29. Two years later, Quaker paid $1.7 billion for a company whose founders had paid just $500 to acquire the name. But the euphoric life cycle was turning down, and the cult following was distracted by imitators, such as Arizona Iced Tea, Mystic, and Nantucket Nectars, as well as Coke and Pepsi through alliances with Nestea and Lipton.

Perhaps what can be learned is that product life cycles are unpredictable, especially where they involve fad or cult followers who may be as fickle as the wind, and where imitation is easy. To bet one's firm on such an acquisition can be risky indeed. But in truth, Smithburg had faced a similar situation with Gatorade, and won big. The moral: Decision making under uncertainty can be a crap shoot. But prudence suggests a more cautious approach.

CONSIDER

Can you think of any other learning insights?

QUESTIONS

1. Why do you think the great Snapple giveaway was ineffective?
2. Do you think Snapple could have been turned around? Why or why not?
3. Do you think the premium retail price for Snapple was a serious impediment? Why or why not?
4. "Pouring more money into a lost cause is downright stupid. Smithburg has got to go." Discuss.
5. "This isn't a case where a guy has gone from a genius to a dummy. Who's better at running the company?" Discuss this statement.
6. "What's all the fuss about? Snapple is going great on our college campus. It's a success, man." Do you agree? Why or why not?
7. Do you drink Snapple? If not, why not? If so, how often—and how much do you like it?

HANDS-ON EXERCISES

Before

1. *Be a Devil's Advocate.* A major decision is at hand. You are a vice-president of the beverage operation at Quaker. William Smithburg is proposing the acquisition of Snapple for some huge sum. Before a decision is made, you have been asked to array any contrary arguments to this expensive acquisition, in other words, to be a devil's advocate (one who takes a contrary position for the sake of argument and clarification of opposing views). What concerns would you raise, and how would you defend them?

After

2. It is late 1996. You are the assistant to Michael Schott, who has just been named president of Snapple. He asks you to formulate a strategic plan for resurrecting Snapple in 1997. What do you propose? Be as specific as you can, and be prepared to defend your recommendations.

3. *Be a Devil's Advocate.* The decision to sell Snapple for $300 million is on the table. What arguments would you array for *not* selling it at this low price? Be as persuasive as you can.

TEAM DEBATE EXERCISE

The acquisition of Snapple is accomplished. Now begins the assimilation. A major debate has ensued regarding whether Snapple should be consolidated with Gatorade or should remain an independent entity. Debate the two positions as persuasively as possible. Be sure and identify any assumptions made.

INVITATION TO RESEARCH

What is the situation with Snapple and Smithburg today? Has Snapple prospered under its new ownership? Is Smithburg running any company? Is Gatorade still a formidable brand?

CHAPTER NINE

Newell's Acquisition of Rubbermaid Becomes an Albatross

J ohn McDonough, CEO of Newell, specialized in buying small marginal firms and improving their operations. In ten years he bought 75 such firms and polished them by eliminating poorer products, employees, and factories, and stressing customer service. This format began to be called "Newellizing." It was hardly surprising that most of the acquisitions had strong brand names but mediocre customer service. Rubbermaid fit this mode, though it was by far the biggest acquisition and would nearly double Newell's sales.

Rubbermaid, manufacturer and marketer of high-volume, branded plastic and rubber consumer products and toys, had been a darling of investors and academicians alike. For ten years in a row, it placed in the *Fortune* survey of America's Most Admired Corporations, and it was No. 1 in both 1993 and 1994. It was ranked as the second-most-powerful brand in a Baylor University study of consumer goodwill, and received the Thomas Edison Award for developing products to make people's lives better. Under CEO Stanley Gault, Rubbermaid's emphasis on innovation often resulted in a new product every day, thereby helping the stock routinely to return 25 percent annually.

Surprisingly, by the middle 1990s, Rubbermaid began faltering, partly because of inability to meet the service demands of Wal-Mart, a major customer. Rubbermaid stock plummeted 40 percent from the 1992 high, leaving it ripe for a takeover. Newell acquired Rubbermaid on March 24, 1999, expecting to turn it around. But then Newell had to wonder . . .

THE ACQUISITION AND WOLFGANG SCHMITT

Former Rubbermaid CEO Wolfgang Schmitt felt a cloak of apprehension settling over him in May 1999. It was only two months after the merger with Newell had been completed, and things were not going as he expected.

Schmitt had become CEO a year after the legendary Stanley Gault retired in 1991. Gault had returned in 1980 to his hometown of Wooster, Ohio (Rubbermaid headquarters), after more than 31 years with the General Electric Company. During Gault's tenure, Rubbermaid stock split four times to the delight of stockholders. It was a tough act to follow.

Wolfgang Schmitt often thought about this, but he was certainly a worthy successor to Gault. He had spent all his working life with Rubbermaid after graduating in 1966 from Otterbein College in Westerville, Ohio (about 60 miles from Wooster) with a degree in economics and business administration. A recruiter visiting the campus convinced him to join Rubbermaid, a rapidly growing company. He started as a management trainee, and in 27 years had worked his way up the corporate ranks to become chairman of the board and chief executive officer in 1993. He was proud of this accomplishment, and thought that his experience was surely an inspiration to young people in the company: Any one of them could dream of becoming CEO, with hard work and loyalty. A significant highlight of his professional life came when he was invited back to Otterbein in November 1997 to inaugurate its Distinguished Executive Lecture Series.

During Schmitt's reign, Rubbermaid reached $2 billion in sales in 1994. When it celebrated its 75-year anniversary a year later, Schmitt set the company's sights on $4 billion in sales for the turn of the century. To do this, he knew it had to become a truly global company, and he instigated four foreign acquisitions that year.

He was an effective CEO; he knew he was. When the Newell Company, a slightly larger multinational firm, expressed an interest in merging, Schmitt thought he owed it to his stockholders, and to himself, to pursue the deal. After all, the two firms' houseware and hardware products and marketing efforts were compatible, and their combination would result in a $7-billion-a-year consumer-products giant. Aiding Schmitt's decision to merge was a nice severance guarantee of $12 million after taxes in addition to his stock options. While Newell's CEO John McDonough would assume the CEO position of the merged corporation, Schmitt was to be a vice chairman and would work closely with McDonough to ensure a smooth merger and help mold the new company.

Now, barely two months later, Schmitt had been shunted aside. He did not have an office at headquarters, his name was not listed on a new report of the seven highest-paid executives, and he was not even included in the list of directors reported to the Securities and Exchange Commission (SEC). He couldn't help feeling betrayed about no longer having a role in the operations of the company, after he had been so instrumental in bringing about the merger. At 55 years of age, he still had many productive years left. More than this, there was the principle of the thing: This was like a kick in the teeth.

But he was not alone. The presidents of three of Rubbermaid's five divisions—Home Products, Little Tykes, Graco-Century, Curver, and Commercial Products—

had already been replaced since the merger. Furthermore, in the Home Products division, only two of the top eight executives were still there.

NEWELL'S ASSESSMENT OF RUBBERMAID

If John McDonough of Newell was so unhappy with Rubbermaid's management and operations, why had he bought Rubbermaid in the first place—and for $6.3 billion dollars, more than twice current sales? At a shareholders' meeting a few months after the acquisition, McDonough tried to explain. He told them that Rubbermaid was a troubled company, but that once it was pulled into the revered operations of Newell, it could be great again.[1]

The shareholders were told that while jobs were being cut, the operations would be stronger in the long run. As a strength, McDonough noted that Rubbermaid commanded 94 percent brand loyalty and generated great customer traffic in stores. But Rubbermaid executives needed to slash unnecessary costs, introduce robotics, and reduce product variety. For example, was it necessary to have dozens of the same type of wastebasket?

Still, McDonough saw poor customer service as Rubbermaid's biggest deficiency, the most unacceptable aspect of its operation, and the one that Newell could most easily correct. After all, Newell had achieved a 98.5 percent on-time delivery rate in dealings with Wal-Mart. He would see that Rubbermaid was brought up to the same performance standard.

Rubbermaid's Customer Service Problems

Perhaps the declining commitment to customer service dated back to Gault's retirement, though Schmitt would likely dispute that. Customer service can erode without being obvious to top management. While some customers complain, many others simply switch their business to competitors. Still, Rubbermaid's lapses in customer service should have been obvious for years. After all, Wal-Mart was not tolerant with vendors not meeting its standards. When McDonough's people began digging deeper into Rubbermaid's operations, they found that the company wasn't even measuring customer service. This deficiency is almost the kiss of death when dealing with major retailers.

Up to the mid-1990s, about 15 percent of Rubbermaid's $2 billion–plus revenues came from Wal-Mart. Rubbermaid had had an impressive earnings growth of at least 15 percent a year to go along with 20 percent operating margins, much of this due to the generous space Wal-Mart gave its plastic and rubber products. This was to change abruptly.

In 1995, Wal-Mart refused to let Rubbermaid pass on much of its higher raw material costs, and began taking shelf space away and giving it to smaller competitors who undersold Rubbermaid. This resulted in a major earnings drop (see

[1] Teresa Dixon Murray, "Newell Details Its Plans for Rubbermaid," *Cleveland Plain Dealer*, May 27, 1999, p. 1-C.

TABLE 9.1.   Rubbermaid Sales and Earnings, 1992–1997

	1992	1993	1994	1995	1996	1997
Sales (in billions)	$1.81	$1.96	$2.17	$2.34	$2.35	$2.40
Net earnings (in millions)	184	211	228	59	152	143
Earnings percent of sales	10.2%	20.0%	18.9%	4.9%	14.2%	13.8%
Earnings per share	1.15	1.32	1.42	.38	1.01	.95

Source: Company reports.

Commentary: This six-year comparison of sales and the various profit indicators shows rather starkly the decline in Rubbermaid's fortunes beginning in 1995. Sales remained practically static from 1995 on, although admittedly they were not growing very robustly in the three years before. The lack of growth occurred during a period of unprecedented economic prosperity.

The earnings comparisons show up worse. While earnings growth was acceptable up to 1995, it greatly worsened beginning in 1995. Not only were net earnings drastically reduced, but they showed little sign of recouping, even though there was some improvement from the bottom of 1995. Of course, net earnings as a percent of sales and per share also drastically declined from what they were in 1992–1994. Rubbermaid's major problems with Wal-Mart occurred in 1995.

Table 9.1) that forced Rubbermaid to shut nine facilities and cut 9 percent of its 14,000 employees. "When you hitch your wagon to a star, you are at the mercy of that star."[2]

Wal-Mart not only complained about poor deliveries but began taking more drastic action. Each day Wal-Mart gives suppliers such as Newell a two-hour time slot in which their trucks can deliver orders placed 24 hours before. Should the supplier miss the deadline, it pays Wal-Mart for every dollar of lost margin. Such a fast replenishment of orders required that factories be tied in with Wal-Mart's computers. Rubbermaid began installing software to do this in 1996 and had spent $62 million by 1999, but still was often not even achieving 80 percent on-time delivery service. This was unacceptable to Wal-Mart, and returns and fines for poor service rose to 4.4 percent of sales in 1998.[3] Finally, Wal-Mart purged most of its stores of Rubbermaid's Little Tykes toy line, giving the space to a competitor, Fisher Price. See the Information Box for a discussion of the power of a giant retailer and the demands it can make.

INFORMATION BOX

THE DEMANDS OF A GIANT RETAILER

Giant retailers, especially the big discount houses, stand in a power position today relative to their vendors. Part of this power lies in their providing efficient access to the

[2] Matthew Schifrin, "The Big Squeeze," *Forbes*, March 11, 1996, p. 46.
[3] Murray, p. 3-C.

marketplace. Imagine the problems of a large consumer goods manufacturer in trying to deal with thousands of small retailers rather than the few big firms that dominate their markets. These giant firms can account for 50 percent and more of many manufacturers' sales. However, if such a major customer is lost or not completely satisfied, the vendor's viability could be in jeopardy.

Retailers like Wal-Mart make full use of their power position. Take paying of invoices, for example. Many vendors give a 2 percent discount if bills are paid within ten days instead of 30. Wal-Mart routinely pays its bills closer to 30 days and still takes the 2 percent discount. Wal-Mart has also led in "partnering" with its vendors. This partnering really means that vendors have to pick up more of the inventory management and merchandising costs associated with Wal-Mart stores, with most of the costs involved in providing fast replenishment so that the stores can maintain lean stocks without losing customer sales through stockouts.

So-called slotting fees are common in the supermarket industry, with manufacturers paying to get things on store shelves. It is estimated that some $9 billion annually changes hands in private, unwritten deals between grocery retailers and food and consumer goods manufacturers.[4]

The following is an example of a slotting fee stipulation of a supermarket chain:

> Effective January 1, 1996
> Our slotting fee is . . . $2,500

> An item authorized will remain authorized for a minimum of six months, (as long as the basic cost does not go up substantially). Many times it is the slotting fee that determines whether we authorize an item or not.

> Given the coercive power of a big retailer, a vendor is practically forced to meet its demands no matter what the cost.

Do you think a big manufacturer, such as Coca-Cola, can be coerced by a big retailer? Why or why not? What might determine the extent of retailer coercion? Can a manufacturer coerce a retailer?

Wal-Mart had such a high regard for Newell's customer service that, upon hearing of the impending merger, it again began carrying Little Tykes toys. McDonough vowed to get Rubbermaid's on-time delivery rate of 80 percent up to Newell's 98.5 percent, and he began ripping out Rubbermaid's computer system and writing off the entire $62 million. In addition, McDonough claimed to be able to squeeze $350 million of costs out of Rubbermaid, which would double its operating income.[5]

---

[4] John S. Long, "Specialty Items to Drive New Market," *Cleveland Plain Dealer*, October 6, 1999, p. 4-F.
[5] Michelle Conlin, "Newellizing Rubbermaid," *Forbes*, May 31, 1999, p. 118.

AFTER THE MERGER

When Newell did not quickly turn Rubbermaid around and Newellize it, stockholders were shocked and disappointed. In a time of rising stock prices, Newell Rubbermaid's shares plunged 20 percent in one day in September 1999 as the now-giant consumer goods firm warned that third-quarter earnings would fall short of expectations. This was only the latest in a string of negatives, and Newell Rubbermaid's stock was to lose almost half of its value since the Rubbermaid acquisition in March. It blamed lower-than-expected sales of Rubbermaid's plastic containers and Little Tykes toys. Still, company officials maintained that "the integration process remains on plan."[6]

A month later, coinciding with a Wal-Mart announcement that it was expanding vigorously in Europe, Newell Rubbermaid said it would focus on expanding overseas to serve domestic retailers who were moving abroad. The company had been getting a quarter of its sales outside the United States. "Our customers are going international," McDonough said. "We have the opportunity to follow them. It's a once-in-a-lifetime opportunity."[7]

The company also maintained that it had sharply reduced the number of late shipments of Rubbermaid products and expected to have 98 percent of orders shipped on time either in the present quarter or next.[8]

Was this a wise merger? Did Newell pay too much for a faltering Rubbermaid? It was hardly likely in the first year of a merger that management would admit to maybe making a mistake. But stockholders were betting with their money. Meantime, Wolfgang Schmitt pondered his exile and the erosion of value of his stock options.

DISAPPOINTMENT

John McDonough resigned as CEO in November 2000, after Newell Rubbermaid cut profit forecasts three times in the year after the Rubbermaid acquisition. Joseph Galli, a "master marketer," as *Forbes* proclaimed him, and the first outsider in the company's 99-year history, became the chief executive in January 2001.

Newell needed a rescuer. McDonough, whose forte was buying underperforming companies and Newellizing them, had met his match. This was the third year of flat or falling profits. For 2001, sales were off 2.4 percent and net income down 42 percent, with share prices reflecting this. The $6 billion purchase of Rubbermaid, its biggest deal, had brought Newell to its knees, and Rubbermaid remained the sickest division.

---

[6] James P. Miller, "Newell Rubbermaid Shares Fall 20% as an Earnings Short Fall Is Predicted," *Wall Street Journal*, September 7, 1999, p. A4.

[7] "Newell Rubbermaid to Resume Acquisitions, Expand Overseas," *Cleveland Plain Dealer*, October 6, 1999, p. 2-C.

[8] *Ibid.*

Joseph Galli

The 43-year-old Galli, in 19 years at Black & Decker, had built a reputation as a marketing wunderkind, a brand builder. He was running the company's crown jewel, the DeWalt brand, a high-margin line of power tools for skilled workers and consumer do-it-yourselfers. Galli recruited teams of college graduates, dubbed "swarm teams," to be super-missionary salespeople hawking the DeWalt brand not only at store openings but at union halls and Nascar races. See the Information Box: Missionary Salespeople.

Galli brought amazing growth to DeWalt, pushing $60 million in sales in 1992 to more than $1 billion by 1999, in the process providing 64 percent of the company's $4.6 billion sales. By age 38, Galli was the second-highest-paid executive at Black & Decker and in line for the top position except that the CEO was not ready to step down anytime soon.

Galli left to be president of *Amazon.com*, staying only a year, then became chief of VerticalNet for 167 days. Some were calling him a tumbleweed, but conceded that if anybody could add sizzle to an unpretentious product line of such things as mop buckets, toilet brushes, and plastic containers, he might be the best.[9]

Galli spent his first three months at Newell Rubbermaid traveling the world and meeting every manager he could. His predecessor, John McDonough, was a diabetic whose leg had been amputated in 1999 and who had spent almost all his time at company headquarters in Beloit, Wisconsin; in his first six months, Galli spent just 36 hours there.

Newell hadn't run a national ad campaign on television in three years. In 2000, the firm spent 0.7 percent on research and development. (Even conservative Colgate spent 2 percent on the innovation of adding a new color of dish detergent.) Sales of the Rubbermaid unit had declined every year since 1998, and were now at $1.8 billion. No-name rivals were taking business away in major retailers such as Wal-Mart, Home Depot, Target, and Bed Bath & Beyond.

Galli tripled spending on new product development for Rubbermaid. He promoted the brand on prime-time TV for the first time in three years with a budget of $15 million, more than was spent in the previous ten years combined. He also budgeted $40 million for swarm teams of well-paid college grads to push Newell Rubbermaid products at mass retailers, as they had done so successfully with power tools at Black & Decker.[10] Galli made his first acquisition in November 2002—buying American Saw and Manufacturing Co., thus expanding into the hand-tool and power-tool market that he knew so well.[11] Could it be that Newell Rubbermaid was on the verge of a turnaround?

---

[9] Bruce Upbin, "Rebirth of a Salesman," *Forbes*, October 1, 2001, pp. 95–104.

[10] Upbin, p. 104.

[11] "Newell Rubbermaid to Buy American Saw in $450 Million Deal," *Wall Street Journal*, November 25, 2002, p. B6.

INFORMATION BOX

MISSIONARY SALESPEOPLE

Missionary or supporting salespeople do not normally try to secure orders. They are used by manufacturers to provide specialized services and create goodwill and more dealer push. They work with dealers, perhaps to develop point-of-service displays, train dealer salespeople to do a better job of selling the product, provide better communication and rapport between distributor and manufacturer, and, in general, aggressively promote the brand. They are particularly important in selling to self-service outlets, such as supermarkets and discount stores, where there are no retail clerks selling to customers, so that displays, shelf space, and in-stock conditions have to be the selling tools.

Galli's super-missionaries or swarm teams were small armies of energetic college recruits who also worked Nascar races, trade shows, new store openings, and the like. A typical super-missionary was given the use of a new Ford Explorer Sport Trac, a territory of 14 Wal-Marts, and a mission: Make sure Newell's pens, bowls, buckets, and blinds are neatly displayed, priced right, and piled high in prominent spots.[12]

Evaluate this statement: "Good customer service doesn't do you much good, but poor customer service can kill you."

ANALYSIS

This case illustrates not only the risks of dealing with behemoth customers, but also the rewards if you can satisfy their demands. After all, in better days Newell Rubbermaid was prepared to follow Wal-Mart to Europe and be a prime supplier of its stores there. But a vendor has to have the commitment and ability to meet stringent requirements. If a 24-hour delivery cycle is demanded, the vendor must achieve this regardless of costs. If selling prices are to be pared to the bone, efficiency must somehow be jacked up and production costs pruned, or else profitability may have to be sacrificed even to the point of extreme concern. Otherwise, the vendor can be replaced.

The alternative? To be content with far less revenue and a host of smaller accounts, or else to have such a powerful brand name as to be partly insulated from price competition. Rubbermaid thought it had this, due to its public accolades of past years. Perhaps this contributed to the apathy regarding its delivery service. But Wal-Mart was hardly impressed with the superiority of the brand's products, which cost more than alternative suppliers and could not be delivered on time.

But note that improving service and shortening replenishment time is not easily or cheaply done. Rubbermaid spent $62 million on computer technology to enable it to meet Wal-Mart's demands, but it was not enough. Better control of warehouse

[12] Upbin, p. 100.

inventories and production schedules is essential. The vendor will need to carry more of the inventory burden traditionally assumed by the retailer and incur additional expenses and investment for more personnel and trucks and other equipment. Perhaps the most damning indictment of Rubbermaid's service deficiencies was how long they continued without being corrected. The problem initially surfaced in 1995, but by 1999 on-time deliveries had still not improved appreciably. What was Rubbermaid's top management doing all this time? Wolfgang Schmitt can hardly escape the blame, since in almost five years he had not corrected this serious problem with the most important customer.

The eagerness to merge, as seen in both McDonough of Newell and Wolfgang Schmitt of Rubbermaid in this case, may not always be in the best interests of shareholders, and certainly not of employees. Communities also suffer, as plants are closed and headquarters moved. It may even not be in the best interest of the executives involved, as Schmitt realized to his dismay, despite taking home a sizable severance package. But is this enough to make up for losing the power and prestige of a top management position, and all the perks that go with it? And what if the value of the stock in the severance package crashes, as Schmitt found to his further dismay? And McDonough in his holdings?

In this era of merger mania, a more sober appraisal is needed by many firms. Not all mergers are in the best interests of both parties. Too often a firm pays too much to acquire another firm, as we saw in the preceding chapter, where Quaker Oats bought Snapple for $1.7 billion and three years later got rid of it for $300 million. Frequently the glowing prospects do not work out.

When an acquisition finally turns out to be unwise, especially where too much is paid for the acquired firm, the conclusion may be that someone fumbled the homework, that the research and investigation of the firm to be acquired was hasty, biased, or downright incompetent. Admittedly, in some cases several suitors may be bidding for the same acquisition candidate, and this then becomes a contest: Who will make the winning bid? The only beneficiaries to such a situation—besides the consultants, lawyers, and investment bankers—are the shareholders of the firm to be acquired.

UPDATE

Early in 2003, Galli announced plans to move the headquarters of Newell Rubbermaid from the "cornfields surrounding the hometown of Freeport, Illinois" to Atlanta, "the city of the future," as Galli depicted it. He thought moving would be a signal that big changes were happening inside and out. He saw that the key to a new image was being in a city that symbolized change and innovation. It didn't hurt that Atlanta offered a sweet deal, potentially giving the company up to $25 million in tax breaks, as well as $1.3 million in cash for land and equipment purchases, as well as other tax relief.[13]

---

[13] Peralte C. Paul and Patti Bond, "Out with the Old," Cox News, as reported in *Cleveland Plain Dealer*, March 8, 2003, pp. C1, C3.

Galli's tenure since 2001 had not provided any breakthrough in sales, profits, and stock prices. The company had 2003 sales of about $7 billion, not much higher than the 2000 sales of $6.9 billion. For the first quarter of 2004, the net loss was $74.9 million on sales of $1.54 billion, and the share price was in the low $20s. Newell sold three subsidiaries in early 2004, part of its strategy to divest underperforming "non-strategic" businesses. Now Galli announced that it was abandoning its growth-by-acquisition strategy "to reconfigure our portfolio through divestitures and the exit of low-margin product lines."[14] Hardly a growth company anymore.

On October 18, 2005, Newell announced that Joseph Galli had resigned by "mutual agreement," after an inability to turn around the company. This capped his disappointing 4 1/2-year tenure, during which he closed 84 facilities, cut 12,000 jobs, and sold $1 billion of low-margin businesses. He was one of the hottest young CEOs when he came to Newell, but "his enthusiasm and his feeling that he was Superman probably made him overoptimistic about what he could accomplish," noted Scott Cowen, a Newell director.[15]

❊ ❊ ❊

Invitation to Make Your Own Analysis and Conclusions

What went wrong with the Rubbermaid acquisition? Why couldn't it be corrected?

❊ ❊ ❊

WHAT CAN BE LEARNED?

Customer service is vital in dealing with big customers—We saw in this case the consequences of not being able to meet the service demands of Wal-Mart. A vendor's very viability may depend on somehow gearing up to meet the service expectations. This should be a top priority if a major customer is not to be lost. Correcting the situation should be a matter of weeks or months, and not years.

The well-known brand name does not always compensate for higher prices or poor service when dealing with big retailers.—Generally we think of a well-respected brand name as giving the vendor certain liberties, of insulating the vendor at least somewhat from vicious price competition, and even excusing the vendor from some service standards, such as prompt and dependable delivery. After all, a respected brand name gives an image of quality that lesser brands do not have, as well as an assured body of loyal customers.

Well, Wal-Mart's dealings with Rubbermaid before the merger certainly disprove that notion.

---

[14] Marcia Pledger, "Newell Rubbermaid Continues Divesting," *Cleveland Plain Dealer*, May 9, 2004.
[15] Evan Perez and Joann S. Lublin, "Newell CEO Resigns After Turnaround Bid Falters," *Wall Street Journal*, October 18, 2005, p. A-11.

How can this be? It still becomes a matter of power position. Not having Rubbermaid, or Little Tykes toys, was hardly damaging to Wal-Mart with its eager alternative suppliers. But the loss of Wal-Mart, even only the partial loss of being given less shelf space, was serious for Rubbermaid.

The positive aspects of organizational restructuring for acquisitions are mixed.—The idea of restructuring generally means downsizing. Some assets or corporate divisions may be sold off or eliminated, and the remaining organization thereby streamlined. This usually means layoffs, plant closings, and headquarters relocations. In Rubbermaid's case, the small Ohio town of Wooster faced the loss of its headquarters and some 3,000 jobs. Of course, management's defense is always that while jobs are being cut, the operations will be stronger in the long run. Perhaps; but not always.

Where an organization has become fat and inefficient with layers of bureaucracy, some pruning of personnel and operations is necessary. But how much is too much, and how much is not enough? Certainly those personnel who are not willing to accept change may have to be let go. Weak persons and operations that show little probability of improvement need to be cut, just as the athlete who can't perform up to expectations can hardly be carried. Still, it is usually better to wait for sufficient information as to the "why" of poor performance before assigning blame for unsatisfactory operational results. (You may want to review Chapter 2 and the Scott Paper and Al Dunlap case for the worst scenario here.)

Periodic housecleaning produces competitive health.—In order to minimize the buildup of deadwood, all aspects of an organization periodically ought to be objectively appraised. Weak products and operations should be pruned, unless solid justification exists for keeping them. Such justification might include good growth prospects or complementing other products and operations or even providing a desired customer service. In particular, staff and headquarters personnel and functions should be scrutinized, perhaps every five years, with the objective of weeding out the redundant and superfluous. Most important, these evaluations should be done objectively, with decisive action taken where needed. While layoffs may result, they sometimes can be avoided by suitable transfers.

Going back to Rubbermaid, the five-year-long tolerance of little improvement in customer service was inexcusable, and one would think that heads should roll (as undoubtedly some did and quickly when Newell took over).

Is there life without Wal-Mart for a big mass-market consumer goods manufacturer?—Can such a large manufacturer be strong and profitable without selling to the giant retailers? Certainly other distribution channels are available for reaching consumers, such as smaller retailers, different types of retailers, wholesalers, and the Internet. For smaller manufacturers, some of these are viable alternatives to Wal-Mart, Target, Kmart, and the various large department store corporations.

Newell's and Rubbermaid's products were diversified but still geared to rather pedestrian household and hardware consumer use, hardly the grist to create a fashion or fad demand. A limited distribution strategy, such as through boutiques, would hardly produce the sales volume needed. Only the mega-retailers could provide the mass distribution and sales volume needed. Of course, Wal-Mart was not the only large retailer, but it was the biggest. Kmart, Target, and the chain department stores were alternatives. But these tended to be just as demanding as Wal-Mart. This suggests that somehow the demands of giant retailers have to be catered to, regardless of costs or inclinations, by firms like Newell and Rubbermaid.

Missionary salespeople can enhance customer service in dealing with large retailers.—Many vendors are realizing this today, and sales-support staff are frequently used to provide the service, rapport, and feedback desirable in dealing with these most important clients. The vendor that provides the best support may well win out over competitors. Furthermore, missionaries may alert the vendor to emerging problems or competitive situations that need to be countered. Where they are swarm teams like Galli's, they can be a powerful tool in winning the battle for shelf space. But they do not guarantee success, as Galli found in his $4\frac{1}{2}$-year stint as Newell CEO.

Once the growth mode is lost, it is difficult to win back.—Newell and its albatross acquisition, Rubbermaid, certainly are examples of this. Both were high flying in the early 1990s, but even Galli, a hot-shot marketer with his previous firm, had not been able to turn Newell Rubbermaid around before he was ousted in 2005.

CONSIDER

Can you add any additional learning insights?

QUESTIONS

1. "Periodic evaluations of personnel and departments aimed at pruning dead-wood cause far too much harm to the organization. Such axing evaluations should themselves be pruned." Argue this position as persuasively as you can.

2. Now present your most persuasive arguments for axing evaluations.

3. How do you account for Rubbermaid's inability to improve its delivery service to Wal-Mart? What factors do you see as contributing to this on-going deficiency?

4. Do you think Newell acted too hastily in discharging Schmitt and other top executives so soon after the merger? Why or why not?

5. Do you think Wal-Mart and the other large retailers are going too far in their demands on their suppliers? Where would you draw the line?

6. Stanley Gault's strategy of trying to introduce a new product every day was lauded as the mark of a successful firm permeated by innovative thinking. Do you agree?

7. Is it likely that a decades-old organization, such as Rubbermaid, would be bloated with excessive bureaucracy and overhead? Why or why not?

8. Why do you think Galli's swarm teams, which were so successful with Black & Decker power tools, did not apparently improve the operations of Newell Rubbermaid?

HANDS-ON EXERCISES

1. Be a Devil's Advocate (one who argues a contrary position). You have been asked by several concerned board members to argue against John McDonough's avid Newellizing policy at the next board meeting. Marshal as many contrary or cautionary arguments as you can and present them persuasively, yet tactfully.

2. You are one of the three divisional presidents fired by McDonough in the first two months of the merger. Describe your feelings and your action plan at this point. (If you want to make some assumptions, state them specifically.)

3. You are a vice president of Rubbermaid, reporting to Wolfgang Schmitt in 1995. The first serious complaints have surfaced from Wal-Mart concerning unacceptable delivery problems. Schmitt has ordered you to look into the complaints and prepare a course of action. Be as specific as you can on how you would approach this and what recommendations you would make.

TEAM DEBATE EXERCISE

It is early 1998. The demands of Wal-Mart are intensifying, and Newell is making overtures to acquire Rubbermaid. Debate these two courses of action in this turnabout year for Rubbermaid: (1) We must gear up to meet Wal-Mart's demands, even though estimated costs of complying are $300 million in a new computer network and other capital and operating costs; versus: (2) It is better to sacrifice the increasingly dictatorial Wal-Mart account and seek alternative distribution. (For this option you need to come up with some creative alternatives, and defend them.)

YOUR ASSESSMENT OF THE LATEST DEVELOPMENTS

Evaluate Galli's actions after he became CEO. Where did he go wrong, or was it a lost cause to begin with?

INVITATION TO RESEARCH

What has Wolfgang Schmitt been doing since his ouster from an active role with Newell Rubbermaid? Have Newell Rubbermaid's fortunes improved since Galli was ousted? How about the stock price? What is Galli doing now?

CHAPTER TEN

DaimlerChrysler—Blatant Misrepresentation

*I*t was supposed to be so right, almost a merger made in heaven, some said at the beginning. Chrysler was the smallest but since 1994 the most efficient U.S. auto producer, with the highest profit margin. Now its productivity and innovative strength would be blended with the prestige of Daimler's legendary Mercedes-Benz. Furthermore, during one of its periodic crises Chrysler had sold off its international operations to help raise needed money, and this merger would increase international exposure in a big way and mate it with a rich partner. The instigator, Juergen Schrempp of Daimler, was lauded for his intentions of building a new car company that would have global economies of scale.

Of course, there were two cultures involved, German and American. But in the executive offices, decision making would be shared, with Chrysler's CEO, Robert Eaton, being a co-chairman with Schrempp.

Chrysler management's expectations of equality with its prestigious merger partner were soon dashed. Schrempp, as it turned out, never intended equality. He had flagrantly misrepresented the merger package, and quickly got rid of Chrysler's top managers. Was this deception unacceptable ethical conduct, or was it rather a hard-nosed negotiating ploy that Chrysler's management should have recognized?

In any case, in November 1998 this merger of "equals" was finalized. And the s__t hit the fan.

CHRYSLER BEFORE THE MERGER

During the last several decades, Chrysler had had a checkered history.

Some said that Lee Iacocca had performed a miracle at Chrysler. He became president of an almost-moribund firm in November 1978. Its condition was so bad that he turned to Washington to bail out the company, and obtained federal loan guarantees of $1.5 billion to help it survive. By 1983, Iacocca had brought Chrysler to profitability, and then to a strong performance for the next four years. He paid back the entire loan seven years before it was due. Like a phoenix, the reeling number-three auto-maker had been given new life and respectability. Some said Iacocca should be president of the United States, that his talents were needed in the biggest job of all.

Iacocca turned to other interests in the latter half of the decade, but by 1988, the company was hurting again. To a large extent the new problems reflected capital deprivation: sufficient money had not been invested in new car and truck designs. This lack of funds was the result of the 1987 acquisition of American Motors Corporation (AMC). The crown jewel of this buyout was the Jeep line of sport-utility vehicles, which appealed to younger, more affluent buyers than Chrysler's older, lower-income customers. Still, Chrysler found itself saddled with the substantial inefficiencies that had bedeviled AMC.

An aging Iacocca again turned his full attention back to the car business, now seven years after retiring his company's horrendous bank debt. He staked the company's resources on four high-visibility cars and trucks: a minivan, the Jeep Grand Cherokee, LH sedans, and a full-size pickup. Fearful that the company might not survive until the new models came out, especially if a recession were to occur before then, Iacocca instituted a far-reaching austerity program, which cut $3 billion from the company's $26 billion annual operating costs.

By 1992, the company was riding high. Iacocca retired on December 31, 1992, with a job well done. As he said on TV, "When it's your last turn at bat, it sure is nice to hit a home run."[1] Robert Eaton, formerly with GM of Europe, replaced Iacocca as Chrysler chairman.

As it moved to the millennium, Chrysler prospered because of a combination of innovative designs, segment-leading products, and rising sales throughout the auto industry. See Table 10.1 for the sales and net profit statistics of these golden years for Chrysler relative to its two U.S. competitors, General Motors and Ford.

AFTER THE MERGER

Seldom has a merger turned out worse, and so quickly. Perhaps because of morale problems and too much attention given to smoothing relations between Detroit and Stuttgart, the bottom line of Chrysler was wracked. Or maybe the problems at Chrysler had been latent, below the surface, and only needed the disruption of a massive takeover to surface. Or could the problems have been triggered by an unwise dictatorship by the German master?

On November 16, 1998, Daimler-Benz issued an additional $36 billion of its stock to buy Chrysler. This, when added to the $48 billion value of its existing stock, brought the total market value of DaimlerChrysler to $84 billion. Early in December 2000, barely two years later, the collapsing DaimlerChrysler stock had a market value of only $39 billion, less than Daimler alone was worth before the deal.

---

[1] Alex Taylor III, "U.S. Cars Come Back," *Fortune*, November 16, 1992, p. 85.

TABLE 10.1.   Sales and Profit Comparisons, Big Three U.S. Automakers, 1993–1998 (millions of dollars)

	1993	1994	1995	1996	1997	1998
Ford						
Sales	108,521	128,439	137,137	146,991	153,637	144,416
Net Profit	2,529	5,308	4,139	4,371	6,920	6,579
	2.3%	4.1%	3.0%	3.0%	4.5%	4.5%
GM						
Sales	138,220	154,951	168,829	164,069	173,168	161,315
Net Profit	2,466	5,659	6,933	4,668	5,972	3,662
	1.8%	3.7%	4.1%	2.8%	3.4%	2.3%
Chrysler						
Sales	43,600	52,235	53,195	61,397	61,147	NA
Net Profit	(2,551)	3,713	2,025	3,529	2,805	NA
	(5.9)%	7.1%	3.8%	5.7%	4.6%	

Note: These are total company sales, the bulk of which are autos/trucks. But with nonvehicle diversifications, the sales will be somewhat overstated for autos/trucks.

Sources: Company public records. NA = Not applicable because of merger with Daimler.

Commentary: After a poor year in 1993—a $2.5 billion loss—Chrysler really bounced back, making a profit of $3.7 billion, which was over 7 percent of sales, far above that of its two major competitors. Chrysler continued the strong showing with multibillion-dollar profits from 1994 on. In 1995, its 3.8 percent profit was well above Ford, but slightly less than GM; in 1996 and 1997 its profit margin again was the best. While we do not have specific figures for 1998, we know that it was also a good year. The collapse came in 1999.

Chrysler was bleeding money. During the second half of 2000, Chrysler lost $1.8 billion and went through $5 billion in cash, this at a time when GM and Ford were still doing well.

By 2000, Eaton was long gone, along with nine other top Chrysler executives, including the renowned designer, Thomas Gale. Then, in November 2000, Eaton's successor, James Holden, a Canadian, the last high-level non-German remaining, was also given the ax. His replacement was a Daimler executive, Deiter Zetsche, 47, a tall German with a walrus mustache. As chief operating officer, Zetsche brought with him Wolfgang Bernhard, 39, an intense young engineer with an MBA from Columbia who was a stickler for cost-cutting. It could have been worse: Zetsche could have brought a big team from Germany instead of only one other man. Still, indignation surfaced at his putting German executives in top positions of this old American firm—a firm that had played an important part in defeating the Germans in World War II.

Eaton and the rest of the Chrysler hierarchy found to their dismay that this was not a merger of equals, despite Chairman Schrempp's 1998 statements to the contrary, not only to Chrysler's top management but also to the SEC (Securities and Exchange Commission), and the inclusion of the Chrysler name in the corporation name. In reality, Chrysler had become only a division of Daimler. In interviews with the media, Schrempp admitted that subjugation of Chrysler had always been his intention, this a duplicity of no small moment.[2]

Later we will analyze why the merger so quickly proved a disaster, at least in the short and intermediate terms.

Jurgen Schrempp

DaimlerChrysler Chairman Jurgen Schrempp, a trim 56, had an untarnished reputation going into the Chrysler merger. He had begun his career with Mercedes as an apprentice mechanic nearly 40 years before, and had moved steadily upward. Now he acknowledged that he faced "outstanding" challenges with Chrysler. But he pointed out, "Five years ago in 1995, Daimler-Benz posted a loss of 6 billion marks ($3 billion). We turned it around in a matter of two years. I think we have the experience and know-how to attend to matters, and if necessary we'll do that at Chrysler . . . Our aim is to be the No. 1 motor company in the world."[3]

Still, there are those who think that he destroyed Chrysler, that "he didn't realize it was the people who counted, not the factories, which were old, or the sales and profits, which could come and go."[4] Schrempp either forced or encouraged key people to leave, and some would say that these departures were of the heart and soul of Chrysler. His duplicity in misleading Chrysler's top managers and shareholders that this was to be a merger of equals could hardly be viewed as anything but ambitious conniving.

During the merger finalization, it was predicted that Chrysler would earn more than $5 billion in 2000, this being what it had earned in 1998. In late 1999, however, Chrysler president James Holden reduced the prediction to only $2.5 billion because of having to spend billions retooling for new-model introductions at a time when an economic slowdown seemed to be looming.

The reduced profit expectation coming so soon after the merger was unacceptable to Schrempp, and he pressured Chrysler to pump up earnings for the first half of the year by building 75,000 more cars and trucks than could readily be sold, with these quickly shipped to dealers. (The accepted accounting practice was to consider a car as revenue to Chrysler when it reached a dealer's lot, not when it was sold by the dealer.) As a result, Chrysler was just short of its $2.5 billion target in the first half of 2000.

Not surprisingly, the inventory buildup resulted in showrooms overflowing with old-model minivans just as new models began arriving in August. With car sales in general now slowing because of the economy, Chrysler had to cut prices even on popular minivans, and it was necessary to increase rebates up to $3,000 on the old models. These price cuts destroyed profitability all the more because Chrysler, in its optimism after record profits in the 1990s, had upgraded its cars and trucks, expecting to charge more for them. But with competition increasing and car pricing

[2] For example, "A Deal for the History Books: The Auto Takeover May Be Remembered for All of the Wrong Reasons," *Newsweek*, Dec. 11, 2000, p. 57.

[3] William J. Holstein, "The Conquest of Chrysler," *U.S. News & World Report*, Nov. 27, 2000, p. 54.

[4] Jerry Flint, "Free Chrysler!" *Forbes*, Oct. 30, 2000, p. 132.

turning deflationary, the price hikes did not hold up, and this and the rebates severely affected profits in the third and fourth quarters. (See the following Information Box for a discussion of rebates.)

INFORMATION BOX

REBATES

A rebate is a promise by a manufacturer to return part of the purchase price directly to the purchaser. The rebate is usually given to consumers, although it can be offered to dealers instead, in the expectation that they will pass some or all of the savings along to consumers.

Obviously, the objective of a rebate is to increase sales by giving purchasers a lower price. But why not simply reduce prices? The rebate is used instead of a regular markdown or price reduction because it is perceived as less permanent than cutting the list price. It can give more promotional push by emphasizing the savings off the regular price, but only for a limited time. Rebates can be effective in generating short-term business, but they may affect business negatively once they have been lifted.

Do you see any dangers with rebates from the manufacturer's viewpoint? As a consumer, would you prefer a rebate to a price reduction, or does it make any difference?

Schrempp Takes Action

With the huge losses in the second half of 2000, Schrempp sent Zetsche to Detroit with simple instructions: "My orders were to fix the place."[5] On his first day Zetsche fired the head of sales and marketing. Then in two months he developed a three-year turnaround plan. It called for cutting 26,000 jobs (29 percent of the workforce), reducing the cost of parts by 15 percent, and closing six assembly plants. Zetsche projected a breakeven point by 2002 and an operating profit of $2 billion in 2003.[6] This would still be well below the operating profit of Chrysler in 1993–1997, before the merger, as shown in Table 10.1.

His colleague from Stuttgart, Wolfgang Bernhard, organized engineers and procurement specialists into 50 teams to find ways to save money on parts. Suppliers were told to reduce prices by 5 percent as of January 2001, with a further 10 percent reduction over the next two years. Some companies, such as Robert Bosch GmbH, the world's second-largest parts maker, and Federal Mogul, said they would not cut prices. Zetsche observed, "If they do not support us to get to the 15 percent, we have to consider that in our future decisions."[7]

---

[5] Alex Taylor III, "Can the Germans Rescue Chrysler?" *Fortune*, April 30, 2001, p. 109.
[6] *Ibid.*
[7] "Daimler Threatens to Drop Some Suppliers," Bloomberg News, as reported in *Cleveland Plain Dealer*, Feb. 28, 2001, P. 6-C.

Bernhard also focused attention on improving quality as a way to cut costs. In particular, the four-wheel-drive trucks showed up poorly on quality surveys. The company began rigorously evaluating new models for quality while they were still in the design stage, so that parts or manufacturing processes could be changed before too much money had been committed.

Zetsche began to direct much of his attention to bringing back standout designs that Chrysler had been noted for in the 1990s. Of late, design and engineering efforts, such as the 2001 minivan and the 2002 Ram, seemed more evolutionary than revolutionary, with leadership allowed to slip while Toyota and Honda became stronger competitors.

Despite increased competition, Zetsche had a unique asset that he thought should help his company regain the edge: the prestige and competence of Mercedes-Benz technology. Mercedes previously had feared diluting its premium brand, but now it was directed to share components with Chrysler. New rear-wheel versions of the Chrysler Concorde and 300 M coming out in 2004 and 2005, for example, were planned to make use of Mercedes electronics, transmissions, seat frames, and other parts. "If Zetsche can sprinkle some Mercedes magic on the Chrysler brand without damaging the premium status of Mercedes, Chrysler has a shot at doing well in the future."[8]

To his credit, Zetsche worked hard to overcome the anti-German feelings that initially followed his and Bernhard's arrival. To stem the potential brain drain, he persuaded some senior Chrysler executives and technicians to stay. And the drastic cutback of workers and closing of factories before long came to be viewed as necessary cost cutting to keep the company viable. Even UAW president Steve Yokich endorsed these actions: "[Otherwise] I don't think there would be a Chrysler."[9]

Other Problems for Schrempp

Two other major problems confronted Schrempp. In October 2000, despite misgivings by Chrysler executives, he acquired 34 percent of Mitsubishi Motors, with the option to up that to 100 percent after three years. Hardly had the deal been finalized than Mitsubishi admitted it had misled consumers about product quality for decades. It also announced that losses for the last six months had nearly doubled. Schrempp reacted by installing a turnaround expert as chief operating officer at Mitsubishi, accompanied by dozens of Japanese-speaking Daimler executives. All the while the new chief executive, Takashi Sonobe, was quoted as saying that he, not the German team, remained in charge, and that he saw no need for big changes. A contest of wills, this.[10]

DaimlerChrysler's Freightliner, the leading North American heavy-truck maker, was also struggling as the North American market hit one of the steepest slumps in a decade. After an aggressive growth policy that involved acquisitions of other truck makers and a heavy investment in a facility for reconditioning used trucks to sustain Freightliner's sale-buyback strategy, demand for new and used heavy trucks

---

[8] Detroit manufacturing consultant Ron Harbour, as reported in *Fortune*, April 30, 2001, p. 110.

[9] Taylor, p. 107.

[10] Holstein, "The Conquest of Chrysler."

plummeted 50 percent, and prices fell sharply. It was expected that Schrempp would install a German national as head of this unit.[11]

PROGNOSIS

As of mid-2001, many observers were pessimistic of the probabilities of Schrempp's resurrecting Chrysler any time soon. In the long term, perhaps; but they questioned whether creditors and shareholders would tolerate a long period of profit drain by Chrysler and low share prices for DaimlerChrysler stock. Rumors were that Deutsche Bank, DaimlerChrysler's largest shareholder, was getting ready to oust Schrempp, and that Chrysler would be broken up into smaller pieces and sold off.[12]

Still, friendly German banks and shareholders might be more patient than Wall Street. DaimlerChrysler was the first German firm to be listed on the New York Stock Exchange, and this listing subjected Schrempp to the impatience of the international financial markets and their obsession with meeting quarterly earnings expectations. In an age of volatile markets, failure to meet such expectations often resulted in a company's stock price collapsing. This bothered Schrempp: "I don't think [it] is advantageous: focusing on quarterly results. It might well be that because we increase our spending, investment, whatever, for a very good reason, that I might occasionally miss what they [investors] expect from me."[13]

Schrempp would have another worry imperiling his job if Chrysler did not improve soon. The third-largest holder of DaimlerChrysler stock was the Las Vegas takeover tycoon Kirk Kerkorian, a powerful man with a reputation for being easily offended. Rumor held that Schrempp had not made himself available to see Kerkorian, but instead went to his ranch in South Africa.[14]

Chrysler executives, much as they might dislike Schrempp, would be worse off if he were ousted. Mercedes executives ruled in Stuttgart headquarters, and without Chrysler's main supporter, Schrempp, Chrysler might not receive the resources needed to make a comeback. It might be broken up and sold, or left withering within the DaimlerChrysler's empire.[15]

ANALYSIS

This case illustrates the downside of mergers and acquisitions. (We use these terms somewhat similarly, but will consider "merger" as closer to the idea of equals coming together, while "acquisition" suggests a larger firm absorbing a smaller one.) The

---

[11] Joseph B. White, "Head of Truck Maker Freightliner Is Leaving Post," *Wall Street Journal*, May 25, 2001, p. A4.
[12] "Can the Germans Rescue Chrysler?" pp. 106–107.
[13] Holstein, p. 69.
[14] Reported in "A Deal for the History Books," p. 57.
[15] See Robyn Meredith, "Batman and Robin," *Forbes*, March 5, 2001, pp. 67–68, and Jerry Flint, "Free Chrysler," *Forbes*, October 30, 2000, p. 132, for more discussion of these scenarios.

causes of these problems are diverse, although certain commonalities occur time and again.

We will examine the salient factors that led to the collapse of Chrysler soon after the merger under (a) those mainly Daimler's fault, (b) those Chrysler's fault, and (c) the externals that made the situation worse. Then we will examine the whole concept of a "merger of equals." Can there really be a merger of equals?

Daimler's Contribution to the Problem

The Morale Factor

Different cultures are often involved when a merger or acquisition takes place, even among seemingly similar firms. For example, one business culture may be more conservative and the other aggressive and even reckless; one may be formal and the other informal; one culture may insist on standard operating procedures (SOPs) being followed, while the other may be far less restricted; one may be dominated by an accountant or control mentality, which emphasizes cost analysis and rigidity of budgets, and the other by the sales mentality, which seeks maximum sales production and flexibility of operations even if expenses sometimes get out of line. Such differences impede easy assimilation.

The assimilation challenge for divergent corporate cultures becomes all the more difficult when different nationalities are involved, for example, Germanic versus American. National pride, and even prejudice, may complicate the situation.

It is hardly surprising that this mammoth merger of a proud German firm and an American firm with a long heritage should have presented morale problems. Especially with one party misled as to the sharing of leadership, the seeds were laid for extreme resentment. Some of this resentment among rank-and-file workers even went back to World War II.

But there were other obstacles to a smooth melding of the two firms. Daimler had to adjust from being an old-line German firm to becoming a huge international firm confronted with a diversity of cultures. "The German instinct is for hierarchy, order, planning. Daimler executives use Dr. or Prof. on their business cards. Many wear dark three-piece suits. Chrysler, by contrast, was known for a freewheeling creativity."[16]

Chrysler's company culture had been highly successful in the very recent past, as shown in Table 10.1 and also in Table 10.2, which presents the gain in market share or competitive position during the 1990s. Its rather unrestrained-by-rules culture seemed to many to be the key to innovative thinking and technical leadership. With the merger it was not only being challenged but repudiated and supplanted by Germans who little appreciated the contributions of designers like Bob Lutz, who came up with products customers wanted that were not engineered at great cost and research. "The daring and imagination of the old Chrysler [is] buried under German management."[17]

---

[16] Holstein, p. 56.
[17] Flint, p. 132.

TABLE 10.2. Chrysler's Market Share of the Big Three U.S. Automakers, 1991–1998

	Chrysler's Sales Percentage of U.S. Car/Truck Automakers
1991	12.2
1992	13.7
1993	15.0
1994	15.6
1995	14.8
1996	16.5
1997	15.8
1998	NA

Sources: Calculated from publicly reported sales figures; 1998 figures not applicable due to merger in November.

Commentary: The improvement in Chrysler performance in the middle and late 1990s is clearly evident. Market-share improvement of even 0.05 percent translates into a gain in competitive position. And here we see a gain of more than 4.0 percent in 1996 and 3.6 percent in 1997. You can see how Chrysler's improving performance in the latter years of the 1990s would be attractive to Daimler.

Schrempp's Major Blunder

A miscalculation by Schrempp little more than a year after the merger was to have drastic consequences. His order to produce and ship 75,000 more older-model vehicles than could reasonably be sold before the new models came out, thus beefing up sales and profits for the first half of the year, resulted in huge imbalances of inventories in the last half and destroyed year-2000 results as well as the early months of 2001. This overproduction was the trigger that brought Chrysler its huge losses and even jeopardized the soundness of Schrempp's acquisition decision.

Chrysler's Contribution

One could argue that Chrysler had grown fat and inefficient after its years of success in the last half of the 1990s, that it was on the verge of a drastic decline in profits even if Daimler had not come on the scene to stir things up. By 1999, Chrysler showrooms were saddled with aging models, including the important minivans that were in their fifth year. While still the leader in minivan sales, Chrysler was losing market share to competitors with newer models, including the Honda Odyssey.

The prosperity of Chrysler in the mid-1990s may have reflected not so much inspired management as a combination of good-luck factors: innovative designs and segment-leading products, yes, but also rising sales throughout the auto industry and a ground swell of demand for high-profit minivans and pickup trucks. Maybe the success of those years paved the way for the disaster that came shortly after

Daimler took over. The great demand for vehicles like the Ram pickup truck, Jeep Grand Cherokee, and Dodge Durango brought a heady confidence that the good times would continue. Accordingly, Chrysler projected market share to increase to 20 percent by 2005, far above anything ever attained before. (You can see from Table 10.2 that reaching a 20 percent market share was not very close.) So Chrysler spent heavily refurbishing plants and buying new equipment. It went from having the fewest workers per point of market share in 1996 to the most by 1999. It was spending money extravagantly, and its entrepreneurial culture was operating unchecked. "The company lost its purpose and lost its direction," the former chief engineer Francois Castaing said.[18]

The uncontrolled entrepreneurial culture led to poor communication and coordination, with each team buying its own components, such as platforms and parts for the different cars, thus not taking advantage of economies of scale. For example, the Durango and the Jeep had different windshield wipers, and Chrysler's five teams specified three different kinds of corrosion protection for the rolled steel used to reinforce plastic bumper surfaces.[19]

Other lapses of good judgment included continuing production of old-model minivans as it was switching production to the new one, thus flooding the market. This yielding to the pressure by Schrempp, as we have seen earlier, was a major factor in the disastrous 2000 results. Could Chrysler executives have protested more vigorously? The practice of the old management to introduce new models in batches rather than spread them over several years brought a feast-or-famine situation: very good years, and rather bad years in between.

External Factors

Certainly the merger was consummated at a time when the auto industry, and the economy in general, was on the threshhold of a downturn. Chrysler apparently miscalculated such an eventuality, spending heavily for costlier models just before demand turned down, and its brands were not strong enough to command higher premiums from customers. By early 2001, Chrysler was outspending all other major automakers on rebates and other incentives.

Chrysler also seemed to be oblivious to the threat of competitors during its golden years. Despite heavy use of incentives, Chrysler lost market share for the first three months of 2001: a 14.2 percent market share vs. 15.1 percent for the same three months in 2000.

CAN THERE REALLY BE A MERGER OF EQUALS?

In reality there is seldom a merger of equals. Unless the two parties actually recapitalize themselves with new stock—and this is seldom done—there is always an acquirer and an acquiree. Even if both parties to the merger have equal seats on

---

[18] As quoted in "Can the Germans Rescue Chrysler?" p. 109.
[19] *Ibid.*

the board of directors, still the acquiring firm and its executives are more dominant. Even if the name of the new combined firm is completely changed, this does not assure a merger of equals. For example, in the well-publicized merger "of equals" in 2000 between Bell Atlantic and GTE, the name *Verizon* was created. But no one was fooled: Bell Atlantic was in charge. Furthermore, there can be no true merger of equals if one firm owns more of the consolidated stock (usually reflecting its larger size) than the other, and this is almost always the case. Daimler was certainly the larger firm in this merger, having paid $36 billion for Chrysler, while its own shares just before the merger had a market value of about $48 billion.

How important is this merger of equals to the executives of acquired firms? Apparently to many it is not of major consequence as long as they get a good price for their stake, or as long as they believe the acquiring firm will honor their importance. Occasionally a merger negotiation will fall apart over the issue of who will be in charge. Take the example of Lucent and Alcatel of France, two of the world's biggest makers of communications equipment: At the last minute, on May 29, 2001, Henry B. Schacht, chairman of Lucent, called off the merger talks. "It started to feel more like an acquisition than a merger," one of the Lucent participants explained. They could not accept the probability that Alcatel would be in charge.[20]

UPDATE

At the beginning of 2002, Chrysler reported that it had lost a staggering $2 billion in 2001, and this brought a new wave of criticism of the merger—after all, it was four years after the deal. For the first years after the merger, Mercedes closely guarded its parts and designs for fear of eroding the Mercedes mystique. Now headquarters in Stuttgart, Germany, finally began forcing its far-flung operations to begin working together. In the spring of 2003, Chrysler introduced two models that reflected more German engineering: the Pacifica, a cross between a station wagon and an SUV; and the Crossfire, a sleek sports car. Waiting in the wings were the LX sedan and an SUV called the Magnum. Headquarters also began bringing engineers from its Mitsubishi subsidiary to Stuttgart in order to integrate some ideas for smaller cars.[21] High time that assimilation efforts should begin, in this now five-year merger.

By 2004, nearly seven years after the merger, Chrysler was on a upswing, with its profits and market share growing because of improvements in quality and design, and drastic cost-cutting. Not the least of the contributors to the turnaround was a hot new car, the 300 C. (The Pacifica, introduced in 2003, had been a dud, partly because it was priced too high.) The new car was not only distinctive but significantly cheaper than equivalent competitive models. For example, a well-equipped version sold for $36,000, while a similarly powered BMW retailed at $60,000. Chrysler gave

[20] For more details, see Seth Schiesel, *New York Times*, reported in *Cleveland Plain Dealer*, June 3, 2001, p. 1-H.

[21] Neal E. Boudette, "At Daimler Chrysler, a New Push to Make Its Units Work Together," *Wall Street Journal*, March 12, 2003, pp. A1 and A15.

a 300 C to Snoop Dogg, in return for a promise he'd include it in a music video, and with crowds being pulled into dealerships, Chrysler's market share inched up to 13 percent from 12.7 percent a year earlier, this at a time when both Ford and GM were losing market share.

Alas, now that Chrysler was making money, Mercedes-Benz was faltering, with serious quality problems. Back in 1998 at the merger, Mercedes was the world's No. 1 luxury brand. Now it had slipped to the fifth largest. This reversal of fortune—whenever one part of the empire turns a corner, another part stumbles—raises doubt about the belief that vast size brings huge economies of scale. Jurgen Schrempp's global vision inspired other auto industry tie-ups, such as Ford's acquisition of Land Rover and Volvo, and GM's stake in Fiat, which also have had mixed results.

The see-sawing performance continued into 2006, now with Chrysler struggling to clear out a large inventory of unsold vehicles, while Mercedes seemed to have rebounded and recovered from its quality problems.[22] By the end of 2006, the situation was worsening as Chrysler recorded a $1.5 billion loss for the third quarter, joining GM and Ford in posting whopping losses. The U.S. auto industry was on the ropes as Tokyo-based Honda reported a profit. Chrysler's losses were blamed on falling sales of large sport-utility vehicles, and also on the highest labor costs among the Big Three, thanks to the UAW's rejection of concessions similar to those given to Ford and GM. Rumors surfaced that Chrysler might be put up for sale by parent DaimlerChrysler.[23]

∗ ∗ ∗

Invitation to Make Your Own Analysis and Conclusions

Could the early problems of the merger have been avoided? What are your recommendations?

∗ ∗ ∗

WHAT CAN BE LEARNED?

Was the flagrant deception that this would be a merger of equals unethical?— Outright deception and lies would seem the essence of unethical behavior, and perhaps illegal as well. They are certainly so viewed when it comes to deceiving consumers. But in the hard negotiating climate of a merger, is a less truthful and trusting stance more the norm? Should we define ethical standards differently than when the hapless consumer is involved?

---

[22] Stephen Power and Neal E. Boudetter, "Slide in Mercedes Performance Dent's Chrysler's Recent Revival," *Wall Street Journal*, February 9, 2005, pp. A1 and A6; Steven Power, "DaimlerChrysler, VW Profits Rise, But Challenges Persist in the U.S.," *Wall Street Journal*, July 28, 2006, p. A2.

[23] Rick Popely, "Crisis at Chrysler After News of $1.5 Billion Loss," *Chicago Tribune*, as reported in *Cleveland Plain Dealer*, October 26, 2006, p. C3.

The situation is indeed different. The consumer is substantially disadvantaged before the greater product knowledge of the seller, and can easily be deceived by false claims. In a business-to-business situation, one would think that information would be shared equally, unless some fraud was involved. And even this could be uncovered if a careful audit was made before the transaction was finalized.

But verbal promises of sharing the administration? Even if written, such promises may be difficult to enforce. What does a "merger of equals" really mean: Is it "a genuine business model, or is it a takeover cloaked in the high-toned language of amity?" as Robert Bruner of the University of Virginia's Darden Graduate Business School phrases it.[24]

Chrysler's top managers should have suspected that their position might be temporary. After all, there is precedent for top-management displacement in mega-"mergers of equals": for example, David Coulter of Bank of America, and John Reed of Citigroup, due to political infighting and disappointed expectations.

Mergers are no panacea.—For years in recurrent cycles of exuberance and caution, businesses have tried to solve the problem of growth with mergers and acquisitions. What you didn't have you could acquire, faster and better than developing it yourself, so the reasoning went. The term *synergy* was widely used, especially in the 1980s, to tout the great benefit and advantages of such mergers and acquisitions. (The following Information Box describes the concept of synergy.)

INFORMATION BOX

SYNERGY

Synergy results from creating a whole that is greater than the sum of its parts, and thus can accomplish more than the total of individual contributions. In an acquisition, synergy occurs if the two firms, when combined, are more efficient, productive, and profitable than they were as separate operations before the merger. Sometimes this is referred to as $2 + 2 = 5$.

How can such synergy occur? If duplication of efforts can be eliminated, if operations can be streamlined, if economies of scale are possible, if specialization can be enhanced, if greater financial, technical, and managerial resources can be tapped or new markets made possible—then a synergistic situation is likely to occur. Such an expanded operation should be a stronger force in the marketplace than the individual single units that existed before.

The concept of synergy is the rationale for mergers and acquisitions. But sometimes combining causes the reverse: negative synergy, where the consequences are worse than the sum of individual efforts. If friction arises between the entities, if organizational missions are incompatible, if the new organizational climate creates fearful, resentful,

---

[24] Robert F. Bruner, "A Merger of Equals?" *Wall Street Journal*, January 20, 2004, p. B2.

and frustrated employees, then synergy is unlikely, at least in the short and intermediate term. Furthermore, if because of sheer optimism or an uncontrolled acquisitive drive, more is paid for the acquisition than it is really worth, then we have a grand blunder. Could that have been the case with the Chrysler acquisition, in addition to the culture problem?

Do you think that a committee or group typically has more synergy than the same individuals working alone? Why or why not?

Wall Street dealmakers, investment bankers, and lawyers reap the bonanza from merger activities, but many mergers do not work out as well as expected, and some are even outright disasters.

We have seen the cultural conflict in the DaimlerChrysler merger. But this is just one of the things that can go wrong. Many acquisition seekers are so eager to get the target company, because it has strength in market share or access to strategic technologies, or because it will make their firm so much bigger in its industry (with all the glamour and prestige of large size for the executives involved), that they are prepared to pay well, and often too much. Funds for borrowing are usually readily available, heavy debt has income tax advantages, and profits may be distributed among fewer shares so that return on equity is enhanced. But all too often the best of the acquired human assets are soon sending out resumes to prospective new employers, and the assimilation and effective consolidation of the two enterprises may be years away. Furthermore, acquiring companies may be left with mountains of debt from over-ambitious mergers and acquisitions, thus greatly increasing the overhead to cover with revenues before profits can be realized.

Cultural differences should be considered in mergers and acquisitions. — Cultural differences in perceptions, customs, ways of doing things, and prejudices often are not given enough heed. The acquiring firm expects to bulldoze its culture on the acquired firm (despite how this may affect pride and willingness to cooperate). As we saw with the Daimler merger with Chrysler—in reality a merger of unequals—arrogance and resentments surfaced.

Should the acquiring company express its dominance quickly, or should it try to be as soothing as possible? Morale will probably not be savaged in a soothing takeover, but there can be serious problems with this approach also. Permitting an acquisition to continue operating with little control can be a disaster waiting to happen, especially if the acquisition is a foreign firm.

How much can you trust? —Both parties to a merger negotiation may express a commitment to equality. But their lip service may prove a facade. Even if executive positions are as evenly balanced as possible, one person may be a more dominant personality than the other, perhaps by dint of bigger stock ownership. Consequently, the merger of equals is in name only, with any equal standing of the acquired firm existing only at the convenience of the acquirer.

The danger of cannibalization.—Cannibalization occurs when a new product takes away sales from an existing product. This is likely to occur whenever a new product is introduced, but flooding the market with the old product just before a new-model introduction, as Daimler pressured Chrysler to do, is asking for problems. DaimlerChrysler found that it took both massive rebates of the old models and substantial price reductions of the new ones to move the inventory—all this destructive to profitability. The same scenario has confronted computer makers and other firms at the cutting edge of new technology. When do you let go the old model without jeopardizing lost sales in the interim?

We do not advocate stopping production of the older model when the new model is first announced. But it seems judicious to reduce production in the months after the announcement. Then the newer, technologically advanced model should command a higher price than the older version. DaimlerChrysler's problems in 2000 were aggravated by the fact that the new models were not so much technologically superior as provided with expensive options that some buyers found not worth the extra money.

Let us not denigrate the desirability of cannibalizing. As products are improved, they should be brought to the marketplace as soon as possible, and not held back because there may be some cannibalization. The temptation to hold back is there, especially when the new product may have a lower profit margin than the product it is supplanting, perhaps because of competition and higher costs. Invariably, the firm that restrains an innovation because of fear of cannibalizing a high-profit product winds up making the arena attractive for competitors to gain an advantage. *Fear of cannibalization should not impede innovation.*

CONSIDER

Can you think of other learning insights?

QUESTIONS

1. Do you think Schrempp was wise to replace the top Chrysler executives? Why or why not?
2. How could Chrysler boss Robert Eaton have been so naive as to permit himself to be ousted from power in a negotiation that he actively campaigned for and accepted? Do you see any way he might have protected his position in the merger?
3. How specifically can a firm protect itself from the extreme risks of cannibalization?
4. Do you think the culture problems could have been largely avoided in this merger? How?
5. Dieter Zetsche was sent from Stuttgart headquarters to fix all-American Chrysler after the disastrous year 2000. On his first day in Detroit he fired

the head of sales and marketing. Discuss the advisability of such a quick action, considering as many ramifications and justifications as possible.

6. Evaluate the desirability of rebates rather than regular markdowns or price cuts.

7. Do you personally think the use of Mercedes parts in Chrysler vehicles would diminish the prestige of the Mercedes brand? Would it help Chrysler that much?

8. Do you think good times can ever be lasting in the auto industry? Why or why not?

HANDS-ON EXERCISES

1. You are one of Chrysler's biggest suppliers of certain parts. You are shocked at the decree by the new management of Chrysler that you must cut your prices by 5 percent immediately, and another 10 percent within two years. What do you do now? Discuss and evaluate as many courses of action as you can. You can make some assumptions, but spell them out specifically.

2. Place yourself in the position of Robert Eaton, CEO of Chrysler before the merger, and now "co-chairman" with Jurgen Schrempp. You have just been told that your services are no longer needed, that the co-chairman position has been abolished. What do you do at this point? Try to be specific and support your recommendations.

3. You are Steve Yokich, president of the United Auto Workers. You initially endorsed Dieter Zetsche's plan to cut costs severely. Although it called for laying off 26,000 workers and closing six plants, you had been convinced that downsizing was necessary to save Chrysler. Now many of your union members are storming about such arbitrary cuts. They are castigating you for supporting the plan, and you may be ousted. Discuss your actions.

TEAM DEBATE EXERCISES

1. In this case we have the great controversy of German top executives replacing Americans. Debate the desirability of replacing versus keeping most of the American incumbents. I would suggest dividing up into two groups, with one arguing for bringing in fresh blood from German headquarters, and the other strongly contesting this. Be prepared to attack your opponents' arguments, and defend your own.

2. Debate the ethics of Daimler's flagrant deception that this was a merger of equals.

YOUR ASSESSMENT OF THE LATEST DEVELOPMENTS

Do you think Chrysler can again be a viable entity in the U.S. auto industry?

INVITATION TO RESEARCH

What is the situation with DaimlerChrysler today? Has Chrysler been sold or spun off? Have the Big Three U.S. automakers been able to counter the great inroads by Honda and Toyota? How does the future look for the U.S. firms?

PART FOUR

PLANNING

CHAPTER ELEVEN

Euro Disney: Bungling a Successful Format

With high expectations, Euro Disney opened just outside Paris in April 1992. Success seemed assured. After all, the Disneylands in Florida, California, and, more recently, Japan were all spectacular successes. But somehow all the rosy expectations became a delusion. The opening results cast even the future continuance of Euro Disney into doubt. How could what seemed so right have been so wrong? What mistakes were made?

PRELUDE

Optimism

Perhaps a few early omens should have raised some cautions. Between 1987 and 1991, three $150 million amusement parks had opened in France with great fanfare. All had fallen flat, and by 1991 two were in bankruptcy. Now Walt Disney Company was finalizing its plans to open Europe's first Disneyland early in 1992. This would turn out to be a $4.4 billion enterprise sprawling over 5,000 acres 20 miles east of Paris. Initially it would have six hotels and 5,200 rooms, more rooms than the entire city of Cannes, and lodgings were expected to triple in a few years as Disney opened a second theme park to keep visitors at the resort longer.

Disney also expected to develop a growing office complex, this to be only slightly smaller than France's biggest, La Defense, in Paris. Plans also called for shopping malls, apartments, golf courses, and vacation homes. Euro Disney would tightly control all this ancillary development, designing and building nearly everything itself, and eventually selling off the commercial properties at a huge profit.

Disney executives had no qualms about the huge enterprise, which would cover an area one-fifth the size of Paris itself. They were more worried that the park might not be big enough to handle the crowds:

"My biggest fear is that we will be too successful."

"I don't think it can miss. They are masters of marketing. When the place opens it will be perfect. And they know how to make people smile—even the French."[1]

Company executives initially predicted that 11 million Europeans would visit the extravaganza in the first year alone. After all, Europeans accounted for 2.7 million visits to the U.S. Disney parks and spent $1.6 billion on Disney merchandise. Surely a park in closer proximity would draw many thousands more. As Disney executives thought about it, the forecast of 11 million seemed too conservative. They reasoned that since Disney parks in the United States (population 250 million) attracted 41 million visitors a year, then if Euro Disney attracted visitors in the same proportion, attendance could reach 60 million with Western Europe's 370 million people. Table 11.1 shows the 1990 attendance at the two U.S. Disney parks and the newest Japanese Disneyland, as well as the attendance/population ratios.

Adding fuel to the optimism was the fact that Europeans typically have more vacation time than U.S. workers. For example, five-week vacations are commonplace for French and Germans, compared with two to three weeks for Americans.

The failure of the three earlier French parks was seen as irrelevant. Robert Fitzpatrick, Euro Disneyland's chairman, stated, "We are spending 22 billion French francs before we open the door, while the other places spent 700 million. This means we can pay infinitely more attention to details—to costumes, hotels, shops, trash

TABLE 11.1. Attendance and Attendance/Population Ratios, Disney Parks, 1990

	Visitors	Population	Ratio
		(millions)	
United States			
Disneyland (Southern California)	12.9	250	5.2%
Disney World/Epcot Center (Florida)	28.5	250	11.4%
Total United States	41.4		16.6%
Japan			
Tokyo Disneyland	16.0	124	13.5%
Euro Disney	?	310[a]	?

[a]Within a two-hour flight.

Source: Euro Disney, *Amusement Business Magazine.*

Commentary: Even if the attendance/population ratio for Euro Disney is only 10 percent, which is far below that of some other theme parks, still 31 million visitors could be expected. Euro Disney "conservatively" predicted 11 million the first year.

[1] Steven Greenhouse, "Playing Disney in the Parisian Fields," *New York Times,* February 17, 1991, Section 3, pp. 1, 6.

baskets—to create a fantastic place. There's just too great a response to Disney for us to fail."[2]

Nonetheless, a few scattered signs indicated that not everyone was happy with the coming of Disney. Leftist demonstrators at Euro Disney's stock offering greeted company executives with eggs, ketchup, and "Mickey Go Home" signs. Some French intellectuals decried the pollution of the country's cultural ambiance with the coming of Mickey Mouse and company: They called the park an American cultural abomination. The mainstream press also seemed contrary, describing every Disney setback "with glee." And French officials negotiating with Disney sought less American and more European culture at France's Magic Kingdom. Still, such protests and bad press seemed contrived and unrepresentative, and certainly not predictive. Company officials dismissed the early criticism as "the ravings of an insignificant elite."[3]

The Location Decision

In the search for a site for Euro Disney, Disney executives examined 200 locations in Europe. The other finalist was Barcelona, Spain. Its major attraction was warmer weather. But the transportation system was not as good as around Paris, and it also lacked level tracts of land of sufficient size. The clincher for the decision for Paris was its more central location. Table 11.2 shows the number of people within two to six hours of the Paris site.

The beet fields of the Marne-la-Vallée area were the choice. Being near Paris seemed a major advantage, since Paris was Europe's biggest tourist draw. And France was eager to win the project to help lower its jobless rate and also to enhance its role as the center of tourist activity in Europe. The French government expected the project to create at least 30,000 jobs and to contribute $1 billion a year from foreign visitors.

TABLE 11.2. Number of People within 2–6 Hours of the Paris Site

Within a 2-hour drive	17 million people
Within a 4-hour drive	41 million people
Within a 6-hour drive	109 million people
Within a 2-hour flight	310 million people

Source: Euro Disney, *Amusement Business Magazine.*

Commentary: The much more densely populated and geographically compact European continent makes access to Euro Disney far more convenient than in the United States.

---

[2] *Ibid.*, p. 6.
[3] Peter Gumbel and Richard Turner, "Fans Like Euro Disney But Its Parent's Goofs Weigh the Park Down," *Wall Street Journal*, March 10, 1994, p. A12.

To encourage the project, the French government allowed Disney to buy up huge tracts of land at 1971 prices. It provided $750 million in loans at below-market rates, and also spent hundreds of millions of dollars on subway and other capital improvements for the park. For example, Paris's express subway was extended out to the park; a 35-minute ride from downtown cost about $2.50. A new railroad station for the high-speed Train à Grande Vitesse was built only 150 yards from the entrance gate. This enabled visitors from Brussels to arrive in only 90 minutes. And when the English Channel tunnel opened in 1994, even London was only 3 hours and 10 minutes away. Actually, Euro Disney was the second-largest construction project in Europe, second only to construction of the Channel tunnel.

Financing

Euro Disney cost $4.4 billion. Table 11.3 shows the sources of financing in percentages. The Disney Company had a 49 percent stake in the project, which was the most that the French government would allow. For this stake, it invested $160 million, while other investors contributed $1.2 billion in equity. The rest was financed by loans from the government, banks, and special partnerships formed to buy properties and lease them back.

The payoff for Disney began after the park opened. The company received 10 percent of Euro Disney's admission fees and 5 percent of the food and merchandise revenues. This was the same arrangement Disney had with the Japanese park. But in the Tokyo Disneyland, the company took no ownership interest, opting instead only for the licensing fees and a percentage of the revenues. The reason for the conservative position with Tokyo Disneyland was that Disney money was heavily committed to building Epcot Center in Florida. Furthermore, Disney had some concerns about the Tokyo enterprise. This was the first non-American Disneyland and also the first cold-weather one. It seemed prudent to minimize the risks. But this turned out to be a significant blunder of conservatism, for Tokyo became a huge success, as the following Information Box discusses in more detail.

TABLE 11.3. **Sources of Financing for Euro Disney (percent)**

Total to Finance: $4.4 billion	100%
Shareholders' equity, including $160 million from Walt Disney Company	32
Loan from French government	22
Loan from group of 45 banks	21
Bank loans to Disney hotels	16
Real estate partnerships	9

Source: Euro Disney.

Commentary: The full flavor of the leverage is shown here, with equity comprising only 32 percent of the total expenditure.

INFORMATION BOX

THE TOKYO DISNEYLAND SUCCESS

Tokyo Disneyland opened in 1983 on 201 acres in the eastern suburb of Urazasu. It was arranged that an ownership group, Oriental Land, would build, own, and operate the theme park, with advice from Disney. The owners borrowed most of the $650 million needed to bring the project to fruition. Disney invested no money, but received 10 percent of the revenues from admission and rides and 5 percent of sales of food, drink, and souvenirs.

While the start was slow, Japanese soon began flocking to the park in great numbers. By 1990, some 16 million a year passed through the turnstiles, about one-fourth more than visited Disneyland in California. In fiscal year 1990, revenues reached $988 million with profits of $150 million. Indicative of the Japanese preoccupation with things American, the park served almost no Japanese food, and the live entertainers were mostly American. Japanese management even apologized for the presence of a single Japanese restaurant inside the park: "A lot of elderly Japanese came here from outlying parts of Japan, and they were not very familiar with hot dogs and hamburgers."[4]

Disney executives were soon to recognize the great mistake they had made in not taking substantial ownership in Tokyo Disneyland. They did not want to make the same mistake with Euro Disney.

Would you expect the acceptance of the genuine American experience in Tokyo to be indicative of the reaction of the French and Europeans? Why or why not?

Special Modifications

With the experiences of the previous theme parks, and particularly that of the first cold-weather park in Tokyo, Disney construction executives were able to bring state-of-the-art refinements to Euro Disney. Exacting demands were placed on French construction companies, and a higher level of performance and compliance resulted than many thought possible to achieve. The result was a major project on time if not completely on budget. In contrast, the Channel tunnel was plagued by delays and severe cost overruns.

One of the things learned from the cold-weather project in Japan was that more needed to be done to protect visitors from wind, rain, and cold. Consequently, Euro Disney's ticket booths were protected from the elements, as were the lines waiting for attractions, and even the moving sidewalk from the 12,000-car parking area.

Certain French accents—and British, German, and Italian accents as well—were added to the American flavor. The park had two official languages, English and French, but multilingual guides were available for Dutch, Spanish, German, and

[4] James Sterngold, "Cinderella Hits Her Stride in Tokyo," *New York Times*, February 17, 1991, p. 6)

Italian visitors. Discoveryland, based on the science fiction of France's Jules Verne, was a new attraction. A theater with a full 360-degree screen acquainted visitors with the sweep of European history. And, not the least modification for cultural diversity, Snow White spoke German, and the Belle Notte Pizzeria and Pasticceria were right next to Pinocchio.

Disney foresaw that it might encounter some cultural problems. This was one of the reasons for choosing Robert Fitzpatrick as Euro Disney's president. While American, he spoke French and had a French wife. However, he was not able to establish the rapport needed, and was replaced in 1993 by a French native. Still, some of his admonitions that France should not be approached as if it were Florida fell on deaf ears.

RESULTS

As the April 1992 opening approached, the company launched a massive communications blitz aimed at publicizing the fact that the fabled Disney experience was now accessible to all Europeans. Some 2,500 people from various print and broadcast media were lavishly entertained while being introduced to the new facilities. Most media people were positively impressed with the inauguration and with the enthusiastic spirit of the staffers. These public relations efforts, however, were criticized by some for being heavy-handed and for not providing access to Disney executives.

As 1992 wound down after the opening, it became clear that revenue projections were, unbelievably, not being met. But the opening turned out to be in the middle of a severe recession in Europe. European visitors, perhaps as a consequence, were far more frugal than their American counterparts. Many packed their own lunches and shunned the Disney hotels. For example, a visitor named Corine from southern France typified the "no spend" attitude of many: "It's a bottomless pit," she said as she, her husband, and their three children toured Euro Disney on a three-day visit. "Every time we turn around, one of the kids wants to buy something."[5] Perhaps investor expectations, despite the logic and rationale, were simply unrealistic.

Indeed, Disney had initially priced the park and the hotels to meet revenue targets, and assumed that demand was there at any price. Park admission was $42.25 for adults—higher than at the American parks. A room at the flagship Disneyland Hotel at the park's entrance cost about $340 a night, the equivalent of a top hotel in Paris. It was soon averaging only a 50 percent occupancy. Guests were not staying as long or spending as much on the fairly high-priced food and merchandise. We can label the initial pricing strategy at Euro Disney as *skimming pricing*. The following Information Box discusses skimming and its opposite, penetration pricing.

[5] "Ailing Euro May Face Closure," *Cleveland Plain Dealer*, January 1, 1994, p. E1.

INFORMATION BOX

SKIMMING AND PENETRATION PRICING

A firm with a new product or service may be in a temporary monopolistic situation. If there is little or no present and potential competition, more discretion in pricing is possible. In such a situation (and, of course, Euro Disney was in this situation), one of two basic and opposite approaches may be taken in the pricing strategy: (1) skimming or (2) penetration.

Skimming is a relatively high-price strategy. It is the most tempting where the product or service is highly differentiated, since it yields high per-unit profits. It is compatible with a quality image. But it has limitations. It assumes a rather inelastic demand curve, in which sales will not be appreciably affected by price. And if the product or service is easily imitated (which was hardly the case with Euro Disney), then competitors are encouraged because of the high profit margins.

The penetration strategy of low prices assumes an elastic demand curve, with sales increasing substantially if prices can be lowered. It is compatible with economies of scale, and discourages competitive entry. The classic example of penetration pricing was the Model T Ford. Henry Ford lowered his prices to make the car within the means of the general public, expanded production into the millions, and in so doing realized new horizons of economies of scale.

Euro Disney correctly saw itself in a monopoly position; it correctly judged that it had a relatively inelastic demand curve with customers flocking to the park regardless of rather high prices. What it did not reckon with was the shrewdness of European visitors: Because of the high prices they shortened their stays, avoided the hotels, brought their own food and drink, and only sparingly bought the Disney merchandise.

What advantages would a lower-price penetration strategy have offered Euro Disney? Do you see any drawbacks?

Disney executives soon realized they had made a major miscalculation. While visitors to Florida's Disney World often stayed more than four days, Euro Disney—with one theme park compared to Florida's three—was proving to be a two-day experience at best. Many visitors arrived early in the morning, rushed to the park, staying late at night, then checked out of the hotel the next morning before heading back to the park for one final exploration.

The problems of Euro Disney were not public acceptance (despite the earlier critics). Europeans loved the place. Since the opening it had been attracting just under 1 million visitors a month, thus easily achieving the original projections. Such patronage made it Europe's biggest-paid tourist attraction. But large numbers of frugal patrons did not come close to enabling Disney to meet revenue and profit projections and cover a bloated overhead.

Other operational errors and miscalculations, most of them cultural, hurt the enterprise. The policy of serving no alcohol in the park caused consternation in a country where wine is customary for lunch and dinner. (This policy was soon reversed.) Disney thought Monday would be a light day and Friday a heavy one, and allocated staff accordingly, but the reverse was true. It found great peaks and valleys in attendance: The number of visitors per day in the high season could be ten times the number in slack times. The need to lay off employees during quiet periods came up against France's inflexible labor schedules.

One unpleasant surprise concerned breakfast. "We were told that Europeans don't take breakfast, so we downsized the restaurants," recalled one executive. "And guess what? Everybody showed up for breakfast. We were trying to serve 2,500 breakfasts at 350-seat restaurants. The lines were horrendous."[6]

Disney failed to anticipate another demand, this time from tour bus drivers. Restrooms were built for 50 drivers, but on peak days 2,000 drivers were seeking the facilities. "From impatient drivers to grumbling bankers, Disney stepped on toe after European toe."[7]

For the fiscal year ending September 30, 1993, the amusement park had lost $960 million, and the future of the park was in doubt. (As of December 31, 1993, the cumulative loss was 6.04 billion francs, or $1.03 billion.) The Walt Disney corporation made $175 million available to tide Euro Disney over until the next spring. Adding to the problems of the struggling park were heavy interest costs. As depicted in Table 11.3, against a total cost of $4.4 billion, only 32 percent of the project was financed by equity investment. Some $2.9 billion was borrowed primarily from 60 creditor banks, at interest rates running as high as 11 percent. Thus, the enterprise began heavily leveraged, and the hefty interest charges greatly increased the overhead to be covered from operations. Serious negotiations began with the banks to restructure and refinance.

ATTEMPTS TO RECOVER

The $960 million lost in the first fiscal year represented a shortfall of more than $2.5 million a day. The situation was not quite as dire as these statistics would seem to indicate. Actually, the park was generating an operating profit. But nonoperating costs were bringing it deeply into the red.

While operations were far from satisfactory, they were becoming better. It had taken 20 months to smooth out the wrinkles and adjust to the miscalculations about hotel demand and the willingness of Europeans to pay substantial prices for lodging, meals, and merchandise. Operational efficiencies were slowly improving.

By the beginning of 1994, Euro Disney had been made more affordable. Prices of some hotel rooms were cut—for example, at the low end, from $76 per night to $51. Expensive jewelry was replaced by $10 T-shirts and $5 crayon sets. Luxury sit-down restaurants were converted to self-service. Off-season admission prices were

[6] Gumbel and Turner, p. A12.
[7] *Ibid.*

reduced from $38 to $30. And operating costs were reduced 7 percent by streamlining operations and eliminating over 900 jobs.

Efficiency and *economy* became the new watchwords. Merchandise in stores was pared from 30,000 items to 17,000, with more of the remaining goods being pure U. S. Disney products. (The company had thought that European tastes might prefer more subtle items than the garish Mickey and Minnie souvenirs, but this was found not so.) The number of different food items offered by park services was reduced more than 50 percent. New training programs were designed to remotivate the 9,000 full-time permanent employees, to make them more responsive to customers and more flexible in their job assignments. Employees in contact with the public were given crash courses in German and Spanish.

Still, as we have seen, the problem had not been attendance, although the recession and the high prices had reduced it. Some 18 million people passed through the turnstiles in the first 20 months of operation. But they were not spending money as people did in the U.S. parks. Furthermore, Disney's high prices had alienated some European tour operators, and it diligently sought to win them back.

Management had hoped to reduce the heavy interest overhead by selling the hotels to private investors. But the hotels only had an occupancy rate of 55 percent, making them unattractive to investors. While the recession was a factor in the low occupancy rates, most of the problem lay in the calculation of lodging demands. With the park just 35 minutes from the center of Paris, many visitors stayed in town. About the same time as the opening, the real estate market in France collapsed, making the hotels unsalable in the short term. This added to the overhead burden and confounded business-plan forecasts.

While some analysts were relegating Euro Disney to the cemetery, few remembered that Orlando's Disney World showed early symptoms of being a disappointment. Costs were heavier than expected, and attendance was below expectations. But Orlando's Disney World turned out to be one of the most profitable resorts in North America.

A FAVORABLE PROGNOSIS

Euro Disney had many things going for it, despite the disastrous early results. In May 1994, a station on the high-speed rail running from southern to northern France opened within walking distance of Euro Disney. This helped fill many of the hotel rooms too ambitiously built. The summer of 1994, the fiftieth anniversary of the Normandy invasion, brought many people to France. Another favorable sign for Euro Disney was the English Channel tunnel's opening in 1994, which potentially could bring a flood of British tourists. Furthermore, the recession in Europe was bound to end, and with it should come renewed interest in travel. As real estate prices became more favorable, hotels could be sold and real estate development around the park spurred.

Even as Disney chairman Michael Eisner threatened to close the park unless lenders restructured the debt, Disney increased its French presence, opening a Disney store on the Champs Élysées. The likelihood of a Disney pullout seemed remote, despite Eisner's posturing, since royalty fees could be a sizable source of revenues even if the park only broke even after servicing its debt. With only a 3.5 percent increase in revenues in 1995 and a 5 percent increase in 1996, these could yield $46 million in royalties for the parent company. "You can't ask, 'What does Euro Disney mean in 1995?' You have to ask, 'What does it mean in 1998?' "[8]

SUMMARY OF MAJOR MISTAKES

Euro Disney, as we have seen, fell far short of expectations in the first 20 months of its operation, so much so that its continued existence was questioned. What went wrong?

External Factors

A serious economic recession that affected all of Europe was undoubtedly a major impediment to meeting expectations. As noted before, it adversely affected attendance—although still not all that much—but drastically affected spending patterns, with frugality being the order of the day for many visitors. The recession also affected real estate demand and prices, thus saddling Disney with hotels it had hoped to sell at profitable prices to eager investors, thereby taking the strain off its hefty interest payments.

The company assumed that European visitors would not be greatly different from the visitors, foreign and domestic, to U.S. Disney parks. Yet, at least in the first few years of operation, visitors were much more price conscious. This suggested that those who lived within a two- to four-hour drive of Euro Disney were considerably different from the ones who traveled overseas, at least in spending ability and willingness.

Internal Factors

Despite the decades of experience with the U.S. Disney parks and the successful experience with the newer Japan park, Disney still made serious blunders in its operational planning, such as the demand for breakfasts, the insistence on wine at meals, the severe peaks and valleys in scheduling, and even such mundane things as sufficient restrooms for tour bus drivers. It had problems in motivating and training its French employees in efficiency and customer orientation. Did all these mistakes reflect an intractable French mindset or a deficiency of Disney management? Perhaps both. But shouldn't Disney's management have researched all the cultural differences more thoroughly? Further, the park needed major streamlining of inventories and operations after the opening. The mistakes suggested an arrogant mindset by Disney management: "We were arrogant," concedes one executive. "It was like, 'We're building the Taj Mahal and people will come—on our terms.' "[9]

The miscalculations in hotel rooms and in pricing of many products, including food services, showed an insensitivity to the harsh economic conditions. But the greatest mistake was taking on too much debt for the park. The highly leveraged

---

[8] Lisa Gubernick, "Mickey N'est Pas Fini," *Forbes*, February 14, 1994, p. 43.
[9] Gumbel and Turner, p. A12

situation burdened Euro Disney with such hefty interest payments and overhead that the breakeven point was impossibly high, and even threatened the viability of the enterprise. See the following Information Box for a discussion of the important inputs and implications affecting breakeven, and how these should play a role in strategic planning.

INFORMATION BOX

THE BREAKEVEN POINT

A breakeven analysis is a vital tool in making go/no go decisions about new ventures and alternative business strategies. This can be shown graphically as follows: Below the breakeven point, the venture suffers losses; above it, the venture becomes profitable.

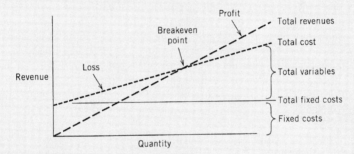

Figure 11.1.

Let us make a hypothetical comparison of Euro Disney with its $1.6 billion in high interest loans (some of these as high as 11 percent) from the banks, and what the situation might be with more equity and less borrowed funds:

For this example, let us assume that other fixed costs are $240 million, that the average interest rate on the debt is 10 percent, and that average profit margin (contribution to overhead) from each visitor is $32. Now let us consider two scenarios: (a) the $1.6 billion of debt, and (b) only $0.5 billion of debt.

The number of visitors needed to breakeven are determined as follows:

$$\text{Breakeven} = \frac{\text{Total fixed costs}}{\text{Contribution to overhead}}$$

Scenario (a): Interest = 10%($1,600,000,000) = $160,000,000

Fixed costs = Interest + $240,000,000

= 160,000,000 + 240,000,000

= $400,000,000

$$\text{Breakeven} = \frac{\$400,000,000}{\$32} = 12,500,000 \text{ visitors needed to breakeven}$$

Scenario (b): Interest = 10%(500,000,000) = $50,000,000

Fixed costs = 50,000,000 + 240,000,000

$$= \$290,000,000$$

$$\text{Breakeven} = \frac{\$290,000,000}{\$32} = 9,062,500 \text{ visitors needed to breakeven}$$

Because Euro Disney expected 11 million visitors the first year, it obviously was not going to break even while servicing $1.6 billion in debt with $160 million in interest charges per year. The average visitor would have to be induced to spend more, thereby increasing the average profit or contribution to overhead.

In making go/no go decisions, many costs can be estimated quite closely. What cannot be determined as surely are the sales figures. Certain things can be done to affect the breakeven point. Obviously it can be lowered if the overhead is reduced, as we saw in Scenario (b). Higher prices also result in a lower breakeven because of greater per-customer profits (but would probably affect total sales quite adversely). Promotion expenses can be either increased or decreased and affect the breakeven point; but they probably also have an impact on sales. Some costs of operation can be reduced, thus lowering the breakeven. But the hefty interest charges act as a lodestone over an enterprise, greatly increasing the overhead and requiring what may be an unattainable breakeven point.

Does a new venture have to break even or make a profit the first year to be worth going into? Why or why not?

Were such mistakes and miscalculations beyond what we would expect of reasonable executives? Probably not, with the probable exception of the crushing burden of debt. Any new venture is susceptible to surprises and the need to streamline and weed out its inefficiencies. While we would have expected this to have been done faster and more effectively at a well-tried Disney operation, European, and particularly French and Parisian, consumers and employees showed different behavioral and attitudinal patterns than expected.

The worst sin that Disney management and investors could make would be to give up on Euro Disney and not to look ahead a few years. A hint of the future promise was Christmas week of 1993. Despite the first year's $920 million in red ink, some 35,000 packed the park most days. A week later on a cold January day, some of the rides still had 40-minute waits.

POSTSCRIPT

On March 15, 1994 an agreement was struck, aimed at making Euro Disney profitable by September 30, 1995. The European banks would fund another $500 million and make such concessions as forgiving 18 months interest and deferring all principal payments for three years. In return, Walt Disney Company agreed to spend about $750 million to bail out its Euro Disney affiliate. Thus, the debt would be halved, with interest payments greatly reduced. Disney also agreed to eliminate for five years the lucrative management fees and royalties it received on the sale of tickets and merchandise.[10]

The problems of Euro Disney were still not resolved by mid-1994. The theme park and resort near Paris remained troubled. However, a new source for financing had emerged. A member of the Saudi Arabian royal family agreed to invest up to $500 million for a 24 percent stake in Euro Disney. Prince Alwaleed had shown considerable sophistication in investing in troubled enterprises in the past. Now his commitment to Euro Disney showed a belief in the ultimate success of the resort.[11]

Finally, in the third quarter of 1995, Euro Disney posted its first profit, some $35 million for the period. This compared with a year earlier loss of $113 million. By now, Euro Disney was only 39 percent owned by Disney. It attributed the turnaround partly to a new marketing strategy in which prices were slashed both at the gate and within the theme park in an effort to boost attendance, and also to shed the nagging image of being overpriced. A further attraction was the new "Space Mountain" ride that mimicked a trip to the moon.

However, some analysts questioned the staying power of the movement into the black. In particular, they saw most of the gain coming from financial restructuring in which the debt-ridden Euro Disney struck a deal with its creditors to temporarily suspend debt and royalty payments. A second theme park and further property development were seen as essential in the longer term, as the payments would eventually resume.

To the delight of the French government, plans were announced in 1999 to build a movie theme park, Disney Studios, next to the Magic Kingdom, to open in 2002. It was estimated that this expansion would attract an additional 4.2 million visitors annually, drawing people from farther afield in Europe. In 1998, Disneyland Paris had 12.5 million visitors, making it France's number-one tourist attraction, beating out Notre Dame.

Also late in 1999, Disney and Hong Kong agreed to build a major Disney theme park there, with Disney investing $314 million for 43 percent ownership while Hong Kong contributed nearly $3 billion. Hong Kong's leaders expected that the new park would generate 16,000 jobs when it opened in 2005, certainly a motivation for the unequal investment contribution.[12]

The Walt Disney Studios theme park opened in March 2002, as planned. It blended Disney entertainment with the history and culture of European film.

---

[10] Brian Coleman and Thomas R. King, "Euro Disney Rescue Package Wins Approval," *Wall Street Journal*, March 15, 1994, pp. A3, A5.
[11] Richard Turner and Brian Coleman, "Saudi to Buy as Much as 24% of Euro Disney," *Wall Street Journal*, June 2, 1994, p. A3.
[12] "Hong Kong Betting $3 Billion on Success of New Disneyland," *Cleveland Plain Dealer*, November 3, 1999, p. 2 C; Charles Fleming, "Euro Disney to Build Movie Theme Park Outside Paris," *Wall Street Journal*, September 30, 1999, pp. A15, A21.

Marketing efforts reflected a newfound cultural awareness, and efforts were focused largely on selling the new park through travel agents, whom Disney initially neglected in promoting Disneyland Paris. The timing could have been better, as theme parks were reeling from the recession and the threat of terrorist attacks. A second Disney park opened in Tokyo in 2001 and was a smash hit. But the new California Adventure park in Anaheim, California had been a bust.[13]

By the end of 2004, Euro Disney was again facing record losses. Partly this was because of the resumption of full royalty payments and management fees to Walt Disney Co. But deeper problems were besetting it. Attendance had remained flat at about 12.4 million. The new Disney Studios Park opened to expectations of 4 million visitors, but only 2.2 million came in 2004, and many complained that it did not have enough attractions. Three major new attractions were scheduled to open in 2006 to 2008, with two of these for the Studios Park. For the first three months of 2005, the popular Space Mountain was closing for upgrading. In this scenario, the company planned "regular admission-price increases." "The business model does not seem viable," observed one portfolio manager.[14]

UPDATE 2005

Something happened in January 2005. The French government realized that it really wanted Euro Disney to succeed. Despite the American-bashing that came after the invasion of Iraq and President Jacques Chirac's calling the spread of American culture an "ecological disaster," another French preoccupation surfaced: the top priority of reducing France's high unemployment. Euro Disney's site was the biggest employer in the Paris region, with 43,000 jobs, and it had created a booming urban sprawl on once-barren land.

Now Prime Minister Jean-Pierre Raffarin vowed not to let Euro Disney go bankrupt: "We are grateful to the American people and have lots of respect for their culture." A state-owned bank contributed around $500 million in investments and loan concessions. The hope was that new and expensive attractions and a better economic climate would bring a turnaround. Still, if the Tower of Terror ride and other new attractions failed to attract millions of new visitors, Disney and the French government might have to pour more money into this venture that had once seemed such a sure thing. Under consideration was the opening of Charles de Gaulle Airport to more low-cost airlines to make Euro Disney a cheaper destination.[15]

Disney also had a lot at stake in the success of Euro Disney. Failure would hurt its global brand image as it prepared to expand into China and elsewhere in the Far

---

[13] Bruce Owwall, "Euro Disney CEO Named to Head Parks World-Wide," *Wall Street Journal*, September 30, 2002, p. B8; Paulo Prada and Bruce Orwall, "A Certain 'Je Ne Sais Quoi' at Disney's New Park," *Wall Street Journal*, March 12, 2002, pp. B1 and B4.

[14] Jo Wrighton, "Euro Disney's Net Loss Balloons, Putting Financial Rescue at Risk," *Wall Street Journal*, November 10, 2004, p. B3.)

[15] Jo Wrighton and Bruce Orwall, "Despite Losses and Bailouts, France Stays Devoted to Disney," *Wall Street Journal*, January 26, 2005, pp. A1 and A6.

East. Perhaps the lessons learned in Paris of trying to keep visitors longer while saving on fixed costs would transfer.

o o o

Invitation for Your Analysis and Conclusions

How do you account for Disney's management erring so badly, both at the beginning and even for years afterwards. Any suggestions?

o o o

WHAT CAN BE LEARNED?

Beware the arrogant mindset, especially when dealing with new situations and new cultures.—French sensitivities were offended by Disney corporate executives who often turned out to be brash, insensitive, and overbearing. A contentious attitude by Disney personnel alienated people and aggravated planning and operational difficulties. "The answer to doubts or suggestions invariably was: Do as we say, because we know best."[16]

Such a mindset is a natural concomitant of success. It is said that success breeds arrogance, but this inclination must be fought against by those who would spurn the ideas and concerns of others. For a proud and touchy people, the French, this almost contemptuous attitude by the Americans fueled resentment and glee at Disney miscues. It did not foster cooperation, understanding, or the willingness to smooth the process. One might speculate that had not the potential economic benefits to France been so great, the Euro Disney project might never have been approved.

Great success may be ephemeral.—We often find that great successes are not lasting, that they have no staying power. Somehow the success pattern gets lost or forgotten or is not well rounded. Other times an operation grows beyond the capability of the originators. Hungry competitors are always in the wings, ready to take advantage of any lapse. As we saw with Euro Disney, having a closed mind to new ideas or needed revisions of an old success pattern—the arrogance of success—makes expansion into different environments more difficult and even risky.

While corporate Disney has continued to have good success with its other theme parks, competitors are moving in with their own theme parks in the United States and elsewhere. We may question whether this industry is approaching saturation, and we may wonder whether Disney has learned from its mistakes in Europe.

Highly leveraged situations are extremely vulnerable.—During most of the 1980s, many managers, including corporate raiders, pursued a strategy of debt

---

[16] Gumbel and Turner, p. A1.

financing (leveraging) in contrast to equity financing (stock ownership). Funds for such borrowing were usually readily available, heavy debt had income tax advantages, and profits could be distributed among fewer shares so that return on equity was enhanced. During this time a few voices decried the over-leveraged situations of many companies. They predicted that when the eventual economic downturn came, such firms would find themselves unable to meet the heavy interest burden. Most lenders paid little heed to these lonesome voices and encouraged greater borrowing.

The widely publicized problems of some of the raiders in the late 1980s, such as Robert Campeau, who acquired major department-store corporations only to find himself overextended and lose everything, suddenly changed some expansionist lending sentiments. The hard reality dawned that these arrangements were often fragile indeed, especially when they rested on optimistic projections for asset sales, for revenues, and for cost savings to cover the interest payments. An economic slowdown hastened the demise of some of these ill-advised speculations.

Disney was guilty of the same speculative excesses with Euro Disney, relying far too much on borrowed funds, and assuming that assets, such as hotels, could be easily sold off at higher prices to other investors. As we saw in the breakeven box, hefty interest charges from over-leveraged conditions can jeopardize the viability of the enterprise if revenue and profit projections fail to meet the rosy expectations.

Be judicious with the skimming price strategy.—Euro Disney faced the classical situation favorable for a skimming price strategy. It was in a monopoly position, with no equivalent competitors likely. It faced a somewhat inelastic demand curve, which indicated that people would come almost regardless of price. So why not price to maximize per-unit profits? Unfortunately for Disney, the wily Europeans circumvented the high prices by frugality. Of course, a severe recession exacerbated the situation.

The learning insight from this example is that a skimming price assumes that customers are willing and able to pay the higher prices and have no lower-priced competitive alternatives. It is a faulty strategy when many customers are unable, or else unwilling, to pay the high prices and can find a way to experience the product or service in a modest way.

CONSIDER

Can you think of other learning insights from this case?

QUESTIONS

1. How could the company have erred so badly in its estimates of the spending patterns of European customers?
2. Could a better reading of the impact of cultural differences on revenues have been achieved?

3. What suggestions do you have for fostering a climate of sensitivity and goodwill in corporate dealings with the French?

4. How do you account for the great success of Tokyo Disneyland and the problems of Euro Disney? What are the key contributory differences?

5. Do you believe that Euro Disney might have done better if located elsewhere in Europe rather than just outside Paris? Why or why not?

6. "Mickey Mouse and the Disney Park are an American cultural abomination." Evaluate this critical statement.

7. Consider how a strong marketing approach might be made to both European consumers and middlemen, such as travel agents, tour guides, even bus drivers.

8. Discuss the desirability of raising admission prices at the very time when attendance is static, profits are nonexistent, and new attractions are months and several years in the future.

HANDS-ON EXPERIENCE

1. As the staff assistant to the president of Euro Disney, you already believe before the grand opening that the plans to use a skimming pricing strategy and to emphasize luxury hotel accommodations is ill advised. What arguments would you marshal to try to persuade the company to offer lower prices and more moderate accommodations? Be as persuasive as you can.

2. It is six months after the opening. Revenues are not meeting target, and a number of problems have surfaced and are being worked on. The major problem remains, however, that the venture needs more visitors and/or higher expenditures per visitor. Develop a business model to improve the situation.

3. How would you rid an organization, such as Euro Disney, of an arrogant mindset? Assume that you are an operational VP and have substantial resources, but not necessarily the eager support of top management.

TEAM DEBATE EXERCISE

It is two years after the opening. Euro Disney is a monumental mistake, profit-wise. Two schools of thought are emerging for improving the situation. One is to pour more money into the project, build one or two more theme parks, and really make this another Disney World. The other camp believes more investment would be wasted at this time, that the need is to pare expenses to the bone and wait for an eventual upturn. Debate the two positions.

YOUR ASSESSMENT OF THE LATEST DEVELOPMENTS

Can you criticize the present business plan for Euro Disney? Do you think the lesson presumably learned should transfer well to the Far East?

INVITATION TO RESEARCH

What is the situation with Euro Disney today? Are expansion plans going ahead? Have other theme parks been opened, and if so, are they encountering any problems?

CHAPTER TWELVE

Boeing: Losing, Then Regaining, Dominance over Airbus

The commercial jet business had long been subject to booms and busts: major demand for new aircraft and then years of little demand. By the second half of the 1990s, demand burgeoned as never before. Boeing, the world's leading producer of commercial aircraft, seemed in the catbird seat amid the worldwide surge of orders. This was an unexpected windfall, spurred by markets greatly expanding in Asia and Latin America at the same time as domestic demand, helped by deregulation and prosperity, boomed. In the midst of these good times, Boeing in 1997 incurred its first loss in 50 years.

During this same period, Airbus (Airbus Industrie), a European aerospace consortium, an underdog, began climbing toward its long-stated goal of winning 50 percent of the over-100-seat airplane market. The battle was all-out, no-holds-barred, and Boeing was vulnerable.

BACKGROUND OF BOEING

Boeing has a fabled past. The company was a major factor in the World War II war effort, and in the late 1950s led the way in producing innovative, state-of-the-art commercial aircraft. It introduced the 707, the world's first commercially viable jetliner. In the late 1960s, it almost bankrupted itself to build a jetliner twice the size of any other then in service, while critics predicted it could never fly profitably. But the 747 dramatically lowered costs and airfares, and brought passenger comfort previously undreamed of in flying. In the mid-1990s, Boeing introduced the high-technology 777, the first commercial aircraft designed entirely with the use of computers.

In an effort to reduce the feast-or-famine cycle of the commercial aircraft business, Boeing acquired Rockwell International's defense business in 1996, and in 1997 purchased McDonnell Douglas for $16.3 billion.

In 1997, Boeing's commercial aircraft segment contributed 57 percent of total revenues. This segment ranged from 125-passenger 737s to giant 450 to 500-seat 747s. The potential seemed enormous: Over the next 20 years, air passenger traffic worldwide was projected to rise 4.9 percent a year and airlines were predicted to order 16,160 aircraft to expand their fleets and replace aging planes.[1] As the industry leader, Boeing had 60 percent of this market. At the end of 1997, its order backlog was $94 billion.

Defense and space operations comprised 41 percent of 1997 revenues. This included airborne warning and control systems (AWACS), helicopters, B-2 bomber subcontract work, and the F-22 fighter, among other products and systems.

PROBLEMS WITH THE COMMERCIAL AIRCRAFT BUSINESS SEGMENT

Production Problems

Boeing proved to be poorly positioned to meet the surge in aircraft orders. Part of this resulted from its drastic layoffs of experienced workers during the industry's last slump, in the early 1990s. Though Boeing hired 32,000 new workers over 18 months starting in 1995, the experience gap upped the risk of costly mistakes. Boeing had also cut back its suppliers in a strenuous effort to slash parts inventories and increase cost efficiency.

But Boeing had other problems. Its production systems were a mess. It had somehow evolved some 400 separate computer systems, and these were not linked. Its design system was labor intensive and paper dependent, and very expensive as it tried to cater to customer choices. A $1 billion program had been launched in 1996 to modernize and computerize the production process. But it was too late: The onslaught of orders had already started. (It is something of an anomaly that a firm that had the sophistication to design the 777 entirely by computers was so antiquated in its use of computers otherwise.)

Demands for increased production were further aggravated by unreasonable production goals and too many plane models. Problems first hit with the 747 Jumbo, and then with a new version of the top-selling 737, the so-called next-generation 737NG. Before long, every program was affected: also the 757, 767, and 777. While Boeing released over 320 planes to customers in 1997 for a 50 percent increase over 1996, this was far short of the planned completion rate. For example, by early 1998 a dozen 737NGs had been delivered to airlines, but this was less than one-third of the 40 supposed to have been delivered by then. Nonetheless, the company maintained through September 1997 that everything was going well, that there was only a month's delay in the delivery of some planes.

Soon it became apparent that the problems were much greater. In October, the 747 and 737 assembly lines were shut down for nearly a month to allow workers to

---

[1] *Boeing 1997 Annual Report.*

catch up and ease part shortages. The *Wall Street Journal* reported horror stories of parts being rushed in by taxicab, of executives spending weekends trying to chase down needed parts, of parts needed for new planes being shipped out to replace defective parts on an in-service plane. Overtime pay brought some assembly-line workers incomes over $100,000, while rookie workers muddled by on the line.[2]

Despite its huge order backlog, Boeing took a loss for 1997, the first in over 50 years. See Table 12.1 for the trend in revenues and net income from 1988 to 1998.

The loss mostly resulted from two massive write-downs. One, for $1.4 billion, arose from the McDonnell Douglas acquisition and in particular from its ailing commercial-aircraft operation at Long Beach, California. The bigger write-off, $1.6 billion, reflected production problems, particularly on the new 737NG. Severe price competition with Airbus resulted in not enough profits on existing business to bring the company into the black. Production delays continued, with more write-downs on the horizon.

As Boeing moved into 1998, analysts wondered how much longer it would take to clear up the production snafus. It would be longer than anyone had been led

TABLE 12.1. Boeing's Trend of Revenues and Income, 1988–1998

	(millions)	
	Revenue	Net Income
1988	16,962	614
1989	20,276	675
1990	27,595	1,385
1991	29,314	1,567
1992	30,184	1,554
1993	25,438	1,244
1994	21,924	856
1995	19,515	393
1996	22,681	1,095
1997	45,800	−177
1998	56,100	1,100

Source: Boeing Annual Reports.

Commentary: Note the severity of the decline in revenues and profits during the industry downturn in 1993, 1994, and 1995. It is little wonder that Boeing was so ill-prepared for the deluge of orders starting in 1995. Then, in an unbelievable anomaly, the tremendous increase in revenues in 1997 to the highest ever—partly reflecting the acquisitions—was accompanied by a huge loss.

[2] Frederic M. Biddle and John Helyar, "Behind Boeing's Woes: Clunky Assembly Line, Price War with Airbus," *Wall Street Journal*, April 24, 1998, p. A16.

to believe. Unexpectedly, a new problem arose for Boeing. Disastrous economic conditions in Asia now brought major order cancellations.

Customer Relations

Not surprisingly, the delayed shipments resulting from Boeing's production problems had a serious impact on customer relations. For example, Southwest Airlines had to postpone adding service to another city because the ordered planes were not ready. Boeing paid Southwest millions of dollars of compensation for the delayed deliveries. Continental also had to wait for five overdue 737s.

Other customers switched to Boeing's only major competitor, Airbus Industrie, of Toulouse, France.

AIRBUS INDUSTRIE

Airbus had to have been salivating at Boeing's troubles. It had been a distant second in market share to the 60 percent of Boeing. Now this was changing, and Airbus could see the possibility of achieving a sustainable 50 percent market share. See the Information Box: Importance of Market Share for a discussion of market share.

INFORMATION BOX

IMPORTANCE OF MARKET SHARE

The desire to surpass a competitor is a common human tendency, whether in sports or business. A measurement of performance relative to competitors encourages this desire and can be highly motivating for management and employees alike. Furthermore, market-share performance is a key indicator in ascertaining how well a firm is doing and in spotting emerging problems, as well as sometimes allaying blame. As an example of the latter, if a firm's sales declined over the preceding year, but its market share steadily improved, this may mean that the firm is doing a good job, but that certain factors have adversely affected the whole industry.

Market share is usually measured by (1) share of overall sales, and/or (2) share relative to certain competitors, usually the top one or several in the industry. Trend data is particularly important: Are things getting better or worse? If worse, why, and what needs to be done to improve the situation?

Since Boeing and Airbus were the only real competitors in this major industry, relative market shares became critical. The perceived importance of gaining, or not losing, market share led to severe price competition that cut into the profits of both firms, as will be discussed later.

How would you respond to the objection that market share data is not all that useful, since "it doesn't tell us what the problem really is"?
Can emphasizing market share be counterproductive? If so, why?

Background of Airbus

Airbus was founded in 1970 as a consortium that came to include four countries: British Aerospace, DaimlerChrysler Aerospace (Germany), France's Aérospatiale, and Spain's Casa. Each of the partners supplied components, such as wings and fuselages; the partners also underwrote the consortium's capital expenses (sometimes with government loans), and were prepared to cover its operating losses.

The organizational structure seemed seriously flawed. It was politicized, with the partners voting on major issues in proportion to their country's ownership stakes. From this fragmented leadership, public squabbles frequently arose, some very serious. For example, plans to produce a new 107-seat A318 were held up by the French, who thought they were not getting their fair share of the production. Finances were also tangled, with components supplied by the various countries charged to Airbus at suspiciously high prices.

The result was that in 1998, Boeing made $1.1 billion on sales of $56.1 billion, while Airbus was losing $204 million on sales of $13.3 billion. Boeing accused Airbus of selling below cost in order to steal business, and Airbus blamed Boeing for the low bids.

The competition between the two companies became increasingly bitter after 1996. In that year, Boeing and several Airbus partners discussed the joint development of a superjumbo. The talks ended when they could not agree on a single design. But Airbus suspected that Boeing was not sincerely interested in collaboration, that its main purpose in the talks was to stall Airbus's plans.

Airbus went ahead with its plans, while Boeing pooh-poohed the idea of such a huge plane.

Airbus Chairman Noel Forgeard

A slight Frenchman with a cheery disposition, Noel Forgeard, 52, joined the consortium in 1998 from Matra, a French aerospace manufacturer. He came with several major goals: to centralize decision-making, to impose sensible bookkeeping, and to make Airbus consistently profitable. The task was not easy. For example, plans to build the world's largest airplane, code-named A3XX, were threatened by disagreements over where it would be assembled. Both France and Germany thought it should be produced in their country. Forgeard stated, "The need for a single corporate entity is well recognized. Everybody here is focused on it."[3] Still, while the need for reorganizing into something like a modern corporation was evident to most executives, the major partners were divided over how to proceed.

The World's Largest Plane

The A3XX was designed as a double-decker plane that could carry 555 passengers comfortably—137 more than a Boeing 747-400 (it could even carry 750 people on routes around Asia where people did not care as much about seating comfort). It was expected to fly by 2004, with prices starting somewhat over $200 million. Development

[3] Alex Taylor II, "Blue Skies for Airbus," *Fortune*, August 2, 1999, p. 103.

costs could reach $15 billion, so essentially the A3XX was a bet-the-company project with an uncertain outlook, much as Boeing's 747 had been 30 years before. To pay for these costs, Airbus expected to get 40 percent from suppliers such as Sweden's Saab, 30 percent from government loans arranged by its partners, and the rest from its own resources.

The huge financing needed for this venture could hardly be obtained without a corporate reorganization, one that would provide a mechanism for handling internal disputes among the various partner countries, not the least of which was where the plane would be assembled. So Forgeard had necessity on his side for reorganizing. But the A3XX faced other issues and concerns.

Should a Plane Like the A3XX Even be Built?

Boeing's publicly expressed opinion stated that the plane would never be profitable. "Let them launch it," said one Boeing official, with a hint of malice.[4] Boeing took the position that consumers want frequent, nonstop flights, such as Southwest Airlines had brought to prominence with its saturation of city-pair routes with frequent flights. An ultra-large aircraft would mean far less frequency.[5]

Airbus, meantime, surveyed big airlines and discerned enough interest in a superjumbo to proceed. It also consulted with more than 60 airports around the world to determine whether such a big plane would be able to take off and land easily. Weight is critical to these maneuvers, and Airbus pledged that the A3XX would be able to use the same runways as the 747 because of a new lightweight material. Instead of regular aluminum, the planes would use a product called Glare, made of aluminum alloy and glass-fiber tape.

Airbus promised ambitious plans for passenger comfort in this behemoth. It built a full-size 237-foot mockup of the interior to show prospective customers, and enlisted 1,200 frequent flyers to critique the cabin mockup. To reduce claustrophobia, the designers added a wide staircase between the upper and lower decks. Early plans also included exercise rooms and sleeping quarters fitted with bunk beds.

Airbus claimed that the 555-seat A3XX would be 15 percent cheaper to operate per seat-mile than Boeing's 747. Boeing maintained that this was wildly optimistic. Frederick Brace, United Airlines vice president of finance, also expressed doubts: "The risk for Airbus is whether there's a market for A3XX. The risk for an airline is: Can we fill it up? We have to be prudent in how we purchase it."[6]

Competitive Position of Airbus

Airbus was well positioned to supply planes to airlines whose needs Boeing couldn't meet near term. Some thought it was even producing better planes than Boeing.

United Airlines chose Airbus's A320 twinjets over Boeing's 737s, saying passengers preferred the Airbus product. Several South American carriers also chose

---

[4] Steve Wilhelm, "Plane Speaking," *Puget Sound Business Journal*, June 18, 1999, p. 112.
[5] *Ibid.*
[6] "Blue Skies for Airbus," p. 108.

A320s over the 737, placing a $4 billion order with Airbus. For 1997, Airbus hacked out a 45 percent market share, the first time Boeing's 60 percent market share had eroded.

The situation worsened drastically for Boeing in 1998. US Air, which had previously ordered 400 Airbus jets, announced in July that it would buy 30 more. But the biggest defection came in August, when British Airlines announced plans to buy 59 Airbus jetliners and take options for 200 more. This broke its long record as a Boeing-loyal customer. The order, worth as much as $11 billion, would be the biggest victory of Airbus over Boeing.[7]

Beyond Boeing's production delays, Airbus had other competitive strengths. While it had less total production capability than Boeing (235 planes vs. Boeing's 550), the Airbus production line was efficient and the company had done better in trimming its costs. This meant it could go head-to-head with Boeing on price. And price seemed to be the name of the game in the late 1990s. This contrasted with earlier days when Boeing rose to world leadership with performance, delivery, and technology more important than cost. "They [the customers] do not care what it costs us to make the planes," Boeing chairman and chief executive Philip Condit admitted. With airline design stabilized, he saw the airlines buying planes today as chiefly interested in how much carrying capacity they could buy for a buck.[8]

Increasingly passengers were grousing about the cramped interiors of planes designed for coast-to-coast trips, and the dearth of lavatories to accommodate 126 to 189 passengers on long flights. Passenger rage appeared to be cropping up more and more. *Forbes* magazine editorialized that "the first carrier that makes an all-out effort to treat passengers as people rather than oversized sardines will be an immense money-maker."[9]

Boeing's new 737-700s and 737-800s were notorious for giving customer comfort low priority. Airbus differentiated itself from Boeing by designing its A320 150-seat workhorse with a fuselage 7 1/2 inches wider than Boeing's, thus adding an inch to every seat in a typical six-across configuration.

In the first four months of 1999, Airbus won an amazing 78 percent of orders. US Airways chairman Stephen Wolf, whose airline had ordered 430 Airbus planes since 1996, said, "Airbus aircraft offer greater flexibility for wider seats, more overhead bin space, and more aisle space—all important in a consumer-conscious business."[10]

A Donnybrook

An interesting competitive brawl that occurred in mid-1999 was indicative of the intensity of this airliner war. Boeing won a $1.9 billion order for ten of its 777 jetliners from Singapore Airlines. This in itself would not have raised eyebrows, but there was

---

[7] "British to Order Airbus Airliners," *Cleveland Plain Dealer*, August 25, 1998, p. 6-C.

[8] Howard Banks, "Slow Learner," *Forbes*, May 4, 1998, p. 54.

[9] "Plane Discomfort," *Forbes*, September 6, 1999, p. 32.

[10] "Blue Skies for Airbus," p. 104.

more to it. As a condition, Boeing agreed to purchase 17 competing Airbus A340-300 jets from Singapore Airlines for resale, thereby enabling the airline to phase them out.

Airbus officials claimed that Boeing had agreed to unprofitable terms out of desperation to close a 777 sale agreement, and that this signaled a new price war involving trade-ins to provide a discount rather than direct price cutting. Boeing crowed that the carrier's decision to eliminate the competing version of the A340 from its fleet was a victory for Boeing.[11]

A month later, still stung by the Boeing sales thrust, and in an effort to thwart it, Airbus announced that it would not provide its standard support services for the jets it sold to Singapore Airlines if Boeing bought and resold them. This countermove could have proved costly to Boeing. On the other hand, Boeing was likely to offer the jets first to airlines with fleets of the same planes, several of which had already expressed interest. Refusing to provide support service would put Airbus in the position of denying support for a small number of planes in the fleet of a major customer. Move and countermove, this.[12]

WHO CAN WE BLAME FOR BOEING'S TROUBLES?

Was it CEO Philip Condit?

Philip Condit became chief executive in 1996, just in time for the emerging problems. He had hardly assumed office before he was deeply involved in the defense industry's merger mania, first buying Rockwell's aerospace operation and then McDonnell Douglas. Condit later admitted that he probably spent too much time on these acquisitions, and not enough time on watching the commercial part of the operation.[13]

Condit's credentials were good. His association with Boeing began in 1965 when he joined the firm as an aerodynamics engineer. The same year, he obtained a design patent for a flexible wing called the sailwing. Moving through the company's engineering and managerial ranks, he was named CEO in 1996 and chairman in 1997. Along the way, he earned a master's degree in management from the Massachusetts Institute of Technology in 1975, and in 1997 a doctorate in engineering from Science University of Tokyo, where he was the first Westerner to earn such a degree.

Was Condit's pursuit of the Rockwell and McDonnell Douglas mergers a major blunder? While analysts did not agree on this, prevailing opinion was more positive than negative, mostly because these businesses could smooth the cyclical nature of the commercial sector.

Interestingly, in the face of severe adversity, no heads rolled, as they might have in other firms. See the Issue Box: Management Climate During Adversity.

---

[11] Jeff Cole, "Airbus Industrie Charges Boeing Is Inciting Price War in Asian Deal," *Wall Street Journal*, June 21, 1999, p. A4.
[12] Daniel Michaels, "Airbus Won't Provide Support Service for Jets It Sold to Singapore Air if Boeing Resells Them," *Wall Street Journal*, July 28, 1999, p. A17.
[13] Howard Banks, "Slow Learner," *Forbes*, May 4, 1998, p. 56.

ISSUE BOX

MANAGEMENT CLIMATE DURING ADVERSITY: WHAT IS BEST FOR MAXIMUM EFFECTIVENESS?

Management shake-ups during adversity can range from practically none to widespread head-rolling. In the first scenario, a cooperative board is usually necessary, and it helps if the top executive(s) controls a lot of stock. But the company's problems will probably continue. In the second scenario, at the extreme, wielding a mean ax with massive worker and management layoffs can wreak havoc on a company's morale and longer-term prospects.

In general, neither extreme—complacency or upheaval—is good. A sick company usually needs drastic changes, but not necessarily widespread bloodletting that leaves the entire organization cringing and sending out resumes. But we need to further define sick. At what point is a company so bad off it needs a drastic overhaul? Was Boeing that sick? Would a drastic overhaul have quickly changed things? Certainly Boeing's management made some miscalculations, mostly in the area of too much optimism and too much complacency, but these were finally recognized.

Major competitor Airbus was finally aggressively attacking, and that certainly had something to do with Boeing's problems. Major executive changes and resignations might not have helped.

How do you personally feel about the continuity of management at Boeing during these difficult times? Should some heads have rolled? What criteria would you use in your judgment of whether to roll heads or not?

Were the Problems Mostly due to Internal Factors?

The airlines' unexpected buying binge, which was brought about by worldwide prosperity fueling air travel, maybe should have been anticipated. However, even the most prescient decision maker probably would have missed the full extent of the boom. For example, orders jumped from 124 in 1994 to 754 in 1996. With hindsight, we know that Boeing made a grievous management mistake in trying to bite off too much, by promising expanded production and deliveries that were wholly unrealistic. We know what triggered such extravagant promises: trying to keep ahead of arch-rival Airbus.

Huge layoffs in the early 1990s contributed to the problems of gearing up for new business. An early-retirement plan had been taken up by 9,000 of 13,000 eligible people. This was twice as many as Boeing expected, and it removed a core of production-line workers and managers who had kept a dilapidated system working. New people could not be trained or assimilated quickly enough to match those lost.

Boeing had begun switching to the Japanese practice of lean inventory management that delivers parts and tools to workers precisely as needed, so that production costs could be reduced. Partly due to this change, and also to the early 1990s downturn, Boeing's supplier base changed significantly. Some suppliers quit the aviation business; others had suffered so badly in the slump that their credit was affected and they were unable to boost capacity for the suddenly increased business. The result was serious parts shortages.

Complicating production problems was Boeing's long-standing practice of customizing. Because it permitted customers to choose from a host of options, Boeing was fine-tuning not only for every airline, but for every order. For example, it offered the 747's customers 38 different pilot clipboards, and 109 shades of the color white.[14] Such tailoring added significantly to costs and production time. This may have been acceptable when these costs could be easily passed on to customers in a more leisurely production cycle, but it was far from maximizing efficiency. With deregulation, fare wars made extreme customizing archaic. Boeing apparently got the message with the wide-bodied 777, designed entirely by computers. Here, choices of parts were narrowed to standard options, much like those carmakers offer in their transmissions, engines, and comfort packages.

Cut-rate pricing between Boeing and Airbus epitomized the situation by the mid-1990s. Then costs became critical if a firm was to be profitable. In this climate, Boeing was so obsessed with maintaining its 60 percent market share that it fought for each order with whatever price it took. Commercial airline production had somehow become a commodity business, with neither Boeing nor Airbus having products all that unique to sell. Innovation seemed disregarded, and price was the only factor in getting an order. So, every order became a battleground, and prices might be slashed 20 percent off list in order to grab all the business possible.[15] And Boeing did not have the low-cost advantage over Airbus.

Price competition worked to the advantage of the airlines, and they grew skillful at gaining big discounts from Boeing and Airbus by holding out huge contracts and negotiating hard.

Boeing's cumbersome, cost-inefficient production systems became a burden in this cost-conscious environment. While some of the problems could be attributed to computer technology not well applied to the assembly process, others involved organizational myopia regarding even such simple things as a streamlined organization and common parts. For example, before recent changes the commercial group had five wing-design groups, one for each aircraft program. This was reduced to one. Another example cited in *Forbes* tells of different tools needed in the various plane models to open their wing-access hatches.[16] Why not use the same tool?

There is a paradox in Boeing's dilemma. Its 777 was the epitome of high technology, computer design, and efficient production planning. But much of its other production was mired in a morass with supplies, parts management, and production inefficiency.

Harry Stonecipher, CEO of McDonnell Douglas before the acquisition and then president and chief operating officer of Boeing, cited arrogance as the mindset behind Boeing's problems. He saw this as coming from a belief that the company could do

---

[14] John Greenwald, "Is Boeing Out of Its Spin?" *Time*, July 13, 1998, p. 68.
[15] "Behind Boeing's Woes," pp. A1, A16.
[16] Banks, p. 60.

no wrong, that all its problems came from outside, and that business as usual would solve them.[17]

The Role of External Factors

Adding to the production and cost-containment difficulties at Boeing were increased regulatory demands. These came not only from the U.S. Federal Aviation Administration, but also from the European Joint Airworthiness Authority (a loose grouping of regulators from more than 20 European countries). The first major consequence of the increased regulatory climate concerned the new 730NG. Boeing apparently thought it could use the same over-the-wings emergency exits as it had on the older 737. But the European regulators wanted a redesign. They were concerned that the older type of emergency exits would not permit passengers in the larger version of the plane to evacuate quickly enough. So Boeing had to design two new over-the-wing exits on each side. This was no simple modification, since it involved rebuilding the most crucial aspect of the plane. The costly refitting accounted for a major part of the $1.6 billion write-down Boeing took in 1997.

Europe's Airbus Industrie had made no secret of its desire to achieve parity with Boeing and have 50 percent of the international market for commercial jets. This mindset led to the severe price competition of the latter 1990s as Boeing stubbornly tried to maintain its 60 percent market share even at the expense of profits. While its total production capacity was somewhat below that of Boeing, Airbus had already overhauled its manufacturing process and was better positioned to compete on price. Airbus's competitive advantage seemed stronger with single-aisle planes, those in the 120–200 seat category, mostly Boeing 737s and Airbus A320s. But this accounted for 43 percent of the $40 billion expected to be spent on airliners in 1998.[18]

The future was something else. Airbus placed high stakes on a superjumbo successor to the 747, with seating capacity well beyond that of the 747. This huge plane would operate from hub airports like New York City's JFK. Meantime, Boeing staked its own future on its 767s and 777s, which could connect smaller cities around the world without any need for passenger concentration at a few hubs.

Have you ever heard of a firm complaining of too much business? Probably not, but then we're confronted with Boeing's immersion in red ink, caused by trying to cope with too many orders. However, Boeing's feast of too much business abruptly ended. Financial problems in Asia brought cancellations and postponements of orders and deliveries.

In October 1998, Boeing disclosed that 36 completed aircraft were sitting in company storage areas in the desert, largely because of canceled orders. By December 1998, Boeing warned that its operations could be hurt by the Asian situation for as long as five years, and it announced that an additional 20,000 jobs would be

---

[17] Bill Sweetman, "Stonecipher's Boeing Shakeup," *Interavia Business & Technology*, September 1998, p. 15.
[18] Banks, p. 60.

eliminated and production cut 25 percent.[19] Of course, it didn't help that Airbus was capitalizing on Boeing's production difficulties by wresting orders from the stable of Boeing's long-term customers, nor that Airbus planned a 30 percent production increase for 1999.

COMPETITION AT THE NEW MILLENNIUM

By 2001 the competition between Airbus and Boeing continued unabated. Airbus had gone ahead with its superjumbo A380, the world's largest passenger jet, with delivery to start in 2006 for a list price of $239 million. In its standard configuration, it would carry 555 passengers between airport hubs. With delivery still five years away, Airbus already had orders for 72 of the jumbos, and expected to reach the 100 milestone early in 2002. It would break even with 250 of the wide bodies.

In March 2001, Boeing scrapped plans for an updated but still smaller 747-X project. Instead it announced plans for a revolutionary delta-winged "Sonic Cruiser," carrying 150 to 250 passengers higher and faster than conventional planes. The savings in time would amount to 50 minutes from New York City to London, and almost 2 hours between Singapore and London. Further time savings would come from the plane's ability to fly to point-to-point destinations, bypassing layovers at such congested hubs as London and Hong Kong. Delivery was expected in 2007 or 2008.

Both companies had undergone major organizational changes. As of January 1, 2001, Airbus was no longer a four-nation consortium; it was now an integrated company with centralized purchasing and management systems. Operations were streamlined toward bottom-line responsibilities.

Boeing had previously diversified itself away from too much dependence on commercial aircraft through its acquisitions of Rockwell's aerospace and defense business, McDonnell Douglas, Hughes Space & Communications, and several smaller companies. Boeing expected that within five years more than half its revenues would come from new business lines, including financing aircraft sales, providing high-speed Internet access, and managing air-traffic problems.[20]

Everything changed with 9/11.

The airline industry's woes that began with 9/11 intensified in 2002. By late that year two major carriers, US Airways and United, were in bankruptcy, and other airlines—with the exception of a few discount carriers, notably Southwest and JetBlue—were experiencing horrific losses. Airlines were placing no new orders and even reneging on accepting delivery of previously ordered planes. Boeing's jet production fell to half of what it had been a year earlier, and forecasts for 2003 and 2004 were little better.

---

[19] Frederick M. Biddle and Andy Pasztor, "Boeing May Be Hurt Up to 5 Years by Asia," *Wall Street Journal*, December 3, 1998, p. A3.

[20] Compiled from David J. Lynch, "Airbus Comes of Age with A380," *USA Today* (June 21, 2001), pp. 1B, 2B; J. Lynn Lunsford, Daniel Michaels, and Andy Pasztor, "At Paris Air Show, Boeing-Airbus Duel Has New Twist," *Wall Street Journal* (June 15, 2001), p. B4; and other sources.

In this environment, the competition between Airbus and Boeing for the few customers still buying became even more fierce and was influenced almost entirely by price. The biggest prize was capturing the 120-plane order from British budget carrier easyJet, and this customer milked its power position to the utmost, repeatedly sending Boeing and Airbus back to improve their offers.

During the aviation slump in the early 1990s, Boeing had beefed up its order backlog by selling at steep discounts—only to find itself in a serious bind in 1997, when it could not keep up with the built-up demand, and production costs skyrocketed. Now Boeing refused to follow Airbus into unprofitable terrain, and Airbus got the easyJet order. Though Airbus claimed it was not selling its planes at a loss, many people in the industry thought otherwise.

In late December 2002, Boeing announced it was shelving the ambitious development program for its high-speed Sonic Cruiser. In talks with potential customers to gauge interest in the plane in this post-9/11 environment, few expressed any interest; most wanted a replacement plane that would be cheaper to operate than existing ones. Boeing began changing its focus to developing a new 250-seat plane that would be 20 percent cheaper to operate than existing jetliners.[21]

Boeing's Continuing Problems

The competition between Boeing and Airbus grew ever more fierce in 2003. This was to prove a watershed year—for the first time, Airbus delivered more planes than Boeing. By selling fleets of A320 variations to low-cost carriers like JetBlue, Airbus captured 52 percent of the commercial jet market. It already had 95 orders for its A380 superjumbo jet seating 550 passengers, which was expected to enter service in 2006, and this was very close to its declared goal of 100. Furthermore Airbus thought it had a chance to sell to the U.S. military. A $23 billion deal for Boeing to supply the U.S. Air Force with 100 modified 767 jetliners for midair refueling was terminated as the company became immersed in a contract-for-job scandal that cost CEO Philip Condit his job and landed chief financial officer Michael Sears in prison. Further shenanigans involved documents stolen from Lockheed, resulting in the loss of $1 billion in space-launch contracts.

Meanwhile, Boeing announced that it would stop making its twin-engine 757 because of waning interest. It was in preliminary planning for a new model, the 7E7, a long-range jet that would seat 200–250 and be 20 percent cheaper to own and operate than other planes. The 7E7 could enter service around 2008. Boeing had not had a new model since 1995, and badly needed a success with the new plane. The company suffered serious setbacks elsewhere. It had to take write-offs on its slow-selling single-aisle 717, and also had written off $2.4 billion of its commercial satellite and launch business.

[21] J. Lynn Lunsford, "Boeing to Drop Sonic Cruiser, Build Plane Cheaper to Operate," *Wall Street Journal*, December 19, 2002, p. B4; Daniel Michaels and J. Lynn Lunsford, "Airbus Is Awarded easyJet Order for 120 New Planes over Boeing," *Wall Street Journal*, October 15, 2002, pp. A3 and A6; Scott McCartney and J. Lynn Lunsford, "Skies Darken for Boeing, AMR and UAL as Aviation Woes Grow," *Wall Street Journal*, October 17, 2002, pp. A1 and A9.

But Boeing achieved profitability by revamping assembly lines, contracting out fabrication of parts, and laying off 32,000 workers after 9/11. Union leaders claimed that the result was an aging skilled workforce and rock-bottom morale.[22]

In early 2004, Airbus captured a $7 billion 110-plane order from Air Berlin, a discount airline that was Germany's No. 2 carrier. What made the situation all the more galling for Boeing chairman and CEO Harry Stonecipher was that Air Berlin had always flown Boeing 737s. A debate brewed among executives and customers over why the once-dominant Boeing was losing order after order.

Stonecipher blamed the company's sales force for not doing a better job of nurturing relationships. But some in the industry blamed Boeing's failures on poor pricing strategy, unwillingness to bend, and a distorted notion that quality was still more important to airlines than price—all this at a time when airlines were struggling mightily to reduce costs.

Compounding the situation, Boeing was trying to gain commitments for its new 7E7 widebody, soon to be renamed the 787 Dreamliner. Airbus was countering with its A350, which would be derived from its current A330 model. Japan Airlines late in 2004 upped the prospects for Boeing's 787 by agreeing to order 30 and taking options for 20 more. This brought total orders and commitments for the plane to 112, but this was still well short of the goal of 200 by the end of 2004.

Boeing continued to attribute Airbus's success in the marketplace to the billions of dollars of European subsidies that allowed it to underbid Boeing. Airbus maintained that its success was planes that could be built more quickly and cheaply than Boeing's.[23]

In December 2004, Boeing had one source of satisfaction. Airbus disclosed that its flagship A380 superjumbo jetliner had cost overruns approaching $2 billion, or about 12 percent in excess of the plane's original budget. The first flight of the huge A380 was expected in March 2005. Airbus saw no problem with the budget overage, and said it would have "no impact on the overall profitability of the program."[24]

Harry Stonecipher was brought back from retirement in early 2004 to try to repair Boeing's relationships with Washington, which had been damaged by legal and ethics problems involving some of its employees following a string of scandals, mostly involving conflicts of interest on government interactions. For example, Boeing's finance chief improperly engaged in employment talks with an Air Force procurement official while she had authority over billions of dollars worth of Boeing contracts. Stonecipher helped draft a code of conduct that prohibited any behavior that might embarrass the company. Alas, after 15 months, Stonecipher himself was

[22] J. Lynn Lunsford, "Boeing, Losing Ground to Airbus, Faces Key Choice," *Wall Street Journal*, April 21, 2003, pp. A1, A8; J. Lynn Lunsford, "Boeing May Risk Building New Jet," *Wall Street Journal*, October 15, 2003, pp. A1, A13; Daniel Michaels, "Airbus Sees Military-Sales Opening," *Wall Street Journal*, September 15, 2003, p. A8.

[23] J. Lynn Lunsford, "Behind Slide in Boeing Orders: Weak Sales Team or Firm Prices?" *Wall Street Journal*, December 23, 2004, pp. A1 and A6; Daniel Michaels, "Airbus Firms Up Plans for a New Jet," *Wall Street Journal*, September 30, 2004, p. A3.

[24] David Gauthier-Villars, Pierre Briancon, and Daniel Michaels, "Airbus Discloses Cost Overruns on Big A380 Jet," *Wall Street Journal*, December 16, 2004, pp. A3 and A10.

dismissed for unethical conduct after directors learned about an extramarital affair that violated this very code of conduct.[25]

THE TIDE TURNS FOR BOEING

In 2005, Jim McNerney, 56 years old, became the third top executive at Boeing in three years. He was the former head of 3M Corp. and of General Electric's jet engine division. While many people expected him to take immediate and drastic action, he spent months at what he called "deep dives" to learn as much as possible about Boeing's massive commercial airplane and defense units. In January 2006, he presented an agenda to "help Boeing lose the baggage of its rocky past while using its size and intellectual talent to produce better financial results."[26]

The year 2006 was to see a monumental swing in the two competitors' fortunes. Boeing's new 787 Dreamliner was proving a real winner, with orders surging even though delivery would not be until 2008. This was no ordinary plane. With its plastic fuselage, it was a sleek aircraft that could carry 250 to 330 people, cruise near the speed of sound (650 mph), had a range of over 10,000 miles, and, Boeing claimed, would cut fuel bills by 20 percent and maintenance costs 30 percent. No one had ever built a commercial airplane with a plastic fuselage (actually, it was carbon fiber embedded in epoxy). As a further production innovation, for the first time Boeing was *outsourcing* more than half the parts of the plane to be manufactured in six different countries. The projected $130 million cost per plane was modest compared with the alternatives, and especially the Airbus's superjumbo A380, now projected to cost about $300 million.

Airbus faltered in 2006 as the A380 delivery schedule experienced further delays. These delays were already costing the company at least $2.5 billion over the $12 billion originally planned; the cost of fines, canceled orders, and lost future orders is additional. The blow to prestige might be even greater. Rising fuel prices and a recent trend toward long-haul flights that avoid connecting at busy hub airports cast doubt on the whole A380 decision of a huge plane designed to fly between major hub airports. Boeing's new 787 and 777 models were marketed as more comfortable and more efficient. Shares of Airbus's parent company, European Aeronautic Defence & Space Co. (EADS), fell sharply and forced the departure of Noel Forgeard and his colleague, Gustav Humbert, on July 2, 2006. Forgeard was criticized for selling some of his EADS shares a few months before the profit warning, but denied accusations of insider trading.[27]

Going into the last quarter of 2006, Airbus's production problems became a crisis situation, and talk was of shifting more work to other nations and other restructuring

---

[25] Carol Hymowitz, "The Perils of Picking CEOs," *Wall Street Journal*, March 15, 2005, pp. B1 and B4.

[26] J. Lynn Lunsford, "Piloting Boeing's New Course," *Wall Street Journal*, June 13, 2006, pp. B1 and B3.

[27] Compiled from Mark Tatge, "Global Gamble," *Forbes*, April 17, 2006, pp. 78–82; J. Lynn Lunsford and Daniel Michaels, "Bet on Huge Plane Trips Up Airbus," *Wall Street Journal*, June 15, 2006, pp. A1 and A11; J. Lynn Lunsford, "Piloting Boeing's New Course," *Wall Street Journal*, June 13, 2006, pp. B1 and B3; Daniel Michaels, "Airbus Problems Lead to Ouster of Key Executives," *Wall Street Journal*, July 3, 2006, pp. A1 and A2.

efforts. Airline executives publicly complained about their inability to plan schedules and related investments due to the uncertainty about A380 delivery. On top of this, European and U.S. aviation regulators determined that the A380's powerful wake required changes in air-traffic-control rules. These new requirements could increase congestion at some large airports and reduce the attractiveness of operating the A380. The giant plane on which Airbus was staking so much was assuming the stance of an albatross.[28]

❖ ❖ ❖

Invitation to Make Your Own Analysis and Conclusions:

What do you see as the major preventative steps that should have been taken by Boeing in the bust and boom of the 1990s?

Do you think that at this point, 2007, the superjumbo A380 should be abandoned? Defend your recommendation.

What would it take to resurrect Airbus?

❖ ❖ ❖

WHAT CAN BE LEARNED?

Again, beware the "king-of-the-hill" three-Cs mindset—Firms that are well entrenched in their industry and that have dominated for years tend to fall into a mindset that leaves them vulnerable to aggressive and innovative competitors. (This was first described in Chapter 7, IBM.)

These "three Cs" are detrimental to a front-runner's continued success:

Complacency
Conservatism
Conceit

Complacency is smugness—a complacent firm is self-satisfied, content with the status quo, no longer hungry and eager for innovative growth. *Conservatism*, when excessive, characterizes a management wedded to the past, to the traditional, to the way things have always been done. Conservative managers see no need to change because they believe nothing is different today (e.g., "Our 747 jumbo jet is the largest that can be profitably used"). Finally, *conceit* further reinforces the myopia of the mindset: conceit regarding current and potential competitors. The beliefs that "we are the best" and "no one else can touch us" can easily permeate an organization that has dominated its industry for years. Usually the three Cs insidiously move in at the highest levels and filter down to the rest of the organization.

---

[28] Simon Clow and Daniel Michaels, "Airbus Work May Move Elsewhere as a Broad Revamp Is Considered," *Wall Street Journal*, September 29, 2006, p. A10.

Stonecipher, former CEO of McDonnell Douglas and then president of Boeing, admitted to company self-confidence bordering on arrogance. The struggle with Airbus should have destroyed any vestiges of the three Cs mindset.

Growth must be manageable.—Boeing certainly demonstrated the fallacy of attempting growth beyond immediate capabilities in a growth-at-any-cost mindset. The rationale for embracing great growth is that firms "need to run with the ball" if they ever get that rare opportunity to suddenly double or triple sales. But there are times when slower, more controlled growth is prudent.

Risks lie on both sides as businesses reach for these opportunities. When a market begins to boom and a firm is unable to keep up with demand without greatly increasing capacity and resources, it faces a dilemma: (1) Stay conservative in fear that the opportunity will be short-lived, but thereby abdicate some of the growing market to competitors, or (2) Expand vigorously to take full advantage of the opportunity, but risk being overextended and vulnerable should the potential suddenly fade. Regardless of the commitment to great growth, a firm must develop an organization and systems and controls to handle it, or find itself in the same morass as Boeing, with quality-control problems, inability to meet production targets, alienated customers, and costs far out of line. And not the least, having its stock price savaged by Wall Street investors while its market share tumbles. Growth must not be beyond the firm's ability to manage it.

Downsizing has its perils.—Boeing presents a sobering example of the risks of downsizing in this era when downsizing is so much in fashion. With incredibly bad timing, Boeing encouraged many of its most experienced and skilled workers and supervisors to take early retirement just a few years before the boom began. Boeing found out the hard way that it could replace bodies, but not the skills needed to produce the highly complex planes under severe deadlines for output. The company would have been better off maintaining a core of experienced workers during the downturn rather than lose them forever. It would have been better suffering higher labor costs during the lean times and disregarding management's typical attitude of paring costs to the bone during such times. Yet, when we look at Table 12.1 and see the severe decreases of revenue and income in 1993, 1994, and lasting well into 1995, we can understand the mindset of Boeing's management.

Problems of competing entirely on price.—Price competition almost invariably leads to price-cutting and even price wars to win market share. In such an environment, the lowest-cost, most efficient producer wins.

More often, all the firms in an industry have rather similar cost structures, and severe price competition hurts the profits of all competitors without bringing much additional business. Any initial pricing advantage is quickly matched by competitors unwilling to lose market share. In this situation, competing on nonprice bases has much to recommend it. Nonprice competition emphasizes uniqueness, perhaps in some aspects of product features and quality, perhaps through service and quicker deliveries or better quality control. A firm's reputation, if good, is a powerful nonprice advantage.

Usually new and rapidly growing industries face price competition as marginal firms are weeded out and more economies of operation are developed. The more mature an industry, the greater likelihood of nonprice competition, since cutthroat pricing causes too much hardship to all competitors.

Certainly the commercial aircraft industry is mature, and much has been made of airlines being chiefly interested in how much passenger-carrying capacity they can buy for the same buck, and of their pitting Airbus and Boeing against each other in bidding wars.[29] Nonprice competition badly needed to be reinstated in this industry. At that point, Airbus appeared to be doing a better job of finding uniqueness, with its passenger-friendly planes and its charting new horizons with the superjumbo. But the pendulum of uniqueness had swung to Boeing by 2006.

The synergy of mergers and acquisitions is suspect.—The concept of synergy says that a new whole is better than the sum of its parts. In other words, a well-planned merger or acquisition should result in a better enterprise than the two separate entities. Theoretically, this seems possible, if operations are streamlined for more efficiency, and greater management and staff competence is achieved as more financial and other resources are tapped—or in Boeing's case, if the peaks and valleys of commercial demand are countered by defense and space business.

Unfortunately, as we have seen in other cases, such synergy often is absent, at least in the short and intermediate terms. More often such concentrations incur severe digestive problems—problems with people, systems, and procedures—that take time to resolve. Furthermore, greater size does not always beget economies of scale. The opposite may in fact occur: an unwieldy organization, slow to act, and vulnerable to more aggressive, innovative, and agile smaller competitors. The siren call of synergy is often an illusion.

The assimilation of the McDonnell Douglas and Rockwell acquisitions came at a most troubling time for Boeing. The Long Beach plant of McDonnell Douglas alone led to a massive $1.4 billion write-off, and contributed significantly to the losses of 1997. Less easily calculated, but certainly a factor, was the management time involved in coping with these new entities.

CONSIDER

Can you think of additional learning insights?

QUESTIONS

1. Do you think Boeing should have anticipated the impact of Asian economic difficulties long before it did?

2. If it had more quickly anticipated the drying up of the Asian market for planes, could Boeing have prevented most of the problems that confronted it? Discuss.

---

[29] For example, Banks, p. 54.

3. Do you think top management at Boeing should have been fired after the disastrous miscalculations in the late 1990s? Why or why not?

4. A major stockholder grumbles, "Management worries too much about Airbus, and to hell with the stockholders." Evaluate this statement. Do you think it is valid?

5. What do you see for Boeing three to five years down the road? For Airbus?

6. Do you think Stonecipher should have been fired for having an affair with an employee? Why or why not?

7. Discuss synergy in mergers. Why does synergy so often seem to be lacking despite expectations?

8. You are a skilled machinist for Boeing and have always been quite proud of participating in the building of giant planes. You have just received notice of another lengthy layoff, the second in five years. Discuss your likely attitudes and actions.

9. How wise do you think it was for Airbus to "bet the company" on the superjumbo A380, the world's largest jet?

10. Do you think Airbus's more passenger-friendly planes gave it a significant competitive advantage? Why or why not? Discuss as many aspects of this as you can.

HANDS-ON EXERCISES

Before

1. You are a management consultant advising top management at Boeing. It is 1993, and the airline industry is in a slump, but early indications are that things will improve greatly in a few years. What would you advise that might have prevented the problems Boeing faced a few years later? Be as specific as you can, and support your recommendations as to practicality and probable effectiveness.

After

2. It is late 1998; Boeing has had to announce drastic cutbacks, with little improvement likely before five years, and Boeing's stock has collapsed, while Airbus is charging ahead. What do you recommend now? (You may need to make some assumptions; if so, state them clearly and keep them reasonable.)

3. It is 2005, and you have been brought in as vice president of sales. What do you propose to counter the aggressive and successful efforts of Airbus to win customers?

4. *Be a Devil's Advocate.* You are a union leader and the 32,000 layoffs after 9/11 appall you. Array all the arguments you can muster for Boeing to reconsider these massive layoffs. Be as persuasive as you can.

TEAM DEBATE EXERCISES

1. A business columnist writes: Boeing could "have told customers 'no thanks' to more orders than its factories could handle . . . [It] could have done itself a huge favor by simply building fewer planes and charging more for them."[30] Debate the merits of this suggestion.

2. Debate the controversy of Airbus Chairman Forgeard's decision to go for broke with the A3XX superjumbo. Is the risk/reward probability worth such a mighty commitment? Debate as many pros and cons as you can, and also consider how much each should be weighted or given priority consideration. (Do not consider what actually happened in 2006. You are not prescient at the time of the decision.)

INVITATION TO RESEARCH

What is the situation with Boeing today? Has it remained profitable? How is the competitive position with Airbus? What is the situation with the A380 superjumbo of Airbus? Has it been abandoned? What is the situation with the 787 Dreamliner. Is it meeting all expectations, or have unexpected engineering problems assailed it?

---

[30] Holman W. Jenkins Jr., "Boeing's Trouble: Not Enough Monopolistic Arrogance," *Wall Street Journal*, December 16, 1998, p. A23.

CHAPTER THIRTEEN

Vanguard: Success in Taking the Road Less Traveled

By the turn of the twenty-first century, Vanguard Group had become the largest mutual fund family in the world, besting Fidelity Investments. While Fidelity was increasing its fund assets about 20 percent a year, Vanguard was growing at 33 percent. Fidelity advertised heavily, while Vanguard did practically no advertising, spending a mere $8 million for a few ads to get people to ask for prospectuses. The Kaufmann Fund, one-hundredth Vanguard's size, spent the same amount for advertising, and General Mills spent twice as much just to introduce a new cereal, Sunrise.[1]

What was Vanguard's secret? How wise is it with such a consumer product to spurn advertising? The answer lies in the vision and steadfastness of John C. Bogle, the founder and now retired chairman.

JOHN BOGLE AND THE CREATION OF VANGUARD

In 1950, as a junior at Princeton, Bogle was groping for a topic for his senior thesis. He wanted a topic that no one had written about in any serious academic paper. In December 1949 he had read an article in *Fortune* on mutual funds. At that time, all mutual funds were sold with sales commissions often 8 percent of the amount invested, and this was taken off the top as a front-end load. (This meant that if you invested $1,000, only $920 would be earning you money. Today we find no funds with a front-end load more than 6.5 percent, so there has been some improvement.) In addition, these funds had high yearly overheads or expense ratios. As Bogle thought about this, he wondered why funds couldn't be bought without salespeople or brokers and their steep commissions, and whether growth could not be maximized by keeping overhead down.

[1] Thomas Easton, "The Gospel According to Vanguard," *Forbes*, February 8, 1999, p. 115.

Right after graduation he joined a tiny mutual fund, Wellington Management Company, and moved up rapidly. In 1965, at age 35, he became the chief executive. Unwisely, he decided to merge with another firm, but the new partners turned out to be active managers, buying and selling with a vengeance, and generating high overhead costs. The relationship was incompatible with Bogle's beliefs, and in 1974 he was fired as chief executive.

He decided to go his own way and change the "very structure under which mutual funds operated" into a fund-distribution company mutually owned by shareholders. The idea came from his Princeton thesis, and included such heresies as "reduction of sales loads and management fees," and "giving investors a fair shake" as the rock on which the new enterprise would be built. He chose the name "Vanguard" for his new company after the great victory of Lord Nelson over Napoleon's fleet with his flagship, HMS *Vanguard*. Bogle launched the Vanguard Group of Investment Companies on September 26, 1974, and he hoped "that just as Nelson's fleet had come to dominate the seas during the Napoleonic wars, our new flagship would come to dominate the mutual fund sea."[2]

But success was long in coming. Bogle brought out the first index fund the next year, a fund based on the Standard & Poor's 500 Stock Price Index, and named it Vanguard 500 Index Fund. It was designed to mirror the market averages, and thus required minimal management decisions and costs. It flopped initially. Analysts publicly derided the idea, arguing that astute management could beat the averages every time, though they ignored the costs of high-priced money managers and frequent trading.

Twenty-five years later, this Vanguard flagship fund, which tracks the 500 stocks on the Standard & Poor's Index, had more than $92 billion in assets and had beat 86 percent of all actively managed stock funds in 1998, and an even higher percentage over the past decade. By early 2000 it overtook Fidelity's famed Magellan Fund as the largest mutual fund of all. The relative growth between Magellan and Vanguard's 500 Index for the five salient years of 1994 to 1999 is shown in Table 13.1.

TABLE 13.1. Relative Growth Comparisons of the Two Largest Mutual Funds, 1994–1999

	Assets (millions $)		5-Year Gain
	6/30/94	6/30/99	(Percent)
Fidelity Magellan	$33,179	$97,594	194.2%
Vanguard 500 Index	8,443	92,644	997.3

Source: Company reports.

Commentary: Especially notable is the tremendous growth of Vanguard's 500 Index Fund in these five years, growing from $8 billion in assets to over $92 billion.

---

[2] John C. Bogle, *Common Sense on Mutual Funds*, New York: Wiley, 1999, pp. 402–403.

The Vanguard family of funds had become the world's largest *no-load* mutual fund group, with 12 million shareholders and $442 billion in assets as of the beginning of 1999. Fidelity, *partly load and partly no-load*, had nearly $700 billion, but the gap was closing fast.

Bogle, The Messiah

A feature article in the February 8, 1999 issue of *Forbes* had this headline:

> The Gospel According to Vanguard—How do you account for the explosive success of that strange business called Vanguard? Maybe it isn't really a business at all. It's a religion.[3]

Bogle's religion was low-cost investing and service to customers. He believed in funds being bought and not sold; thus, no loads or commissions to salespeople or brokers. Customers had to seek out and deal directly with Vanguard. The engine was frugality, with the investor-owner's best interests paramount. This was not advertised, not pasted on billboards, but the gospel was preached in thousands of letters to shareholders, editors, Securities & Exchange Commission members, and members of Congress. Bogle made many speeches, comments to the news media, appearances on such TV channels as CNBC, and wrote two best-selling books. With his gaunt face and raspy voice, he became the zealot for low-cost investing, and the major critic of money managers who trade frenetically, in the process running up costs and tax burdens for their investors. As the legions of loyal and enthusiastic clients grew, word-of-mouth from past experiences, and favorable mentions in business and consumer periodicals such as *Forbes*, *Wall Street Journal*, *Money*, and numerous daily newspapers, as well as TV stations, brought a ground swell of new and repeat business to Vanguard.

Bogle turned 70 in May 1999, and was forced to retire from Vanguard's board. The new chairman, John J. Brennan, 44, seemed imbued with the Bogle philosophy and vision. He said, "We're a small company, and we haven't begun to explore our opportunities, yet." He noted that there's Europe and Asia, to say nothing of the trillions of dollars held in non-Vanguard funds. "It's humbling."[4]

GREAT APPEAL OF VANGUARD

Performance

Each year *Forbes* presents "Mutual Funds Ratings" and "Best Buys." The Ratings lists the hundreds of mutual funds that are open-end, that is, can be bought and sold at current net asset prices. (**Note**: A far smaller number of mutuals are closed-end funds that have a fixed number of shares and are traded like stocks. These generally have higher annual expenses, yet sell at a discount from net asset value. We will disregard these in this case.)

[3] Easton, p. 115.
[4] Easton, p. 117.

The Best Buys are the select few funds that *Forbes* analysts judge to "invest wisely, spend frugally, and you get what you pay for," and that have performed best in shareholder returns over both up and down markets. Vanguard equity and bond funds dominate *Forbes'* Best Buys:

> Of 43 U.S. equity funds listed in the various categories, 12 were Vanguard funds. Of 70 bond funds, 27 were Vanguard.[5]

Forbes explains that "the preponderance of Vanguard funds in our Best Buy Tables is a testament to the firm's cost controls. Higher expenses, for most other fund families, are like lead weights. Why carry them?"[6] Table 13.2 shows representative examples of the substantially lower expenses of Vanguard funds relative to others on the Best Buy list.[7]

Looking at total averages, the typical mutual fund has an expense ratio of 1.24 percent of assets annually. The ratio for Vanguard's 101 funds was 0.28 percent, almost a full percentage point lower.[8]

How does Vanguard achieve such a low expense ratio? We noted before its reluctance to advertise; nor does it have a mass sales force. Its commitment has been to pare costs to the absolute minimum. But there have been other economies.

Fidelity and Charles Schwab have opened numerous walk-in sales outposts. Certainly these bring more sales exposure to prospective customers. But are such sales-promotion efforts worth the cost? Vanguard decided not. It had one sales outpost in Philadelphia, but closed it to save money.

Vanguard discouraged day traders and other market timers from in-and-out trading of its funds. It even prohibited telephone switching on the Vanguard 500 Index; redemption orders had to come by mail. Why such market timing discouragement? Frequent redemptions run up transaction costs, and a flurry of sell orders might impose trading costs that would have to be borne by other shareholders if some holdings had to be sold.

Not the least of the economies is what Bogle calls passive investing, tracking the market rather than trying to actively manage the funds by trying to beat the market. The funds with the highest expense ratios are hedge funds, and these usually are the most active traders, with heavy buying and selling. They seldom beat the market, but squander a lot of money in the effort and burden shareholders with sizable capital gains taxes because of the flurry of transactions. Still, the common notion prevails that more is better, that the more expensive car or service must be better than its less expensive alternative. See the following Information Box for another discussion of the price-quality perception.

---

[5] *Forbes*, August 23, 1999, pp. 128, 136–137.
[6] *Ibid.*, p. 136.
[7] *Ibid.*, pp. 128, 137.
[8] Easton, p. 116.

TABLE 13.2. **Comparative Expense Ratios of Representative Mutual Funds**

	Annual Expenses per $100
Balanced Equity Funds:	
Vanguard Wellington Fund	0.31
Columbia Balanced Fund	0.67
Janus Balanced Fund	0.93
Ranier Balanced Portfolio	1.19
Index Equity Funds:	
Vanguard 500 Index	.18
T. Rowe Price Equity Index 500	.40
Dreyfus S&P 500 Index	.50
Gateway Fund	1.02
Municipal Long-Term Bonds:	
Vanguard High Yield Tax Exempt	.20
Dreyfus Basic Muni Bond	.45
Strong High Yield Muni Bond	.66
High-Yield Corporate Bonds:	
Vanguard High Yield Corp.	.29
Fidelity High Income	.75
Value Line Aggressive Income	.81
Ivesco High Yield	.86

Source: Company records as reported in *Forbes Mutual Fund Guide*, August 23, 1999.

Commentary: Vanguard's great cost advantage shows up very specifically here. It is not a slightly lower expense ratio, but is usually three or four times lower than similar funds. Take, for example, the category of Index Equity Funds, where the goal is to simply track the Index averages, which suggests passive management rather than free-wheeling buying and selling. Vanguard's costs are far below the other funds; in one case, the Gateway fund is five times higher.

INFORMATION BOX

THE PRICE-QUALITY PERCEPTION REVISITED

We had a similar box in Chapter 3 on Perrier, and will have another in Chapter 22. But the topic is worth further discussion. In the Perrier case, we considered whether high-priced bottled water was that much better than regular tap water or lower-priced bottled water, and concluded that it usually was not. The same thing applies to perfume, to beer and liquor, and to many other consumer products. "You get what you pay for" is a common perception, and its corollary is that you judge quality by price: The higher the price, the higher the quality. But this notion leads many consumers to be taken advantage of, and enables top-of-the-line brands and products to command a higher profit margin than lower-priced alternatives. Admittedly, sometimes we are led to the more expensive brand or item for the prestige factor.

When it comes to money management, by no means do high fees mean better quality; the reverse is usually true. And prestige should hardly be a factor, since we are not inclined to show off our investments as we might a new car. Does a high-overhead index fund deliver better performance than a cheap one, than Vanguard? Not at all. And hedge funds, as we noted before, seldom even beat the averages despite running up some of the highest expenses in the mutual fund industry. Looking at Table 13.2, which shows typical expense ratios of Vanguard and its competitors, are the other funds doing a better job than Vanguard with their expenses three to five times higher? No, because their high expense ratios take away from any performance advantage, even if frequent trading results in somewhat better gains, and that seldom is achieved.

If Vanguard advertised its great expense advantage aggressively to really get the word out, do you think it would win many more customers? Why or why not?

Another factor also contributes to the great cost advantage of Vanguard. It is a mutual firm, organized as a nonprofit owned by its customers. Almost all other financial institutions, except TIAA-CREF (and we will discuss this shortly), have stock ownership with its heavy allegiance to profit maximization.

Customer Service

Many firms espouse a commitment to customer service. It is the popular thing to do, rather like motherhood, apple pie, and the flag. Unfortunately, pious platitudes do not always match reality. Vanguard's commitment to service seems to be more tangible.

Service to customers is often composed of the simple things. Such as just answering the phone promptly and courteously, or responding to mail quickly and completely, or giving complete and unbiased information. Vanguard's 2,000 phone representatives are ready to answer the phone by the fourth ring. During a market panic or on April 15, when the tax deadline stimulates many inquiries, CEO John Brennan brings a brigade of executives with him to help man the phones. Vanguard works to make its monthly statements to investors as complete and easy to understand as possible, and it leads the industry in this.

The philosophy of a customer-service commitment was espoused by Bogle. "Our primary goal: to serve, to the best of our ability, the human beings who are our clients. To serve them with candor, with integrity, and with fair dealing. To be the stewards of the assets they have entrusted to us. To treat them as we would like the stewards of our own assets to treat us."

In a talk he gave at Harvard Business School in December 1997, Bogle described to the students how "our focus on human beings had enabled Vanguard to become what at Harvard is called a 'service breakthrough company.' I challenged the students to find the term *human beings* in any book they had read on corporate strategy. As far as I know, none could meet the challenge. But 'human beingness' has been one of the keys to our development."[9]

Not the least of the consumer best interests has been a commitment to holding down taxable transactions for shareholders. Vanguard has led the industry with tax-managed funds aimed at minimizing the capital gains that confront most mutual fund investors to their dismay at the end of the year.

COMPETITION

Why is Vanguard's low-expense approach not matched by competitors? All the other fund giants that sell primarily to the general public are for-profit companies. Are they willing to sacrifice profits to win back Vanguard converts? Hardly likely. Are they willing to reduce their hefty marketing and advertising expenditures? Again, hardly likely. Why? Because advertising, not word-of-mouth, is vital to their visibility and to seeking out customers.

TIAA-CREF

One potential competitor looms, another low-cost fund contender. TIAA-CREF, which manages retirement money for teachers and researchers, in 1997 launched six no-load mutual funds that are now open to all investors. The funds' annual expenses range from 0.29 percent to 0.49 percent, comparable to Vanguard's. A significant potential attraction over Vanguard is that each fund's investment minimum is just $250, compared with Vanguard's usual minimum of $3,000. As of late August 1999, the combined assets of the six TIAA-CREF funds was $1.5 billion, far less, of course, than the near $500 billion of Vanguard at the time.

TIAA-CREF is also run solely for the benefit of its shareholders, being another mutual with the long-term aim of providing fund-management services at cost. Still, there is some doubt that expense ratios can be kept low should the new funds fail to attract enough investors.

Is this a gnat against the giant Vanguard? Perhaps; however, the low investment requirement of only $250 should certainly attract cost-conscious investors who cannot come up with the $3,000 that Vanguard requires on most of its funds. Still, six fund choices versus the more than 100 of Vanguard is not very attractive yet. Efforts to be as tax-efficient as Vanguard are also unknown.

ANALYSIS

The success of Vanguard with its disavowal of most traditional business strategies flies in the face of all that we have come to believe. It suggests that heavy advertising

[9] Bogle, pp. 423, 424.

expenditures may at least be questioned as not always desirable—and what a heresy this is. It suggests that relying on word-of-mouth and whatever free publicity can be garnered may sometimes be preferable to advertising. All you need is a superior product or service. It supports the statement that textbooks like to shoot down: "If you build a better mousetrap, people will come." Conventional wisdom maintains that without advertising to get the message out, the better mousetrap will fade away from lack of buyer knowledge and interest. But the planning of Bogle and Vanguard to tread a different path and not be dissuaded, despite the critics, illustrates a remarkable and enduring commitment first formulated more than three decades ago.

How do we reconcile Vanguard with the commonly accepted notion that communication is essential to get products and services to customers (except perhaps when selling solely to the government or to a single customer)?

Maybe we should not try to fit Vanguard into these traditional beliefs. Maybe it is the exception, the anomaly, in its seeming repudiation of them. Still, let us not be too hasty in this judgment.

I do not believe that Vanguard contradicts traditional principles of marketing and business strategy. Rather, it has revealed another approach to the communication component: the effective use of word-of-mouth publicity. If we have a distinctive product that can be tangibly demonstrated as superior in relative cost advantages to competitors, then demand may be stimulated without mass advertising. Word-of-mouth, enhanced or developed through formal publicity—from media, public appearances, and publications—can replace massive advertising expenditures of competitors. But is there a downside to all this? Let us examine the role of word-of-mouth in more detail in the following Information Box.

INFORMATION BOX

THE POTENTIAL OF WORD-OF-MOUTH AND UNPAID PUBLICITY

Word-of-mouth advertising, by itself, is almost always frowned on by the experts. It is the sign of the marginal firm, one without sufficient resources to do what is needed to get established. Such a firm is bound to succumb to competitors that are better managed and have more resources. The best the experts can say for word-of-mouth advertising is that if the firm manages to survive for a few years, and if it *really* has a superior product or service, then it might finally attain some modest success.

Compared to spending for advertising, word-of-mouth takes far longer to have any impact, and firms seldom have the staying power to wait years, so the belief holds. The best strategy would be to have both, with healthy doses of advertising to jump-start the enterprise, and let favorable word-of-mouth reinforce the advertising.

As we have seen, Bogle and his Vanguard repudiated the accepted strategy, yet became highly successful. Still, it took time, even decades. If you look at Table 13.1, in 1994, after 16 years, the flagship Index 500 Fund had reached $8 billion in assets; not bad, but far below the heavily advertised Magellan Fund of Fidelity. The growth of the Index 500 fund has accelerated only in recent years. Would more advertising have shortened the period?

Bogle would maintain that advertising would have destroyed Vanguard's uniqueness by making its expenses like those of other funds. He would also likely contend that the favorable publicity enhanced the word-of-mouth influence of satisfied shareholders, and thus there was no need for expensive advertising. But in the early years, Vanguard did not have much favorable publicity. On the contrary, it took experts a long time to admit that a low-expense fund with passive management could do as well or better than aggressively managed funds with a lot of buying and selling and big trading and marketing expenses.

So the success of Vanguard without much formal advertising attests to the success of word-of-mouth heavily seasoned by favorable free publicity. But was it too conservative, especially in the early years?

Do you think Vanguard should have advertised more, especially in its early days? Why or why not? If yes, how much more do you think it should have spent?

Vanguard illustrates a commendable application of one important business strategy principle: the desirability of uniqueness or product differentiation. It differentiated itself from competitors in two respects: (1) its resolve and ability to bring out a low-priced product and at the same time one of good quality, and (2) its achievement of good customer service despite the low price.

Even today, after several decades of competitors seeing this highly effective strategy, Vanguard still is virtually unmatched in its uniqueness, except for one newcomer that is hardly a contender, but could be a factor should Vanguard let down its guard and be tempted to seek more profits.

Prognosis—Can Vanguard Continue as Is?

Is it likely that Vanguard can continue its success pattern without increasing advertising and other costs and becoming more like its competitors? Why should it change? It has become a giant with its low-cost strategy. The last decade saw a growing momentum created by favorable word-of-mouth and publicity that made the need for heavy advertising and selling efforts far less than in the early years. It took bravery, or audacity, in those early years not to succumb to the Lorelei beguilement that advertising and commission selling was the only viable strategy. Something would be lost if Vanguard were to change its strategy and uniqueness and become a higher-cost imitation of its competitors.

If Vanguard is so good, why are so many investors still doing business with the higher-cost competitors? We can identify four groups of consumers who are not customers of Vanguard:

1. Those who have not studied the statistics and editorials of publications like *Forbes*, *Money*, and *Wall Street Journal*, and are not aware of the Vanguard advantage.

2. Those who are naive in investing and content to let someone else—a broker or a banker—advise them and reap the commissions.

3. Those who are swayed by the massive advertisements of firms like Fidelity, Dreyfus, Rowe Price, and others.

4. Those who put their faith in the price-quality perception: the higher the price, the higher the quality, with quality guaranteeing higher investor returns.

In addition to continued investments by its ardent customers, Vanguard should find potential in the gradual eroding of the commitment of these four consumer groups. Of course, the overseas markets also offer a huge and virtually untapped potential for Vanguard.

❖ ❖ ❖

Invitation for Your Own Analysis and Conclusions

You do not have to agree with Bogle's planning strategy. Playing the *devil's advocate*, persuasively present another perspective. (You may want to do some research on American Funds, and also on the next case, Edward Lampert, hedge fund manager extraordinaire.)

❖ ❖ ❖

UPDATE

In the new millennium, several shifts in the relative positions of the major players in the mutual fund industry began to take place. By 2005, the assets of the three largest fund houses and their percent change from 2000 were:

Assets($billion):	2000	2005	Percent Change
Vanguard	$448.3	$747.1	67%
American	333.2	714.4	114
Fidelity	569.3	629.7	11

As you can see, Vanguard had forged to the top, easily surpassing Fidelity. But American Funds was charging fast, more than doubling its assets, and seemed likely to soon overtake Vanguard as the largest mutual fund family. What is there about American that makes it so appealing to investors?

American Funds is the complete opposite of Vanguard in almost all respects. Its funds try to beat the market by being actively managed, with, of course, the higher expenses coming from this. Adding to the costs, it is distributed through brokers who love to sell the American family of funds because of a nice 5.75 percent sales commission. It does no advertising (similar to Vanguard in this), and its stock pickers shun the limelight and do not appear on TV chat shows. CEO Paul Haaga scorns the self-proclaimed virtues of arch-rival Vanguard. He refers to Bogle as "a saint with his own statue." Unlike most funds that have a chief stock-picking manager, with American it is difficult to know who is selecting specific stocks, since each fund has as many as eight managers, all seemingly equal—so who is an investor to blame for a poor performance? Still, American's biggest funds have mostly done better than the S&P 500, and this performance along with eager broker recommendations has lured investors. However, skeptics point to academic studies of the difficulty of beating the market over long periods, especially as funds get larger. Vanguard doesn't have to worry about this, because many of its assets are in index funds that aim only to match the market.

A harbinger that it is becoming more difficult for American to beat the market were the latest asset figures for the largest equity funds. As of July 31, 2006, Vanguard's equity assets (i.e., stock only) were $532.7 billion. Fidelity was next with $444.7 billion, while American, with only 29 funds, was third at $386.3. Matching *Forbes* Best Buys recommendations for 1999 with those of 2006, Vanguard stock funds had 25 percent of the recommendations in 2006—slightly below 1999—but its bond funds recommendations were 49 percent for 2006, well above the 1999 figures.[10]

WHAT CAN BE LEARNED?

Marketing can be overdone.—Vanguard's success shows that marketing can be overdone. Too much can be spent for advertising without realizing congruent benefits. Sales expenses and branch office overhead may get out of line. Yet, few firms dare reduce such costs lest they be competitively disadvantaged. For example, it is the brave executive who reduces advertising in the face of increases by competitors, though the results of the advertising may be impossible to measure with any accuracy.

Still, despite Vanguard's success in downplaying advertising, one has to wonder how much faster the growth might have been if it had budgeted more dollars for selling, at least in the early years.

Can word-of-mouth by itself do the job of advertising?—In Vanguard's case, word-of-mouth combined with favorable unpaid publicity from the media made it the largest mutual fund family in the industry. However, the time needed for word-of-mouth, even eventually with good publicity, to build demand has to be a negative. Without such favorable publicity, it would have taken far longer.

The benefits of frugality.—There is far too much waste in most institutions, business and non-business. Some waste comes from undercontrolled costs and such extravagances as lavish expense accounts and entertainment, and expenditures that do little to benefit the bottom line. Other factors may be a top-heavy bureaucratic organization saddled with layers of staff personnel, and/or too many debt payments due to heavy investments in plant and equipment or mergers. Heavy use of

[10] "Fund Survey: Family Counseling," *Forbes*, September 18, 2006, pp. 186, 188–189. Also used in this update: Michael Maiello, "The Un-Vanguard," *Forbes*, September 19, 2005, pp. 182–185; "How the Largest Funds Fared," *Wall Street Journal*, December 4, 2006, p. R6.

advertising may not always pay off enough to justify the expenditures. In money management, trading costs may get far out of line.

Vanguard shows the benefit of austerity in greatly reduced expense ratios for its funds compared to competitors. More and more astute investors are at last recognizing this unique cost advantage that not only gives a better return on their investment dollars but some of the best customer service in the industry.

The power of differentiation.—Firms seek to differentiate themselves, to come up with products or ways of doing business that are unique in some respect from competitors. This is a paramount quest of business strategy and accounts for the massive expenditures for advertising. Too often attempts to find uniqueness are fragile, not very substantial, and easily lost or countered by competitors. Sometimes, though, they can be rather enduring, as, for example, the quality-image perception perpetrated by advertisements featuring the lonely Maytag repairman, as described in Chapter 20. If a firm can effectively differentiate itself from competitors, it gains a powerful advantage and may even be able to charge premium prices.

While Vanguard seemingly disregarded marketing, John Bogle found a powerful and enduring way to differentiate through low-cost quality products and superb customer service. For decades no competitor has been able to match this attractive uniqueness.

Beware placing too much faith in the price-quality relationship.—We are drawn to judge quality by a product's price relative to other choices. Often this is justified, although the better quality may not always match the higher price. In other words, the luxury item may not be worth the much higher price, except for the significant psychological value that some people see in the prestige of a fine brand name. Unfortunately, there are some products and services where the higher price does not really reflect higher quality, better workmanship, better service, and the like. Then we are taken advantage of with this price-quality perception. Beware of always judging quality by price.

CONSIDER

Can you think of additional learning insights?

QUESTIONS

1. "The success of Vanguard is due to media exploitation of what would otherwise be a very ordinary firm." Discuss.

2. Why do you think people continue to buy front-end load mutual funds with 5–6 percent commission fees when there are numerous no-load funds to be had?

3. Do you think Bogle's shunning advertising was really a success, or was it a mistake?

4. Was Vanguard's failure to open walk-in sales outposts a mistake and an example of misplaced frugality? Why or why not?

5. What are the differences between passive and active fund management? How significant are they?

6. "Vanguard seems too good. There must be a downside." Discuss.

7. What is a service-breakthrough company?

8. Can publicity ever take the place of massive advertising expenditures?

HANDS-ON EXERCISES

1. You are an executive assistant to John Brennan, the new CEO of Vanguard now that Bogle has retired. Brennan is thinking of judiciously adding some marketing and advertising expenditures to the paucity that Bogle insisted on. He has directed you to draw up a position paper on the merits of adding some advertising and even some walk-in sales outposts such as other big competitors have already done. (You may be instructed to make a cost/benefit analysis, which is described in a box in Chapter 20.)

2. You are John Brennan, CEO. It is 2009; TIAA-CREF is turning out to be a formidable competitor, and is gaining fast on your first-place position in the industry. What actions would you take, and why? Discuss all the ramifications of the actions you can think of?

TEAM DEBATE EXERCISES

1. You are a member of the board of directors of Vanguard. John Bogle is approaching the retirement age as set forth in the company policies. However, he wants to continue as chairman of the board, even though he is willing to let Brennan assume active management. Debate the issue of whether to force Bogle to step down or bow to his wishes.

2. Debate Bogle's no-advertising policy.

INVITATION TO RESEARCH

Is Vanguard still No. 1 in the mutual fund industry? Has it increased its advertising expenditures? Has Brennan made any substantial changes? What happened to Fidelity's Magellan Fund in the 1990s and before? How is TIAA-CREF doing?

CHAPTER FOURTEEN

A Hedge Fund Manager Finds Opportunity in Two Faltering Firms—Kmart and Sears

On November 17, 2004, Kmart Holding Corp. chairman Edward Lampert and Sears chairman and CEO Alan Lacy announced a deal for Kmart to buy the once-dominant Sears department store chain for $11.5 billion. This merger of battered retail giants would propel the combination into the No. 3 position behind behemoth Wal-Mart and Home Depot. This would be the second-largest retail merger ever. It would take the Sears name and be called Sears Holdings Corp.

Some analysts questioned how a merger of two faltering firms—both long hampered by weak management, outdated stores, and inefficient operations—could make one winner. However, investors thought otherwise, and bid up the stocks of both companies. While the name of the new company was to be Sears Holdings Corp., Kmart would be dominant. Part of the investor zeal was faith in Edward Lampert as a turnaround expert extraordinaire. That, and the suspected value of the combined companies' real estate.

EDWARD LAMPERT

The 42-year-old Lampert had built a fortune buying struggling companies and turning them around. He had hitherto shunned publicity, though now this was difficult to do in such a highly visible merger. In 2003, any desire for secrecy was thwarted when he was kidnapped from the garage of his office building in Greenwich, Connecticut, with his captors demanding a $1 million ransom. This tested Lampert's persuasive skills, and they were not found wanting, for he eventually convinced the kidnappers to let him go for $40,000.

209

The son of a lawyer in a comfortable New York City suburb, Lampert's life became more focused after his father died when he was 14. Interested in finance, he graduated from Yale and joined Goldman Sachs upon graduating. There he found a mentor, Robert Rubin, who later became U.S. Secretary of the Treasury. Lampert left the firm in 1988 at age 28 to start a hedge fund, ESL Investments, with about $25 million to invest. He had long been an admirer of Warren Buffett, second only to Bill Gates of Microsoft as the richest American. Buffett had gained his wealth by concentrating on undervalued, old-line companies that threw off lots of cash. And just as Buffett did in the 1960s with Berkshire, then just a declining textile mill in New Bedford, Massachusetts, Lampert did with bankrupt Kmart, gaining control in 2003 and turning it into a powerful investment vehicle. His investors included the wealthy and famous, and he made them even wealthier. His hedge fund's annual returns since 1988 have averaged almost 30 percent.

Unlike other hedge funds, ESL did not trade stocks actively, but tended to take big positions and hold them long-term. As an example of his investment style, Lampert in 1997 bought an initial stake in AutoZone, a leading auto-parts retailer that was struggling. By 1999, he had a seat on the board, installed a new CEO, and boosted cash flow. To help profits, he raised prices, cut store-management budgets, and shifted to less-experienced staff—and the company's stock price surged from the low $20s in late 1999 to more than $100 in October 2003.[1]

Kmart had filed for Chapter 11 bankruptcy protection in January 2002, finding itself unable to compete with the likes of Wal-Mart and Target. After the filing, more than 600 unprofitable stores were closed, 57,000 Kmart employees were terminated, and Kmart stockholders' common stock was wiped out. Lampert began buying Kmart debt after the filing, while a subsequent controversy over accounting and perks given to former executives reduced the value of its bank debt to less than 70 cents on the dollar, and its bonds to about 35 cents on the dollar. He came to hold debt with a face value of about $1 billion. But bad news continued for Kmart, and Lampert faced paper losses of $100 million.

He demanded a seat on the court-sanctioned committee of holders of bank debt and bonds. There he argued against the slowness of the bankruptcy process and the "excessive" fees paid to lawyers and consultants. Lampert forced the resignation of Kmart's chief executive and installed Julian Day, a former Sears executive, as CEO. He pushed hard to get the company out of bankruptcy quickly. "He was absolutely confident that the business was worth something, despite an enormous amount of skepticism by most parties," said Henry Miller, a financial adviser to Kmart during its bankruptcy restructuring.[2]

But Lampert's hedge fund had to pour in more money to buy out Kmart's banks, and when the retailer emerged from bankruptcy in May 2003, he held more than 50 percent of Kmart's new stock through conversion of his debt holdings into equity. He then led an aggressive strategy of closing or selling another 600 stores. The

---

[1] Rachel Beck, "So, Does 2 + 2 = 5 for Kmart, Sears?" Associated Press, as reported in *Cleveland Plain Dealer*, November 23, 2004, p. C5.

[2] Gregory Zuckerman and Mitchell Pacelle, "Sears Suitor Faces a Tough Bet," *Wall Street Journal*, November 18, 2004, p. C4.

proceeds from these, no longer having the burden of billions of dollars of debt, and from severe cost-cutting brought a speedy financial turnaround, with profits being posted in each of the next four quarters after Lampert took over. The stock price meantime increased sevenfold from its price of $15 a share when it emerged from bankruptcy, and the hedge fund gained almost $4 billion from its Kmart holdings. ESL Investments now owned 43 million shares of Kmart and 31 million shares of Sears. In the wake of the merger news, in one day it recorded paper profits of nearly $600 million.

THE EVOLUTION OF KMART

Kmart had been a newcomer to the discount scene. The early discounters started a few years after World War II, offering goods in barns, lofts, warehouses, abandoned factories, all places of low overhead. Shopping amenities were few. Goods were displayed on pipe racks, maybe jumbled on tables, and there were no services and hardly any employees except those at the checkouts. But prices were far lower than traditional retailers could offer. Most of the early discounters were ill-managed, undercapitalized, and very vulnerable to the sophisticated management that S. S. Kresge Co. had developed in more than half a century of being the second-largest variety chain, behind only Woolworth. The name Kresge was changed to Kmart in 1977.

Kmart destroyed its weaker competitors and was second only to Sears in sales until 1990. Sears, however, carried appliances, furniture, tools, some machinery, automobile accessories and tires as well as other goods that Kmart and department stores did not carry, so that Sears' sales statistics were not entirely comparable with Kmart's.

Sam Walton started Wal-Mart in 1969, and in the late 1970s, Wal-Mart sales were only 5 percent of Kmart's. It had 150 stores to Kmart's more than 1,000 that were mostly in urban locations. Wal-Mart stayed in rural small towns where it developed technology to have lean inventories, reduce overhead to the lowest in the industry, yet keep shelves well stocked and be able to offer lowest prices.

When Wal-Mart finally began invading Kmart's turf, it had a significant price advantage that Kmart never was able to overcome. In addition, the Wal-Mart stores were newer than the Kmart aging stores. In 1990, Wal-Mart caught up with Kmart, and then irresistibly surged ahead while Kmart faltered. In a desperate effort to win back customers, Kmart's management increased its inventory investment and tried to match Wal-Mart's prices. But with Wal-Mart's efficiency and low overhead, Kmart could not match its prices without going into the red. Unable to compete with Wal-Mart and an aggressive Target aimed at a slightly more affluent customer, Kmart became ripe for Lampert's takeover.

THE EVOLUTION OF SEARS

Sears spanned three centuries of being a dominant force in the retail industry. It started in the late nineteenth century when it sent thousands of rural Americans the

Sears Roebuck catalog, quickly dubbed the "consumer's bible." This offered a huge variety of goods at prices far cheaper than they could be bought elsewhere. Sears advertised itself as the "Cheapest Supply House on Earth," and turned America into a consumer democracy, where everyone had equal access to the same goods at the same price.[3] Sears surpassed Montgomery Ward as the largest retailer in 1900, with sales of $10 million to Ward's $8.7 million. Never again would Ward surpass Sears. The catalog became a fixture in millions of American homes—and outhouses—and enabled farm families to keep up with changing fashions and the raft of manufactured goods becoming available.

By the 1920s, with many of its customers migrating to the cities or else having cars and better roads, Sears' founding principle of bringing cheap merchandise to remote areas of the country was becoming obsolete. In a major strategic decision, it opened its first retail store in Chicago in 1925, and by 1933 had 400 stores. It launched its famous Kenmore and Craftsman brands in 1927, and started the Allstate Insurance Co. in 1931. In 1953, Sears issued its own credit card, and it started the Discovery Card in 1985. In 1981 it diversified, acquiring Dean Witter Reynolds and Coldwell Banker. In 1993, with much handwringing, Sears discontinued the catalog and sold its interests in its financial units. In 2002 it acquired Lands' End for $1.9 billion.

By the 1990s, Sears found itself squeezed by a changing retail environment. Its lower- and middle-class customers were flocking to the powerful and efficient Wal-Marts and Targets for low prices. Those wanting quality were drawn to Nordstrom or specialty retailers like Gap. Those looking for home improvement and building supplies were drawn to surging category-killer chains such as Home Depot and Lowe's.

At the time of the merger with Kmart, Sears had 870 mostly mall-based stores and 1,100 specialty stores, with net income for partial 2004 of $648 million; Kmart had 1,504 stores, almost all standing alone and not in malls, with net income for partial 2004 of $533 million after Lampert had taken it out of bankruptcy and closed or sold about 600 losing stores.[4] With its sluggish sales in recent years, Sears had also lost favor with investors until the announced merger.

LAMPERT'S CHALLENGE

Possible Problems

In order to generate the most short-term profit possible after buying distressed Kmart and thus drive share prices up, Lampert put no money into improving its stores—though many were old and drab—in the 18 months after it came out of bankruptcy protection. He reduced inventories, avoided most discounting, and cut advertising and other expenses. He was able to sell some stores to chains such as Home Depot and also some to Sears. Other unsaleable money-losing stores were

---

[3] Cynthia Crossen and Kortney Stringer, "A Merchant's Evolution," *Wall Street Journal*, November 18, 2004, p. B1.
[4] WSJ Research, "Down the Aisles," *Wall Street Journal*, November 18, 2004, p. B1.

closed. But his cash flow shored up the balance sheet with a $3 billion cash hoard, and dazzled investors in the planned merger.

Since he made no significant investments, same-store sales slid drastically, 13 percent in one recent quarter. In the highly competitive retail environment, such frazzled stores would likely be lodestones for the chain's efforts to revive itself without major rejuvenation. But any major investments would reduce profits.

One objective of mergers is to combine and coordinate operations and products wherever possible, so to avoid redundancies and strengthen existing product lines. Could some Sears' goods be readily sold in Kmart stores, and vice versa? Sears had strong brands in its Kenmore appliances and Craftsman tools. Wal-Mart was not much of a factor with such goods. But would it be practical to move these bulky appliances into Kmarts? They would require considerable space, which would mean less room for groceries, paper goods, household staples, and similar products. They would also require a much higher level of employee than typically found in a Kmart, as well as major remodeling to support such high-priced and bulky products. None of the three competitors—Sears, Kmart, and Wal-Mart—was strong in apparel, although Wal-Mart was improving its quality, and had introduced the more stylish George line. In 2002, Sears bought the Lands' End apparel brand, and this had done well in upscale markets, but not so well in less-affluent ones.

It was doubtful that either Kmart or Sears had the merchandising/computer technology to match Wal-Mart in preventing out-of-stocks and overstocks of other goods. Anecdotal incidents of Kmart and Sears merchandising expertise were troubling. Visits to Kmart and Sears stores in Ohio by retail consultants after the merger was announced found Kmart depleted in some grocery items, while Sears still had baseball caps in November for faraway teams, such as Oakland, Atlanta, and San Francisco.[5]

Kmart was not alone in having steadily declining same-store sales. Sears had also had sliding sales almost every month over the four years before the merger. CEO Alan Lacy had tried. He had reorganized departments, dropped product lines, changed store signs, added clothing lines, and laid off thousands of employees. He sold the credit-card business to Citigroup in 2003, at about the same time that Kmart was beginning its credit card. The Lands' End acquisition brought more expertise in apparel. Still, same-store sales declined. Would Lampert do any better?

Lampert's Goals for the New Merger

Lampert had a reputation for keeping his cards close to his vest. A plethora of analysts began speculating about how he would proceed, and how successful he would be. Investors seemed dazzled by his past successes in turning around distressed companies. At a news conference after the announced merger, Lampert and Lacy of Sears talked about potential synergies, a buzz word often used to support merger decisions. See the following Information Box for an analysis of the synergy of Lands' End in fitting in with the Kmart/Sears merger.

[5] Amy Merrick and Ann Zimmerman, "Can Sears and Kmart Take On a Goliath Named Wal-Mart?" *Wall Street Journal*, November 19, 2004, p. B1.

INFORMATION BOX

LANDS' END: DOES IT FIT IN WITH THE NEW MERGER?

Lands' End was a longtime catalog seller that had built a strong following with its high-quality items such as cashmere sweaters, its wide range of sizes and assortments, and its high level of customer service. It was based in a small Wisconsin town, and its most direct competitor was L. L. Bean, also from a small town, but in Maine.

Sears bought the company in 2002 for $1.9 billion, hoping it would be a cornerstone brand that would beef up apparel sales and draw customers who were buying appliances and other non-clothing items. Lands' End thought the exposure to potential customers in Sears' 870 locations would be healthy. The reverse was more the case. The wider exposure weakened Lands' End's exclusivity, and it was often poorly positioned "in between men's suits, snow blowers, tools, denim and work clothes." Charlie O'Shea, an analyst for Moody's, said, "It hasn't done what I think Sears wanted it to do. The general idea was to take the higher-income demographic, the hard-line appliance shopper, and have them walk across the store and buy apparel." But this was not happening enough.[6]

Kmart's takeover of Sears caused more consternation for Lands' End. The blue-collar image of Kmart seemed incompatible with the quality image Lands'End had built up over the years. Kmart had to wonder, too, whether Lands'End merchandise would sell at all in its stores, or simply take up precious space better used for other goods. Instead of the synergy $2 + 2 = 5$ effect, with the total result better than the two separate operations before, it seemed more a $2 + 2 = 3$, with the combined result worse than the two separate operations were before.

Do you think Lands' End goods would sell in Kmart stores? What would it take? How could Lands' End do better in Sears stores?

Lambert and Lacy talked of squeezing suppliers, thanks to the $40 billion a year in buying power of the two companies. They talked of streamlining back-office operations. They predicted annual savings of $500 million within three years. They would aim to synchronize such areas as merchandising and planning, with cross-selling between stores, bringing Craftsman tools, Diehard batteries, and possibly Kenmore appliances into Kmarts and Martha Stewart goods into Sears.

Most Sears stores were in traditional malls, but malls were losing some favor with consumers. Research found that 80 percent of consumer shopping dollars were now spent elsewhere than malls, compared to about 60 percent in 1995. Furthermore, six of the nation's largest retailers were not in malls, this being twice the number of the late 1990s.[7] Several hundred more Kmart stores could be converted into Sears stores, which would enable Sears to address the location problem in its business model,

---

[6] Aaron Nathans, "Sears-Kmart Union Puts Lands' End in Double Jeopardy," *New York Times*, as reported in *Cleveland Plain Dealer*, January 13, 2005, C6.)

[7] Amy Merrick and Dennis K. Berman, "Kmart to Buy Sears for $11.5 Billion," *Wall Street Journal*, November 18, 2004, p. A8.

and begin to adapt to a retailing environment that had shifted to stand-alone big-box stores. Some of this adaptation would be to a new chain called Sears Grand, which is closer to the popular off-mall format of the Wal-Marts and Home Depots.

Sears Grand stores had a mix of appliances, lawn and garden goods, hardware, and clothing. Since these stores were bigger than regular Sears department stores, they could add such products as books and magazines, CDs and DVDs, as well as groceries and everyday necessities. Sears was testing such stores in different sizes and formats. See the following Information Box for a discussion of the advantage that chains offer of being able to test different strategies in a few stores, and hone their effectiveness before going larger-scale. These stores were thought to be better able to compete in the home-improvement market against the likes of Wal-Mart, Home Depot, Lowe's, and Best Buy.

INFORMATION BOX

ADVANTAGES OF CHAINS: OPPORTUNITY FOR EXPERIMENTATION

An organization with numerous similar outlets has an unparalleled opportunity for experimenting with new ideas in the quest for what might be most productive and compelling. Prospective strategy changes can be tested in a few stores, any promising modifications determined, and the success of the strategy ascertained from concrete sales and profit results.

All this can be done with relatively little risk since only a few outlets of the total chain are involved, and the strategy will be adopted throughout the organization only if results are favorable. Similar experimentation is hardly possible for a firm with few comparable units, which usually is the case with manufacturers; but where it can be done, the risks in making major strategy changes are greatly reduced, and the arena for creative innovation is enhanced.

How would you design such an experiment for Sears Grand? Be as specific as you can, and make any assumptions needed.

What should be of concern to investors is whether Lampert can make this third-largest retailer sufficiently competitive in today's hostile environment. This suggests some semblance of growth, with some new stores and rejuvenated ones—it might be called a patient turnaround strategy. But perhaps that is not what Lambert is expecting to do. Do Sears and Kmart need to grow, or would a status quo situation be acceptable as long as steady income is generated at least in the intermediate future?

If Lampert succeeds in the turnaround, and the stock of the combined companies rises accordingly, then he will be well armed to pull off more deals, to be well on the way to becoming another Warren Buffett. But maybe he doesn't need to be a hero. By squeezing cash out of every aspect of Kmart's operation over 18 months, he has already built a war chest of $3 billion. Sears also has a $2.7 billion cash reserve that can probably be increased as he wrings inefficiencies out of the aging firm. Kmart furthermore has $3.8 billion in tax credits carried over from previous losses that should shield profits for some years to come. Maybe simply continuing to accumulate a cash hoard is enough to give Lampert the ammunition to pursue his goal of great wealth by investing in other promising distressed bargains.

Some analysts felt that Lampert's best course of action would be in liquidating the underlying real estate of Kmart and Sears. However, once the best locations have been sold off, there would not be much left. In an economy of rising interest rates, the speculative hope that liquidating real estate would fuel ever-rising stock prices could be wistful thinking.[8] The real estate fall-back plan might well be more limited by other retailers unloading stores as well. Federated Department Stores and May Department Stores reportedly plan to sell off mall space. Other retail chains, such as Toys "Я" Us and Office Depot, are expected to follow suit. If the economy approaches a recession, this trend will probably accelerate, with prices and demand decreasing.[9]

UPDATE

On March 24, 2005, with shareholders signing off, Kmart officially bought Sears for $12.3 billion. Lampert told reporters, "It's an opportunity to transform two companies that once were great—to transform them into a great company relative to the 21st century. I think there's a presumption that you're going to see a lot of store closings. That's a wrong presumption. Our program is to keep as many stores open as we can." Lampert also denied that the company had plans to get rid of Lands' End: "Lands' End isn't for sale. It's a great American brand, and I think it's a brand that we could run very, very well."

Some layoffs would be forthcoming from among the 5,000 people working at the two firms' headquarters—the Kmart headquarters in Troy, Michigan, would be combined with Sears' headquarters in Hoffman Estates, Illinois—but the vast majority of the 400,000 workforce would keep their jobs. Plans were to convert about 400 of the Kmart stores over the next three years to a new midsize "Sears Essentials" store format being launched outside its traditional malls.

Standard & Poor's analysts cautioned investors that "the combination of heightened business risk, intense competition and possible under-achievement in the company's off-mall strategy could lead to sales and margin problems, as well as deteriorating credit measures."[10]

Sixty-nine percent of Kmart shareholders voted to approve the deal in a sparsely attended session lasting five minutes. Two hours later, Sears shareholders also voted

---

[8] Jesse Eisinger, "Will Lampert Get It All to Fit?" *Wall Street Journal*, November 24, 2004, p. C1.
[9] Jesse Eisinger, "Lampert Faces a Long Shot in Reviving Sears," *Wall Street Journal*, September 14, 2005.
[10] Andrew Leckey, "Analysts Rate Sears Stock as a 'Hold,'" Tribune Media Services, as reported in *Cleveland Plain Dealer*, March 30, 2005, p. C5.

69 percent in favor of the deal, but the scene was raucous, with retired and former Sears employees, upset about the acquisition by Kmart, clamoring against the deal. "This is a sad and dark day for Sears Roebuck," a former auto center manager fumed at the meeting. "It is unbelievable that Kmart, two years out of bankruptcy, would be strong enough to purchase Sears, a company in business for over a century."[11]

By early 2006, speculation in the business press focused on the possibility of Lampert's taking Sears private. While acquiring the 60 percent of Sears that his hedge fund did not own could cost $12 to $15 billion, there would be no public shareholders to scrutinize and criticize his efforts. He could do this gradually by billion-dollar buybacks each year. Then, when the lofty share price eventually falls, he would be poised to buy the rest via a tender offer.[12]

ANALYSIS

Whether operational gains can be achieved from the Sears/Kmart merger is uncertain, especially against the might of competitors Wal-Mart, Target, and Home Depot. Adding to the competitive uncertainties is the length of time needed to assimilate the merger in the disparate organizations and operations. It might be years before any synergies could be realized. This suggests that this third-largest retailer may be quite vulnerable for some years, and will probably steadily lose market share.

The great cash hoard that Lampert can generate from a stripped-down Kmart and Sears operation, and the inflated stock prices influenced by all this cash and by the optimistic assessment of real estate values for liquidation, promises only a short-term reprieve. Perhaps long enough to get these two dinosaur retailers on the growth track again? Probably not. A better expectation would be of slowing the market-share erosion—provided that most of the cash is reinvested in the company.

How is the cash to be spent? If it is spent in seeking acquisitions of other declining businesses, leaving Kmart and Sears to fend for themselves with deteriorating and sparsely funded stores in the arena of the world's greatest retailers, then their eventual survival is not promising. In ten years will there still be a Kmart and a Sears? But Lampert's cash may grow considerably. Then he may be left with the reputation of a raider who guts his acquisitions. I wonder whether he really wants that. I also wonder whether he can pull off a turnaround of even modest proportions. Such a turnaround would undoubtedly take all of the accumulated cash—and probably more, taking on debt again—to rejuvenate stores, increase inventories and advertising, and perhaps introduce new computer technology.

Another option might be to gradually close down the weaker chain and pour resources into making the other stronger. This stronger entity would probably be Sears, and it appeals to a more affluent customer than Kmart's blue-collar customer. Some Kmarts in more affluent neighborhoods might be convertible to Sears. But still, this is going to take major investment.

---

[11] Dave Carpenter, "Sears Sale to Kmart Gets Blue, er, Green Light," Associated Press, as reported in *Cleveland Plain Dealer*, March 25, 2005, pp. C1 and C3.

[12] Mark Tatge and Miriam Gottfried, "What Is Eddie Buying?" *Forbes*, January 9, 2006, p. 40.

Will Lampert succeed with Sears and Kmart? It really depends on how he defines "succeed." Does it mean becoming a bigger force in the marketplace? Does it mean accumulating more cash bonanza? We can see a clue to the longer-term prospects for Lampert's enterprise in the fortune of AutoZone, his first acquisition in 1997, and the initial testing of his strategy of cutting promotions, service, and investment in stores. AutoZone's stock rose fourfold between 2001 and 2003 from the severe cost-cutting. In 2005, same-store sales fell 2 percent, while two rivals' same-store sales were up 8 percent. The stock price has never again reached its October 2003 high. The lack of investment in stores drove customers to the competition. In the first quarter of 2006, Sears' shares jumped 13 percent on news that first-quarter profits more than doubled. But same-store sales fell 8.4 percent. An ill wind on the horizon?[13]

✿ ✿

Invitation to Make Your Own Analysis and Conclusions:

The issue is in doubt regarding Lampert's long-term success with his strategy. Draw your own prediction, and give your persuasive rationale.

✿ ✿

WHAT CAN BE LEARNED?

Beware optimistic projections for mergers.—Optimistic assumptions have no place in merger decisions. Most mergers are consummated with rather high expectations of synergy and growth. Many of them do not work out as expected, at least within the desired timeframe of a year or two. Some never work out, and eventually the losing acquisitions are given up on, or hung on to while draining financial and managerial resources.

Will the great merger of Kmart and Sears to become the country's third-largest retailer meet Lampert's declared expectations, or will he flee from the scene with a hoard of cash and two gutted former retail empires?

Assumptions should be defended in merger decisions.—Objectivity and conservative projections are called for in merger decisions. These are often the most important decisions the managers will ever have to make, and deserve thorough investigation and research. Top management should insist that assumptions and their reasoning be defended, at least as much as possible in an uncertain future. It is prudent to consider a worst-case scenario: "What if?" The use of a devil's advocate can often be worthwhile in such major decisions to bring out all aspects of the opposing position.

Don't depend on stock prices to support a risky merger.—The stock market is a volatile instrument. The get-rich motivation of some investors can foster wild and unreasonable speculations. It is not unusual for the share prices of

---

[13] Bernard Condon, "Cheapskate," *Forbes*, June 19, 2006, pp. 136–138.

some firms to be bid up far beyond their fair value, with more and more investors living in a dream world and jumping on the bandwagon, only to have prices come tumbling down as more sobering realities become evident. Kmart's and Sears' prices seem to conform to this pattern: a gamble bid up to unrealistic levels.

What happens to Lampert's grand scheme if the inflated stock prices of Kmart and the new enterprise, Sears Holdings Corp., should lose their lofty valuations? This would mean fewer financial assets for future acquisitions. If the loss of valuation is quite severe, sufficient capital to rejuvenate the aging stores of Sears and Kmart may be limited. We wonder how Lampert's hedge fund, ESL Investments, and its wealthy clients would tolerate sharply falling share prices of this major holding in the fund. But if the intent is to take Sears private, then the collapse of the share price might mean a buying opportunity.

Use same-store sales instead of total sales statistics in evaluating retail performance.—A key measure of how a retail chain is doing (aside from income statistics) is same-store sales. The total sales figure reflects new store openings; it tells nothing about how existing stores are doing, and may hide a deteriorating situation. For example, if existing stores are showing steadily declining sales—as both Kmart and Sears stores were at the time of the merger, and are still today—this is a major indicator of how vulnerable these stores are. One wonders if any can be converted to a growth mode again. For decisions regarding which stores to close, the trend in same-store sales has to be a major input. This is especially true if different store managers have still been unable to turn things around. A further analysis should be made before any decision to cut: Why is the store not doing better? Is it incompetence, bad location, aggressive competitors, untrained or unmotivated staff—what? What would it take to correct these problems, or correct them reasonably?

Old facilities are vulnerable to newer competitors.—Kmart and Sears stores are generally older than most of the Wal-Marts, Targets, Home Depots, and Lowe's. This presents a quandary in trying to compete without major investments to rejuvenate and open new state-of-the-art stores. Customers prefer to shop at nicer stores, it is easier to attract better employees, and even suppliers tend to give preferential treatment to firms they see as growing rather than stagnant. This is a conundrum for the retailer with old stores trying to compete. Where is the money coming from for major rejuvenation of existing stores? Would it be better to spend the limited resources on new stores? What is this going to do to overhead and ability to compete against lowest prices?

Minimum reinvestment may be desirable in some circumstances.—Sometimes marginal property is not worth much additional investment, but it still may not be a candidate for closure, even though little or no growth is on the horizon. It depends on how much overhead is required and whether it can generate some profit even at low sales. If the store or operation is debt free—and debt is a major factor in overhead—then it may be worth keeping for a while at least. (At this point, you may want to review the Breakeven Box in Euro Disney, Chapter 11, for the effect on sales needed to breakeven and make a profit if debt overhead can be reduced.) With Lampert's buying up the debt of Kmart in exchange for equity, the overhead was greatly reduced and these operations were grinding out a cash flow of $3 million in the first 18 months of his control. The problem, from Lampert's perspective, is whether stock prices will stabilize at a high level once the no-growth future becomes evident.

CONSIDER

Can you think of other learning insights?

QUESTIONS

1. Do you think this merger will fly? Why or why not?
2. Explain why total sales information for a retail chain is insufficient in evaluating performance.
3. Visit a Kmart store and a Wal-Mart store. What was your overall impression as to strengths and weaknesses?
4. Visit a Sears store and a Target store. What was your overall impression of their strengths and weaknesses?
5. Do you think you would like to be a Kmart store manager? A Sears manager? Do you see any implications for the companies from your attitude?
6. Does the size of the Kmart/Sears entity after the merger give it a competitive advantage? Why or why not?
7. Is market share all that important in this case? Discuss.
8. "Kmart does not really have to match the low prices of Wal-Mart. It should not even try." Evaluate this statement by an analyst.

HANDS-ON EXERCISES

1. *Be a Devil's Advocate.* Lampert has about decided to limit any additional investment in Kmart either for rejuvenating stores or building up inventory. Argue as persuasively as you can against this draconian decision. (Be somewhat diplomatic; you don't want to antagonize him.)
2. You are an ambitious Sears store manager. Describe how you might design your career path to achieve a high executive position in Lampert's new retail behemoth. (Assume that Lampert is not going to abandon the enterprise.)
3. You are the principal adviser to Sears' Alan Lacy. He wants you to develop a plan for positioning the new Sears Grand stores. Develop a plan of action for these stores, identifying various options, and then persuasively presenting one. If you prefer, do the same thing with the Sears Essentials store format.

TEAM DEBATE EXERCISES

1. A controversy has developed regarding whether Kmart and Sears should continue as two separate entities, or whether one or the other should be phased out, with resources directed to only one. Debate the two positions using all the salient arguments you can muster for your position. Be prepared to attack the other side.

2. You represent a group of shareholders of Lampert's hedge fund, ESL. Your group is opposed to the merger, and believes everyone would be better off if the over $3 billion cash hoard generated so far by Kmart is used for other growth opportunities. You will be debating another group of shareholders who stand solidly behind the merger with Sears.

INVITATION TO RESEARCH

How has the merger gone? Is it generally deemed to be successful? Has Lampert stayed with his initial plan to be instrumental in turning around the Kmart and Sears operations? Has the stock market continued to be kind to this endeavor? Have Lampert and his hedge fund turned their attention to buying out any other troubled firms yet?

LEADERSHIP AND EXECUTION

CHAPTER FIFTEEN

Hewlett-Packard Under Carly Fiorina, and After Her

In July 1999, Hewlett-Packard, the world's second-biggest computer maker, chose Carly Fiorina to be its CEO. Thus she became the first outsider to take the reins in HP's 60-year history. Never before had the company ever filled any top job with an outsider, and now this. Fiorina now became one of only three women to head a *Fortune* 500 company.

Three years later in May 2002, Fiorina engineered the biggest merger in high-tech history, with Compaq Computer. To do so she had to convince government regulators in the United States and Europe that the merger was not anti-competitive. She also had to get stockholder approval in the face of bitter opposition by Walter Hewlett, son of co-founder Bill Hewlett. She even had to survive a court challenge by Hewlett, who claimed she had misled stockholders into voting for the merger.

By August 2003, it looked like the massive merger and the differing corporate cultures were being well assimilated—unlike the problems of many mergers, including several discussed in this book. Was HP to be the model, a paragon, for bringing together two organizations?

CARLY FIORINA

Carleton (Carly) Fiorina disappointed her father, a federal court judge and law professor, by dropping out of law school after one semester at UCLA. (The name Carleton was a tradition that began during the Civil War, when her father's family lost all its men named Carleton. In remembrance, each descendant named either a son Carleton or a daughter Cara Carleton. Carly is the ninth Cara Carleton since the Civil War.)

Before dropping law, Fiorina earned a BA in medieval history and philosophy from Stanford University in 1976. She received an MBA in marketing from the University of Maryland in 1980, and an MS from MIT's Sloan School.

She was 44 years old when chosen for the CEO post at Hewlett-Packard, after nearly 20 years at AT&T and Lucent Technologies. At Lucent, she spearheaded the spin-off from AT&T in 1996, overseeing the company's initial public offering and the marketing campaign that positioned Lucent as an Internet company. In 1998, she became president of Lucent's global service-provider business, a $19 billion operation that sold equipment to the world's largest telephone companies.

Fiorina is known for having a "silver tongue and an iron will," being articulate and persuasive. She has a personal touch that inspires intense loyalty, even giving little gifts like balloons and flowers to employees who land big contracts. Her coddling of customers at Lucent was legendary, as were her sales and marketing skills.[1]

Still, how did a student of philosophy, medieval history, and marketing succeed in being the winning candidate for CEO by HP's search committee? Each member of the committee listed 20 qualities they would like to see in the new CEO. Then they boiled these down to four essential criteria: the ability to conceptualize and communicate sweeping strategies, the operations savvy to deliver on quarterly financial goals, the power to bring urgency to the organization, and the management skills to drive a nascent Internet vision throughout the company. Carly was selected from 300 potential candidates.[2] She was the first outsider in the company's history to become CEO; indeed, no outsiders had even been high-level executives. What qualities did Carly apparently manifest that swayed the search committee to choose her over 300 other candidates. See the following Issue Box for a discussion of two extremes of leadership: charismatic and visionary versus shunning the limelight and emphasizing execution.

ISSUE BOX

CHARISMATIC VERSUS DOWN-TO-EARTH OPERATIONAL LEADERSHIP

From the four essential criteria that the search committee settled on as needed for the CEO, both extremes apparently were sought. It is unlikely that any one person would possess each in abundance. The ability and emphasis would favor either one or the other. In Fiorina's case, she favored, and was good at, being a charismatic leader, one who could communicate sweeping strategies, bring a sense of urgency to the organization, and drive a vision throughout the company. Undoubtedly her "silver tongue" and persuasive skills influenced the committee and represented the extreme of charismatic leadership. As we will see later in the case, she was fired by the board of directors less than six years later; an operations man replaced her, and the stock price doubled. This raises some provocative questions: Can a person be too charismatic? Is an organization better served by operational leadership, shunning the spotlight and lofty visions?

---

[1] Peter Burrows, with Peter Elstrom, "HP's Carly Fiorina: The Boss," *Business Week Online*, August 2, 1999.
[2] *Ibid.*

What does a charismatic leader bring to an organization? Change. And this can be highly desirable for organizations mired in complacency, bureaucracy, and conservatism (the three Cs again). But it can also bring resentment, jealousy, and even fear of having positions eliminated or reduced. A charismatic leader is seldom inclined to give priority to details, and unless this mindset is delegated to competent subordinates, operations may suffer.

The major merger with Compaq Computer that Fiorina instigated and pushed through, despite criticism and serious opposition from Walter Hewlett, a member of the board and family with 24 percent of the vote, would probably not have been consummated without her charisma and steadfastness. But a charismatic leader can run roughshod over subordinates, and, as in Carly's case, may be disdainful of the board's efforts to change her ways. As we shall see in the Update, the Compaq merger turned out to be a triumph, but not until after her departure.

If Fiorina were a man, do you think he would have been fired as she was?

THE HEWLETT-PACKARD COMPANY (HP)

HP was founded by Stanford University classmates Bill Hewlett and Dave Packard in 1938. They invented their company's first product in a tiny Palo Alto, California garage. It was an audio oscillator, an electronic test instrument used by sound engineers. One of their first customers was Walt Disney Studios, which purchased the oscillators to develop and test an innovative sound system for the movie *Fantasia*. From 1938 to 1978, Bill and Dave built a company that became a model for thousands of subsequent Silicon Valley enterprises. In so doing, they created an informal egalitarian culture where brilliant engineers could flourish. Their emphasis on teamwork and respect for co-workers was dubbed the "HP Way."

From 1978 to 1992, John Young directed HP into becoming a major computer company, something AT&T, Honeywell, RCA, and other first-generation electronics companies never were able to do. But Young's efforts to consolidate HP's independent units bogged the company down in bureaucracy.

From 1992 to 1999, Lew Platt, a well-liked engineer who had joined the firm in 1966, guided HP for its growth in the mid-1990s, but he encountered difficulties when PC prices and Asian sales plummeted in the late 1990s. By now, HP had become a staid company, but one with deep engineering roots and old-fashioned dependability.

THE SITUATION WHEN CARLY FIORINA TOOK OVER

"Some might say we're stodgy, but no one would say this company doesn't have a shining soul," Fiorina said when she took over.[3] HP had not had a major breakthrough

[3] *Ibid.*

product since the inkjet printer in 1984. And the "HP Way" had evolved into a bureaucratic, consensus-style culture, somehow not conducive to being in the forefront in a time of rapid technological innovations.

A bloated bureaucracy seems to be a concomitant of many old, successful organizations. We have encountered others in this book, such as Sunbeam and Scott Paper, IBM, and Boeing. Examples abounded of the bureaucracy run amok that had developed at HP. The company had 130 different product groups. When retailer Best Buy wanted to buy computer products, 50 HP salespeople showed up to push their units' goods. When a vice president at HP wanted an operational change, 37 different internal committees had to approve it.[4]

The dearth of new products went along with the cumbersome bureaucracy and the many different product groups. Managers often were reluctant to invest in new ideas for fear of missing their sales goals. If the proposed new product did not seem assured of healthy profits, or might cannibalize or take away business from existing products, it was not considered further.

The crown jewel of HP's arsenal of products was its printer business, which it had dominated since the 1980s. Ink and toner refills brought HP some $10 billion annually, 15 percent of total revenues. The profitability of the refills enabled the company to sell printers at low prices, much as Gillette sells its razors for bare-bones prices, but makes huge profits on the sales of blades.

In 1998, with revenue growth slowing to the low single-digits, CEO Platt began to act more decisively in combating the malaise. He hired McKinsey & Co. consultants to explore restructuring, which led to the spin off of HP's $8 billion test-and-measurement division, which had little relevance to the faster-growing computer and printer businesses. Platt put his own job on the line, suggesting that the board hire a new CEO. This led to Fiorina's hiring.

FIORINA'S ACTIONS

The Merger with Compaq

Fiorina began searching for a big deal soon after becoming CEO. HP and Compaq Computer agreed to the rough outline of a merger in June 2001, then spent four months planning it before the formal announcement. But she could hardly have expected the controversy of the ensuing merger battle, in which Walter Hewlett, an HP board member, first voted in favor of the deal and then waged a bitter public campaign against it. He voted his family's 24 percent of the ballots against the merger, and it passed by only three percentage points. Not content with this defeat, Hewitt sued, charging that Fiorina and HP had illegally manipulated the vote, but he was unsuccessful and the merger went ahead.

What might have led to serious divisiveness in the organization, and particularly among the higher executive staff, making Fiorina's job difficult at best, had more of the opposite effect. While some had initially resented her as an outsider who

---

[4] Examples cited in Burrows and Elstrom, pp. 4–5.

didn't understand the HP Way, now most united behind their controversial new leader. "None of us anticipated the conflict. Carly was characterized as someone who destroyed the soul of HP, and we were her willing accomplices," Susan Bowick, HPs personnel chief said.[5] Still, one would expect many employees to resist change, knowing that Fiorina's arrival most likely heralded substantial changes and jobs lost.

Forcing the Integration with Compaq

The planning and tradeoffs that went into merging the two firms could serve as a model for other successful mergers. One month after the merger announcement, and before it had been officially approved, executives and staff from both firms met to come up with decisions on thousands of matters that would be involved in bringing a smooth integration. These ranged from what product lines to keep to which pension plan to use. The group started with almost 100 employees and grew to 2,500 by the merger's completion. Of the 15 highest-ranking executives, 10 were to come from HP and 5 from Compaq.

When the books of both organizations were opened, striking contrasts became evident: HP was losing $100 million a quarter on an industry-standard product called NetServer, but was making money on a proprietary model; Compaq had the reverse problem. HP's PC (personal computer) sales were mostly from retail, while Compaq had a profitable Web-based business. One company got a better deal from Microsoft on Windows, the other did better with chips from Intel—these small percentage differences amounted to billions of dollars.

The decision was made early on that the practices of only one of the two companies could be allowed to survive in each of the various areas of the new organization, and these changes could not be delayed. The choices involved jobs; the more consolidation, the more jobs lost. For examples: the HP Jornade handheld was dropped in favor of the Compaq iPAQ; the money-losing HP NetServer was killed and Compaq's rival Proliant line kept; Compaq's consumer PC business was axed in favor of the HP business; HP's corporate PC business was killed and Compaq's kept. Table 15.1 shows how the various product categories of the two firms were meshed.

The companies' four incompatible e-mail systems were consolidated into one, connecting 215,000 PCs and 49,000 other devices. Before the merger, HP and Compaq had more than 1,000 locally set policies on such things as rebates for customers and dental coverage for employees. These were unified into a single set of rules for 160 countries.

Cost Cutting Through Greater Efficiencies

Opportunities for cost cutting abounded. Here are some examples:

- The old HP spent $140 million a year for printing documents, manuals, and brochures, with an estimated $50 million of these unused; expenditures for the combined giant were now reduced to $130 million, with only $10 million of estimated waste.

---

[5] Quentin Hardy, "We Did It," *Forbes*, August 11, 2003, p. 80.

TABLE 15.1. How HP and Compaq Meshed

Servers

HP servers made money on Unix, not Linus.

Compaq made money on Linus, not Unix.

Commercial PCs

Compaq made money. HP lost.

Consumer PCs

HP made money. Compaq lost. (In order to maximize retail shelf space, HP closed the Compaq commercial line, but kept the brand.)

Printers

HP was the world leader. Compaq contracted it out.

Handhelds

Compaq's iPAQ won over HP's money-losing Jornada.

Software

Compaq had software for individual servers to work harder. HP had software to manage big groups of servers.

Direct sales over the Internet

Compaq had a $500 million engine. HP needed one.

Headquarters

Compaq's Houston base was closed. HP stayed in Palo Alto, California.

Sources: Company; and Quentin Hardy, "We Did It," *Forbes,* August 11, 2003, p. 80.

Commentary: We can see from this meshing of the various products and systems that there was no major duplication. In most areas, where one was weak, the other was strong. The weak one then was eliminated or absorbed. This probably accounted for Fiorina's success in getting the merger approved by U.S. and European antitrust regulators.

- HP's manufacturing costs in the first year of the merger were down 26 percent. All HP vendors were organized into just five supply chains, and most suppliers were connected to HP via the Internet and got consumption data and replenished orders automatically, for a saving of $1 billion. Inventory was sliced from 48 days' supply to 40 days, thereby freeing up $1.2 billion in working capital.

- Accounts receivable were shrunk by 4 days, and the faster customer payments freed up $800 million.

- 17,000 jobs were eliminated after the merger.

Through these and other cost savings from the complex merger, Fiorina was able to cut $3.5 billion in annual costs—a billion more and a year earlier than promised.[6]

New Products and New Business

In the first full year after the merger, the results were impressive. Some 3,000 new patents had been racked up and 367 new products introduced. The patents spanned

[6] *Ibid.*, pp. 76–82.

every part of the technology complex, from print technology to molecular computing. HP gained market share in key categories, and won a ten-year, $3 billion outsourcing deal with Procter & Gamble. Combined sales to Disney more than doubled since 2001. HP built technology for Walt Disney World's newest ride, Mission: Space, and wireless headsets that explained the theme park in five languages.

The sales and profit quarterly results for fiscal 2002 are shown in Table 15.2. The first two quarters reflect the figures for the two companies before the merger, the last two quarters are after the merger. The last quarter's figures, ending October 31, 2002, made Carly Fiorina particularly proud: "During the fourth quarter of fiscal 2002, we returned to profitability after incurring nearly $3 billion in significant restructuring and other acquisition-related charges, which led to an overall operating loss of $2.5 billion in the third fiscal quarter. The charges were primarily for eliminating redundant positions and offices around the world, in-process research and development, and employee retention bonuses incurred in accordance with the acquisition-integration plans we drew up in the first half of the year."[7]

On the basis of HP's apparent success in its merger with Compaq, Fiorina began pitching to corporate America that you have to consolidate and you have to cut, and we can help you do it because we have done it ourselves. HP portrayed itself as The Greatest Case Study Ever Told. In merging its systems with Compaq's, HP could boast that it had erected a single communications network linking more than a quarter million PCs and handhelds; it handled 26 million e-mails a day. It also cut the number of software applications used from 7,000 to 5,000, and of components bought from 250,000 to 25,000.

We can perform similar miracles for you, Fiorina and her colleagues told such clients as General Electric, the Department of Homeland Security, and the Walt Disney Company, as well as many smaller firms. HP's approach, known as "adaptive enterprise," used new technology and smarter consulting to help organizations lower their overhead. HP guaranteed in written contracts that its adaptive model would save

TABLE 15.2. Quarterly HP Results Before and After the Merger

For Fiscal Year Ended October 31, 2002 (millions)			
	Before Merger		After Merger
	Jan. 31	April 30	July 31	Oct. 31
Net revenue	$11,383	$10,621	$16,536	$18,048
Earnings (loss) from operations	625	414	(2,476)	425

Source: Hewlett-Packard Company Reports.

Commentary: You can see from the profit realized for the fourth quarter ended October 31, 2002 that Fiorina had reason to feel that the merger had been well orchestrated and the two firms rather quickly integrated. The big loss in the third quarter reflected the extraordinary expenses and write-offs due to the merger, and these were now behind the company as it looked to 2003 and beyond.

[7] *HP Annual Report, 2002*, CEO Carly Fiorina's Statement, January 31, 2003, p. 25.

15–30 percent in operating costs. HP claimed that its own information technology budget had fallen 24 percent after the merger by making use of this adaptive approach.

The Threat of IBM

The most awesome competitor to HP's services and consulting business was IBM. IBM called its approach "on-demand computing," and it was well equipped to dominate this market. While IBM's annual revenue was only $9 billion more than HP's $72 billion, the market value of its stock, at $142 billion, was more than twice HP's. IBM made huge profits, more than double HP's, even though IBM employed more than twice as many people. IBM was already a major factor in higher-profit services, whereas HP still got most of its revenue from hardware, such as printers, servers, and PCs, many of which barely covered their costs. In a recent quarter, for example, HP's $5 billion PC business had a profit margin of only 0.025 percent. Furthermore, IBM had several years up on HP in promoting its Business Consulting Services, part of its $36.3 billion Global Services unit. And it could boast that it too had recently slashed $3 billion in costs by selling off three factories, shifting manufacturing to cheaper locations such as China and Ireland, and simplifying product designs. In the process it reduced inventories by a third, cut suppliers by half, and found other economies, such as packaging PCs in cheaper cardboard boxes and recycling components from old mainframes.[8] Table 15.3 shows selected comparisons between IBM and HP.

TABLE 15.3.   IBM and HP Selected Comparisons, 2002

	IBM	HP
Sales (000,000)	81,186	63,082
Profits (000,000)	8,060	(680)
Assets (000,000)	96,484	72,093
Annual Cash Flow	$13.8 bil.	$4.8 bil.
Annual R&D	about $5 bil.	about $4 bil.
Total patents	38,000	19,000
Patents in past year	3,288	3,000
Size of sales army	35,000	21,750

Sources: "The Top 500 Companies in America," *Forbes*, April 14, 2003, p. 144; Quentin Hardy, "We Did It," *Forbes*, August 11, 2003, p. 82.

Commentary: With the Compaq merger, HP approaches the size of IBM in sales and in assets. The loss in income is hardly a true comparison with IBM because of the nonrecurring expenses of the merger. HP shows surprising strength in R&D spending and in patents in the past year. But its much lower cash flow is an impediment against IBM, and the sales staff is far smaller.

---

[8] Daniel Lyons, "Back on the Chain Gang," *Forbes*, October 13, 2003, pp. 114, 116.

Still, HP could claim one of the fastest and most effective mergers in all of business, and by far the biggest in the computer industry. It saw its adaptive model as a technology and strategy that could be sold to other firms contemplating mergers and strategic changes. The first big test was a $3 billion Procter & Gamble contract, for which the bidding specifications ran 10,000 pages. HP was the underdog against the likes of IBM and Electronic Data Services. But it won the contract on the first round, selling the potential cost savings, data virtualization, and new across-the-company roles for the 2,000 P&G technicians that it agreed to involve in the deal. IBM claimed that HP took a big future loss on the P&G contract to get a trophy win. "It's good news to hear that," said HP veteran Ann Livermore, who ran the services business. "They're still underestimating our capabilities."[9]

With this win, selling moved into high gear at HP. See the following Information Box for a discussion of the importance of selling at all levels of an organization.

INFORMATION BOX

IMPORTANCE OF SELLING AT ALL LEVELS

Whether you are working for a small or a big company, whether you are the lowest employee, or a professional sales rep, or a high-level corporate executive, or even the CEO, you should always be selling—to employees, customers, your bosses, Wall Street. Maybe you don't realize it, but what you're really selling is yourself, although it may more ostensibly be a product, the company, or an idea.

Carly Fiorina certainly sold herself, to those who could make her CEO—for she was chosen from 300 other candidates. And she sold herself to the organization, if not to Walter Hewlett, so that its people accepted her and were motivated far beyond what they had been.

Including Fiorina, each of HP's 15 highest-ranking executives became a seller as well as a manager, calling on 7 to 15 major customer accounts. For example, Peter Blackmore, a former Compaq top executive, who ran the $11 billion-a-year large computer business, spent almost every weekday on an HP jet calling on major accounts, and also managed sales reps who brought in as much as $400 million a year each. "The thing you have to learn is the sheer scale of all this. Wherever you are, you have to get each process implanted right, or it won't work. People watch you all the time, your body language—you can't have an off day," he said. But Blackmore further expounded, "It's worth the exhaustion. It took IBM eight years to get their act together. We're going to beat them in two or three."[10]

Do you agree with this assessment of the importance of selling at all levels in an organization. Can you think of some exceptions?

---

[9] Hardy, p. 82.
[10] Adapted from Carol Hymowitz, "Business Leaders List Books That Inspire and Inform Their Work," *Wall Street Journal*, October 14, 2003, p. B1; Quentin Hardy, "We Did It," *Forbes*, August 11, 2003, pp. 80, 82.

IS THE "SUCCESSFUL" MERGER A DONE DEAL?

Skeptics of the HP merger with Compaq for a while appeared to be proven wrong. CEO Fiorina impressed analysts with cost cuts faster and deeper than they had ever imagined. She unveiled a host of new consumer products, and a new vision. Investors were willing to attribute anemic revenue growth to the deep recession in technological spending.

As the economy and stock market began to improve in 2003, HP stock flirted with a 52-week high of $24 a share until August 20, the day after HP announced it had missed its third-quarter earnings expectations. The explanation was slack European markets, which counted for 40 percent of company sales, plus price-cutting in personal computers and weakness in HP's enterprise businesses. The stock slid 11 percent on this news.

Dell was the big culprit affecting HP's computer sales, and it had turned in a strong quarter by contrast. HP failed to raise PC prices fast enough to keep pace with such components as computer memory. It also missed the boat in forecasting sales for flat-panel computer screens, and had to use expensive air freight to meet the demand. Then Dell announced it was cutting the prices of business computers by 22 percent.[11]

Fiorina planned to excite consumers, who had been steadier customers than corporate clients—consumer-related sales comprised 30 percent of total HP sales—with 150 new products in time for the back-to-school and Christmas seasons of 2003. HP was also testing a "store-in-store" concept at consumer electronics retailers like Circuit City. The HP area within these large retailers would emphasize how all HP products can work together, with assortments well beyond just PCs and printers, as, for example, media-center PCs that link home entertainment and computers together. But adding to HP's worries, Dell announced that it would cut prices on its personal computers and network servers. Sales for HP's personal-systems division, which included notebooks and desktops, rose 4.5 percent in the third quarter, but the division remained unprofitable.

Printers and ink refills have long carried HP, with rising sales and profits. Yet the enterprise-systems group, which generated about 20 percent of total revenue, remained the last of HP's four main businesses to still be in the red as fiscal 2003 drew to a close. The turnaround of the systems group, which made server computers, storage devices, and related software used by large corporations and agencies, was plagued by competition from Dell and IBM, and slow tech spending by corporate customers. Unless this could quickly be turned around, it would represent a continuing black mark on the controversial $19 billion Compaq purchase, which had partly been undertaken to repair the enterprise business.[12]

Whether the merger with Compaq was a model of how best to handle mergers was still unproven at this point.

---

[11] Quentin Hardy, "HP Slips Up," *Forbes*, September 15, 2003, p. 42.

[12] For more details, see Amy Tsao, "Carly Fiorina's Next Big Challenge," *Business Week online*, August 22, 2003; Pui-Wing Tam, "Man on the Hot Seat at HP's Struggling Enterprise Unit," *Wall Street Journal*, August 19, 2003, pp. B1 and B5.

The situation—and especially the stock price of HP—had not improved by the beginning of 2005. The closing price by the end of January was under $20 a share, which was 15 percent less than when the Compaq deal was announced in September 2001, and 50 percent less than when Fiorina was named CEO in July 1999. (Admittedly, the tech sector had not been robust in the previous four years, but HP had fallen considerably more than its major competitors, IBM and Dell.) The HP board began considering a reorganization that would distribute some of Fiorina's key day-to-day responsibilities to other executives. "She has tremendous abilities" one person close to the situation said. "But she shouldn't be running everything every day. She is very hands on, and that slows things."[13]

Other criticisms centered on the Compaq merger. This was Fiorina's "Get-Big" strategy to compete with IBM. But it seemed to have led to complex and myriad problems. HP's PC unit was taking a beating from Dell. It found itself faltering against IBM in servicing big corporate clients, and had been unable to come up with any big new consumer gadgets. A controversy was brewing around the issue of whether HP would be better off broken into pieces rather than keeping the company whole. The example of IBM was given to support breaking up: "IBM had the courage recently to exit the bleak PC business. By contrast, HP continued to hold fast."[14]

HP's Board Ousts Fiorina

Abruptly, on February 9, 2005, the board fired Fiorina, after she resisted the directors' plan for her to cede some day-to-day authority to the heads of HP's key business units. This was just before she had been scheduled to attend a meeting at the White House with members of the Business Roundtable. Just a few weeks later, HP reported a 10 percent increase in revenue for its first fiscal quarter, better than expected.

AFTER CARLY

Mark Hurd was the man chosen to succeed Fiorina. He had spent 25 years at electronic cash-register maker NCR, working up from a sales job to CEO. Some critics thought Carly was "full of herself and out of touch," whereas Mark Hurd was the anti-Carly, "ignoring all fluff for execution." He became a star of Wall Street, as manifested by HP shareholder value pushing up over 50 percent after he took over. Dell had been almost flat during this time, while IBM shareholders lost money.

The biggest criticisms against Fiorina focused on the 2002 Compaq acquisition. But Hurd saw nothing wrong with this and other elements of her strategy. He did not break up the company along pre-merger lines, as Fiorina's loudest critics sought. She had planned to cut 10,000 to 12,000 jobs; Hurd cut 15,000. She had predicted

---

[13] Pui Wing Tam, "Hewlett-Packard Board Considers a Reorganization," *Wall Street Journal*, January 24, 2005, pp. A1 and A5.

[14] Jesse Eisinger, "Carly Fiorina Fails at Hewlett-Packard After Betting Badly," *Wall Street Journal*, January 26, 2005, pp. C1 and C2; Ben Elgin, "Carly's Challenge," *Business Week*, December 13, 2004, pp. 98–108.

that HP would be the biggest tech company in the world, and its revenue in 2006 was $87 billion, about even with IBM's. HP was number two worldwide to Dell in PCs, number one in windows, Linux servers, and printers, and number four in tech services. Total operating expenses were 21.5 percent in 2001. By 2006, they were down to about 16 percent. But all but one percentage point of the decline happened before Hurd's cost-cutting campaign took hold.

Some analysts began asking who deserved the credit. Hurd is quick to say that in HP's PC business, "there has been a prolonged sustained march in performance that, frankly, predates me." One analyst suggested that HP's directors "in the end, got the best of both worlds—a charismatic CEO who brought about a hotly contested but transformational merger, and a no-nonsense, operations-oriented CEO determined to make the combined company work."[15]

Latest Developments

In the summer of 2006, a nasty scandal wracked HP. The company began investigating suspected leaks by directors to the *Wall Street Journal, Business Week,* and the *New York Times* that the board was unhappy with then-CEO Fiorina. The hired investigators used a range of extraordinary tactics, including "pretexting," or the use of deception to obtain phone records of board members and employees, booby-trapped e-mail to invade a reporter's computer, impersonating corporate officials, and physical surveillance of at least one director and a journalist. Criminal investigations were under way by the FBI and the California attorney general. In this atmosphere, chairman Patricia Dunn resigned, as did the general counsel and several directors. The House Energy and Commerce Committee demanded to know how such tawdry tactics could have been used. Pretexting is "an invasion of privacy and probably is illegal," the chairman of the panel said, and wondered why no one "had the good sense and courage to say 'Stop.'" Patricia Dunn and Mark Hurd refused to "accept personal responsibility for what happened." The former general counsel and nine other HP attorneys and investigators invoked the Fifth Amendment right against self-incrimination, and refused to testify.[16]

ANALYSIS

Unlike many other mergers that quickly soured, such as Snapple in Chapter 8 and Newell Rubbermaid in Chapter 9, HP's merger with Compaq at first seemed a qualified success, even though the combined company still had profitability problems. After all, despite being larger now, it still faced the formidable competition of IBM

---

[15] Alan Murray, "HP Lost Faith in Carly, But Not in Merger," *Wall Street Journal,* May 24, 2006, p. A2. For a sampling of the many articles on this newsworthy story, also see Chana R. Schoenberger, "Carly Resurrected," *Forbes,* July 24, 2006; Christopher Lawton, "Hewlett-Packard's Net Income Increases 51%," *Wall Street Journal* , May 17, 2006, p. A3.

[16] Marilyn Geewax, *Cox News Service,* as reported in *Cleveland Plain Dealer,* September 29, 2006, pp. C1 and C5.

and Dell Computer. The boom in corporate high-tech spending had ended and long-term growth prospects for the industry no longer seemed robust, while a number of marginal firms were on the ropes. With the merger, HP seemed poised to take advantage of a revival of corporate interest, and perhaps a regeneration of consumer interest from appealing new products. All the while, HP still dominated the high-profit ink-refill market. We can identify the major factors that seemed to promise a successful merger:

First of all, it was not a hostile acquisition. Both parties believed that coming together would strengthen the resulting firm, making it a bigger power in the market, and bringing substantial cost savings.

Thorough and objective planning of the merger. For four months before the merger was even announced, a top-level committee was studying the feasibility and planning for the integration of the two organizations. After the approval of the merger, months more of detailed preparation were involved. All conceivable problems or stumbling points were identified and resolved, with prompt implementation once the merger was officially approved.

Involvement of executives and staffs of both firms. The study group began with not quite 100 employees and had 2,500 by the merger's completion. Top-level executives and staff members of both firms participated, apparently in a spirit of equality and objectivity, and many stayed with the new organization.

Redundancies were avoided at all costs. Early disagreements or indecisions were curbed by HP strategist Robert Napier. "Every business decision triggers an IT (information technology) event," he declared. This would force the new HP to reconfigure its systems, which would be costly and time consuming. So a commitment was made to pick just one of the two companies' products and practices and make it law. The new merger mantra became: "Adopt and go."[17]

Compatibility and congeniality were sought. Fiorina joined the rather close-knit HP as an outsider, and had to strive to gain acceptance. The bitter merger battle with Walter Hewlett served to unite most of the organization behind Fiorina. The goodwill apparently carried over with the acceptance of Compaq employees as part of the HP team, even though some 17,000 jobs were eliminated because of redundancies.

Fiorina admitted that one of the toughest aspects of the integration was the reduction of the workforce through a combination of layoffs, early retirements, and attrition. "Although layoffs are never easy, we worked hard to conduct this process with dignity and compassion, recognizing the many contributions our employees had made during their careers."[18]

Monday-Morning Quarterbacking After the Ouster

Perhaps Fiorina could have been a better administrator. Heading a $56 billion firm, perhaps she needed to delegate more, not be too hands-on. Lack of delegation is not an uncommon fault of executives, but it can limit their effectiveness in higher positions. She resisted the idea of an assistant or vice chairman, and maybe this

[17] Hardy, p. 81.
[18] *HP's 2002 Annual Report*, p. 23.

should have been reconsidered. She was in a difficult situation, with the might of Dell in PCs, and the powerful IBM at the other extreme of the industry. Add to this a resentful Walter Hewlett, who was still influential with the board, and perhaps Fiorina's doom was sealed. (At the end of the chapter, in the hands-on and debate exercises, we invite students to address Fiorina's situation in 2005 before the abrupt termination decision, and also whether the company should have been broken up, as some experts thought, perhaps into printing and nonprinting operations, or into consumer and corporate businesses.)

People rushed to judgment in the days following the ouster news. Shareholders blamed her for the sagging stock price. Long-term employees condemned her for upsetting the company's paternalistic culture. Industry analysts faulted her for HP's sluggish computer business. While Fiorina was a dynamic and charismatic leader who was widely esteemed in the business world, inside HP her rather autocratic management style stirred deep animosity from some employees, and several high-level executives had quit for other positions. Some employees reportedly reacted to her ouster with "jubilant" champagne toasts.[19]

Fiorina seems to have received little credit for the planning and organization that made the merger with Compaq what most experts now have to concede is a legitimate success. As the CEO and primary mover in this merger, this may prove to have been her finest hour.

❖ ❖ ❖

Invitation to Make Your Own Analysis and Conclusions

What could Carly have done differently to have secured her position at HP?

❖ ❖ ❖

WHAT CAN BE LEARNED?

Don't rush into the merger or acquisition. — Major blunders occur when firms spend billions of dollars for acquisitions without careful research and reasoned judgment. Sometimes it seems that CEOs are throwing around shareholders' money for a crap shoot. Sometimes they get so caught up in the acquisitions game, especially if another firm is also interested in the acquisition, that a bidding war drives up prices beyond the reasonable.

Enough time should be taken to confirm what is a fair price and where the limit should be. Enough research needs to be done to prevent surprises. Ideally, the investigation should go beyond the numbers and records—the quantitative

---

[19] Pui-Wing Tam, "Fallen Star: HP's Board Ousts Fiorina as CEO," *Wall Street Journal*, February 10, 2005, pp. A1 and A8.

data—and look for qualitative information from employees, customers, and suppliers. For example, do the firm and its brands have a good reputation, a so-so one, or a negative one? Such information can hardly be gained in just a few weeks.

How compatible are the two organizations?—While complete compatibility is hardly possible, especially in hostile acquisitions, it should be a major factor in the decision. Compatibility encompasses not only personnel in the two organizations and any cultural differences that may make assimilation difficult, but products, distribution channels, ways of doing business, and a number of other factors. We have seen the problem of lack of compatibility in several other cases, and the nasty surprises it engendered.

Redundancies should be identified and decisions made about them.—We saw in this case superb attention given to identifying redundant products and operations and the decisions to remove duplications. Sometimes HP's product or way of doing things was eliminated; other times Compaq's. The issues were already being decided before the merger was even announced. Such efforts brought profitable integration of the merger within a year.

One major argument for a merger is that two firms can thereby streamline separate operations by combining their various entities into one. For example, two separate sales forces might be combined into one; similarly with information technology, human resource, and other staff departments. Therefore, total costs should be less than they would be with two separate firms. If the matter of redundancy is not quickly resolved, any cost benefits of the merger are delayed. Yet, sometimes the result of a poorly researched merger is an indigestible mess.

Assumptions should be defended.—It is easy when caught up in the merger game, especially in a bidding war, to assume all kinds of optimistic things, such as a synergy that does not exist, a compatibility that can never be achieved, a sales potential that is not to be realized. Optimistic assumptions have no place in merger decisions. So much money is involved, so much executive and staff time will be needed, that the bad merger decision can torment the firm and its shareholders for years to come. Objectivity and conservative projections seem called for.

Top management should insist that assumptions and their reasoning be defended, at least as much as possible in an uncertain future. It might be prudent to consider a worst-case scenario: What if? A *devil's advocate* can often be very worthwhile, yet is too seldom utilized.

The power of a charismatic leader.—Carly Fiorina was a charismatic leader. Even though new to the HP organization, she seemed able to motivate employees and managers to jump-start the innovation machine, to escape the staid bureaucratic culture that had crept into the organization in recent years. She appeared able to get key people in both firms to support the Compaq merger and work together to make it work. Mergers can succeed without charisma, but it helps if enthusiasm and commitment can be instilled. Yet a charismatic leader can make enemies, can arouse jealousies that undermine and detract. One wonders if this was not a factor in the HP organization.

CONSIDER

Can you think of other learning insights?

QUESTIONS

1. We noted the four criteria proposed by the HP search committee for the new CEO. Do you think human relations skills should have been a fifth? Why or why not? Can you think of other criteria that might have been added?

2. "Tradition has no place in corporate thinking today." Discuss this statement.

3. Giant organizations are often plagued with cumbersome bureaucracies. Discuss how this tendency could be prevented as an organization grows to large size over many years.

4. Playing a *devil's advocate*, present the case against the Compaq merger. (You may want to research the arguments raised by Walter Hewett in his aggressive campaign against the merger.)

5. "HP is gouging the consumer in charging such high prices for its ink-refill cartridges. Sure, it's a high-profit item, but such profits cross the line and are obscene." Discuss.

6. Do you think the loss of 17,000 jobs in the merger was laudatory, or should it be condemned? What would swing your opinion?

7. Should all redundancies be eliminated? Can you think of any that might be worth continuing?

HANDS-ON EXERCISES

1. You have been asked by Carly Fiorina to draw up a rationale for eliminating 17,000 jobs. She wants it to be as tactful and persuasive as possible.

2. Be a *devil's advocate* and argue against the elimination of 17,000 jobs.

3. Michael Dell, founder and CEO of Dell Computer, had his sights set on invading HP's lucrative printer and ink-refill business. As an adviser to Carly Fiorina, what action, if any, would you recommend taking to try to thwart Dell's incursion. Be prepared to support your recommendations.

4. Place yourself in the position of Carly Fiorina at the beginning of 2005, facing a critical board, skeptical stockholders, and a negative press. Lay out your strategy to protect your position. Do you think this would have saved her job? Why or why not?

TEAM DEBATE EXERCISES

1. The search committee for a new CEO is seriously considering Carly Fiorina. Based on the information in the case, debate the controversy: should we hire this woman who is an outsider, or look for someone else among our 300 candidates?

2. In the planning for the implementation of the merger, it has been proposed that all redundancies should be eliminated, and that any commonalities of products and practices be resolved by axing one and combining into the other. Debate this draconian proposal.

3. Debate the controversy of breaking up HP into two or three separate units. The group proposing the breakup will need to specify which parts should be spun off, and why.

INVITATION TO RESEARCH

How has HP's operating performance fared since 2006? Has the stock price continued to rise above the 30s? Has Dell become a bigger factor in this market? Has price competition become more aggressive in the ink-refill market? Whatever happened to Walter Hewlett? What is Fiorina doing now?

CHAPTER SIXTEEN

Wal-Mart: A Tottering Giant

*I*n March 1992, Sam Walton passed away after a two-year battle with bone cancer. Perhaps the most admired businessman of his era, he had founded Wal-Mart Stores with the concept of discount stores in small towns and had brought it to the lofty stature of the biggest retailer in the United States, and then the world—ahead of the decades-long leaders, Sears and JCPenney, and in 1990, pushing ahead of an earlier great discount-store success, Kmart.

Walton's successors continued his legacy well. By the end of fiscal 1998, Wal-Mart's sales of $137.6 billion made it one of the largest corporations in the world; by 2002 sales were $217.8 billion, and it had knocked ExxonMobil out of first place.

Yet a growing number of people were questioning how Wal-Mart was using its gargantuan power, some seeing it becoming the antithesis of fair competition through questionable practices toward suppliers, competitors, employees, and the communities where its stores were located. Was Wal-Mart becoming too big? Would its growth rate ever slow?

THE EARLY YEARS OF SAM WALTON

Samuel Moore Walton was born in Kingfisher, Oklahoma, on March 29, 1917. He and his brother, James, born three years later, were reared in a family that valued hard work and thrift. They grew up in Missouri in the depths of the Great Depression.

By the time Walton entered eighth grade in Shebina, Oklahoma, he was already exhibiting the character traits that would dominate his future life: quiet and soft spoken, but a natural leader who became class president and captain of the football team. He even became the first Eagle Scout in Shebina's history.

At the University of Missouri, Walton excelled in academics and athletics. He worked his way through college by delivering newspapers, working in a five-and-dime store, life-guarding, and waiting tables at the university.

After his graduation in 1940, Walton joined the JCPenney Company and became a management trainee at the store in Des Moines, Iowa. There he applied his work ethic, competed to become Penney's most promising new man, and became imbued with the Penney philosophy of catering to smaller towns and having "associates" instead of employees or clerks. He also met J. C. Penney himself and was intrigued with his habit of strolling around stores and personally meeting and observing customers and salespeople. After 18 months, Walton left Penney's for the U.S. Army, but what he had learned in the Penney store in Des Moines was to shape his future ideas.

WAL-MART'S GROWTH TO THE BIGGEST RETAILER

Sam Walton was discharged from the Army in August 1945. By chance he stumbled on an opportunity to buy the franchise of a Ben Franklin variety store in Newport, Arkansas, and he opened it a month later. The lease arrangement with the building's owner did not work out, so he eventually relocated in Bentonville, Arkansas, in 1950. During the 1950s and early 1960s, Walton worked up to 15 Ben Franklin franchises. In the winter of 1962, he proposed at a Ben Franklin board meeting that the company should aggressively turn its efforts to discounting, citing the great potential of this emerging retail phenomenon. The company refused to consider such an innovative idea, so Walton and his brother went ahead anyway. They opened a Discount City in Rogers, Arkansas, in 1962; and then a second store in Harrison, Arkansas, in 1964. They incorporated the business as Wal-Mart Stores on October 31, 1969, and it became a publicly held company a year later. In 1970, Walton also opened his first distribution center and general office: a 72,000-square-foot complex in Bentonville, Arkansas. In 1972, Wal-Mart became listed on the New York Stock Exchange.

In 1976, Walton severed ties with Ben Franklin in order to concentrate on expanding Wal-Mart. His operations now extended to small towns in Arkansas, Missouri, Kansas, and Oklahoma. The essence of Walton's management philosophy during these building years was that of an old-fashioned entrepreneur; Walton personally roamed through his own stores, as well as those of competitors, always looking for new ideas in mass-merchandising to maximize sales at attractive prices.

Rather than confront the major retailers—department stores, chains such as Penney's and Sears, and the strong discounters such as Kmart—Walton confined his efforts to smaller cities, places shunned by the major retailers as having insufficient market potential. But he saw these small markets as a strategic window of opportunity if tapped by an aggressive firm.

Growth accelerated. By the end of 1975 Walton had 104 stores with nearly 6,000 employees and annual sales of $236 million, which generated $6 million net profit. The next year, the number of stores increased to 125, employees to 7,500, and sales to $340 million, with $11.5 million in profit.

Table 16.1 compares Wal-Mart's sales growth and number of stores with Kmart, its major competitor, from 1980 to 1990, the decade that ended with Wal-Mart forging ahead to become the biggest retailer. By the end of 1990, Wal-Mart had 1,573 stores located in 35 states.

TABLE 16.1.   **Comparison of Growth in Sales and Number of Stores, Wal-Mart and Kmart, 1980–1990**

	Kmart		Wal-Mart	
	Sales (millions)	Number of Stores	Sales (millions)	Number of Stores
1980	$14,204	1,772	$1,643	330
1981	16,527	2,055	2,445	491
1982	16,772	2,117	3,376	551
1983	18,597	2,160	4,667	642
1984	20,762	2,173	6,401	745
1985	22,035	2,332	8,451	859
1986	23,035	2,342	11,909	980
1987	25,627	2,273	15,959	1,114
1988	27,301	2,307	20,649	1,259
1989	29,533	2,361	25,810	1,402
1990	32,070	2,350	32,602	1,573

Source: Company annual reports.

Commentary: Several of these statistics are of particular interest. First, the comparison of Wal-Mart and Kmart sales from 1980 to 1990, slightly more than one decade, show Wal-Mart's tremendous growth rate, starting at little more than 10 percent of Kmart sales figures to forge ahead by 1990. And Kmart was no slouch during this period.

Second, Wal-Mart achieved its leadership in total sales with almost 800 fewer stores than Kmart had. This means that Wal-Mart's stores were achieving much higher sales volume than Kmart's, a fact that is further borne out by the statistics in Table 16.3

Some of these new stores were Wal-Mart SuperCenters, considerably larger than regular Wal-Marts, having a warehouse-style food outlet under the same roof as the discount store. While these food stores carried items comparable to the products in a regular urban supermarket, the assortment and service were superior to most direct competitors in the smaller cities. The key advantage of adding food to general-merchandise discount stores was greater traffic: Because customers shop weekly for groceries, they are exposed to other merchandise in the stores far more than would otherwise be the case.

Wal-Mart by now was also opening another category of stores: Sam's Wholesale, also known as Sam's Clubs. First introduced in 1984, by 1991 there were 148. The wholesale-club concept came about as regular discount stores seemed to be reaching saturation in some locations. The wholesale warehouse went a step further in discounting.

Sam's Clubs were large, ranging up to 135,000 square feet. Each store was a membership-only operation, and qualified members included businesses and members of certain groups, such as government employees and credit union members. Although the stores were huge, they carried less than 5 percent of the total variety of items carried by regular discount stores. Assortments were limited to fast-moving home goods and apparel, generally name brands, with prices 8 to 10 percent over cost, well under those of discount stores and department and specialty stores. Sam's Clubs were the initial entry for Wal-Mart into the big metropolitan markets it had avoided in its early years.

In December 1987 Wal-Mart opened its newest merchandising concept, Hyper-mart USA, in Garland, Texas, a suburb of Dallas. The hypermart offered a combination of groceries and general merchandise in over 200,000 square feet of selling space. The stores also included a variety of fast-food and service shops, such as beauty shops, shoe repair, and dry cleaners. Thus, an atmosphere was created of one-stop shopping. But in spite of optimistic beginnings, the hypermart idea proved unsuccessful and it was replaced with the scaled-down version, the SuperCenter.

For a comparison of the sales and profitability of Wal-Mart with Kmart, Sears, and JCPenney from 1980 to 1990, see Table 16.2. Note that profitability comparisons include both operating profit as a percentage of sales, and the more valid measure of profitability, the return on equity, that is, the return on the money invested in the enterprise. From this table we see the awesome growth of Wal-Mart in sales and profitability compared with its nearest competitors. Table 16.3 shows another operational comparison, this time the average sales per store for Wal-Mart and Kmart. And again, the comparison shows the great growth performance of Wal-Mart.

THE FUTURE WITHOUT SAM WALTON

On March 17, 1992, President George H.W. Bush awarded Sam Walton the Medal of Freedom, a capstone among his other honors, which included Man of the Year, the Horatio Alger Award in 1984, and Retailer of the Decade in 1989. Unfortunately, Walton did not live long to enjoy this high honor; he died of cancer nine days later, on March 26, 1992, just four days short of his seventy-fifth birthday.

David Glass, 53 years old, assumed the role of president and chief executive officer. Glass was known for his hard-driving managerial style. He had gained his retail experience at a small supermarket chain in Springfield, Missouri, and joined Wal-Mart as executive vice president for finance in 1976. He was named president and chief operating officer in 1984, while Sam Walton kept the position of chief executive officer. About the transition, Glass said: "There's no transition to make, because the principles and basic values he [Walton] used in founding this company were so sound and so universally accepted . . . We'll be fine as long as we never lose our responsiveness to the customer."[1]

A new generation now was entrusted to continue the successful growth as Wal-Mart entered the tougher competitive environment of U.S. metropolitan areas, and then the world. By 1995, sales were $82 billion and only three Fortune 500 companies had higher sales: General Motors, Ford, and Exxon.

---

[1] Susan Caminiti, "What Ails Retailing," *Fortune*, January 30, 1989, p. 61.

TABLE 16.2. 10-Year Comparison of Gross Revenues, Percentage of Operating Margin, and Return on Equity for Wal-Mart and Its Competitors[a]

| | Wal-Mart | | | Kmart | | | Sears | | | JCPenney | | |
| | Gross Revenue | % Operating Profit Margin | Equity Return % | Gross Revenue | % Operating Profit Margin | Equity Return % | Gross Revenue | % Operating Profit Margin | Equity Return % | Gross Revenue | % Operating Profit Margin | Equity Return % |
Year												
1981	$2,445.0	5.6	25.6	$16,527.0	2.2	9.0	$27,357	7.2	8.2	$11,860	7.5	13.2
1882	3,376.3	7.8	25.4	17,040.0	4.3	10.1	30,020	8.8	10.1	11,414	8.3	13.3
1983	4,666.9	8.3	26.6	18,878.9	6.0	16.7	35,883	9.7	14.4	12,078	8.7	13.1
1984	6,400.9	8.5	27.5	21,095.9	6.7	15.4	38,828	10.5	14.1	13,451	7.8	11.4
1985	8,451.5	7.2	25.6	22,420.0	6.2	14.4	40,715	9.5	11.5	13,747	7.7	9.8
1986	11,909.1	7.1	26.6	23,812.1	5.7	14.5	44,282	9.1	10.4	15,151	8.6	11.0
1987	15,959.3	6.8	27.8	25,626.6	5.8	15.7	48,439	8.5	12.1	15,747	9.1	14.6
1988	20,649.0	6.4	27.8	27,301.4	6.5	16.0	50,251	9.2	3.0	15,296	8.3	20.4
1989	25,810.7	6.5	27.1	29,532.7	5.8	6.5	53,794	9.2	10.6	16,405	9.2	18.4
1990	32,601.6	6.0	24.1	32,070.0	5.4	14.0	55,971	7.4	7.0	16,365	2.4	15.6

[a]Gross revenue is in $ billions.

Source: Company annual reports.

Commentary: The comparison with major competitors shows Wal-Mart far exceeding its rivals in revenue growth. The operating profit percentage exceeds Kmart's for most years, but Sears and Penney look better here. However, the true measure of profitability is return on equity, and here Wal-Mart shines: It indeed is a very profitable operation, while offering consumers attractive prices.

TABLE 16.3. Average Sales per Store,
Wal-Mart and Kmart, 1980–1990

	Kmart	Wal-Mart
1980	$8,015,801	$4,978,788
1981	8,042,338	4,979,633
1982	7,922,532	6,127,042
1983	8,609,722	7,269,470
1984	9,554,533	8,591,946
1985	9,448,970	9,838,184
1986	9,835,611	12,152,040
1987	11,274,527	14,325,852
1988	11,833,983	16,401,111
1989	12,508,682	18,409,415
1990	13,646,808	20,726,001

Source: Computed from Table 16.1.

Commentary: The great increase in sales per store for
Wal-Mart is particularly noteworthy. In 1980 an average
Wal-Mart store's sales was hardly one-half that of an average
Kmart. By 1990 the average Wal-Mart store was generating
more than 50 percent more sales than an average Kmart.

INTO THE NEW MILLENNIUM

In 2001 Wal-Mart knocked off ExxonMobil to become the world's biggest firm in
revenues, with sales of $217.8 billion to ExxonMobil's $187.5 billion. General Motors's
sales were $177.3 billion, and Ford, in fourth place, had sales of $162.4 billion.[2] Table
16.4 shows selected statistics of operating performance at the beginning and end of
the decade 1992–2002. Wal-Mart's former closest retail rivals had been left in the
dust by 2002, as can be readily seen below:

2002	Revenues (billions)	% Change since 2001
Sears	$41.1	0.3
Target	39.9	8.1
Kmart	36.9	1.1
Penney	32.0	0.5
Wal-Mart	217.8	13.8

Its nearest rival up to 1990, the one that dominated the retail environment in the
early days of Wal-Mart, was Kmart. But Kmart slid into Chapter 11 bankruptcy, and
subsequently a hedge fund merged it with Sears (see Chapter 14 for the details).

[2] "Sales Super 500," *Forbes*, April 15, 2002, p. 168.

TABLE 16.4. Wal-Mart Selected Growth Statistics,
1993–2002

	2002	1993
Net sales (millions)	$217,799	$55,484
Net income (millions)	$6,671	$1,995
Number of associates	1,383,000	434,000
Number of U.S. Wal-Mart stores	1,647	1,848
Number of U.S. SuperCenters	1,066	34
Number of U.S. Sam's Clubs	500	256
International units	1,170	10

Source: Wal-Mart annual reports

Commentary: Here we see a fourfold increase in sales in these 10 years. Income had only a little more than a threefold increase, but was still impressive. Of particular interest is the decrease in number of U.S. Wal-Mart stores in producing these increases, but the big growth was in Supercenters and Sam's Clubs, and the biggest of all was in international units, but then Wal-Mart had barely entered the international arena in 1993.

With the millennium approaching, and only a short step away from becoming the world's largest firm, Wal-Mart turned to other growth opportunities. It bought Asda Group PLC, a large British supermarket chain, thereby expanding its international presence. In the United States, it not only accelerated building discount-grocery SuperCenters, but also expanded its smallish, (40,000-square-foot) Neighborhood Markets, designed to fill the gaps between convenience stores and Wal-Mart's big SuperCenters. Wal-Mart also bought a small savings bank in Oklahoma that could pave the way for bringing to banking its low prices for such services as check cashing, credit cards, and loans.

Invasion of Foreign Markets

Overseas expansion created the most waves. European merchants and labor unions ran scared, but consumers stood to benefit enormously: "Its low-pricing policies and customer-friendly attitude is likely to change the face of British retailing and its reputation for high prices and surly service," one scribe wrote.[3]

The Wal-Mart threat led two rival French retailers to merge in a $16-billion-dollar deal, though the combined company would still be far smaller than Wal-Mart. The battle was perhaps fiercest in Germany, where Wal-Mart had 95 stores. Competitors began staying open longer and improving customer courtesy. The biggest obstacle, however, was Germany's regulatory agency, which closely monitored whether prices were too low, while powerful trade unions worried that price wars would result in store closures and job losses.

---

[3] Ernest Beck, "The Wal-Mart Is Coming! And Shopping for the British May Never Be the Same," *Wall Street Journal*, June 16, 1999, p. A23.

To reduce costs, Wal-Mart began buying globally, negotiating one price for stores worldwide. In so doing, it changed the organization to combine some domestic and international operations, including buying, new store planning and marketing.[4]

With few prime sites in the United States remaining untapped for stores, Wal-Mart continued an aggressive expansion worldwide, but some of its efforts were not very successful. For example, in Germany Wal-Mart still had losses five years after buying two local chains to gain entry into the market. German consumers were very price sensitive, and Wal-Mart failed to beat competitors who quickly undercut it and beefed up their private-label goods. Wal-Mart's use of greeters was met with disdain by German shoppers. These experiences cast doubt on whether the Wal-Mart model was suitable in every international market.

More than 80 percent of Wal-Mart's international revenue came from Canada, Mexico, and the U.K. In China it struggled with a primitive supply chain. In Japan it faced a powerful but backward retail ecosystem. While Wal-Mart has done well in Mexico, it faced stronger competitors in the huge markets of Brazil and Argentina. It made some mistakes along the way. It entered Hong Kong in 1994 and left two years later after bad decisions on merchandise selection and location. It entered Indonesia in 1996, but fled after a Jakarta store was looted and torched in the 1997–98 riots. In South Korea, its SuperCenters misread local tastes, and locations were too far outside city centers.

Wal-Mart's impact on the world went beyond its store openings overseas. It imported many goods from low-wage countries such as China, thereby eliminating manufacturing jobs and depressing wage growth in the United States. But by selling goods for less, Wal-Mart raised living standards and created 800,000 jobs worldwide, in addition to the labor needed for construction and distribution in these countries.[5]

INGREDIENTS OF SUCCESS

Management Style and Employee Orientation

Sam Walton cultivated a management style that emphasized individual initiative and autonomy over close supervision. He constantly reminded employees that they were vital to the success of the company, that they were essentially "running their own business," that they were "associates" or "partners" in the business, rather than simply employees.

In his employee-relations philosophy, Walton borrowed from James Cash Penney, founder of the JCPenney Company, and his formulation of the "Penney idea" in 1913. The Penney idea also stressed the desirability of constantly improving the human factor, of rewarding associates through participation in what the business produces, and of appraising every policy and action to see whether it squares with what is right and just.

[4] Emily Nelson, "Wal-Mart Revamps International Unit to Decrease Costs," *Wall Street Journal*, August 10, 1999, p. A6; David Woodruff and John Carreyrou, "French Retailers Create New Wal-Mart Rival," *Wall Street Journal*, August 31, 1999, p. A14.
[5] Bruce Upbin, "Wall-to-Wall Wal-Mart," *Forbes*, April 12, 2004, pp. 76–85.

Walton emphasized bottoms-up communication, thereby providing a free flow of ideas throughout the company. For example, the "people greeter" concept (described in the Information Box: Greeters) was implemented in 1983 as a result of a suggestion received from an employee in a store in Louisiana. This idea proved so successful that it has been adopted by Kmart, some department stores, and even shopping malls.

INFORMATION BOX

GREETERS

All customers entering Wal-Mart stores encounter a store employee assigned to welcome them, give advice on where to find things, and help with exchanges or refunds. These "greeters" thank people exiting the store, while unobtrusively observing any indications of shoplifting.

Many retailers staff exits and entrances; what makes Wal-Mart's greeters unique is their friendliness and patience. Wal-Mart has found that retirees supplementing pensions usually make the best greeters and are most appreciated by customers. As noted before, this idea was suggested by an employee (associate); Sam Walton liked the idea, and it became a company-wide practice.

Do you personally like the idea of a store employee greeting you as you enter and leave an establishment? On balance, do you think the greeter idea is a plus or a minus? Explain.

Another example of listening to employees' ideas came when an assistant manager in an Alabama store ordered too many Moon Pie marshmallow sandwiches. The store manager told him to use his imagination to sell the excess, so John Love came up with the idea of holding the first World Championship Moon Pie Eating Contest. It was held in the store's parking lot and became so successful that it became a yearly event, drawing spectators not only from the community but from all over Alabama as well as surrounding states.[6]

In 1972 Wal-Mart instituted a profit-sharing plan that enabled associates to share in the company's yearly profits. As one celebrated example of the benefits of profit sharing, Shirley Cox worked as an office cashier earning $7.10 an hour. When she retired after 24 years, her profit sharing amounted to $220,127.[7] In addition, associates could participate in a payroll stock-purchase plan with Wal-Mart contributing part of the cost.

The Sam Walton philosophy was to create a friendly, "down-home," family atmosphere in his stores. He described it as a "whistle while you work philosophy," one that stressed the importance of having fun while working because you can work

---

[6] Don Longo, "Associate Involvement Spurs Gains," *Discount Store News*, December 18, 1989, p. 83.
[7] Cited in Vance H. Trimble, *Sam Walton: The Inside Story of America's Richest Man*, New York: Dutton, 1990, p. 233.

better if you enjoy yourself. He was concerned about losing this atmosphere: "The bigger Wal-Mart gets, the more essential it is that we think small. Because that's exactly how we have become a huge corporation—by not acting like one."[8]

Another incentive spurred employees to reduce shrinkage (i.e., the loss of merchandise due to shoplifting, carelessness, and employee theft). Employees were given $200 each a year if shrinkage limits were met, and they became detectives watching shoppers and each other. In 1989, Wal-Mart's shrinkage rate was 1 percent of sales, well below the industry average.[9]

A rather simple way to make employees feel part of the operation was regular sharing of statistics about the store's performance, including profits, purchases, sales, and markdowns. Many employees thought of Wal-Mart as their own company.

Not the least of the open and people-oriented management practices was what Walton called MBWA, Management by Walking Around. Managers, from store level to headquarters, walked around the stores to stay familiar with what was going on, talk to the associates, and encourage associates to share their ideas and concerns. Such interactions brought a personal touch usually lacking in large firms.

Not surprisingly, unions have not fared well at Wal-Mart. Walton argued that in his "family environment," associates had better wages, benefits, and bonuses than any union could get for them. In addition, he maintained that the bonuses and profit sharing were inducements far better than anything a union could negotiate. (Today, Wal-Mart has come under criticism for some of its employee relations, especially health benefits and handling of overtime.)

State-of-the-Art Technology

The decentralized management style led to a team approach to decision-making. A huge telecommunications system permitted headquarters to easily communicate with stores. In addition, home-office management teams, using company airplanes, visited stores to assess their operations and any problems and to coordinate needed merchandise transfers among stores. A master computer tracked the company's complex distribution system.

Small-Town Invasion Strategy

Adopting a strategy similar to that of the JCPenney Company over half a century before, Wal-Mart for many years shunned big cities and kept to smaller towns where competition consisted only of local merchants and small outlets of a few chains, such as Woolworth, Gamble, and Penney.

These merchants typically offered only limited assortments of merchandise, had no Sunday or evening hours, and charged substantially higher prices than would be found in the more competitive big-city environments. Larger retailers, especially discount stores, had shunned small towns as not affording enough potential to support

---

[8] *Ibid.*, pp. 104 and 105.
[9] Charles Berstein, "How to Win Employee and Customer Friends," *Nation's Restaurant News*, January 30, 1989, p. F3.

the sales volume needed for the low-price strategy. But Wal-Mart found abundant potential with customers flocking from surrounding towns and rural areas for its variety of goods and prices. (In the process of captivating these consumers, Wal-Mart wrecked havoc on the existing small-town merchants. See the Issue Box: Impact of Wal-Mart on Small Towns for a discussion of the sociological impact of Wal-Mart on small towns.) The company honed its skills in such markets isolated from aggressive competitors, and then flexed its muscles and moved confidently into the big cities, whose retailers were as fearful of Wal-Mart as the thousands of small-town merchants had been.

ISSUE BOX

IMPACT OF WAL-MART ON SMALL TOWNS

During most of its growth years, Wal-Mart pursued a policy of opening stores on the outskirts of small rural towns, usually with populations between 25,000 and 50,000. Attractive both in prices and assortment of goods, a Wal-Mart store drew customers from miles around; and was often the biggest employer in the town, giving jobs to 200–300 locals.

But the dominating presence of Wal-Mart was a mixed blessing for many communities. Small-town merchants were devastated and unable to compete. Downtowns became decaying vestiges of what perhaps a few months previously had been prosperous centers. But consumers benefited.

Wal-Mart brought tradeoffs and controversy: Was rural America better or worse off with the arrival of Wal-Mart? While most experts saw the economic development brought on by Wal-Mart as more than offsetting the business destruction it caused, few could dispute the sociological trauma.

What is your assessment of the desirability of Wal-Mart coming into a rural small town? How might your assessment differ depending on your position or status in that community?

Controlling Costs

Sam Walton was a stickler for holding down costs in order to offer customers the lowest prices. Cost control started with vendors, and Wal-Mart gained the reputation of being hard to please, of constantly pressuring suppliers to give additional price breaks and advertising, and to provide prompt deliveries. (In Chapter 9, on Newell Rubbermaid, we saw the difficulty vendors faced in trying to meet Wal-Mart's demands.) In its efforts to buy goods at the lowest possible prices, Wal-Mart attempted to bypass middlemen and sales reps and buy all goods direct from manufacturers. In so doing, a factory presumably would save money on sales commissions of 2 to 6 percent, and was expected to pass the savings on to Wal-Mart. Understandably, this aroused a heated controversy from groups representing sales reps.

Wal-Mart achieved great savings with its sophisticated distribution centers and its own fleet of trucks that enabled it to buy in bulk directly from suppliers. Most goods were processed through one of the company's distribution centers. For example, take the distribution center in Cullman, Alabama, situated on 28 acres with 1.2 million square feet. Some 1,042 employees loaded 150 outbound Wal-Mart trailers a day and unloaded 180. On a heavy day, laser scanners routed 190,000 cases of goods on an 11-mile-long conveyor.[10]

Each warehouse used the latest in optical scanning devices, automated materials-handling equipment, bar coding, and computerized inventory. With a satellite network, messages could be quickly flashed between stores, distribution centers, and corporate headquarters in Bentonville, Arkansas. Handheld computers assisted store employees in ordering merchandise. These advanced technologies cut distribution expenses to half those of most chains.

Wal-Mart had previously been able to achieve great savings in advertising costs, compared to major competitors. While discount chains typically spent 2 to 3 percent of sales for advertising, Wal-Mart held it to less than 1 percent of sales. Some of this difference reflected low media rates in its small-town markets. But advertising costs were also kept low in larger markets by using very little local advertising, relying instead on national TV institutional commercials showing prices being slashed and Wal-Mart as a good and caring firm. See the Issue Box: Institutional Advertising? for a discussion.

ISSUE BOX

SHOULD WE USE INSTITUTIONAL ADVERTISING?

Institutional advertising is nonproduct advertising designed to create goodwill for the firm rather than immediate and specific product sales. While the intent is laudable, the payoff is murky, because it is difficult to measure goodwill and its effect on sales. With specific product advertising, of course, a retailer can determine the effectiveness of an ad by the specific sales it produces compared to previous periods when the product was not advertised. We suggest that most institutional advertising is based on faith—faith that enough people will see the ad or commercial and gain a favorable attitude toward the company, the assumption being that a favorable attitude translates into more sales.

Wal-Mart's heavy use of institutional commercials on TV originally was two-pronged: (1) showing its employees as friendly and helpful, not only to customers but to the community at large; and (2) showing prices enthusiastically being slashed. As Wal-Mart confronted more and more negative publicity, it increased its institutional advertising as never before, trying to reinforce the image of Wal-Mart as a good citizen. In January 2005, CEO Lee Scott authorized full-page ads in more than 100 newspapers around the nation to highlight the message that Wal-Mart provides great opportunity for employee advancement, with stores providing mainly full-time jobs and a broad benefits package.[11]

---

[10] John Huey, "America's Most Successful Merchant," *Fortune*, September 23, 1991, p. 54.
[11] Chuck Bartels, Associated Press, as reported in "Wal-Mart Hits Critics with Media Blitz," *Cleveland Plain Dealer*, January 14, 2005, pp. C1 and C5.

> Despite the greater use of institutional advertising, the criticisms just would not go away, as we will discuss in the next section.
>
> Be a *devil's advocate*. Argue as persuasively as you can that institutional advertising may have improved Wal-Mart's image, but had little definitive effect on sales.

Wal-Mart's operating and administrative costs reflected a rigidly enforced, spartan operation. A lean headquarters organization and a minimum of staff assistants, compared with most other retailers, completed the cost-control philosophy and reflected Sam Walton's frugal thinking, which dated back to the company's earliest days.

A DARKER SIDE

Despite the good-citizen image that Walton sought to cultivate, Wal-Mart has provoked controversy almost from its beginnings. As it honed its skills and resources, and moved into more and more small towns, its impact on these local communities was profound. As discussed in a box, many downtowns were devastated when local merchants could not compete with the giant newcomer opening on the outskirts of town. Still, most people thought Wal-Mart brought more good than bad to their community—although some communities voted to keep Wal-Mart out.

Today, Wal-Mart is the most powerful firm in the world, with its huge size and buying clout, and this invites allegations that it may be crossing the line of unfair competition. Suppliers have felt the power of Wal-Mart and the price and service demands that it imposes on those wishing to do business with it. For many suppliers, losing Wal-Mart's business would be life-threatening; they have to meet its dictates, or else.

Wal-Mart led the retail industry in "partnering" with its vendors. If this were truly a two-way relationship, it would be of mutual benefit and would be an example of a symbiotic relationship in which the two parties gain from one another's success. However, Wal-Mart's "partnering" more often meant that vendors had to assume most of the inventory management and merchandising costs associated with their products in Wal-Mart stores; it also compelled them to guarantee fast replenishment, often saddling them with huge costs, so that the stores could maintain lean stocks. Wal-Mart's power position made some of these demands on vendors a do-it-or-else situation: "If you can't do it, we'll find another vendor."

In 1998, Wal-Mart entered grocery retailing, and in only four years, by 2002, became the nation's largest grocer with over $53 billion in grocery sales. Its nonunionized workforce and legendary efficiency enabled it to drive prices down in every market it entered—good for customers, but deadly for rivals. In the decade of the 1990s, 29 grocery chains sought bankruptcy-court protection, with Wal-Mart the catalyst in 25 of these cases.[12]

---

[12] Patricia Callahan and Ann Zimmerman, "Price War in Aisle 3," *Wall Street Journal*, May 27, 2003, pp. B1 and B16.

In recent years, Wal-Mart found toys to be a big traffic generator, especially during the important Christmas season, and expanded its emphasis on toys until it bested Toys "R" Us to become the biggest toy retailer.

For Christmas 2003, Wal-Mart moved to increase its market share even more. It drastically reduced prices on many of the hottest toys in late September, long before the peak selling season. This essentially denied its smaller competitors a profitable Christmas season, forcing them to match the low prices or lose most of their customers. As a result, two major toy chains, famed FAO Schwarz, along with its Zany Brainy and Right Start stores, and KB Toys filed for bankruptcy protection, unable to profitably match Wal-Mart's prices. Wal-Mart could afford to sell popular toys at a loss to generate traffic for its other merchandise. But its smaller competitors could not. Toys "R" Us, the nation's second-largest toy chain behind Wal-Mart, also suffered.[13]

Despite Wal-Mart's profit sharing and bonuses, scattered allegations surfaced about dictatorial employee relations and refusal to pay earned overtime. Wal-Mart led in pruning employee health benefits by requiring a six-month wait for hourly workers to be eligible for benefits, while deductibles ranged up to $1,000, triple the norm. It refused to pay for flu shots, eye exams, child vaccinations, and numerous other treatments normally covered by other employers, nor would it usually pay for treatment of preexisting conditions in the first year of coverage. As a result, Wal-Mart spent 40 percent less per employee for health care than the national average. To Wal-Mart's credit, some saw its approach to health care as a positive influence at a time when health care costs were soaring.[14]

Wal-Mart has also been the target of lawsuits accusing it of bias toward women and not paying employees for all the hours they work. The company vigorously fought such court actions, and as we saw in the box on institutional advertising, had in early 2005 begun a massive media blitz to defend itself. Joseph Sellers, an attorney in a gender-discrimination suit, observed, "It is hard to reconcile Wal-Mart's claim that it is serving everybody when it systematically underpaid and under-promoted its 1.6 million women employees for over a decade."[15]

In late 2003, Wal-Mart faced serious allegations of subcontracting its daily cleaning chores in many stores to firms that employed illegal immigrants at low wages with no overtime or benefits, and without collecting payroll taxes. These illegalities purportedly saved the company millions. If its executives knew of such practices, they could be indicted. In a company so tightly controlled, some doubted that the executives could have been oblivious.[16]

Going into 2004, Wal-Mart faced increasing criticism and legal action. The lawsuits had been granted class-action status in Massachusetts, California, Indiana, and Minnesota, and 35 similar suits were pending. It was alleged that Wal-Mart understaffed its stores, banned overtime, and consequently required workers to

---

[13] Lisa Bannon, "An Icon's Last Christmas?" *Wall Street Journal*, December 12, 2003, pp. B1 and B2.

[14] Bernard Wysocki Jr. and Ann Zimmerman, "Wal-Mart Cost-Cutting Finds a Big Target in Health Benefits," *Wall Street Journal*, September 30, 2003, pp. A1 and A16.

[15] Bartels, p. C5.

[16] Dan K. Thomasson, "Underpriced and Overgrown," *Cleveland Plain Dealer*, November 15, 2003, p. B7.

continue to work after their shifts, as well as during rest and meal breaks, without compensation. Wal-Mart denied that it required workers to work without pay.

The Los Angeles City Council was trying to prevent Wal-Mart from opening its SuperCenters in the city. Similar bans on the giant stores had been approved in the San Francisco Bay area, as well as in communities from Atlanta to Albuquerque. City leaders feared that the stores would drive local wages down as rival businesses struggled to survive, wipe out more jobs than they created, and leave more people without health insurance, thereby putting additional burden on overtaxed public hospitals and clinics.

Wal-Mart fought back aggressively, taking the battle to the ballot box. A spokesman declared, "The reality is that this is not some huge grass-roots uprising. Most communities in the state do not believe the government should be restricting the shopping choices of their residents."[17]

UPDATE

On July 28, 2006, Wal-Mart admitted defeat in Germany's giant but cutthroat retail market, and announced it would sell its 85 stores there to a German retailer, incurring a loss of $1 billion. After eight years of trying, Wal-Mart said it had been unable to turn around the stores, which had lost money every year. This decision came two months after Wal-Mart sold its 16 stores in South Korea to a local retailer, for $882 million. These actions amounted to a severe retreat from its aggressive global expansion, and a serious challenge to its image of power and efficiency. Strong unions, restrictive operating laws, poorly chosen retail acquisitions, and difficulty in adjusting to German shopping customs contributed to the failure. But unrelenting price competition from local discounters made the situation worse. Despite these setbacks, Wal-Mart maintained that it continued to thrive in many countries, particularly Mexico, Canada, Brazil, and Britain.

Still, Wal-Mart's largest non-American operation, that in Britain, had been struggling of late, and its top local rival, Tesco, was thriving. Tesco is Britain's largest retailer, with a market share in groceries of 31 percent, nearly double the 16 percent held by Wal-Mart, and it was planning to invade Wal-Mart's home turf on the West Coast in 2007. As the U.S. market became saturated, Wal-Mart had been looking at overseas markets for growth. But the Japanese unit had also suffered losses. India and China were also presenting challenges. There were restrictions on stores in India, and a state-run union in China was trying to force Wal-Mart to allow unions in its 60 stores.

With its stock price trading in a narrow range over the preceding six years because investors saw scant growth ahead, with the international market losing its luster, Wal-Mart launched a major effort to remake itself in 2005. It shifted its

---

[17] "Wal-Mart Suit Gets Class-Action Status in Massachusetts," *Wall Street Journal*, January 19, 2004, p. A2; Rene Sanches, "L.A. Isn't Buying Wal-Mart's Sales Job," *Washington Post*, reported in *Cleveland Plain Dealer*, February 4, 2004, p. C2.

image from "always low prices" to building an image as a "lifestyle" retailer offering trendy apparel and housewares. It planned to remodel 1,800 U.S. stores by mid-2007, adding faux-wood floors, wider aisles, and nicer rest rooms, among other things. While the stores would remain open during the remodeling, some analysts predicted that same-store sales would drop 3 to 7 percent due to the disruption.

Wal-Mart's attempts to expand its empire into the banking business encountered opposition from the banking industry, unions, and consumer groups; and some lawmakers urged federal regulators to reject the bid. Representative Tubbs Jones of Cleveland called Wal-Mart "a poor corporate citizen . . . one of the most often sued companies in history," with claims of gender discrimination and wage and hour violations. "Its employees' reliance on state federal medical programs . . . and its violations of the Clean Water Act, raise serious questions about the character of Wal-Mart's management and business practices."[18]

In a late-breaking lawsuit, a state jury found that Wal-Mart violated Pennsylvania labor laws by forcing employees to work through rest breaks and off the clock, a decision that the plaintiffs' lawyers said would result in at least $62 million in damages. Wal-Mart was facing a slew of similar suits around the country. It settled a Colorado case for $50 million, and was appealing a $172 million award handed down by a California jury.[19]

On October 6, 2006, in an effort perhaps aimed more at improving public image than profitability, Wal-Mart launched a $4 drug program for 143 generics in 235 Florida pharmacies. The program was quickly expanded to 14 additional states on October 19, and Wal-Mart filled more than 152,000 new prescriptions in four days. Rivals Target Stores and Publix Super Markets quickly matched the offer with their own $4 drug programs, and over the next few weeks, more supermarket chains, Kmart, and some independent pharmacies followed. Critics were quick to point out that these drugs were mostly older medications that had been replaced by newer drugs, and they represented only 1 percent of the total number of drugs available. The National Community Pharmacists Association, representing 24,000 independent pharmacies, called this a public relations stunt and a marketing ploy to get more people to come into Wal-Mart. Wal-Mart said that it can offer the drugs more cheaply than its competitors because of efficiencies in the way it does business, and that the company is not selling them at a loss. It announced plans to expand both the number of states participating and the number of eligible drugs.[20]

For all the criticisms of Wal-Mart, the decision to cut pharmacy prices should be a significant benefit to consumers. With competitors quickly following in reducing

---

[18] Compiled from Stephen Koff, "Deny Wal-Mart Bank Bid, FDIC Told," *Cleveland Plain Dealer*, April 11, 2006, p. C2; Cecilie Rohwedder, "No. 1 Retailer in Britain Uses 'Clubcard' to Thwart Wal-Mart," *Wall Street Journal*, June 6, 2006, pp. A1, A16; Ann Zimmerman and Emily Nelson, "With Profits Ellusive, Wal-Mart to Exit Germany," June 29–30, 2006, pp. A1, A6; Kris Hudson, "Wal-Mart's Bid to Remake Itself Weighs on Sales," *Wall Street Journal*, July 21, 2006, pp. C1, C4.

[19] Maryclaire Dale, "Jurors Find Wal-Mart Required Off-Clock Work," Associated Press, as reported in *Cleveland Plain Dealer*, October 13, 2006, p. C2.

[20] Janet H. Cho, "$4 Wal-Mart Drugs Reach Ohio," *Cleveland Plain Dealer*, October 27, 2006, pp. C1 and C3.

their prices, Wal-Mart became a catalyst in crumbling sky-high pharmaceutical costs that the government has been unable to rein in.

Wal-Mart can also be lauded for being a paragon of efficiency. Never was this more obvious than in its reaction when Katrina devastated New Orleans and the Gulf Coast. See the following Information Box about Wal-Mart and Katrina.

INFORMATION BOX

WAL-MART'S HANDLING OF THE KATRINA EMERGENCY PUTS FEMA TO SHAME

The Federal Emergency Management Agency (FEMA) could learn a lot from Wal-Mart. By Friday, August 26, when the hurricane touched down in Florida, 33-year-old Jason Jackson, the retailer's director of business continuity, had been joined by 50 Wal-Mart managers and support personnel, ranging from trucking experts to loss-prevention specialists, at the company's emergency command center. On Sunday, before the storm made landfall on the Gulf Coast, Jackson ordered warehouses to deliver a variety of emergency supplies to designated staging areas, ranging from generators to dry ice and bottled water, and even including such essential goods as mops and bleach. Then the storm knocked out the computerized system for automatically updating store inventory levels, and communication had to be by phone. By Tuesday, scores of Wal-Mart trucks, some escorted by police, were delivering essential goods to company stores across the Gulf. Wal-Mart beat FEMA by days in getting trucks filled with emergency supplies to relief workers and people whose lives had been devastated by the storm.

As one example: the store in LaPlace, Louisiana, lost power and water, as did all its neighbors in suburban New Orleans. Jackson's emergency center sent six loss-prevention employees, who helped secure the building and merchandise. The center also sent generators and the store's immediate supply needs. It soon became a refuge for evacuees. Store employees showed up for work in small and then growing numbers. Soon, more than 100 customers were waiting in 95-degree heat for their turn to shop. Elsewhere, 600 law-enforcement officers from around the state gathered in Gonzalez to start rescue operations, but they had no supplies. They called Wal-Mart the day after the hurricane and two days later got truckloads of water and other essential items. And still no sign of FEMA.

While Katrina was the biggest disaster Wal-Mart had ever faced, it has encountered other areas hit by less destructive hurricanes, tornadoes, and floods.[21]

Do you think the organizational and planning skills of Wal-Mart in dealing with massive catastrophes should be transferable to governmental agencies like FEMA? Why or why not?

---

[21] Ann Zimmerman and Valerie Bauerlein, "At Wal-Mart, Emergency Plan Has Big Payoff," *Wall Street Journal*, September 12, 2005, pp. B1 and B3.

COMMENTARY

Wal-Mart is a success story of no small moment. It has certainly been good for consumers and for the country, and it is a symbol of one man's vision and leadership. Nonetheless, there are legitimate questions: In its quest to provide customers with the lowest prices, has it become guilty of predatory practices, crossing the line in coercing suppliers, and using its size to deliberately drive out less efficient competitors? Have its executives been guilty of going too far in hard-nosed cost-cutting? Has it practiced gender discrimination? Is it polluting the environment with abandoned old box stores?

Of late, questions are also being raised about whether Wal-Mart can continue to grow. It already has over $300 billion in sales. The following Issue Box discusses Wal-Mart's growth prospects and their impact.

ISSUE BOX

IS THERE A LIMIT TO WAL-MART'S GROWTH?

Geoffrey Colvin, senior editor of *Fortune*, has postulated what would be the operational statistics if Wal-Mart were to grow at the same rate in the next 15 years as it has in the last 15 years, and the results are mind-boggling. Its revenues would be $3.2 trillion, the size of Japan's total economic output, or of France's and Britain's economies combined. If its workforce were to grow for the next 15 years at the same rate it has in the past 15, Wal-Mart would employ 8.2 million people: this would be equivalent to the entire working population of Los Angeles, San Francisco, and six other large American cities being employed by Wal-Mart. Looking at these figures, can anyone doubt that Wal-Mart's growth rate will decelerate? Colvin sees three forces "that look almost certain to do the job."

Societal resistance. Wal-Mart is already feeling the heat emanating from its size. Its unprecedented PR campaign of full-page ads in 100 newspapers suggests that. Critical media attention has exploded in recent years, neighborhoods and towns are agitating against allowing another Wal-Mart in their communities, over 5,000 lawsuits are pending against it, and at least one crusader (or agitator, depending on your point of view), Albert Norman, is making a good living rousing merchants, townspeople, unions, and environmental groups to rise up against new additional Wal-Marts. He also decries Wal-Mart's "boneyard"—371 empty hulks of former Wal-Mart stores.[22]

It is not improbable that labor unions and small businesses will persuade Congress to enact some kind of small-business protection. Colvin also raises an interesting speculation: "As Wal-Mart expands into ever more lines of business, maybe consumers will limit the dollars they're willing to hand to one company."

Competition. While most businesses quail when confronted with a new Wal-Mart in their vicinity, there is enough anecdotal evidence that some can prosper in the shadow

[22] "Giant Slayer," *Forbes*, September 6, 2004, pp. 73–76.

of Wal-Mart. Particularly in overseas markets, Wal-Mart is often having a very difficult time of it. Competition may rise up to delimit the growth rate of Wal-Mart in the future.

Cultural exhaustion. We have had massive firms in earlier decades—such as Sears, General Motors, IBM, AT&T, U.S. Steel, Standard Oil—and their dominance is no more. A few have been broken up by antitrust efforts. But most have seen a withering of their driving spirit, their eagerness to innovate, their flexibility—they have instead become encumbered with bureaucracy, enamored with process rather than execution. A 3Cs mind-set of vulnerability—complacency, conservatism, and conceit—have overtaken all the great firms in the past. While Wal-Mart seems to be stubbornly resisting this, it shows increasing signs of vulnerability, both domestically and around the world.[23]

Do you agree with Colvin's speculations? Why or why not?

Take a *devil's advocate* position against Albert Norman. Present as many arguments against his criticisms of Wal-Mart as you can—in other words, defend Wal-Mart.

✿ ✿ ✿

Invitation for Your Own Analysis and Conclusions

Wal-Mart is planning rather drastic and expensive changes domestically by upgrading stores, merchandise, and advertising to appeal to a more upscale market (more like Target, it seems). It is also limiting the depth of its assortments in some areas. Do you think these plans are overdue, a mistake at this time, or what? Defend your conclusions.

✿ ✿ ✿

WHAT CAN BE LEARNED?

Take good care of people.—Sam Walton was concerned with two groups of people: his employees and his customers. By motivating and even inspiring his employees, he found that customers also were well served. Somehow, in the exigencies of business, especially big business, the emphasis on people tends to be pushed aside. Walton made caring for people common practice.

By listening to his employees, by involving them, exhorting them, and giving them a real share of the business—all the while stressing friendliness and concern for customers—Walton fostered a business climate almost unique in any large organization. In addition to providing customers with the friendliest of employees, his stores also offered honest values and great assortments, and catered to the concerns of many middle-income Americans for the environment and American jobs.

But is Walton's philosophy eroding?

---

[23] Geoffrey Colvin, "Wal-Mart's Growth Will Slow Down—Eventually," *Fortune*, February 7, 2005, p. 48.

Go for the strategic window of opportunity.—Strategic windows of opportunity sometimes come in strange guises. They represent areas of potential business overlooked or untapped by existing firms. But in the formative and early growth years of Wal-Mart, no window could have seemed less promising than the one Walton milked to perfection and to great growth. Small towns and cities in many parts of rural America were losing population and economic strength, partly because of the decline in family farms and the accompanying infrastructure of small businesses. It was hardly surprising that the major discount chains focused their growth efforts on large metropolitan areas. Although many small towns had Penney's and Sears outlets as well as Woolworth, Gamble, and Coast to Coast stores, these were often marginal old stores in the backwater of corporate consciousness. The retail environment was one of small stores with limited assortments of merchandise and relatively high prices.

Here Walton saw something no other merchants had: that the limited total market potential meant a dearth of competition. He also saw the potential as far greater than the population of the small town and its immediate environs. Indeed, a Wal-Mart store in an isolated rural community could draw customers from many miles away.

Do such windows of opportunity still exist today? You bet they do, for the entrepreneur with vision, an ability to look beyond the customary, and the courage to follow up on the vision.

Consider the marriage of old-fashioned ideas and modern technology.—Walton embraced this strategy and made it work throughout his organization, even as it grew to large size. In the forefront of retailers in the use of communication technology and computerized distribution, he still was able to motivate his employees to offer friendly, helpful customer services to a degree that few large retailers have consistently achieved.

Other firms can benefit from the example of Wal-Mart in cultivating homespun friendliness with awesome technology, and competitors are trying to emulate it. The difficulty that many are finding, however, is in achieving consistency.

Beware the arrogance of power.—Wal-Mart is no longer a humble company. Maybe it hasn't been since the days of Sam Walton. (Other firms fall into the same mindset: for example, Euro Disney in Chapter 11, and Boeing in Chapter 12.) It is difficult not to succumb to this arrogant attitude—which can permeate an entire organization—to the detriment of relations with employees, customers, suppliers, the communities with which it does business, and eventually even the government (despite heavy lobbying and political pandering). Arrogance must be combated, must not be permitted to become obvious, for it makes for huge public relations problems and negative press relations.

How is arrogance to be combated? It starts at the top, and only then can percolate down through the rest of the organization until it reaches those who have contact with customers and the various other publics with which the firm deals. Any large firm is highly visible, and actions that might be overlooked for smaller firms can sometimes mushroom to serious proportions. When a firm is the biggest in the world, and knows it, and uses its power to drive hard bargains and coerce dissenters—such as vocal opponents of a proposed new store in their community—then it sets itself up for a public relations situation that denigrates its public image even if it wins.

For the large and powerful firm, its public image should be of major importance. Many decisions should be made with the probable impact on public image in mind.

Buy American and environmental programs help the public image.—As foreign manufacturers increasingly took market share away from American producers—in the process destroying some American jobs—public sentiment mounted for import restrictions to save jobs. In March 1985, Walton became concerned about what seemed to him a national problem. He ordered his buyers to find products that American manufacturers had stopped producing because they couldn't compete with foreign imports. Thus began Walton's Buy American program, which became a cooperative effort between retailers and domestic manufacturers to reestablish the competitive position of American-made goods in price and quality. At the time, Magic Chef, 3M, Farris Fashions, and many other manufacturers joined Walton's crusade, and Wal-Mart pledged to support domestic production of items ranging from film to microwave ovens to flannel shirts and other apparel. Regardless of the great controversy over the desirability of free trade, many middle-class Americans applauded Wal-Mart's leadership in this widely publicized "Buy American" policy. Now the policy has quietly slipped away, and cheaper imports are the rule.

Wal-Mart also became a leader in challenging manufacturers to improve their products and packaging in order to protect the environment. As a result, manufacturers made great improvements in eliminating excessive packaging, converting to recyclable materials, and getting rid of toxic inks and dyes. Has this policy been abandoned?

Other environmental activities at the time included participation in Earth Day events, with tree plantings, information booths, and videos to show customers how to improve their environment. Wal-Mart was also active in fund-raising for local environmental and charitable groups, and in adopt-a-highway programs, in which store personnel volunteered at least one day a month to collect trash and clean up local highways and beaches.

The firm that acts for environmental protection stands to benefit in customer relations and, not the least, from positive media attention. Firms catering to the general public—as Wal-Mart certainly is—should be alert to their increasing concerns and where possible take on a leadership role.

Can a firm become too big?—We cannot answer this. But we can warn of the danger of bigness as far as the public interest and trusting relationships are concerned. The phrase "arrogance of power" describes the temptation of bigness. Some would even see this as a natural evolution of size. Years ago, major firms like U.S. Steel and Standard Oil were broken up because enough people believed they had become too big; General Motors for years feared this, until foreign competition destroyed its dominance. Could Wal-Mart be approaching the same fate as it increasingly dominates certain sectors of the retail scene? When it can tyrannize its suppliers, drive competitors in the food and toy industries into bankruptcy, bring fear to others as it searches for new areas to assert its power—may it be in danger of losing its humanity?

CONSIDER

Can you identify additional learning insights that could be applicable to firms in other situations?

QUESTIONS

1. How might you attempt to compete with Wal-Mart if you were:
   a. a small hardware merchant?
   b. a small men's clothing store?
   c. a supermarket?
   d. a toy store?

2. Do you think Wal-Mart is vulnerable today to governmental intervention, and if so, in what way? If you do not think it is vulnerable, do you see any limits to its growth?

3. When you shop at Wal-Mart, do you usually find the employees far superior in friendliness and knowledge to those of other retailers? If not, what are your conclusions regarding Wal-Mart's employee-relations programs?

4. What weaknesses do you see Wal-Mart as having either now or potentially? How can the company overcome them?

5. Can discounting go on forever? What are the limits to growth by price competition?

6. Discuss Wal-Mart's business practices (especially in regard to unions, invading small towns, and supplier relations) in terms of their ethical ramifications for the industry and for society. Should students be encouraged to emulate these practices?

7. Do you think Wal-Mart today is a benevolent and humane firm? Why or why not? Is it completely ethical?

8. Do you think Wal-Mart's Buy American program should be reestablished? Why or why not?

HANDS-ON EXERCISES

1. Be a *devil's advocate*. The decision is being made to phase out the hypermarts. Argue as persuasively as you can that Wal-Mart is being too hasty and that the hypermart concept should be continued, if necessary with some changes.

2. You are an ambitious Wal-Mart store manager. Describe how you might design your career path to achieve a high executive position. Be as creative as you can.

3. You are the principal adviser to David Glass, who replaced Sam Walton as chief executive. Even though Wal-Mart has expanded aggressively overseas in recent years, he still thinks the greatest potential lies in foreign markets. He has charged you to develop a strategy to make greater inroads. What do you advise, and why? (Hint: you may need to do some research on Wal-Mart's overseas presence at this time, and what specific problems it seems to be encountering in some countries.)

TEAM DEBATE EXERCISES

1. Debate the notion of Wal-Mart aggressively seeking to enter small communities in places like rural New England, where many people oppose it. Should Wal-Mart bow to the public pressure (which the company deems to be from a small minority of vehement agitators), or should it carry on with "right on its side"?

2. Can the great growth of Wal-Mart continue indefinitely? Debate the pros and cons of this.

3. Is Wal-Mart today in danger of losing its humanity?

YOUR ASSESSMENT OF THE LATEST DEVELOPMENTS

How would you evaluate Wal-Mart's latest move to $4 for certain generic prescriptions? Do you think it will be a significant factor in reining in health costs? Why or why not?

INVITATION TO RESEARCH

Have higher energy costs had a negative influence on Wal-Mart's fortunes? Are Wal-Mart's same-store sales comparing favorably with Target and Home Depot? Has the drastic renovation and upgrading of stores and merchandise been successful? Are there any ominous signs on the horizon? Have the management style and employee relations changed since what was described in the case? Are any stores unionized? Are the overseas efforts becoming more successful?

CHAPTER SEVENTEEN

Southwest Airlines: "Try to Match Our Prices"

In 1992, the airlines lost a combined $2 billion, matching a dismal 1991, and bringing their three-year red ink total to a disastrous $8 billion. Three carriers—TWA, Continental, and America West—were operating under Chapter 11 bankruptcy, and others were lining up to join them. But one airline, Southwest, was profitable as well as rapidly growing—with a 25 percent sales increase in 1992 alone. Interestingly enough, it was a low-price, bare-bones operation, run by a flamboyant CEO, Herb Kelleher. He had found a niche, a strategic window of opportunity, and oh how he milked it! See the following Information Box for further discussion of strategic windows of opportunity and their desirable accompaniment, SWOT analysis.

INFORMATION BOX

STRATEGIC WINDOW OF OPPORTUNITY AND SWOT ANALYSIS

A strategic window is an opportunity in the marketplace, not at present well served by competitors, that fits well with the firm's competencies. Strategic windows often last for only a short time (although Southwest's strategic window has been much more durable), before they are filled by alert competitors.

Strategic windows are usually found by systematically analyzing the environment, examining the threats and opportunities it holds. The competencies of the firm, its physical, financial, and people resources—management and employees and their strengths and weaknesses—should also be assessed. The objective is to determine what actions might or might not be appropriate for that particular enterprise and its orientation. This is commonly known as a SWOT analysis: analyzing the *strengths* and *weaknesses* of the firm, and assessing the *opportunities* and *threats* in the environment.

The analysis may be a formal part of the planning process, or it may also be informal and even intuitive. We suspect that Herb Kelleher instinctively sensed a strategic window in short hauls and lowest prices. Although he must have recognized the danger that his bigger competitors would try to match his prices, he believed that with his simplicity of operation he would be able to make a profit while bigger airlines were racking up losses.

Why do you think the major airlines so badly overlooked the possibilities in short hauls at low prices?

HERBERT D. KELLEHER

Herb Kelleher impressed people as an eccentric. He liked to tell stories, often with himself as the butt, and many involved practical jokes. He admitted that he sometimes was a little scatterbrained. In his cluttered office, he displayed a dozen ceramic wild turkeys as a testimonial to his favorite brand of whiskey. He smoked five packs of cigarettes a day. As an example of his zaniness, he painted one of his 737s to look like a killer whale, in celebration of the opening of Sea World in San Antonio. Another time, during a flight he had flight attendants dress up as reindeer and elves, while the pilot sang Christmas carols over the loudspeaker as he gently rocked the plane.

Kelleher is a "real maniac," said Thomas J. Volz, vice-president of marketing at Braniff Airlines. "But who can argue with his success?"[1]

Kelleher grew up in Haddon Heights, New Jersey, the son of a Campbell Soup Company executive. He graduated from Wesleyan University and New York University law school, then moved to San Antonio in 1961, where his father-in-law helped him set up a law firm. In 1968, he and a group of investors put up $560,000 to found Southwest; of this amount, Kelleher contributed $20,000.

In the early years he was the general counsel and a director of the fledgling enterprise. But in 1978 he was named chairman, despite his having no managerial experience, and in 1981 he became CEO. His flamboyance soon made him the most visible aspect of the airline. He starred in most of its TV commercials. A rival airline, America West, charged in ads that Southwest passengers should be embarrassed to fly such a no-frills airline, whereupon Kelleher appeared in a TV spot with a bag over his head. He offered the bag to anyone ashamed to fly Southwest, suggesting it could be used to hold "all the money you'll save flying us."[2]

He knew many of his employees by name, and they called him "Uncle Herb" or "Herbie." He held weekly parties for employees at corporate headquarters. And he encouraged such antics by his flight attendants as organizing trivia contests, delivering instructions in rap, and awarding prizes for the passengers with the largest holes in their socks. But the wackiness had a shrewd purpose: to generate a gung-ho spirit to boost productivity. "Herb's fun is infectious," said Kay Wallace, president of the Flight Attendants Union Local 556. "Everyone enjoys what they're doing and realizes they've got to make an extra effort."[3]

[1] Kevin Kelly, "Southwest Airlines: "Flying High with 'Uncle Herb'," *Business Week*, July 3, 1989, p. 53.
[2] *Ibid.*, p. 53.
[3] Richard Woodbury, "Prince of Midair," *Time*, January 25, 1993, p. 55.

THE BEGINNINGS

Southwest was conceived in 1967, folklore tells us, on a napkin. Kelleher was still a lawyer, and Rollin King, one of his clients, had an idea for a low-fare, no-frills airline to fly between major Texas cities. He doodled a triangle on the napkin, labeling the points Dallas, Houston, and San Antonio.

The two tried to go ahead with the plan, but were stymied for more than three years by litigation, battling Braniff, Texas International, and Continental over the right to fly. In 1971, Southwest won, and it went public in 1975. At that time, it had four planes flying between the three cities. Lamar Muse was president and CEO from 1971 until he was fired by Southwest's board in 1978. Then the board of directors tapped Kelleher.

At first, Southwest was in the throes of life-and-death low-fare skirmishes with its giant competitors. Kelleher liked to recount how he came home one day "beat, tired, and worn out. So I'm just kind of sagging around the house when my youngest daughter comes up and asks what's wrong. I tell her, 'Well, Ruthie, it's these damned fare wars.' And she cuts me right off and says, 'Oh, Daddy, stop complaining. After all, you started 'em.' "[4]

For most small firms, competing on a price basis with much larger, well-endowed competitors is tantamount to disaster. The small firm simply cannot match the resources and staying power of bigger competitors. Yet Southwest somehow survived. Not only did it initiate the cutthroat price competition, but it achieved cost savings in its operations that the larger airlines could not. The question then became: How long would the big carriers be content to maintain their money-losing operations and match Southwest's low prices? And the big airlines eventually blinked.

In its early years, Southwest faced other legal battles. Take Dallas and Love Field. The original airport, Love Field, is close to downtown Dallas, but it could not geographically expand at the very time when air traffic was increasing mightily. A major new facility, Dallas/Fort Worth International Airport, replaced it in 1974. This boasted state-of-the-art facilities and enough room for foreseeable demand, but it had one major drawback: it was 30 minutes farther from downtown Dallas. Southwest was able to avoid a forced move to the new airport and to continue at Love. But in 1978, competitors pressured Congress to bar flights from Love Field to anywhere outside Texas. Southwest was able to negotiate a compromise, now known as the Wright Amendment, that allowed flights from Love Field to the four states contiguous to Texas. In retrospect, the Wright Amendment forced onto Southwest a key ingredient of its later success: the strategy of short flights.[5]

GROWTH

Southwest grew steadily, but not spectacularly, through the 1970s. It dominated the Texas market by appealing to passengers who valued price and frequent departures.

[4] Charles A. Jaffe, "Moving Fast by Standing Still," *Nation's Business*, October 1991, p. 58.
[5] Bridget O'Brian, "Southwest Airlines Is a Rare Air Carrier: It Still Makes Money," *Wall Street Journal*, October 28, 1992, p. A7.

Its one-way fare between Dallas and Houston, for example, was $59 in 1987, versus $79 for unrestricted coach flights on other airlines.

In the 1980s, Southwest's annual passenger traffic count tripled. At the end of 1989, its operating cost per revenue mile—the industry's standard measure of cost-effectiveness—was just under 10 cents, which was about 5 cents per mile below the industry average.[6] Although revenues and profits were rising steadily, especially compared with the other airlines, Kelleher took a conservative approach to expansion, financing it mostly from internal funds rather than taking on debt.

Perhaps the caution stemmed from an ill-fated acquisition in 1986. Kelleher bought a failing long-haul carrier, Muse Air Corp., for $68 million, and renamed it TransStar. (This carrier had been founded by Lamar Muse after he left Southwest.) But by 1987, TransStar was losing $2 million a month, and Kelleher shut down the operation.

By 1993, Southwest had spread to 34 cities in 15 states. It had 141 planes, and each of them made 11 trips a day. It used only fuel-thrifty 737s, and still concentrated on flying large numbers of passengers on high-frequency, one-hour hops at bargain fares (average $58). Southwest shunned the hub-and-spoke systems of its larger rivals and took its passengers direct from city to city, often to smaller satellite airfields rather than congested major metropolitan fields. With rock-bottom prices, and no amenities, it quickly dominated most new markets it entered.

As an example of Southwest's impact on a new market, it came to Cleveland, Ohio, in February 1992, and by the end of the year was offering 11 daily flights. In 1992, Cleveland Hopkins Airport posted record passenger levels, up 9.74 percent from 1991. "A lot of the gain was traffic that Southwest Airlines generated," noted John Osmond, air trade development manager.[7]

In some markets, Southwest found itself growing much faster than projected, as competitors either folded or else abandoned directly competing routes. For example, in Phoenix, America West Airlines cut back service in order to conserve cash after a Chapter 11 bankruptcy filing. Of course, Southwest picked up the slack, as it did in Chicago when Midway Airlines folded in November 1992. And in California, Southwest's arrival led several large competitors to abandon the Los Angeles–San Francisco route, unable to meet Southwest's $59 one-way fare. Before Southwest, fares had been as high as $186 one way.[8]

Cities that Southwest did not serve began petitioning for service. For example, Sacramento, California, sent two county commissioners, the president of the chamber of commerce, and the airport director, to Dallas to petition for service. Kelleher consented a few months later. In 1991, the airline received 51 similar requests.[9]

A unique situation was developing. On many routes, Southwest's fares were so low that they competed with buses, and even with private cars. By 1991, Kelleher did not even see other airlines as his principal competitors: "We're competing with the automobile, not the airlines. We're pricing ourselves against Ford, Chrysler, GM,

[6] Jaffe, p. 58.
[7] "Passenger Flights Set Hopkins Record," *Cleveland Plain Dealer*, January 30, 1993, p. 3D.
[8] O'Brian, p. A7.
[9] *Ibid.*

Toyota, and Nissan. The traffic is already there, but it's on the ground. We take it off the highway and put it on the airplane."[10]

Various aspects of Southwest's growth and increasingly favorable competitive position during the salient years from 1987 to 1991 are depicted in Tables 17.1, 17.2, and 17.3, and Figure 17.1. While Southwest's total revenues were still less than those of the major airlines in the industry, its growth pattern indicated a major presence, and its profitability was second to none.

Tapping California

Southwest's formidable competitive power was perhaps never better epitomized than in its 1990 invasion of populous California. By 1992, it had become the second-largest player, after United, with 23 percent of intrastate traffic. This was achieved by pushing down fares as much as 60 percent on some routes. The big carriers, which had tended to surrender the short-haul niche to Southwest in other markets, suddenly faced a real quandary in the "Golden State." Now Southwest was being described as a "500 pound cockroach, too big to stamp out."[11]

The California market was indeed enticing. Some 8 million passengers each year flew between the five airports in metropolitan Los Angeles and the three in the San Francisco Bay area, this being the busiest corridor in the United States. It was also

TABLE 17.1. Growth of Southwest Airlines; Various Operating Statistics, 1982–1991

Year	Operating Revenues ($ millions)	Net Income ($ millions)	Passengers Carried (thousands)	Passenger Load Factor
1991	$1,314	$26.9	22,670	61.1%
1990	1,187	47.1	19,831	60.7
1989	1,015	71.6	17,958	62.7
1988	860	58.0	14,877	57.7
1987	778	20.2	13,503	58.4
1986	769	50.0	13,638	58.8
1985	680	47.3	12,651	60.4
1984	535	49.7	10,698	58.5
1983	448	40.9	9,511	61.6
1982	331	34.0	7,966	61.6

Source: Company annual reports.

Commentary: Note the steady increase in revenues and in number of passengers carried. White the net income and load factor statistics show no appreciable improvement, these statistics still are in the vanguard of an industry that has suffered badly in recent years. See Table 17.2 for a comparison of revenues and income with the major airlines.

[10] Subrata N. Chakravarty, "Hit 'Em Hardest with the Mostest," *Forbes*, September 16, 1991, p. 49.
[11] Wendy Zellner, "Striking Gold in the California Skies," *Business Week*, March 30, 1992, p. 48.

TABLE 17.2.   Comparison of Southwest's Growth in Revenues and Net Income with Major Competitors, 1987–1991

	1991	1990	1989	1988	1987	% 5-year Gain
Operating Revenue Comparisons ($ millions)						
American	$9,309	$9,203	$8,670	$7,548	$6,369	46.0
Delta	8,268	7,697	7,780	6,684	5,638	46.6
United	7,850	7,946	7,463	7,006	6,500	20.8
Northwest	4,330	4,298	3,944	3,395	3,328	30.1
Southwest	1,314	1,187	1,015	860	778	68.9
Net Income Comparisons ($ millions)						
American	(253)	(40)	412	450	225	
Delta	(216)	(119)	467	286	201	
United	(175)	73	246	426	22	
Northwest	10	(27)	116	49	64	
Southwest	27	47	72	58	20	

Source: Company annual reports.

Commentary: Southwest's revenue gains over these five years outstripped those of its largest competitors. While the percentage gains in profitability are hardly useful because of the erratic nature of airline profits during these years, Southwest stands out starkly as the only airline to be profitable each year.

TABLE 17.3.   Market Share Comparison of Southwest with Its Four Major Competitors, 1987–1991

	1991	1990	1989	1988	1987
Total Revenues (millions): American, Delta, United, Northwest	$29,757	$29,144	$27,857	$24,633	$21,835
Southwest Revenues:	1,314	1,187	1,015	860	778
Percent of Big Four	4.4	4.1	3.6	3.5	3.6
Increase in Southwest's market share, 1987–1991: 22%					

Source: Company annual reports.

one of the pricier routes, as the low fares of AirCal and Pacific Southwest Airlines had been eliminated when these two airlines were acquired by American and US Air.

Into this situation Southwest charged, with low fares and frequent flights. While airfares dropped, total air traffic soared 123 percent in the quarter Southwest entered the market. Competitors suffered; American lost nearly $80 million at its San Jose hub, while US Air also lost money even though it cut service drastically. United, the

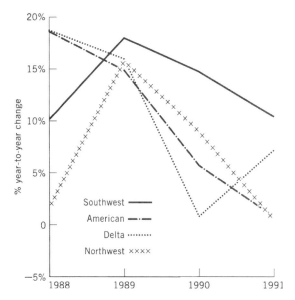

Figure 17.1. Year-to-year percentage changes in revenues, Southwest and its three major competitors, 1988–1991.

market leader, quit flying the San Diego–Sacramento and Ontario–Oakland routes, where Southwest had rapidly built up service. The quandary of the major airlines was all the greater because this critical market fed traffic into the rest of their systems, especially the lucrative transcontinental and trans-Pacific routes. They could hardly abdicate California to Southwest. American, for one, considered creating its own no-frills shuttle for certain routes. But the question remained: could anyone stop Southwest with its formula of lowest prices and lowest costs and frequent schedules? And, oh yes, good service and fun.

INGREDIENTS OF SUCCESS

Although Southwest's operation under Kelleher had a number of rather distinctive characteristics contributing to its success pattern and its seizing of a strategic window of opportunity, the key factors appear to have been cost containment, employee commitment, and conservative growth.

Cost Containment

Southwest has been the lowest-cost carrier in its markets. While its larger competitors might try to match its cut-rate prices, they could not do so without incurring sizable losses. Nor did they seem able to trim their costs to match Southwest. For example, in the first quarter of 1991, Southwest's operating costs per available seat mile (i.e., the number of seats multiplied by the distance flown) were 15 percent lower than America West's, 29 percent lower than Delta's, 32 percent lower than United's, and 39 percent lower than US Air's.[12]

Many aspects of the operation contributed to these lower costs. Since all its planes were aircraft of a single type, Boeing 737s, the costs of training, maintenance, and inventory could be reduced. And since a plane earns revenues only when flying, Southwest was able to achieve a faster turnaround time on the ground than any other airline. Although competitors take upwards of an hour to load and unload passengers and then clean and service the planes, some 70 percent of Southwest's flights have a turnaround time of 15 minutes, while 10 percent have even pared the turnaround time to 10 minutes.

Southwest also curbed costs in areas of customer service. It offered peanuts and drinks, but no meals. Boarding passes were reusable plastic cards. Boarding time was minimal because there were no assigned seats. Southwest subscribed to no centralized reservation service. It did not even transfer baggage to other carriers; that was the passengers' responsibility. Admittedly, such customer service frugality would be less acceptable on longer flights—and this helped to account for the difficulty competing airlines had in cutting their costs to match Southwest's. Still, if the price is right, many passengers might also opt for no frills on longer flights.

Employee Commitment

Kelleher was able to achieve an esprit de corps unmatched by other airlines despite the fact that Southwest employees were unionized. His relationship with the unions was not adversarial, so that Southwest was able to negotiate flexible work rules, with flight attendants and even pilots helping with plane cleanup. Employee productivity continued very high, permitting the airline to be lean staffed. Kelleher resisted the inclination to hire extravagantly when times were good, necessitating layoffs in leaner times. This contributed to employee feelings of security and loyalty. The low-key attitude and sense of fun that Kelleher engendered helped, perhaps more than anyone could have foreseen. Kelleher declared, "Fun is a stimulant to people. They enjoy their work more and work more productively."[13]

Conservative Growth Efforts

Not the least of the ingredients of success was Kelleher's conservative approach to growth. He resisted the temptation to expand vigorously—for example, to seek to fly to Europe or get into head-to-head competition with larger airlines with long-distance routes. Even in its geographical expansion, conservatism prevailed. The philosophy of expansion was to do so only when enough resources could be committed to go into a city with 10 to 12 flights a day, rather than just one or two. Kelleher called this "guerrilla warfare," with efforts concentrated against stronger opponents in only a few areas, rather than dissipating strength by trying to compete everywhere.

---

[12] Chakravarty, p. 50.
[13] *Ibid.*

Even with a conservative approach to expansion, the company showed vigorous but controlled growth. Its debt, at 49 percent of equity, was the lowest among U.S. carriers. Southwest also had the airline industry's highest Standard & Poor's credit rating.

GALLOPING TOWARD THE NEW MILLENNIUM

In its May 2, 1994 edition, prestigious *Fortune* magazine devoted its cover story to Herb Kelleher and Southwest Airlines. It raised an intriguing question: "Is Herb Kelleher America's Best CEO?" It called him a "people-wise manager who wins where others can't."[14] Southwest's operational effectiveness continued to surpass all rivals in such productivity ratios as cost per available seat mile, passengers per employee, and employees per aircraft. Only Southwest remained consistently profitable among the big airlines, by the end of 1998 having been profitable for 26 consecutive years. Operating revenue had grown to $4.2 billion (it was $1.3 billion in 1991—see Table 17.2), and net income was $433 million, up from $27 million in 1991.

In 1999, Herb Kelleher was named CEO of the Year by *Chief Executive* magazine.

Geographical Expansion

Late in October 1996, Southwest launched a carefully planned battle for East Coast passengers that would drive down air fares and pressure competitors to back away from some lucrative markets. It chose Providence, Rhode Island, just 60 miles from Boston's Logan Airport, thus tapping the Boston-Washington corridor. The Providence airport escaped the congested New York and Boston air-traffic-control areas, and from the Boston suburbs was hardly a longer trip than to Logan Airport. Experience had shown that air travelers would drive a considerable distance to fly with Southwest's cheaper fares.

As Southwest entered new markets, most competitors refused any longer to try to compete price-wise; they simply could not cut costs enough to compete. Their alternative then was either to pull out of the short-haul markets or be content to let Southwest have its market share while they tried to hold on to other customers by stressing first-class seating, frequent-flyer programs, and other in-flight amenities.

In April 1997, Southwest quietly entered the transcontinental market. From its major connecting point of Nashville, Tennessee, it began nonstops both to Oakland, California, and to Los Angeles. With Nashville's direct connections with Chicago, Detroit, Cleveland, Providence, and Baltimore-Washington, as well as points south, this afforded *one-stop*, coast-to-coast service, with fares about half as much as the other major airlines.

Two other significant moves were announced in late 1998. One was an experiment. On Thanksgiving Day, a Southwest 737-700 flew *nonstop* from Oakland to the Baltimore-Washington Airport, and back again. It provided its customary no-frills service, but a $99 one-way fare, the lowest in the business. The test was designed to see how pilots, flight attendants, and passengers would feel about spending five

---

[14] Kenneth Labich, "Is Herb Kelleher America's Best CEO?" *Fortune*, May 2, 1994, pp. 45–52.

TABLE 17.4. Cities Served by Southwest, October 1999

Albuquerque	Hartford, CT*	New Orleans	Sacramento
Amarillo	Houston (Hobby &	Oakland	St. Louis
Austin	Bush Intercontinental)	Oklahoma City	Salt Lake City
Baltimore/Washington	Indianapolis	Omaha	San Antonio
Birmingham	Islip (Long Island)	Ontario, CA	San Diego
Boise	Jackson, MS	Orange County	San Francisco
Burbank	Jacksonville	Orlando	San Jose
Chicago (Midway)	Kansas City	Phoenix	Seattle
Cleveland	Little Rock	Portland	Spokane
Columbus	Los Angeles (LAX)	Providence, RI	Tampa
Corpus Christi	Louisville	Raleigh-Durham	Tucson
Dallas (Love Field)	Lubbock	Reno/Tahoe	Tulsa
Detroit (Metro)	Manchester, NH	Rio Grande Valley	
El Paso	Midland/Odessa	(South Padre	
Ft. Lauderdale	Nashville	Island/Harlingen)	

*Service to Hartford began October 31, 1999.

hours in a 737, with only peanuts and drinks served in flight. The older 737s lacked the fuel capacity to fly coast-to-coast nonstop, but with Boeing's new 737-700 series this was no problem. The Thanksgiving Day test was a precursor of more nonstop flights, because Southwest had firm orders for 129 of the new planes to be delivered over the next seven years. This would enable it to compete with the major carriers on their moneymaking transcontinental flights.

In November 1998, plans were also announced for starting service to MacArthur Airport at Islip, Long Island, which would enable Southwest to tap into the New York City market. By late 1999 it was flying to 54 cities in 29 states. Table 17.4 list the cities.

UPDATE TO 2006

By mid-2002, with the 9/11 disaster still affecting airline travel, Southwest was the only major carrier that had been operating profitably in the 18 months since. U.S. airlines were posting losses of as much as $8 billion in 2002—eclipsing the record in 2001 of $7.7 billion, with the loss in the more profitable business travel being particularly acute. The high-cost airlines faced enormous pressure from low-fare carriers, most notably Southwest, but also from Internet sites that allowed bargain hunting. Southwest was now the nation's sixth-largest airline, and it had been profitable for 29 consecutive years.

In June 2001, just months before the September 11 attacks, Herb Kelleher retired. He was replaced by James Parker, who had joined Southwest in 1986, and Parker readily admitted that he was no Herb Kelleher. His immediate challenge was to contain the operating costs of soaring liability insurance and unionized workers' agitation for raises to match the rich contracts negotiated at other airlines before September 11. However, the bankruptcies of United Airlines and US Airways in late 2002 highlighted the need for airlines to slash billions in operating costs, notably through labor givebacks of extravagant union contracts, and this helped subdue new labor demands.[15]

In the increasingly brutal airline market, even Southwest was getting squeezed. It still remained profitable, and its seat capacity for the first half of 2004 was up 29 percent from four years earlier, but because of mounting price competition, revenue had risen only 18 percent during this time. It remained profitable while the worldwide airline industry had incurred losses of about $30 billion since 2001. But Southwest now faced price competition from a new breed of low-price competitors, such as JetBlue Airways, which offered amenities like inflight TV. The bigger airlines also were becoming more competitive, for they had substantially lowered their costs and their ticket prices. Some pilots on major airlines, with their compensation givebacks, were even making less than Southwest pilots. In this environment, CEO James Parker abruptly retired after only three years on the job. He was replaced in July 2004 by 50-year-old Gary Kelly, former chief financial officer of Southwest.

In early 2005 Southwest announced its invasion of the Pittsburgh market, taking advantage of US Airways' major service cuts there. This was the latest move in Southwest's continuing buildup in the East. It had entered the Philadelphia market in May 2004, and with its arrival traffic rose more than 51 percent and average fares fell more than 37 percent. Pittsburgh now had six low-cost carriers, and the dominant hub position of US Airways had eroded.[16]

Southwest also added Fort Myers, Florida, and Denver in 2005, and planned to offer flights to Washington's Dulles Airport by the fall of 2006. Its Baltimore presence already tapped Washington's northern and eastern Maryland suburbs, and now Dulles would expose it to the burgeoning population in northern Virginia.

In these expansions into more competitive airports, the growth was pushing Southwest toward becoming a typical big airline. It even began testing whether it should move to assigned seating instead of its hallmark open-seating policy; early results suggested that assigned seating could shave a minute or so off boarding time, but would lead to more disappointed customers. Still, it remained a different kind of airline, with no first-class seating, no meals, and no posh airport VIP clubs. By the end of 2006, Southwest had 478 planes, more than United's 460 mainline jets. Long promoted as "*the* low-fare carrier," it had raised fares nine times since the middle of 2005, including a $10 increase on some flights over the July Fourth weekend.

CEO Kelly maintains that nothing is imminent, but that "it's a matter of when, not if," Southwest will launch service to Mexico, Canada, or even the Caribbean.

---

[15] Scott McCartney, "Southwest Sets Standards on Costs," *Wall Street Journal*, October 9, 2002; Daniel Fisher, "Is There Such a Thing as Nonstop Growth? *Forbes*, July 8, 2002, pp. 82, 84.

[16] Melanie Trottman, "At Southwest, New CEO Sits in a Hot Seat," *Wall Street Journal*, July 19, 2004, pp. B1 and B3; idem, "Southwest Feels Squeeze," *Wall Street Journal*, August 23, 2004, p. B3; idem, "Southwest Will Fill US Airways' Pittsburgh Gap," *Wall Street Journal*, January 6, 2005, p. D9.

As it grows ever larger, change is on the horizon for diluting Southwest's efficiency built around its all-Boeing 737 fleet. The possibility of flying 100-seat jets to smaller markets is being considered. Further erosion of the successful bare-bones business plan seems probable, such as adding some type of in-flight entertainment. The airline's market niche as the lowest-fare carrier is eroding.

In addition to making some changes reflecting its growing size and seeking new market, several other factors threatened the bare-bones leadership. One was the end of Southwest's advantage over rivals in fuel costs. It had used contracts to lock in future fuel prices—a fuel-hedging program—that saved $900 million in 2005, but this was due to wind down in 2007. The other was largely a factor of its success of 60 consecutive quarterly profits by July 2006, a record of profitability unique in the industry. Labor negotiations were looming, and while Southwest's pilots were the highest paid in the industry, thanks to big pay cuts for the pilots in the major airlines, they maintained that they were entitled to raises.[17]

By the end of 2006, the so-called legacy carriers had been reinvigorated. With their severe price cutting of the previous years, they now had some of the lower costs that only the discounters previously could enjoy, and in addition had the premium overseas traffic that discounters did not have. This situation was affecting the stocks of JetBlue, AirTran, Frontier Airlines, and Southwest, all of which reported sharply lower profits.[18]

✿ ✿ ✿

Invitation to Make Your Own Analysis and Conclusions

Your analysis, please, of CEO Kelly's contemplated new business plan for Southwest.

✿ ✿ ✿

WHAT CAN BE LEARNED?

The power of low prices and simplicity of operation.—If a firm can maintain prices below its competitors, and do so profitably and without sacrificing quality of service, then it has a powerful advantage. We noted in Chapter 13 the great advantage Vanguard had with its lowest expense ratio in the mutual fund industry. Southwest also achieved this with its simplicity of operation and no-frills but dependable service. Competition on the basis of price is seldom used in most mature industries (although the airline industry has been an exception) primarily

---

[17] Compiled from Dan Reed, "At 35, Southwest's Strategy Gets More Complicated," *USA Today*, July 11, 2006, pp. B1 and B2; Susan Warren, "Keeping Ahead of the Pack," *Wall Street Journal*, December 19, 2005, pp. B1 and B3; idem, "Southwest to Offer Flights to Dulles Starting This Fall," *Wall Street Journal*, April 5, 2006, p. B2.

[18] Melanie Trottman and Susan Carey, " 'Legacy' Airlines May Outfly Discount Rivals," *Wall Street Journal*, October 30, 2006, pp. C1 and C4.

because competitors can quickly match prices with no lasting advantage to anyone. As profits are destroyed, only customers benefit, and then only in the short run before the industry realizes the futility of price competition. (In new and rapidly changing industries, price competition is effective as productivity and technology improve and marginal competitors are driven from the market.)

The effectiveness of Southwest's cost controls, however, shows the true competitive importance of low prices. Customers love the lowest-price provider *if* it does not sacrifice too much quality, comfort, and service. While there was some sacrifice of service and amenities with Southwest, most customers found this acceptable because of the short-haul situation; and dependable and reasonable service was still maintained.

An intriguing factor regarding the relationship of customer satisfaction and price is explored in the Information Box: The Key to Customer Satisfaction: Meeting Customer Expectations.

INFORMATION BOX

THE KEY TO CUSTOMER SATISFACTION: MEETING CUSTOMER EXPECTATIONS

Southwest consistently earns high ratings for its customer satisfaction, higher than its giant competitors. Yet the major airlines all offered more food service than Southwest's peanuts and drinks. They also provided such additional amenities as advance seat assignments, in-flight entertainment on longer flights, the opportunity to upgrade, and a comprehensive frequent-flyer program. Yet Southwest gets the highest points for customer satisfaction.

Could something else be involved here?

Let's call it *expectations*. If a customer has high expectations, perhaps because of a high price and/or the advertising promising high-quality, luxury accommodations, dependable service, or whatever, then if the product or service does not live up to expectations, customer satisfaction dives. Turning to the airlines, customers are not disappointed in Southwest's service because they don't expect luxury; Southwest does not advertise luxury. Its customers don't expect frills, but they receive pleasant, courteous treatment by employees, dependable, safe flights, and low prices. On the other hand, expectations are higher for the bigger carriers with their higher prices. This is well and good for the first- or business-class service. But for the many who fly coach—?[19]

Do you think there is a point where a low-price/no frills strategy would be detrimental to customer satisfaction? What might this depend on?

---

[19] Source: The idea of expectations affecting customer satisfaction was suggested by Ed Perkins for Tribune Media Services and reported in "Hotels Must Live Up to Promises," *Cleveland Plain Dealer*, November 1, 1998, p. 11-K.

The power of a niche strategy. — Directing business efforts toward a particular customer segment or niche can be a powerful competitive advantage. Especially is this true if no competitor is directly catering to the niche or is likely to do so with a concerted effort. An untapped niche then becomes a strategic window of opportunity.

Kelleher revealed Southwest's niche strategy: While other airlines set up hub-and-spoke systems in which passengers are shunted to a few major hubs from which they are transferred to other planes going to their destination, "we wound up with a unique market niche: we are the world's only short-haul, high-frequency, low-fare, point-to-point carrier ... We wound up with a market segment that is peculiarly ours, and everything about the airline has been adapted to serving that market segment in the most efficient and economical way possible."[20] See the following Information Box for a discussion of the criteria needed for a successful niche or segmentation strategy.

INFORMATION BOX

CRITERIA FOR SELECTING NICHES OR SEGMENTS

In deciding what specific niches to seek, these criteria should be considered:

1. *Identifiability.* Is the niche identifiable so that the people it encompasses can be isolated and recognized? It was not difficult to identify the short-route travelers, and while their numbers could not easily be estimated at first, this was soon to change as demand burgeoned for Southwest's short-haul services.

2. *Size.* The segment must be of sufficient size to be worth the efforts to tap it. And again, the size factor proved to be significant: Southwest soon offered 83 flights daily between Dallas and Houston.

3. *Accessibility.* For a niche strategy to be practical, promotional media must be able to reach the segments without much wasted coverage. Southwest had little difficulty in reaching its target market through billboards, newspapers, and similar means.

4. *Growth potential.* A niche is more attractive if it shows some growth characteristics. The growth potential of short-haul flyers proved to be considerably greater than for airline customers in general. Partly the growth reflected customers won from higher-cost and less convenient airlines. And some of the emerging growth reflected customers' willingness to give up their cars to take a flight that was almost as economical and certainly more comfortable.

5. *Absence of vulnerability to competition.* Competition, both present and potential, must certainly be considered in making specific niche decisions. By quickly becoming the low-cost operator on its early routes, and gradually expanding without

---

[20] Jaffe, p. 58.

diluting its cost advantage, Southwest became virtually unassailable in its niche. The bigger airlines, with their greater overhead and less flexible operations, could not match Southwest prices without going deeply into the red. And the more Southwest became entrenched in its markets, the more difficult it was to pry it loose.

But nothing remains forever. Today Southwest's position is less unassailable.

Assume you are to give a lecture to your class on the desirability of a niche strategy, and you cite Southwest as a classic example. But suppose a classmate asks: "If a niche strategy is so great, why didn't the other airlines practice it?" How will you respond?

Southwest has been undeviating in its pursuit of its niche. For years, while others tried to copy, none were able to fully duplicate it. For years, Southwest was the nation's only high-frequency, short-distance, low-fare airline. As an example of its virtually unassailable position, Southwest accounted for more than two-thirds of the passengers flying within Texas, and Texas was the second-largest market outside the West Coast. When Southwest invaded California, some San Jose residents drove an hour north to board Southwest's Oakland flights, skipping the local airport where American had a hub. And in Georgia, so many people were bypassing Delta's huge hub in Atlanta and driving 150 miles to Birmingham, Alabama, to fly Southwest that an entrepreneur started a van service between the two airports.[21]

Unlike many firms, Southwest did not permit success to dilute its niche strategy. It has not attempted to fly to Europe or South America, or to match the big carriers in offering amenities on coast-to-coast flights—Yet! In curbing such temptations, it has not sacrificed growth potential. It still has many U.S. cities to embrace. Despite its price advantage now being countered by low-price competitors and even by some major airlines desperately trying to reduce overhead to better compete with discount carriers on certain routes, Southwest is still the market leader in its niche.

Seek dedicated employees.—Stimulating employees to move beyond their individual concerns to a higher level of performance, a truly team-oriented approach, was by no means the least of Kelleher's accomplishments. The esprit de corps enabled planes to be turned around in 15 minutes instead of the hour or more of competitors; it brought a dedication to serving customers far beyond what could ever be expected of a bare-bones, cut-price operation; it brought a contagious excitement to the job obvious to customers and employees alike.

Kelleher's extroverted, zany, and down-home personality certainly helped in cultivating dedicated employees. So did his legendary ability to remember employees' names, his sincere interest in them and, of course, the company parties. Flying in the face of conventional wisdom, which says that an adversarial relationship between management and labor is inevitable with the presence of a

[21] O'Brian, p. A7.

union, Southwest achieved its great teamwork while being 90 percent unionized. It helped, though, that Kelleher started the first profit-sharing plan in the U.S. airline industry in 1974, with employees eventually owning 13 percent of the company stock.

Whether the high degree of worker dedication can pass the test of time, and the test of increasing size, is uncertain. Kelleher himself has retired, and his two successors have different personalities. Yet here is a model for an organization growing to large size and still maintaining employee commitment. In the preceding case we examined the leadership style of Sam Walton and the growth of Wal-Mart to become the largest retailer.

The attainment of dedicated employees is partly a product of the firm itself, and how it is growing. A rapidly growing firm—especially when its growth starts from humble beginnings, with the firm as an underdog—promotes a contagious excitement. Opportunities and advancements depend on growth. And where employees can acquire stock in the company, and see their shares rising, potential financial rewards seem almost infinite. Success tends to create a momentum that generates continued success.

CONSIDER

Can you identify additional learning insights that could be applicable to other firms in other situations?

QUESTIONS

1. In what ways might airline customers be segmented? Which segments or niches would you consider Southwest's prime targets? Which segments probably would not be?

2. Discuss the pros and cons for expansion of Southwest beyond short hauls. Which arguments do you see as most compelling?

3. Evaluate the effectiveness of Southwest's unions.

4. On August 18, 1993, a fare war erupted. To initiate its new service between Cleveland and Baltimore, Southwest announced a $49 fare (a sizable reduction from the then standard rate of $300). Its rivals, Continental and US Air, retaliated. Before long, the price was $19, not much more than the tank of gas it would then take to drive between the two cities—and the airlines also supplied a free soft drink. Evaluate the implications of the price war for the three airlines.

5. A price cut is the most easily matched marketing strategy, and usually provides no lasting advantage to any competitor. Identify the circumstances when you see it desirable to initiate a price cut and potential price war.

6. Do you think it is likely that Southwest will remain dominant in its niche despite the array of discount carriers? Why or why not?

7. What is your forecast for the competitive environment of the airline industry ten years from now?

HANDS-ON EXERCISES

1. Herb Kelleher has just retired. And you are his successor. Unfortunately, your personality is quite different from his: you are an introvert and far from flamboyant, and your memory for names is not good. What would be your course of action to try to preserve the great employee dedication of the Kelleher era? How successful do you think you will be? Did the board make a mistake in hiring you?

2. Herb Kelleher has not retired. He is going to continue until 70, or later. Somehow, his appetite for growth has increased as he has grown older. He has charged you with developing plans for expanding into longer hauls, and maybe to South and Central America, and even to Europe. Be as specific as you can in developing the desired expansion plans.

3. How would you feel personally about a five-hour transcontinental flight with only a few peanuts, and no other food or movies? Would you be willing to pay quite a bit more to have more amenities?

TEAM DEBATE EXERCISES

1. The Thanksgiving Day nonstop transcontinental experiment went fairly well, although customers and even flight attendants expressed some concern about the long, five-hour flight with no food and no entertainment. No one complained about the price.

2. Debate the two alternatives of going ahead slowly with the transcontinental plan with no frills, or adding a few amenities, such as some food, reading material, or whatever else might make the flight less tedious. You might even want to debate the third alternative of dropping the idea entirely at this time.

YOUR ASSESSMENT OF THE LATEST DEVELOPMENTS

The so-called legacy airlines were having resurging revenues and profitability by the end of 2006, to the detriment of Southwest and the other discount carriers. What is your assessment of the situation from Southwest's standpoint? Is this only a short-term phenomenon, or is the discounter model—low fares and rapid, mostly domestic growth—vulnerable long-term?

INVITATION TO RESEARCH

What is Southwest's current situation? What is its market share in the airline industry? Is it still maintaining a high growth rate? Has the decision been made to expand the nonstop transcontinental service, and have any changes been made in the no-frills service for this. How about international flights? Have other discount carriers, such as JetBlue, made any sizable inroads in Southwest's niche?

CHAPTER EIGHTEEN

Herman Miller:
A Beleaguered Role-Model
in Leadership

*H*erman Miller, Inc., an office-furniture maker based in Zeeland, Michigan, had long been a celebrated company, extolled in numerous business texts, including Tom Peters's best-seller, *A Passion for Excellence*, and *The 100 Best Companies to Work for in America* by Robert Levering and Milton Moskowitz. Its furniture designs have been displayed in New York's Museum of Modern Art. It was a model of superb employee relations, and it stood in the forefront with environmentally sensitive policies. The company had been a paragon for almost seven decades.

But in the 1990s, circumstances began changing, and not for the best from Herman Miller's perspective. While sales had generally been increasing, although far from robustly, profits were seriously diminishing. Herman Miller remained the high-price, high-cost contender in an increasingly competitive market, and a market that itself was only expanding modestly. Amid these difficulties, one could wonder whether the enlightened approach to management might be turning out to be an albatross. Should it be modified or even abandoned?

BACKGROUND

D. J. DePree founded the company in 1923 in a small town in west-central Michigan. He named it Herman Miller after his father-in-law, who provided startup capital. For seven decades it was run by the DePree family, devout members of the Dutch Third Reformed Church, and they maintained a paternalistic relationship with their employees through the decades.

Employee Relations

Early on, the family sought to set a kinder, gentler tone with its employees, offering profit-sharing and employee-incentive programs long before they were fashionable.

285

Along with this, participative management almost bordering on democracy was practiced. (See the following Information Box for a discussion of participative management.) This helped create a loyal workforce that turned out well-made products that could be sold at premium prices.

INFORMATION BOX

PARTICIPATIVE MANAGEMENT: IS IT THE BEST?

Directing or issuing instructions to subordinates as to what is to be done can take two extremes. In participative direction, the manager consults with the people responsible for doing the task about how best to accomplish it; the subordinates participate in the decision. Authoritative direction is simply issuing orders unilaterally, with no consultation with or participation by subordinates. Sometimes more extreme positions are identified: dictatorial and democratic. The following diagram depicts the range of managerial styles:

dictatorial	authoritative	participative	democratic

$\longleftarrow$ less   degree of subordinate involvement in planning and decision making   more $\longrightarrow$

    The democratic style is similar to the participative except that the subordinates get to vote, with the decision going to the most votes. In the participative style, the manager may or may not go along with the ideas of subordinates.

    Several advantages come from a greater use of participation. People tend to be more cooperative and enthusiastic when they have some involvement in the planning. Not uncommonly, better decisions also come with the different experiences and points of view. The executive may become more a coordinator of ideas than a "boss." In such an atmosphere employee development is maximized.

    The major drawback is time. Consultation takes time. Many decisions are too minor to be worth such discussion. Other times, actions have to be made quickly and there is little time for participation. And if employees are new and untrained, if they lack interest, or if they are not very competent, no benefit would be likely.

    The best managers tend to use participation whenever they can, especially where the decision directly involves employees. But they choose their opportunities carefully. It can be used with just one or two subordinates, or with a whole group.

Do you think another objection to a participative management style is that it undermines the manager's authority? Why or why not?

    Through the 1960s and 1970s, the company prospered with the expanding office-furniture industry. D.J.'s sons, Hugh and Max, took the enterprise public but continued to nurture employees' commitment to the company. For example:

- In the 1980s, when hostile takeovers threatened many firms, the company instituted "silver parachutes" for all employees so that any who might lose their jobs would receive big checks.

- It may be the only company in the United States to have had a vice-president of people.

- In a time of escalating top executive salaries, reaching more than a hundred times their companies' lowest wages by 1990, Herman Miller limited the top salary to no more than 20 times the average wage of a line worker in the factory.

- Employees were organized into work teams, and every six months workers and their bosses evaluated each other.

- In the middle 1980s, Max DePree, in the interest of ensuring the fullest career development of promising managers, announced that he would be the last member of the family to head up Herman Miller. Henceforth, the next generation of DePrees would not even be permitted to work at the company. See the following Issue Box for a discussion of the desirability of nepotism (favoritism granted by persons in high office to relatives and friends).

Of course, there had never been any serious effort to unionize the workforce.

ISSUE BOX

HOW DESIRABLE IS NEPOTISM?

Max DePree announced that he would be the last DePree to head up Herman Miller, and that the next generation of DePrees would not even be permitted to work at the company. While his rationale for this was to encourage the career development of promising managers, the issue was not so black-and-white, but more complex. We see examples of both good and bad nepotism.

We have no further to look than Ford Motor Company. William Ford, great-grandson of founder Henry Ford, was named CEO of the company in 2001, succeeding Jacques Nasser, who had been involved in the Ford Explorer/Firestone Tire Disaster. William Ford was greeted as a kind of savior at first, bringing the company to profitability in 2002 through 2004 before higher gas prices and tough competition hurt profits on the popular trucks and SUVs. With the Ford family controlling 40 percent of the voting shares, the board was hardly in a position to replace him. Especially since in 1945, Henry Ford II, grandson of the founder, wrested control of a struggling Ford and successfully ran the company for 34 years.

But nepotism can be an anchor to non-aggressive actions, with underperforming executives difficult to sack. When family members are on the board and control the bulk of the voting shares, nepotism can represent the extreme example of inbreeding. And Max DePree was right: relatives working for the company can stifle the ambitions of other able employees, and even make recruiting top-level executives difficult.[1]

---

[1] Related to this, see Phred Dvorak and Jaclyne Badal, "Relative Problems," *Wall Street Journal*, July 24, 2006, pp. B1 and B4.

Do you think Depree went too far in prohibiting any relative from working for Herman Miller, even at the lowest level? Do you see any other drawbacks in prohibiting nepotism?

Product Development

Since 1968, the company had turned its attention to designing products for a so-called Action Office. It introduced components, such as desk consoles, cabinets, chairs, and flexible panels, that could give flexibility, and some degree of privacy, to the workplace. It emphasized innovative designs, and dealt with a number of "enormously gifted but extremely high-strung designers."[2] These vaulted Herman Miller into the top ranks of the industrial-design world.

The company regularly budgeted between 2 and 3 percent of sales for design research, double the industry average. Sometimes its commitment to doing what was right (rather than what was best) brought it to a new level of corporate consciousness. For example:

- In the 1970s, an enormously successful desk chair called the Ergon was introduced. Millions of these designed-for-the-body chairs were sold. Then an advanced desk chair called the Equa was proposed. It would cost about the same as the Ergon. At this point many companies would have scrapped it rather than cannibalize (take sales away from) their star. But Herman Miller introduced it nevertheless.

- In March 1990, the Eames chair, the company's signature piece, was given a routine evaluation of the materials used. This was a distinctive office chair with a rosewood exterior finish, priced at $2,277. The research manager, Bill Foley, realized that two species of trees used, rosewood and Honduran mahogany, came from vulnerable rain forests. The decision was made to ban the use of these woods once existing supplies were exhausted, even though the CEO, Richard H. Ruch, predicted that this decision would kill the chair.[3]

Environmental Sensitivity

Few firms have shown the concern for the environment that Herman Miller has. In addition to the rain forest example above, here are several other instances of its concern:

- The firm cut the trash it hauled to landfills by 90 percent since 1982.
- It built an $11 million waste-to-energy heating and cooling plant, thus saving $750,000 per year in fuel and landfill costs.

[2] Kenneth Labich, "Hot Company, Warm Culture," *Fortune*, February 27, 1989, p. 75.
[3] D. Woodruff, "Herman Miller: How Green Is My Factory?" *Business Week*, September 16, 1991, pp. 54–55.

- Herman Miller employees used 800,000 styrofoam cups, material anathema to waste disposal. So it distributed 5,000 mugs and banished styrofoam. The mugs carried this admonition, "On spaceship earth there are no passengers . . . only crew."[4]

- The company spent $800,000 for two incinerators that burned 98 percent of the toxic solvents coming from the staining of woods, thereby exceeding Clean Air Act requirements. CEO Ruch, under questioning from the board of directors for the costly exceeding of standards, stated that having the machines was "ethically correct."[5]

EMERGING SOBERING REALITIES

By 1995, Herman Miller was a $1 billion corporation. But given that its sales in 1989 had been almost $800 million, this was not a significant accomplishment, especially since profits had slid from over $40 million in most of the 1980s to $4.3 million in 1995. And in 1992, it recorded a net loss of $3.5 million, its first loss ever. Table 18.1 shows the trend in revenues for selected years from 1985 to 1995. Table 18.2 shows the net income disappointments during these years. Earnings by 1995 were 90 percent less, on higher sales, than in many years in the 1980s. And net income as a percentage of revenues had been declining steadily since 1985, from 8.3 percent to only 0.4 percent in 1995.

Perhaps most indicative of the worsening performance of Herman Miller was its "competitive battles." Hon Industries was a very close competitor, one of virtually the same size and aiming at similar markets. Table 18.3 shows Hon's sales and net income during these same years. Unlike Herman Miller, Hon's profits had risen steadily, and

TABLE 18.1. Herman Miller Revenues, 1985–1995

	Millions	Percent Change
1985	$ 492	
1987	574	17.6
1989	793	38.2
1991	879	10.8
1993	856	(2.6)
1995	1,083	26.5

Source: Company public records.

Commentary: While somewhat erratic, the increase in sales should hardly in itself be a cause for alarm. But this does not tell the whole story of Herman Miller's problems. See Table 18.2.

[4] *Ibid.*
[5] *Ibid.*

TABLE 18.2. Herman Miller's Total Net Income,
and Percent of Sales, 1985–1995

	Millions	Percent of Sales
1985	$40.9	8.3
1987	33.3	5.8
1989	41.4	5.2
1991	14.1	1.6
1993	22.1	2.6
1995	4.3	.4

Source: Company public records.

Commentary: Here the trend is far more serious than in Table 18.1. The
trend in total profits is steadily downward since the 1980s, despite the
increase in sales during most of these years. While the results for 1995
are particularly troubling (and resulted in the chairman's "retirement"),
of particular concern is the erosion of profits as a percentage of total
sales. And this is not for a single year but for all of the 1990s.

TABLE 18.3. Sales and Profit Performance of Major Competitor,
Hon Industries, 1985–1994

	Revenues (millions)	Net Income (millions)	Income as Percent of Sales
1985	$473.3	$26.0	
1987	555.4	24.8	5.5
1989	602.0	27.5	4.5
1991	607.7	32.9	5.4
1993	780.3	44.6	5.7
1994	846.0	54.4	6.4

Source: Company public records.

Commentary: Hon and Herman Miller are surprisingly close in total sales. If anything,
Herman has been growing slightly faster than Hon. But looking at profits tells a different
story. While Herman's profits have been eroding badly. Hon's have steadily been
increasing. And the improvement in profits as a percent of sales for Hon is impressive
indeed, while this is the great source of Herman Miller's trepidation.

net income as a percentage of revenues was two to three times better in the 1990s.
Figures 18.1 and 18.2 show the competitive battles graphically.

Any top executive has to be concerned with the fortunes of the company's stock
price and the satisfaction of shareholders. While Hon Industries' stock price had
climbed fourfold in the last decade, Herman Miller's barely moved: in 1985 its

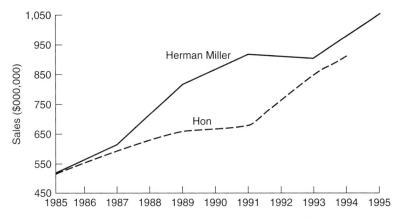

Figure 18.1. *The Competitive War:* sales comparisons, Herman Miller and Hon, 1985–1995.

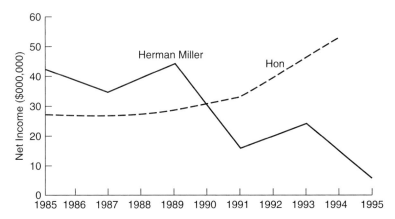

Figure 18.2. *The Competitive War:* net income comparisons, Herman Miller and Hon, 1985–1995.

over-the-counter shares sold at $24; in 1995 they were about the same—this in the midst of the greatest bull market in stock market history.

J. Kermit Campbell became the company's first outsider CEO in 1992, following upon a 32-year career at Dow Corning. In an annual report, he seemed to espouse all the best values of the DePrees: "I truly believe that there is something in human nature that wants to soar."[6]

Campbell was named chairman in May 1995 when Max DePree retired. He acted quickly to cut costs and, in the process, to discharge several top executives. The head of Herman Miller's biggest division, workplace systems, a 20-year veteran, was let go. The company's chief financial officer was also removed. Campbell's goal was to pare selling and administrative costs to 25 percent from the current 30 percent.

[6] Justin Martin, "Broken Furniture at Herman Miller," *Fortune*, August 7, 1995, p. 32.

He wanted to cut about 200 employees from a workforce of 6,000, doing so through early retirements but also from firings. He closed plants in Texas and New Jersey, as well as several showrooms. At this point, Herman Miller was rapidly losing its reputation as one of the best companies to work for in America. But Campbell could point out that survival was more important than preserving a pristine worker relationship.

Campbell's tenure proved to be short. In mid-July, barely two months into his chairmanship, on the same day the company announced its annual results and a nearly 90 percent drop in profits from the previous year, his departure was also announced. What was not clear was whether the board was dissatisfied with Campbell's cost-cutting because it was too little or too much.

In any case, the board named Michael Volkema as new chief executive. Volkema had joined Herman Miller in 1990 when it acquired cabinetmaker Meridian. He had the reputation of being driven and charismatic, and he was young—only 39. He had come to the board's attention for his cost-cutting efforts in the small Meridian operation ($100 million in sales).

Problems in the Changing Market

The marketplace was hardly the same in the 1990s as in the heyday of the 1960s and 1970s. Sales of office furniture were not expected to grow at more than 5 percent, even if corporate profits remained high. A basic shift in demand was blamed for this: Computer technology required fewer layers of management, leading to general downsizing of office-space needs.

Not only was total demand growing slowly, but the premium end of the market, which had long been Herman Miller's niche, was also drying up as businesses in general chose to reduce costs by using lower-priced furniture.

In 1994, Herman Miller introduced a new Aeron chair, made from a mesh material that helped keep the body cooler. Although its design was unique and artistic, it retailed for up to $1,150, hundreds of dollars more than most other office chairs. Sales were disappointing.

Given the limitations in the business market, the company saw opportunity in the home-office sector. "We'll have 40 million to 50 million people working some part of their day at home," Campbell predicted. He hoped that the firm's quality image would be especially appealing to a significant part of this market.[7] So the company introduced its first home-office line, carrying a price tag of $1,799 for a desk. Early results were not promising; hundreds of OfficeMax and Office Depot stores featured fully acceptable desks for no more than $725.

Herman Miller's problem of arousing demand for its admittedly high-quality, well-designed furniture was further impeded by the company's traditional practice of doing very little product advertising. While this strategy worked in decades past, was it still appropriate in the 1990s?

---

[7] Marcia Berss, "Tarnished Icon," *Forbes*, July 31, 1995, p. 45.

ANALYSIS

A central issue in the Herman Miller shift toward operational mediocrity and deterioration in recent years had to do with its enlightened management style toward both employees and the environment. Long the model for superb employee relations, Herman Miller faced a dilemma: In an age of impersonal cost-cutting and downsizing, can a company be competitive with altruistic policies that protect employees and the environment? Perhaps more to the point, were Herman Miller's problems the result of such policies being unrealistic today, or was something else wrong, something having little to do with employee relations and environmental concerns?

Let us address the crucial question: Do the best in employee relations add unacceptable costs? What employee relations are we talking about? Giving employees participation in many decisions? Giving them profit-sharing incentives? Giving them opportunities for advancement as far as their abilities will take them? Making them feel wanted and appreciated, and part of a team? Giving them a feeling of job security at a time when so many firms were downsizing and forcing many employees out, whether under the guise of early retirement or as outright forced discharges? Involving them with products they can take pride in? Do such things add to unacceptable costs against "lean and mean" competitors?

While these questions or issues could be debated at some length, perhaps the only question that really is a detriment to achieving necessary cost savings is that of job security. Some paring down might need to be done to stay competitive cost-wise, especially in a computer age where middle-management and staff positions can be consolidated.

Unfortunately, management and workers alike must face the grim realities of today's environment—the fact that their skills and experience may no longer be needed today, that they must be prepared to shift jobs and learn new skills or else expect early retirement no matter how enlightened the firm. To compete, businesses must be "lean" if not "mean." Early retirements or terminations can be done harshly or empathetically. Empathetically suggests reasonable early-retirement incentives, help with finding alternative employment or with the training needed to develop new skills. Counseling can be important—and time: time to adjust to the harsh realities and to pursue alternative employment opportunities before being cast out. All these add some costs. But an organization does not have to be mean in seeking to be competitive. Can't a firm be kind to loyal employees, even if it adds a little to its costs temporarily?

Regarding the environment, did Herman Miller lose money by not building its chairs from certain tropical hardwoods found in rain forests? Maybe some; but substitute woods should have proven acceptable to virtually all customers. Other costs, such as going beyond the 1990 Clean Air Act requirements for incinerators and building an $11 million waste-to-energy heating and cooling plant, resulted in some cost savings, although not as much as the investments made. On the other hand, substituting reusable mugs for styrofoam cups reportedly resulted in cost savings of

$1.4 million.[8] So environmental concern and action do not have to result in major additional expenditures.

It seems, then, that indicting Herman Miller's altruistic policies for its less-than-laudable recent operating results might be mistaken. Perhaps the blame rather lies in an aging strategy: high-quality, well-designed products, priced at the top of the market, with the major promotional reliance on word-of-mouth rather than advertising. What worked well in the 1980s and before needed to be reevaluated in the 1990s and beyond. This is more an age of austerity, with aggressive competitors and killer-category chains, such as Office Depot, offering good merchandise at prices half or less than Herman Miller's. In particular, perhaps Herman Miller should have tested the waters for medium-priced goods. It would not need—or want to—discard its quality reputation, nor abandon the high end of the market. Rather, it could have expanded its offerings downward from the very high end.

Herman Miller also seemed to have miscalculated in the receptivity of the home-office market to its high-priced furniture. While undoubtedly a few wealthy individuals would willingly pay the steep price for a desk and other furniture of highest quality at the cutting edge of design, this market might not be very sizable.

UPDATE

Michael Volkema changed things for the better, after the painful downsizing and restructuring of Herman Miller in the industry slump of the mid-1990s. By the end of 2000, five years under Volkema, sales almost doubled to $1.938 billion, and operating income went from $1.2 million to $140 million for a net profit percentage of 7.2 percent. Comparing with the major competitor, Hon Industries, revenues were almost the same, but Herman Miller's net income was well above Hon's $106 million and net profit percentage of 5.2 percent.

In January 2000, *Forbes* selected Herman Miller to its "Platinum List" of exceptional corporations that "pass a stringent set of hurdles measuring both long- and short-term growth and profitability.[9]

Volkema had expanded the narrow high-end customer base to emerging and midsize businesses, and homes. In three years he spent more than $200 million on computer systems and other technology aimed at assuring speedy delivery, and another $100-million-plus on research and development for new products. To attract consumers, a Web site was developed featuring office furniture specially designed for this market.

Employees were still catered to, with a bright and airy new plant in Holland, Michigan, where workers assembled furniture to music by U2, the Allman Brothers, and Sting. "A sign near the front door boasted that workers there haven't been late in shipping a single order in 75 days."[10]

---

[8] Woodruff, p. 55.
[9] Brian Zajac, "The Best of the Biggest," *Forbes*, January 10, 2000, pp. 84–85.
[10] "Reinventing Herman Miller," *Business Week*, April 3, 2000, p. EB88; Ashlea Ebeling, "Herman Miller: Furnishing the Future," *Forbes*, January 10, 2000, pp. 94–96.

By 2001, revenues reached beyond $2.2 billion, with net income $144 million, both statistics the best ever. Then the market collapsed in 2002 in the aftermath of 9/11. Since 2004, both revenue and income have shown steady gains, with fiscal 2006 having a 14.6 percent revenue gain, and net earnings 46 percent above the previous year.

Herman Miller was still widely recognized both for its innovative products and its business practices. In fiscal 2004 it was named recipient of the prestigious National Design Award for product design from the Smithsonian Institution's Cooper-Hewitt National Design Museum. In 2005, it was again included in *Business Ethics* magazine's "100 Best Corporate Citizens," and was cited by *Fortune* as the "most Admired" company in its industry.[11]

❀ ❀ ❀

Invitation to Make Your Own Analysis and Conclusions

How would you improve the Herman Miller business model? Support your analysis and recommendations.

❀ ❀ ❀

WHAT CAN BE LEARNED?

A firm has to adapt to changing competitive forces. —Not many firms can afford the luxury of decades of undeviating policies and strategies. Most find that some adaptability is essential for the dynamic environment they face.

Alertness to changing conditions is not difficult. Nor does it require constant research and investigation. Most changes do not occur suddenly and without warning. Indeed, the business press is quick to highlight innovations and changing circumstances. The rise of the super office-equipment chains, such as OfficeMax, Staples, and Office Depot, was widely heralded and discussed, and their great growth was very visible. Before its changeover, Herman Miller made no attempt to cope with the obvious changes in the office-furniture market. The company either did not grasp the significance of change, or else judged its high-end niche to be solid and not contracting.

In adversity, altruistic concerns become dulled. —It is perhaps only natural that when firms face hard times, their benevolent tendencies toward employees and their proactive treatment of the environment lessens, and sometimes even disappears. Where downsizing is indicated, actions toward employees, even long-time ones, sometimes become ruthless. "Voluntary" early retirement may be mandatory, and severance pay far from generous.

But survival of the company is at stake, management counters critics. In a widely quoted statement, Albert Dunlap, the merciless terminator described in

---

[11] Press release, June 28, 2006, http://www.HermanMiller.com.

Chapter 2, said, "I see no point in sacrificing 100 percent of the employees for the 35 percent who ought to leave."[12]

Objectively, one wonders how many companies have grown so fat that more than one-third of the employees should be laid off.

Shareholder discontent is unhealthy for executives.—This is as it should be. Stockholders have the right to agitate for drastic shakeups when the company fortunes, as reflected in unsatisfactory stock prices, show little promise of improving, especially when competitive firms are doing much better, as Hon Industries was. Such comparisons indicate that the disappointing performance is not industry-related but reflects the failings of current and past management.

Executives who wish to keep their jobs should be concerned about shareholder satisfaction. Of course, this is easier said than done. Sometimes a company's problems are too deep-seated for easy remedies. But this leaves the current executives vulnerable to hostile takeovers by those who think the parts of the firm are worth more than the whole entity, and that it should be broken up, or that the bloated cost structure requires severe pruning by a new administration willing to wield a mean ax. Aggressive hedge funds today have little patience with share prices in the doldrums; they want positive action.

On the other hand, a complacent and management-dominated board may perpetuate incompetence far too long, and leave shareholders little recourse but to sell their stock, probably at a sizable loss.

A firm can keep—or regain—the growth mode without abandoning higher ethical standards.—As we see from the rebirth of Herman Miller, a firm can still be true to its desired higher ethical standards. Some deadwood products and employees may have to be phased out, and a leaner, more efficient structure imposed, but environmental concerns and good employee relations are still compatible with running an efficient and highly competitive firm.

CONSIDER

Can you think of additional learning insights?

QUESTIONS

1. "A worker-sensitive firm is bound eventually to face a competitive disadvantage. It cannot control its labor costs." Evaluate this statement.

2. Do you see any risks in Herman Miller's lowering its quality and its prices? Do you think it should have done so?

3. What do you think of the "enlightened" policy announced by Max DePree as he retired that henceforth no DePree would ever work for the firm again, in order that able people could have unimpeded career paths within the company? Discuss as many facets of this policy change as you can.

---

[12] Kenneth Labich, "Why Companies Fail," *Fortune*, November 14, 1994, p. 53.

4. Evaluate the statement by Dunlap of Scott Paper that "I see no point in sacrificing 100 percent of the employees for the 35 percent who ought to leave."

5. What do you think of the decision to forgo using an attractive wood because it was taken from a rain forest that needed to be protected?

6. What would be your prescription for a successful change manager? You might want to compare with Al Dunlap, and with Campbell, who only lasted two months at Herman Miller.

HANDS-ON EXERCISES

Before

1. Operating results for fiscal year 1987 have just come out. They show that net income dropped 11.9 percent from the previous year and 19 percent from 1985. What is even more troubling, net income as a percentage of sales fell from 8.3 percent in 1985 to 5.8 percent. What do you propose at this time?

After

2. It is July 1995. Chairman Campbell has just "resigned" under pressure from the board. You have been named his successor. What do you do now? (You may have to make some assumptions, but keep them reasonable and state them specifically.) Don't be bound by what actually happened. Maybe a different strategy would have been more successful.

TEAM DEBATE EXERCISE

Debate both sides of the controversy of whether a firm with enlightened and empathetic employee relations can compete in a climate of aggressive competitors and severe downsizing.

INVITATION TO RESEARCH

What is the situation with Herman Miller today? Is Michael Volkema still chief executive? Has Herman Miller continued its turnaround? Can you find any recent information about its employee and environmental relations?

PART
SIX

CONTROLLING

CHAPTER NINETEEN

United Way: A Not-for-Profit Organization Also Needs Controls and Oversight

T he United Way of America, the preeminent charitable organization in the United States, celebrated its 100-year anniversary in 1987. It had evolved from local community chests, and its strategy for fund-raising had proven highly effective: funding local charities through payroll deductions. The good it did seemed unassailable.

Abruptly in 1992, the image that United Way had created was jolted by revelations from investigative reporters of free-spending and other questionable deeds of its greatest builder and president, William Aramony. A major point of public concern was Aramony's salary and uncontrolled perks in a lifestyle that seemed inappropriate for a charitable organization that depended mostly on contributions from working people.

We are left to question the callousness and lack of concern with the ethical impact on the public image of this major charitable and not-for-profit entity. After all, unlike business firms that offer products or services to potential customers, charitable organizations depend on contributions that people give freely out of a desire to help society, with no tangible personal benefits. An image of high integrity and honest dealings without any semblance of corruption or privilege would seem essential for such organizations.

THE STATURE AND ACCOMPLISHMENTS OF THE UNITED WAY

Organizing the United Way as the umbrella charity to fund other local charities through payroll deductions established an effective means of fund-raising. As a not-for-profit entity, the United Way became the recipient of 90 percent of all charitable donations. It gained strong support from employers by involving them as leaders of annual campaigns. The extensive publicity would cause participating executives acute loss of face if their own organization did not go "over the top" in meeting campaign goals. As a result, employers sometimes used extreme pressure to achieve 100 percent participation by employees. A local United Way executive admitted that "if participation is 100 percent, it means someone has been coerced."[1]

For many years, outside of some tight-lipped gripes from corporate employees, the organization moved smoothly along, with local contributions generally increasing every year, although the need for charitable contributions invariably increased all the more.

The national organization, United Way of America (UWA), is a separate corporation and has no direct control over the approximately 2,200 local United Way offices. Most of the locals voluntarily contributed one cent on the dollar of all funds they collected. In return, the national organization provided training and promoted local United Way agencies through advertising and other marketing efforts.

Much of the success of the United Way movement in becoming the largest and most respected charity in the United States was due to the 22 years of William Aramony's leadership of the national organization. When he first took over, the United Ways were not operating under a common name. He built a nationwide network of agencies, all operating under the same name and using the same logo of outstretched hands, which became nationally recognized as the symbol of charitable giving. Unfortunately, in 1992 an exposé of Aramony's lavish lifestyle as well as other questionable dealings led to his downfall and burdened local United Ways with serious difficulties in fund-raising.

WILLIAM ARAMONY

During Aramony's tenure, United Way contributions increased from $787 million in 1970 to $3 billion in 1990. He increased his headquarters budget from less than $3 million to $29 million in 1991. Of this, $24 million came from the local United Ways, with the rest coming from corporate grants, investment income, and consulting. He built up the headquarters staff to 275 employees.[2]

Aramony moved comfortably among the most influential people in our society. He attracted a prestigious board of governors, including many top executives from America's largest corporations, but only three of the 37 came from not-for-profit organizations. The board was chaired by John Akers, chairman and CEO of IBM. Other board members included Edward A. Brennan, CEO of Sears; James D. Robinson III, CEO of American Express; and Paul J. Tagliabue, commissioner of the National Football League. The presence of these top executives brought prestige to United Way and spurred contributions from some of the largest and most visible organizations in the United States.

Aramony was the highest-paid executive in the charity field. In 1992, his compensation package was $463,000, nearly double that of the next-highest-paid

---

[1] Susan Garland, "Keeping a Sharper Eye on Those Who Pass the Hat," *Business Week*, March 16, 1992, p. 39.
[2] Charles E. Shepard, "Perks, Privileges and Power in a Nonprofit World," *Washington Post*, February 16, 1992, p. A38.

executive in the industry, Dudley H. Hafner of the American Heart Association. The board fully supported Aramony, regularly giving him 6 percent annual raises.[3]

Investigative Disclosures

The *Washington Post* began investigating Aramony's tenure as president of United Way of America in 1991, raising questions about his high salary, travel habits, possible cronyism, and dubious relations with five spin-off companies. In February 1992, it released the following information on Aramony's expense charges:[4]

- Aramony had charged $92,265 in limousine expenses to the charity during the previous five years.
- He had charged $40,762 on airfares for the supersonic Concorde.
- He had charged more than $72,000 on international airfares that included first-class flights for himself, his wife, and others.
- He had charged thousands more for personal trips, gifts, and luxuries.
- He had made 29 trips to Las Vegas, Nevada, between 1988 and 1991.
- He had expensed 49 journeys to Gainesville, Florida, the home of his daughter and a woman with whom he had a relationship.
- He had allegedly approved a $2 million loan to a firm run by his chief financial officer.
- He had approved the diversion of donors' money to questionable spin-off organizations run by long-time aides and provided benefits to family members as well.
- He had passed tens of thousands of dollars in consulting contracts from the UWA to friends and associates.

United Way of America's corporate policy prohibited the hiring of family members in the actual organization, but Aramony skirted the direct violation by hiring friends and relatives as consultants in the spin-off companies. He paid hundreds of thousands of dollars in consulting fees, for example, to two aides in vaguely documented and even undocumented business transactions.

The use of spin-off companies provided flexible maneuvering. One of the spin-off companies Aramony created to provide travel and bulk purchasing for United Way chapters purchased a $430,000 condominium in Manhattan and a $125,000 apartment in Coral Gables, Florida, for Aramony's use. Another of the spin-off companies hired Aramony's son, Robert Aramony, as its president. Loans and money transfers between the spin-off companies and the national organization raised questions. No records showed that the board of directors had been given the opportunity to approve the loans and transfers.[5]

---

[3] Joseph Finder, "Charity Case," *New Republic*, May 4, 1992, p. 11.
[4] Shepard, "Perks, Privileges and Power"; Kathleen Teltsch, "United Way Awaits Inquiry on Its President's Practices," *New York Times*, February 24, 1992, p. A12; Charles E. Shepard, "United Way Report Criticizes Ex-Leader's Lifestyle," *Washington Post*, April 4, 1992, p. A1.
[5] Shepard, p. A38.

CONSEQUENCES

When the information about Aramony's salary and expenses became public, the reaction was severe. Stanley C. Gault, chairman of Goodyear Tire & Rubber Co., asked: "Where was the board? The outside auditors?" Robert O. Bothwell, executive director of the National Committee for Responsive Philanthropy, said, "I think it is obscene that he is making that kind of salary and asking people who are making $10,000 a year to give 5 percent of their income."[6] At this point, let us examine the issue of executive compensation: Are many executives overpaid? See the Issue Box: Executive Compensation: Is It Too Much?"

ISSUE BOX

EXECUTIVE COMPENSATION: IS IT TOO MUCH?

At the time United Way's Aramony came under criticism, a controversy began mounting over the multi-million-dollar annual compensation of corporate executives. For example, in 1992, the average annual pay of CEOs was $3,842,247; the 20 highest-paid ranged from over $11 million to a mind-boggling $127 million for Thomas F. Frist Jr., of Hospital Corporation of America.[7] Pay of corporate executives has continued to climb robustly since 1992.

Activist shareholders, including some large mutual and pension funds, began protesting the high compensations, especially for top executives of firms that were not even doing well. New disclosure rules imposed in 1993 by the Securities & Exchange Commission (SEC) spotlighted questionable executive-pay practices. In the past—and still not uncommon today—complacent boards, themselves well paid and often closely aligned with the top executives of the organization, condoned liberal compensations. A major argument supporting high executive compensation is that their salaries are modest, compared to some entertainers and athletes, but their responsibilities are far greater. Another argument for high top-executive compensation is that pay incentives are needed to lure top talent, and that the present executive-pay system "has contributed to positive U. S. economic performance."

Institutional investors think a lot differently. Only 22 percent thought the pay system has helped the economy; over 90 percent saw top executives as "dramatically overpaid."[8]

In light of the for-profit executive compensations, Aramony's salary was modest. And the results were on his side: He made $369,000 in basic salary while raising $3 billion; Lee Iacocca, at the same time, made $3 million while Chrysler lost $795 million. Where is the justice?

[6] Garland, p. 39; Felicity Barringer, "United Way Head Is Forced Out in a Furor Over His Lavish Style," *New York Times*, February 28, 1992, p. A1.

[7] John A Byrne, "Executive Pay: The Party Ain't Over Yet," *Business Week*, April 26, 1993, p. A1.

[8] Carol Hymowitz, "Sky-High Payouts to Top Executives Prove Hard to Curb," *Wall Street Journal*, June 26, 2006, p. B1.

As head of a large for-profit corporation, Aramony undoubtedly could have earned several zeros more in compensation and perks, with no raised eyebrows. But isn't the situation different for a not-for-profit organization? Especially when revenues are derived from donations by millions of people of modest means? This is the controversy. On one hand, shouldn't a charity be willing to pay for the professional competence to run the organization as effectively as possible? But how do revelations of high compensation affect the public image and fund-raising of not-for-profit organizations?

What is your position regarding the compensation and perks of an Aramony, relative to the many times greater compensation of for-profit executives? How could CEO compensation be curbed?

As a major consequence of the scandal, some United Way locals withheld their funds, at least pending a thorough investigation of the allegations. John Akers, chairman of the board, noted that by March 7, 1992, dues payments were running 20 percent behind the previous year, and he admitted: "I don't think this process that the United Way of America is going through, or Mr. Aramony is going through, is a process that's bestowing a lot of honor."[9]

In addition to the decrease in dues payments, UWA was in danger of having its not-for-profit status revoked by the Internal Revenue Service because of the loans to the spin-off companies. For example, it loaned $2 million to a spin-off corporation in which the chief financial officer of UWA was also a director, this being a violation of not-for-profit corporate law. Moreover, UWA guaranteed a bank loan taken out by one of the spin-offs, also a violation of not-for-profit corporate law.[10]

The adverse publicity benefited competing charities, such as Earth Share, an environmental group. United Way, at one time the only major organization to receive contributions through payroll deductions, now found itself losing market share to other charities able to garner contributions in the same manner. For all the building that William Aramony had done, the United Way's status as the primary player in the American charitable industry was now in danger of disintegration due to his uncontrolled excesses.

On February 28, amid mounting pressure from local chapters threatening to withhold their annual dues, Aramony resigned. In August 1992, the United Way board of directors hired Elaine Chao, the Peace Corps director, to replace Aramony.

ELAINE CHAO

Chao's story was one of great achievement for a person only 39 years old. She was the eldest of six daughters in a family that came from Taiwan to California when Elaine was 8 years old and did not know a word of English. Through hard work, the family

[9] Felicity Barringer, "United Way Head Tries to Restore Trust," *New York Times*, March 7, 1992, p. 81.
[10] Shepard, "Perks," p. A38.

prospered. "Despite the difficulties ... we had tremendous optimism in the basic goodness of this country, that people are decent here, that we would be given a fair opportunity to demonstrate our abilities," she told an interviewer.[11] Chao's parents instilled in their six daughters the conviction that they could do anything they set their minds to, and all the daughters went to prestigious universities.

Elaine Chao earned an economics degree from Mount Holyoke in 1975, then went on for a Harvard MBA. She was a White House fellow, an international banker, chair of the Federal Maritime Commission, deputy secretary of the U.S. Transportation Department, and director of the Peace Corps before accepting the presidency of the United Way of America.

Chao's salary was $195,000, less than half of Aramony's. She cut budgets and staffs: no transatlantic flights on the Concorde, no limousine service, no plush condominiums. She expanded the board of governors to include more local representatives, and committees on ethics and finance were established. Still, she had no illusions about her job: "Trust and confidence once damaged will take a great deal of effort and time to heal."[12] The Information Box: Public Image discusses the special importance of the public image for not-for-profit agencies.

INFORMATION BOX

PUBLIC IMAGE FOR NOT-FOR-PROFIT ORGANIZATIONS

Product-oriented firms ought to be concerned and protective of their public image; even more so, not-for-profit organizations, such as schools, police departments, hospitals, politicians, and most of all, charitable organizations, should be concerned. Let us consider the importance of public image for representative not-for-profits.

Large city police departments often have a poor image among important segments of the population. The need to improve this image is hardly less important than for a manufacturer faced with a deteriorating brand image. A police department can develop a campaign to win friends; examples of possible activities aimed at creating a better image are promoting tours and open houses of police stations, crime laboratories, police lineups, and cells; speaking at schools; and sponsoring recreation projects, such as a day at the ballpark for youngsters.

Public school systems, faced with taxpayer revolts against mounting costs and image damage owing to teacher strikes, need conscious effort to improve their image in order to obtain more public support and funds.

Many nonbusiness organizations and institutions, such as hospitals, governmental bodies, even labor unions, have grown self-serving, dominated by a bureaucratic mentality so that perfunctory and callous treatment is the rule and the image is in the pits. Improvement of the image can only come through a greater emphasis on satisfying the public's needs.

[11] "United Way Chief Dedicated," *Cleveland Plain Dealer*," March 28, 1993, p. 24A.
[12] *Ibid.*

Not-for-profits are especially vulnerable to public image problems because they depend solely on voluntary support. The need to be untainted by scandal is crucial. In particular, great care must be exerted to ensure that contributions are being spent wisely and equitably, that overhead costs are kept reasonable, and that no opportunities exist for fraud and other misdeeds. The threat of investigative reporting must be feared and guarded against.

How can a not-for-profit organization be absolutely certain that moneys are not being misspent and that there are no ripoffs?

A Local United Way's Concerns

In April 1993, for the second time in a year, United Way of Greater Lorain County (Ohio) withdrew from the United Way of America. The board of the local chapter was still concerned about the financial stability and accountability of the national agency. In particular, it was concerned about the retirement settlement for Aramony. A significant "golden parachute" retirement package was being negotiated with him by the national board; it was in the neighborhood of $4 million. Learning of this triggered the Lorain County board's decision to again withdraw from UWA.

There were other reasons as well for their decision. The national agency was falling far short of its projected budget because only 890 of the 1,400 affiliates that had paid membership dues two years before were still paying. Roy Church, president of the Lorain agency, explained the board's decision: "Since February . . . it has become clear that United Way of America's financial stability and ability to assist locals has been put in question. The benefit of being a United Way of America member isn't there at this time for Lorain's United Way."[13]

Elaine Chao's task of resurrecting United Way of America would not be easy.

ANALYSIS

The lack of accountability to the donating public was a major factor in UWA's problems. The operation was so loosely run, with no one to approve or halt administrators' actions, that questionable practices were encouraged. It also opened the way for great shock and criticism, come the revelation. The fact that voluntary donations were the principal source of revenue made the lack of accountability all the more crucial. In a for-profit organization, lack of accountability primarily affects stockholders; for a major charitable organization, it affects millions of contributors, who see their money and/or commitment being squandered.

Where full disclosure and a system of checks and balances are lacking, the organization invites vulnerability on two fronts. The worst-case scenario is outright "white-collar theft," when unscrupulous people find it an opportunity for personal

---

[13] Karen Henderson, "Lorain Agency Cuts Ties with National United Way," *Cleveland Plain Dealer*, April 16, 1993, p. 7 C.

gain. The absence of sufficient controls and accountability can make even normally honest persons succumb to temptation. Second, insufficient controls tend to promote a mindset of arrogance and allow people to play fast and loose with the system. Aramony seemed to fall into this category with his spending extravagances, cronyism, and other conflict-of-interest activities.

The UWA theoretically had an overseer: the board, like the board of directors of a business corporation. But when the board members act as a rubber stamp, and are solidly in the camp of the chief executive, they are not really exercising control. This appeared to be the case with UWA during Aramony's "reign".

Certainly a board's failure to fulfill its responsibility is not unique to not-for-profits. Corporate boards have often been notorious for promoting the interests of the incumbent executives. Although the problem of compliant boards has received publicity and criticism of late, and is changing in some organizations, it still prevails in others. See the Issue Box: Role of the Board of Directors for a discussion.

ISSUE BOX

WHAT SHOULD BE THE ROLE OF THE BOARD OF DIRECTORS?

In the past, most boards of directors have tended to be rubber stamps, closely allied with top executives and even composed mostly of corporate officials. In some organizations today this is changing, mostly in response to critics concerned about board tendencies to always support the status quo and perpetuate the "establishment." More and more, opinion is shifting to the idea that boards must assume a more activist role:

> The board can no longer play a passive role in corporate governance. Today, more than ever, the board must assume an activist role—a role that is protective of shareholder rights, sensitive to communities in which the company operates, responsive to the needs of company vendors and customers, and fair to its employees.[14]

Incentives for more active boards have been the increasing risk of liability for board decisions, as well as liability insurance costs. Although the board of directors has long been seen as responsible for establishing corporate objectives, developing broad policies, and selecting top executives, this is no longer viewed as sufficient. Boards must also review management's performance to ensure that the company is well run and that stockholders' interests are furthered. And, today, they must ensure that society's best interests are not disregarded. All of this translates into an active concern for the organization's public image or reputation—its ethical conduct.

But the issue remains: To whom should the board owe its greatest allegiance—the entrenched bureaucracy or the external publics? Without having board members

---

[14] Lester B. Korn and Richard M. Ferry, Board of Directors Thirteenth Annual Study, New York: Korn/Ferry International, February 1986, pp. 1– 2.

representative of the many special interests affected by the organization, the inclination is to support the interests of the establishment.

Do you think a more representative and active board will prevent a similar scenario for United Way in the future? Why or why not?

UPDATE

William Aramony was convicted of defrauding the United Way out of $1 million. He was sentenced to seven years in prison for using the charity's money to finance a lavish lifestyle.

Despite this, a federal judge ruled in late 1998 that the charity must pay its former president more than $2 million in retirement benefits. "A felon, no matter how despised, does not lose his right to enforce a contract," U.S. District Judge Shira Scheindlin in New York ruled.[15]

Hurricane Katrina tested United Way in the fall of 2005, and it was not found wanting. United Way of Northeast Louisiana normally handled 7,000 calls a year. It fielded more than 111,000 calls across Louisiana during September and October 2005. Other United Ways throughout the Gulf Coast states as well as in communities with large numbers of Katrina evacuees responded to hundreds of thousands of telephone calls seeking such services as shelters, food, medical assistance, job training, post-disaster assistance, and recovery information (http://national.unitedway.org).

✩ ✩ ✩

Invitation to Make Your Own Analysis and Conclusions

How do you think Aramony's misuse of his position could have been prevented? What controls and accountability would you recommend? How would you persuade the board to be more socially responsible?

✩ ✩ ✩

WHAT CAN BE LEARNED?

Beware the arrogant mindset.—A leader with a mindset of superiority to subordinates and even to concerned outsiders—who sees other opinions as not acceptable—is a formula for disaster, both for an organization and for a society. It promotes dictatorship, intolerance of contrary opinions, and an attitude that "we need answer to no one." The consequences are as we have seen with

---

[15] Reported in *Cleveland Plain Dealer*, October 25, 1998, p. 24A

William Aramony: moving over the edge of what most deem acceptable and ethical conduct, assuming the role of the final authority who brooks no questions or criticism. The absence of real or imagined controls or reviews seems to bring out the worst in humans. We seem to need periodic scrutiny to avoid the trap of arrogant decision-making devoid of responsiveness to other concerns.

Checks and balances are even more important in not-for-profit and governmental bodies than in corporate entities.—For-profit organizations have "bottom-line" performance (i.e., profit-and-loss performance) as the ultimate control and standard. Not-for-profit and governmental organizations do not have this control, so they have no ultimate measure of their effectiveness.

Consequently, not-for-profit organizations should be subject to the utmost scrutiny by objective outsiders. Otherwise, abuses seem to be encouraged and perpetuated. Not-for-profit organizations are sheltered from competition, which usually demands greater efficiency. Thus, without objective and energetic controls, not-for-profit organizations have a tendency to get out of hand, to be run as little dynasties unencumbered by the constraints that face most businesses. Fortunately, investigative reporters and increased litigation by aggrieved parties today act as the needed controls for such organizations. In view of the revelations of investigative reporters, we are left to wonder how many other abusive and reprehensible activities have not as yet been detected.

Marketing of not-for-profits depends on trust and is particularly vulnerable to bad press.—Not-for-profits depend on donations for the bulk of their revenues. They depend on people to give without receiving anything tangible in return (unlike businesses). And the givers must have trust in the organization—trust that the contributions will be well spent, that the beneficiaries will receive maximum benefit, and that administrative costs will be low. Consequently, when publicity surfaces that causes such trust to be questioned, the impact can be devastating. Contributions can quickly dry up or be shunted to other charities.

With governmental bodies, of course, their perpetuation is hardly at stake with bad publicity. However, officials can be recalled, impeached, or not reelected.

CONSIDER

Can you add to these learning insights?

QUESTIONS

1. As a potential or actual giver to United Way campaigns, how do you feel, about Aramony's "high living"? Would these allegations affect your gift giving? Why or why not?

2. What prescriptions do you have for thwarting arrogance in not-for-profit and/or governmental organizations? Be as specific as you can, and support your recommendations.

3. How do you personally feel about the coercion that some organizations exert for their employees to contribute substantially to the United Way? What implications, if any, do you see as emerging from your attitudes about this?

4. "Since there is no bottom-line evaluation for performance, nonprofits have no incentives to control costs and prudently evaluate expenditures." Discuss.

5. How would you feel, as a large contributor to a charity, about its spending $10 million for advertising? Discuss your rationale for this attitude.

6. Do you think the action taken by UWA after Aramony was the best way to salvage the public image? Why or why not? What else might have been done?

HANDS-ON EXERCISES

1. You are an adviser to Elaine Chao, who has taken over the scandal-ridden United Way. What advice do you give her for as quickly as possible restoring the confidence of the American public in the integrity and worthiness of this preeminent national charity organization?

2. You are a member of the board of governors of United Way. Allegations have surfaced about the lavish lifestyle of the highly regarded Aramony. Most of the board members, being corporate executives, see nothing at all wrong with his perks and privileges. You, however, feel otherwise. How would you convince the other board members of the error of condoning Aramony's activities? Be as persuasive as you can in supporting your position.

TEAM DEBATE EXERCISE

Debate this issue: No not-for-profit organization can ever attain the efficiency of a business firm that always has the bottom line to be concerned about.

INVITATION TO RESEARCH

What is the situation with United Way today? Are all local agencies contributing to the national? Have donations matched or exceeded previous levels? Has Elaine Chao restored confidence? What is Elaine Chou doing now?

CHAPTER TWENTY

Maytag: Incredibly Loose Supervision of a Foreign Subsidiary; Also, the Allure of Outsourcing

*T*he atmosphere at the annual meeting in the little Iowa town of Newton had turned contentious. As Leonard Hadley faced increasingly angry questions from disgruntled shareholders, the thought crossed his mind: "I don't deserve this!" After all, he had been CEO of Maytag Corporation for only a few months, and this was his first chairing of an annual meeting. But the earnings of the company had been declining every year since 1988, and in 1992, Maytag had had a $315.4 million loss. No wonder the stockholders in the packed Newton High School auditorium were bitter and critical of their management. But there was more. Just the month before, the company had the public embarrassment and costly atonement resulting from a monumental blunder in the promotional planning of its United Kingdom subsidiary.

Hadley doggedly saw the meeting to its close, and limply concluded: "Hopefully, both sales and earnings will improve this year."[1]

THE FIASCO

In August 1992, Hoover Limited, Maytag's British subsidiary, launched a travel promotion: Anyone in the United Kingdom buying more than 100 U.K. pounds worth of Hoover products (about $150) before the end of January 1993 would get two free round-trip tickets to selected European destinations. For 250 U.K. pounds worth of Hoover products, they would get two free round-trip tickets to New York or Orlando.

[1] Richard Gibson, "Maytag's CEO Goes Through Wringer at Annual Meeting," *Wall Street Journal*, April 28, 1993, p. A5.

A buying frenzy resulted. Consumers had quickly figured out that the value of the tickets easily exceeded the cost of the appliances necessary to be eligible for them. By the tens of thousands, Britishers rushed out to buy just enough Hoover products to qualify. Appliance stores were emptied of vacuum cleaners. The Hoover factory in Cambuslang, Scotland, that had been making vacuum cleaners only three days a week was suddenly placed on a 24-hour, seven-day-a-week production schedule—an overtime bonanza for the workers. What a resounding success for a promotion! Hoover managers, however, were unhappy.

Hoover had never ever expected more than 50,000 people to respond. And of those responding, it expected far fewer would go through all the steps necessary to qualify for the free trip and really take it. But more than 200,000 not only responded but also qualified for the free tickets. The company was overwhelmed. The volume of paperwork created such a bottleneck that by the middle of April only 6,000 people had flown. Thousands of others either never got their tickets, were not able to get the dates requested, or waited for months without hearing the results of their applications. Hoover established a special hot line to process customer complaints, and these were coming in at 2,000 calls a day. But the complaints quickly spread, and the ensuing publicity brought charges of fraud and demands for restitution. This raises the issue of loss leaders—how much should we use loss leaders as a promotional device?—discussed in the following Issue Box.

ISSUE BOX

SHOULD WE USE LOSS LEADERS?

Leader pricing is a type of promotion with certain items advertised at a very low price—sometimes even below cost, in which case they are known as loss leaders—in order to attract more customers. The rationale is that customers are likely to purchase other, regular-price items as well, with the result that total sales and profits will be increased. If customers do not purchase enough other goods at regular prices to more than cover the losses incurred from the attractively priced bargains, then the loss leader promotion is ill-advised. Some critics maintain that the whole idea of using loss leaders is absurd: The firm is just "buying sales" with no regard for profits.

While UK Hoover did not think of its promotion as a loss leader, in reality it was: The company stood to lose money on every sale if the promotional offer was taken advantage of. Unfortunately for its effectiveness as a loss leader, the likelihood of customers purchasing other Hoover products at regular prices was remote, and the level of acceptance was not capped, so that losses were permitted to multiply. The conclusion has to be that this was an ill-conceived idea from the beginning. It violated the two central conditions for loss leaders: that they should stimulate sales of other products, and that the losses should be limited.

Do you think loss leaders really are desirable under certain circumstances? Why or why not?

Maytag dispatched a task force to try to resolve the situation without jeopardizing customer relations any further. But it acknowledged that it's "not 100% clear" that all eligible buyers will receive their free flights.[2] The ill-fated promotion was a staggering blow to Maytag financially. It took a $30 million charge in the first quarter of 1993 to cover unexpected additional costs linked to the promotion. Final costs were expected to exceed $50 million, which would be 10 percent of UK Hoover's total revenues. This for a subsidiary acquired only four years before that had yet to produce a profit.

Adding to the costs were problems with the two travel agencies involved. The agencies were to obtain low-cost space-available tickets, and would earn commissions selling "packages," including hotels, rental cars, and insurance. If consumers bought a package, Hoover would get a cut. Despite the overwhelming demand for tickets, however, most consumers declined to purchase the package, thus greatly reducing support money for the promotional venture. So, Hoover greatly underestimated the likely response, and overestimated the amount it would earn from commission payments.

If these cost-overruns had added greatly to Maytag's and Hoover's customer relations and public image, the expenditures would have seemed more palatable. But with all the problems, the best that could be expected would be to lessen the worst of the agitation and charges of deception. And this was proving to be impossible. The media, of course, salivated at the problems and were quick to sensationalize them:

> One disgruntled customer, who took aggressive action on his own, received the widest press coverage, and even became a folk hero. Dave Dixon, claiming he was cheated out of a free vacation by Hoover, seized one of the company's repair vans in retaliation. Police were sympathetic: they took him home, and did not charge him, claiming it was a civil matter.[3]

Heads rolled also. Initially, Maytag fired three UK Hoover executives involved, including the president of Hoover Europe. Hadley, at the annual meeting, indicated that others might also lose their jobs before the cleanup was complete. He likened the promotion to "a bad accident . . . and you can't determine what was in the driver's mind."[4]

Receiving somewhat less publicity was the question of why corporate headquarters allowed executives of a subsidiary such wide latitude that they could saddle parent Maytag with tens of millions in unexpected costs. Didn't top corporate executives have to approve ambitious plans? A company spokesman said that operating divisions were "primarily responsible" for planning promotional expenses. While the parent may review such outlays, "if they're within parameters, it goes through."[5] This

[2] James P. Miller, "Maytag U.K. Unit Find a Promotion Is Too Successful," *Wall Street Journal*, March 31, 1993, p. A9.

[3] "Unhappy Brit Holds Hoover Van Hostage," *Cleveland Plain Dealer*, June 1, 1993, p. D1; Simon Reeve and John Harlow, "Hoover Is Sued over Flights Deal," *London Sunday Times*, June 6, 1993.

[4] Gibson, p. A5.

[5] Miller, p. A9.

raises the question, discussed in the following Issue Box, of how loose a rein foreign subsidiaries should be allowed.

ISSUE BOX

HOW LOOSE A REIN FOR A FOREIGN SUBSIDIARY?

In a decentralized organization, top management delegates considerable decision-making authority to subordinates. Such decentralization—often called a "loose rein"—tends to be more marked with foreign subsidiaries, such as UK Hoover. Corporate management in the United States understandably feels less familiar with the foreign environment and therefore is more willing to let the native executives operate with fewer constraints than it might with a domestic subsidiary. In the Maytag/Hoover situation, decision-making authority by British executives was evidently extensive, and corporate Maytag exercised little operational control, being content to judge performance by the ultimate results achieved. Major deviations from expected performance goals, or widespread traumatic happenings—all of which happened to UK Hoover—finally gained corporate management's attention.

Major advantages of extensive decentralization or a loose rein, are: (1) top-management effectiveness can be improved, since time and attention are freed for presumably more important matters; (2) subordinates are permitted more self-management, which should improve their competence and motivation; and (3) in foreign environments, native managers presumably better understand their unique problems and opportunities than corporate management, located thousands of miles away, possibly can. But the drawbacks are as we have seen. The parameters within which subordinate managers operate can be so wide that serious miscalculations may not be stopped in time. Since top management is ultimately responsible for all performance, including actions of subordinates, it faces greater risks with extensive decentralization and giving a free rein.

"Since the manager is ultimately accountable for whatever is delegated to subordinates, a free rein reflects great confidence in subordinates." Discuss.

BACKGROUND ON MAYTAG

Maytag is a century-old company. The original business, founded in 1893, manufactured feeder attachments for threshing machines. In 1907, the company moved to Newton, Iowa, a small town 30 miles east of Des Moines, the capital. Manufacturing emphasis turned to home-laundry equipment and wringer-type washers.

A natural expansion of this emphasis occurred with the commercial laundromat business in the 1930s, when coin meters were attached to Maytag washers. Rapid growth of coin-operated laundries took place in the United States during the late 1950s and early 1960s. The 1970s hurt laundromats with increased competition and soaring energy costs. In 1975, Maytag introduced new energy-efficient machines, and "Home Style" stores that rejuvenated the business.

TABLE 20.1. Maytag Operating Results, 1974–1981 (in millions)

	Net Sales	Net Income	Percent of Sales
1974	$229	$21.1	9.2%
1975	238	25.9	10.9
1976	275	33.1	12.0
1977	299	34.5	11.5
1978	325	36.7	11.3
1979	369	45.3	12.3
1980	346	35.6	10.2
1981	409	37.4	9.1

Average net income percent of sales: 10.8%

Source: Company operating statistics.

Commentary: These years show a steady, though not spectacular growth in revenues, and a generally rising net income, except for 1980. Of particular interest is the high net income percentage of sales, averaging 10.8 percent over the 8-year period, with a high of 12.3 percent.

The Lonely Maytag Repairman

For years Maytag reveled in a coup, with its washers and dryers enjoying a top-quality image thanks to decades-long ads in which a repairman laments his loneliness because of Maytag's trouble-free products. (The actor who portrayed the repairman died in early 1997.) The result of this dependability and quality image was that Maytag could command a price premium: "Their machines cost the same to make, break down as much as ours—but they get $100 more because of the reputation," grumbled a competitor.[6]

During the 1970s and into the 1980s, Maytag continued to capture 15 percent of the washing-machine market, and enjoyed profit margins about twice that of competitors. Table 20.1 shows operating results for the period 1974–1981. Whirlpool was the largest factor in the laundry equipment market, with a 45 percent share, but this was largely because of sales to Sears under the Kenmore brand.

Acquisitions

For many years, until his retirement on December 31, 1992, Daniel J. Krumm influenced Maytag's destinies. He had been CEO for 18 years and chairman since 1986, and his tenure with the company encompassed 40 years. In that time, the home-appliance business encountered some drastic changes. The most ominous occurred in the late 1980s with the merger mania, in which the threat of takeovers by

---

[6] Brian Bremmer, "Can Maytag Clean Up Around the World?" *Business Week*, January 30, 1989, p. 89.

TABLE 20.2. Maytag Operating Results, 1989–1992

	Revenue (000,000)	Net Income	% of Revenue
1989	$3,089	131.0	4.3%
1990	3,057	98.9	3.2
1991	2,971	79.0	2.7
1992	3,041	(315.4)	(10.4)

Source: Company annual reports.

Commentary: Note the steady erosion of profitability, while sales remained virtually static. For a comparison with profit performance of earlier years, see Table 20.1 and the net income to sales percentages of this more "golden" period.

hostile raiders often motivated heretofore conservative executives to greatly increase corporate indebtedness, thereby decreasing the attractiveness of their firms. Daniel Krumm was one of these running-scared executives, as rumors persisted that the company was a takeover candidate.

Largely as a defensive move, Krumm pushed through a deal for a $1 billion buyout of Chicago Pacific Corporation (CPC), a maker of vacuum cleaners and other appliances with $1.4 billion in sales. As a result, Maytag was burdened with $500 million in new debt. Krumm defended the acquisition as giving Maytag a strong foothold in a growing overseas market. CPC was best known for the Hoover vacuums it sold in the United States and Europe. Indeed, so dominant was the Hoover brand in England that many people did not vacuum their carpets, but "hoovered" them. CPC also made washers, dryers, and other appliances under the Hoover brand, selling them exclusively in Europe and Australia. In addition, it had six furniture companies, but Maytag sold these shortly after the acquisition.

Krumm had been instrumental in transforming Maytag, the number-four U.S. appliance manufacturer—behind General Electric, Whirlpool, and Electrolux—from a niche laundry-equipment maker into a full-line manufacturer. He had led an earlier acquisition spree in which Maytag expanded into microwave ovens, electric ranges, refrigerators, and freezers. Its brands now included Magic Chef, Jenn-Air, Norge, and Admiral. The last years of Krumm's reign, however, were not marked by great operating results. As shown in Table 20.2, revenues showed no gain in the 1989–1992 period, while income steadily declined.

Trouble

Although the rationale for internationalizing seemed inescapable, especially in view of the recent wave of joint ventures between U.S. and European appliance makers, still the Hoover acquisition was troublesome. While it was a major brand in England and in Australia, Hoover had only a small presence in Europe. Yet, this was where the bulk of the market was, with some 320 million potential appliance buyers.

The probabilities of the Hoover subsidiary being able to capture much of the European market were hardly promising. Whirlpool was strong, having ten plants there in contrast to Hoover's two plants. Furthermore, Maytag faced entrenched European competitors, such as Sweden's Electrolux, the world's largest appliance maker; Germany's Bosch-Siemens; and Italy's Merloni Group. General Electric had also entered the market with joint ventures. The fierce loyalty of Europeans to domestic brands raised further questions about the ability of Maytag's Hoover to penetrate the European market without massive promotional efforts, and maybe not even then.

Australia was something else. Hoover had a good competitive position there, and its refrigerator plant in Melbourne could easily be expanded to include Maytag's washers and dryers. Unfortunately, the small population of Australia limited the market to only about $250 million for major appliances.

Britain accounted for half of Hoover's European sales. But at the time of the acquisition, its major appliance business was only marginally profitable. This was to change: after the acquisition it became downright unprofitable, as shown in Table 20.3 for the years 1990 through 1992, as it struggled to expand in a recession-plagued Europe. The results for 1993, of course, reflected the huge loss from the promotional debacle. Hardly an acquisition made in heaven.

TABLE 20.3. Operating Results of Maytag's Principal Business Components, 1990–1992

	Revenue (000,000)	Income*(000)
1990		
North American Appliances	$2,212	$221,165
Vending	191	25,018
European Sales	497	(22,863)
1991		
North American Appliances	2,183	186,322
Vending	150	4,498
European Sales	486	(865)
1992		
North American Appliances	2,242	129,680
Vending	165	16,311
European Sales	502	(67,061)

*This is operating income, that is, income before depreciation and other adjustments.

Source: Company annual reports.

Commentary: While these years were not particularly good for Maytag in growth of revenues and income, the continuing, and even intensifying, losses in the Hoover European operation had to be troublesome. And this is before the ill-fated early 1993 promotional results.

TABLE 20.4.   Long-Term Debt as a Percent
of Capital from Maytag's Balance Sheets,
1986–1991

Year	Long-Term Debt/Capital
1986	7.2%
1987	23.3
1988	48.3
1989	46.8
1990	44.1
1991	42.7

Source: Company annual reports.

Commentary: The effect of acquisitions, in particular that of the Chicago Pacific Corporation, can be clearly seen in the buildup of long-term debt. In 1986, Maytag was virtually free of such commitments; two years later its long-term debt ratio had increased almost seven-fold.

Maytag's earlier acquisitions also were becoming soured. Its acquisitions of Magic Chef and Admiral were diversifications into lower-priced appliances, and these did not meet expectations. But they left Maytag's balance sheet and cash flow weakened (see Table 20.4). Perhaps more serious, Maytag's reputation as the nation's premier appliance maker was tarnished. Meanwhile, General Electric and Whirlpool were attacking the top end of its product line. As a result, Maytag found itself in the No. 3 or 4 position in most of its brand lines.

ANALYSIS

Flawed Acquisition Decisions

The long decline in profits after 1989 should have triggered strong concern and corrective action. Perhaps it did, but the action was ineffectual, and the decline continued, culminating in a large deficit in 1992 and serious problems in 1993. As shown in Table 20.2, the acquisitions brought neither revenue gains nor profitability. One suspects that in the rush to fend off raiders in the late 1980s, the company bought businesses it might never have in more sober times, and that it paid too much for these businesses. Further, they cheapened the proud image of quality for Maytag.

Who Can We Blame in the U.K. Promotional Debacle?

Maytag's corporate managers were guilty of a common fault in their acquisitions: they gave newly acquired divisions a loose rein, letting them continue to operate independently with few constraints: "After all, these executives should be more knowledgeable about their operations than corporate headquarters would be." Such confidence is sometimes misguided. In the U.K. promotion, Maytag management would seem as derelict as management in England. Planning guidelines or parameters were far too loose and undercontrolled. The idea of subsidiary management being able to burden the parent with $50 million of unexpected charges, and to have this erupt with no warning, borders on the absurd.

Finally, the planning of the U.K. executives for this ill-conceived travel promotion defies all logic. They vastly underestimated the demand for the promotional offer, and they greatly overestimated the paybacks from travel agencies on the package deals. Yet it took no brilliant insight to realize that the value of the travel offer exceeded the price of the appliance—indeed, 200,000 customers rapidly arrived at this conclusion—and that such a sweetheart of a deal would be irresistible to many, and that it could prove to be costly in the extreme to the company. A miscalculation, or complete naivete on the part of executives and their staffs, who should have known better?

How Could the Promotion Have Avoided the Problems?

The great problem resulting from an offer that was too good could have been avoided, and without scrapping the whole idea. A cost-benefit analysis would have provided at least a perspective as to how much the company should spend to achieve certain benefits, such as increased sales, greater consumer interest, and favorable publicity. See the following Information Box for a more detailed discussion of the important planning tool of a cost-benefit analysis.

INFORMATION BOX

COST-BENEFIT ANALYSIS

A cost-benefit analysis is a systematic comparison of the costs and benefits of a proposed action. Only if the benefits exceed the costs would we normally have a "go" decision. The usual way to make such an analysis is to assign dollar values to all the costs and benefits, thus providing a common basis for comparison.

Cost-benefit analyses have been widely used by the Defense Department in evaluating alternative weapons systems. In recent years, such analyses have been sporadically applied to environmental regulation and even to workplace safety standards. As an example of the former, a cost-benefit analysis can be used to determine whether it is socially worth spending X million dollars to meet a certain standard of clean air or water.

Many business decisions lend themselves to a cost-benefit analysis. It provides a systematic way of analyzing the inputs and the probable outputs of major alternatives. In a business setting some of the costs and benefits can be very quantitative, but they often should be tempered by nonquantitative inputs to reach the broadest perspective. Schermerhorn suggests considering the following criteria in evaluating alternatives: [7]

Benefits: What are the benefits of using the alternatives to solve a performance deficiency or take advantage of an opportunity?

---

[7] John R. Schermerhorn, Jr., *Management*, 6th ed. (New York: Wiley, 1999), p. 61.

Costs: What are the costs of implementing the alternatives, including direct resource investments as well as any potentially negative side-effects?

Timeliness: How fast will the benefits occur and a positive impact be achieved?

Acceptability: To what extent will the alternatives be accepted and supported by those who must work with them?

Ethical soundness: How well do the alternatives meet acceptable ethical criteria in the eyes of multiple stakeholders?

What numbers would you assign to a cost-benefit analysis for Maytag Hoover's plan to offer the free airline tickets, under an assumption of 5,000 takers? 20,000 takers, 100,000 takers? 500,000 takers? (Hint: We know that 200,000 people qualified for the free tickets, and that the final costs were expected to reach $50 million. If we assume that costs would have a straight-line relationship with number of takers, then costs for 5,000 takers would be 2.5 percent of $50 million, 20,000 takers would be 10 percent, and so on. Now you need to estimate the value of the benefits for the various levels of takers.) What would be your conclusions for these various acceptance rates? Is there a point of diminishing returns?

A cost-benefit analysis should certainly have alerted management to the possible consequences of various acceptance levels, and of the significant risks of high acceptance. The company could have set limits on the number of eligibles: perhaps the first 1,000, or the first 5,000. Doing this would have held or capped the costs to reasonably defined levels, and avoided the greater risks. Or the company could have made the offer less generous, perhaps by upping the requirements, or by lessening the premiums. These more moderate alternatives would still have made an attractive promotion, but not the major uncontrolled catastrophe that happened.

Final Resolution of the Promotion Mess?

Maytag's invasion of Europe proved a costly failure. In the summer of 1995, Maytag gave up. It sold its European operations to an Italian appliance maker, recording a $135 million loss.

Even by the end of 1996, the Hoover mess was still not cleaned up. Hoover had spent $72 million flying some 220,000 people and had hoped to end the matter. But the fight continued four years later, with disgruntled customers who never flew taking Hoover to court. Even though Maytag had sold this troubled division, it could not escape the emerging lawsuits.[8]

---

[8] "Hoover Can't Clean Up Mess from Free Flights," *Cleveland Plain Dealer,* December 12, 1996, p. 1C; Dirk Beveridge, "Hoover Loses Two Lawsuits Tied to Promotion," *Gannett Newspapers,* February 21, 1997, p. 4F.

LATER DEVELOPMENTS
Leonard Hadley

In the summer of 1998, Leonard Hadley could look forward and backward with some satisfaction. He would retire the next summer when he turned 65, and he had already picked his successor. Since assuming the top position in Maytag in January 1993 and confronting the mess with the U.K. subsidiary during his first few months on the job, he had turned Maytag completely around.

He knew no one had expected much change from him, an accountant who had joined Maytag right out of college. He was known as a loyal but unimaginative lieutenant of his boss, Daniel Krumm, who died of cancer shortly after naming Hadley his successor. After all, he reflected, no one thought that major change could come to an organization from someone who had spent his whole life there, who was a clone, so to speak, and an accountant to boot. Everyone thought that changemakers had to come from outside, like Al Dunlap of Scott Paper and Sunbeam (as described in Chapter 2). Well, he had shown them, and given hope to all number-two executives who resented Wall Street's love affair with outsiders.

Within a few weeks of taking over, he'd fired a bunch of managers, especially those rascals in the U.K. who'd masterminded the great Hoover debacle. He determined to get rid of foreign operations, most of them newly acquired and unprofitable. He just did not see that appliances could be profitably made for every corner of the world, because of the variety of regional customs. Still, he knew that many disagreed with him about this, including some of the board members who thought globalization was the only way to go. Still, over the next 18 months he had prevailed.

He chuckled to himself as he reminisced. He had also overturned the decades-long corporate mindset not to be first to market with new technology because they would "rather be right than be first." His "Galaxy Initiative" of nine top-secret new products was a repudiation of the old mindset. One of them, the Neptune, a front-loading washer retailing at $1,100, certainly proved him right. Maytag had increased its production three times and raised its suggested retail price twice, and still it was selling like gangbusters. Perhaps the thing he was proudest of was getting Maytag products into Sears stores, the seller of one-third of all appliances in the United States. Sears' desire to have the Neptune was what swung the deal.

As an accountant, he probably should be focusing first on the numbers. Well, 1997 was certainly a banner year, with sales up 10.9 percent over the previous year, while profitability, as measured by return on capital, was 16.7 percent, both sales and profit gains leading the industry. And 1998 so far was proving to be even better, with sales jumping 31 percent and earnings 88 percent.

He remembered the remarks of Lester Crown, a Maytag director: "Len Hadley has—quietly, softly—done a spectacular job. Obviously, we just lacked the ability to evaluate him [in the beginning]."[9]

---

[9] Carl Quintanilla, "Maytag's Top Officer, Expected to Do Little, Surprises His Board," *Wall Street Journal*, June 23, 1998, pp. A1, A8.

Leonard Hadley retired August 12, 1999. He knew he had surprised everyone in the organization by going outside Maytag for his successor. He chose Lloyd Ward, 50, Maytag's first black executive, a marketing expert from PepsiCo, and before that Procter & Gamble, who had joined Maytag in 1996 and was currently president and chief operating officer.

However, with extreme regret Hadley found that his choice of a successor was flawed, or maybe Ward was just a victim of circumstances mostly beyond his control. After 15 months, Ward left, citing differences with Maytag's directors amid sorry operating results. Hadley came out of retirement to be interim president and CEO. Some 3,400 Maytag workers, a quarter of Newton's population, roared when they heard the news. They had feared the company would be moved to either Chicago or Dallas, or that it would be sold to Sweden's Electrolux. Hadley assured them that no such thing would ever happen as long as he was at the helm.[10] Hadley retired again in June 2001 when Ralph F. Hake became his successor.

Hake came to Maytag from Fluor Corporation, an engineering and construction firm, where he had been executive vice president. Before that he spent 12 years in various executive positions with Maytag's chief rival, appliance manufacturer Whirlpool.

Hake kept the headquarters in Newton, Iowa, but moved three plants to Reynosa, Mexico, intensifying fears that Maytag might export even more jobs to countries with cheap labor. He tried to allay such concerns: "I do not anticipate multiple plant shutdowns or restructuring here." However, some analysts cautioned that consumers were becoming increasingly cost conscious—and less concerned with whether a product is made in the United States or abroad.

Hake also sought to move the company's product line beyond the traditional to more unusual products. He created a Strategic Initiatives Group with 10 to 12 members to introduce a premium-priced line of mixers, blenders, toasters, and coffee makers under the brand name Jenn-Air Attrezzi. The hope was that a focus on creative thinking would move the company out of its slump.[11]

The Allure (and Necessity?) of Outsourcing

Even though Hake had moved some manufacturing jobs to cheaper labor overseas, Maytag was slower to do this than its competitors, and by 2005, it was hurting, with its stock plummeting, and its dividend slashed in half. While 12 percent of its products were made abroad, larger competitors such as Whirlpool and General Electric had huge cost advantages with more than half their production overseas. In recent years, Maytag also had to compete against nimble Asian newcomers, including South Korean

---

[10] "Maytag Chief Quits as Profits Plummet," *Cleveland Plain Dealer*, November 10, 2000, p. 3C; Emily Gersema, "Maytag Re-hires Former CEO After Time of Internal Turmoil," *Wall Street Journal*, January 15, 2001, p. 3H.

[11] David Pitt, Associated Press, as reported in "Maytag's Moves to Mexico Under Fire," *Cleveland Plain Dealer*, August 6, 2003, p. C2; Fara Warner, *New York Times*, as reported in "Maytag Cookin' With New Twist on Tools for the Kitchen," *Cleveland Plain Dealer*, September 14, 2003, pp. G1, and G6.

LG Electronics, which had brought innovative appliances to the United States a few years earlier.

In 2005, with its sickly stock price, Maytag now became an attractive buyout. Ripplewood Holdings, an investment group, bid $14 a share for the company. This offer was bested by Whirlpool, which offered $21 a share in cash and stock to Maytag shareholders, and the deal was sealed. American jobs and Newton, Iowa, jobs in particular, were in jeopardy.[12]

❊ ❊ ❊

Invitation for Your Own Analysis and Conclusions

How could American jobs have been better saved in the competitive appliance industry?

❊ ❊ ❊

WHAT CAN BE LEARNED?

Again—Beware overpaying for an acquisition.—Hoping to diversify its product line and gain overseas business, Maytag paid $1 billion for Chicago Pacific in 1989. As it turned out, this was far too much, and the debt burden was an albatross. Hadley conceded as much: "In the long view, it was correct to invest in these businesses. But the timing of the deal, and the price of the deal, made the debt a heavy burden to carry."[13]

Zeal to expand, and/or the desire to reduce the attractiveness of a firm's balance sheet with heavy debt and thus fend off potential raiders, does not excuse foolhardy management. The consequences of bad decisions remain to haunt a company, and the ill-advised purchases often have to be sold off at substantial losses (as we saw in Chapter 8). The analysis of potential acquisition candidates must be soberly and thoroughly done, and rosy projections questioned, even if this means the deal may be soured.

In decision planning, consider a worst-case scenario.—There are those who preach the desirability of positive thinking, confidence, and optimism—whether it be in personal lives, athletics, or business practices. But expecting and preparing for the worst has much to commend it, since a person or a firm is then better able to cope with adversity, avoid being overwhelmed, and more likely to make prudent rather than rash decisions.

Apparently the avid acceptance of the promotional offer was a complete surprise; no one dreamed of such wide demand. Yet was it so unreasonable to think that a very attractive offer would meet wild acceptance?

---

[12] Dennis K. Berman and Michael McCarthy, "Maytag to Be Sold to Investor Group for $1.13 Billion," *Wall Street Journal*, May 20, 2005, pp. A3, A10; Joseph T. Hallinan, "Whirlpool Seals Maytag Deal; Antitrust Review Is Next Battle," *Wall Street Journal*, August 23, 2005, p. B10.

[13] Kenneth Labich, "Why Companies Fail," *Fortune*, November 14, 1994, p. 60.

In using loss leaders, put a cap on potential losses.—Loss leaders, as we noted earlier, are items promoted at such attractive prices that the firm loses money on every sale. The expectation, of course, is that the customer traffic generated by such attractive promotions will increase sales of regular-profit items so that total profits will be increased.

The risks of uncontrolled or uncapped loss leader promotions are vividly shown in this case. For a retailer who uses loss leaders, the loss is ultimately capped as the inventory is sold off. With UK Hoover there was no cap. The solution is clear: Attractive loss-leader promotions should be capped, such as the first 100 or the first 1,000 or for one week only. Otherwise, the promotion should be made less attractive.

Beware giving too loose a rein, thus sacrificing controls, especially of unproven foreign subsidiaries.—Although decentralizing authority down to lower ranks is often desirable and results in better motivation and management development than centralization, it can be overdone. At the extreme, where divisional and subsidiary executives have almost unlimited decision-making authority and can run their operations as virtual dynasties, corporate management essentially abdicates its authority. Such looseness in an organization endangers cohesiveness; it tends to obscure common standards and objectives; and it can even dilute unified ethical practices.

Extreme looseness of control is not uncommon with acquisitions, especially foreign ones. It is easy to make the assumption that the foreign executives were operating successfully before the acquisition and have more first-hand knowledge of the environment than the corporate executives.

Still, there should be limits on how much freedom these executives should be permitted—especially when their operations have not been notably successful. In Maytag's case, the U.K. subsidiary had lost money every year since it was acquired. Accordingly, one would expect prudent corporate management to have condoned less decentralization and insisted on tighter controls than it might otherwise.

The power of a cost-benefit analysis.—For major decisions, executives have much to gain from a cost-benefit analysis. It forces them to systematically tabulate and analyze the costs and benefits of particular courses of action. They may find that likely benefits are so uncertain as to not be worth the risk. If so, now is the time to realize this, rather than after substantial commitments have already been made.

Without doubt, regular use of cost-benefit analyses for major decisions improves executives' batting averages for good decisions. Even though some numbers may have to be judgmental, especially as to probable benefits, the process of making the analysis forces a careful look at alternatives and the most likely consequences. For more important decisions, input from diverse staff people and executives will bring greater power to the analysis.

CONSIDER

What additional learning insights can you add?

QUESTIONS

1. How could the promotion of UK Hoover have been better designed? Be as specific as you can.

2. Given the fiasco that did occur, how do you think Maytag should have responded?

3. "Firing the three top executives of UK Hoover is unconscionable. It smacks of a vendetta against European managers by an American parent. After all, their only 'crime' was a promotion that was too successful." Comment on this statement.

4. Do you think Leonard Hadley, the Maytag CEO for only two months, should be soundly criticized for the U.K. situation? Why or why not?

5. Please speculate: Why do you think the UK Hoover fiasco happened in the first place? What went wrong?

6. Evaluate the decision to acquire Chicago Pacific Corporation (CPC). Do this both for the time of the decision and for now—after the fact—as a post-mortem. Defend your overall conclusions.

7. Use your creativity: Can you devise a strategy for UK Hoover to become more of a major force in Europe?

8. Evaluate Hadley's reflections in the summer of 1998. Do you agree with all of his convictions and actions? Why or why not?

HANDS-ON EXERCISES

1. You have been placed in charge of a task force sent by headquarters to England to coordinate the fire-fighting efforts in the aftermath of the ill-fated promotion. There is neither enough productive capacity nor enough airline seating available to handle the demand. How would you propose to handle the situation? Be as specific as you can and defend your recommendations.

2. As a staff vice president at corporate headquarters, you have been charged to develop company-wide policies and procedures that will prevent such a situation from ever occurring again. What would you recommend?

TEAM DEBATE EXERCISES

1. How tightly should you supervise and control a foreign operation? The Maytag example suggests very tightly. But was it an aberration, unlikely to be encountered again? Debate the issue of very tight controls versus relative freedom for foreign operations.

2. Debate the two sides of outsourcing, from the viewpoints of workers, of communities, of stockholders, of company executives, and even of what's best for our economy.

INVITATION TO RESEARCH

Did the merger of Maytag with Whirlpool go through as planned, or was there substantial antitrust opposition to it? What is the competitive situation in the appliance industry today? Are there any Maytag employees still left in Newton, Iowa? Has all production been outsourced?

CHAPTER TWENTY-ONE

MetLife: Poorly Controlled Sales Practices

In August 1993, the state of Florida cracked down on the sales practices of giant Metropolitan Life, a company dating back to 1868, and the country's second-largest insurance firm. MetLife agents based in Tampa were alleged to have duped customers out of some $11 million. Thousands of these customers were nurses lured by the sales pitch to learn more about "something new, one of the most widely discussed retirement plans in the investment world today."[1] In reality, it was a life-insurance policy in disguise, and what clients were led to think were savings deposits were actually insurance premiums.

As we will see, the growing scandal rocked MetLife, and eventually brought it several billion dollars in fines and restitutions. What was not clear for certain was the full culpability of the company: Was it guilty only of not monitoring agent performance sufficiently to detect unethical and illegal activities, or was it the great encourager of such practices?

RICK URSO: THE VILLAIN?

The first premonitory rumble that something bad was about to happen came to Rick Urso on Christmas Eve 1993. Home with his family, he received an unexpected call from his boss, the regional sales manager. In disbelief, he heard there was a rumor going around the executive suites that he was about to be fired. Urso had known that the state of Florida had been conducting an investigation, and that company auditors had also been looking into sales practices. And on September 17, two corporate vice-presidents had even shown up to conduct the fourth audit that year, but on leaving they had given him the impression that he was complying with company guidelines.

[1] Suzanne Woolley and Gail DeGeorge, "Policies of Deception?" *Business Week*, January 17, 1994, p. 24.

Urso often reveled in his good fortune and attributed it to his sheer dedication to his work and the company. He had grown up in a working-class neighborhood, the son of an electrician. He had started college, but dropped out before graduating.

His sales career began at a John Hancock agency in Tampa in 1978. Four years later, he was promoted to manager and was credited with building up the agency to number two in the whole company.

He left John Hancock in 1983 for MetLife's Tampa agency. His first job was as trainer. Only three months later, he was promoted to branch manager. Now his long hours and overwhelming commitment were beginning to pay off. In a success story truly inspiring, his dedication and his talent as a motivator of people swept the branch from a one-rep office to one of MetLife's largest and most profitable. By 1993, the agency employed 120 reps, seven sales managers, and 30 administrative employees. And he was the head. In 1990 and 1991, Urso's office won the company's Sales Office of the Year award. With such a performance history, the stuff of legends, he became the company's star, a person to look up to and to inspire trainees and other employees.

Urso had the passion of an evangelist: "Most people go through life being told why they can't accomplish something. If they would just believe, then they would be halfway there. That's the way I dream and that's what I expect from my people."[2] He soon became known as the "Master Motivator," and increasingly was the guest speaker at MetLife conferences.

On the Monday after that Christmas, the dire prediction came to pass. He was summoned to the office of William Groggans, the head of MetLife's Southeast territory, and there was handed a letter by the sober-faced Groggans. With trembling hands he opened it and read that he was fired. The reason: engaging in improper conduct.

The Route to Stardom

Unfortunately, the growth of his Tampa office could not be credited to simple motivation of employees. Urso found his vehicle for great growth to be the whole-life insurance policy. This was part life insurance and part savings. As such, it required high premiums, but only part earned interest and compounded on a tax-deferred basis; the rest went to pay for the life insurance policy. What made this so attractive to company sales reps was the commission: A Met whole-life policy paid a 55 percent first-year commission. In contrast, an annuity paid only a 2 percent first-year commission.

Urso found the nurse market to be particularly attractive. Perhaps because of their constant exposure to death, nurses were easily convinced of the need for economic security. He had his salespeople call themselves "nursing representatives," and his Tampa salespeople carried their fake retirement plan beyond Florida, eventually reaching 37 states. A New York client, for example, thought she had bought a retirement annuity. But it turned out to be insurance even though as a single woman she didn't need such coverage because she had no beneficiaries.[3]

[2] Weld F. Royal, "Scapegoat or Scoundrel," *Sales & Marketing Management*, January 1995, p. 64.
[3] Jane Bryant Quinn, "Yes, They're Out to Get You," *Newsweek*, January 24, 1994, p. 51.)

As the growth of the Tampa agency became phenomenal, Urso's budget for mailing brochures was upped to nearly $1 million in 1992, ten times that of any other MetLife office. This gave him national reach.

Urso's own finances increased proportionately because he earned a commission on each policy his reps sold. In 1989, he was paid $270,000. In 1993, as compensation exceeded $1 million, he moved his family to Bay Shore Boulevard—the most expensive area of Tampa.

Early Warnings

A few complaints began surfacing. In 1990, the Texas insurance commissioner warned MetLife to stop its nursing ploy. The company made a token compliance by sending out two rounds of admonitory letters. But apparently nothing changed. See the following Information Box about the great deficiency of token compliance without follow-up.

INFORMATION BOX

THE VULNERABILITY OF COMPLIANCE IF IT IS ONLY TOKEN

A token effort at compliance to a regulatory complaint or charge tends to have two consequences, neither good in the long run for the company involved:

1. Tokenism gives a clear message to the organization: "Despite what outsiders say, this is acceptable conduct in this firm." Thus is set the climate for less-than-desirable practices.

2. Vulnerability to harsher measures in the future. With the malpractice continuing, regulators, convinced that the company is stalling and refusing to cooperate, will eventually take more drastic action. Penalties will move beyond warnings to become punitive.

Actually, the firm may not intend to stall, but that is the impression conveyed. If the cause of the seemingly token effort is really faulty controls, one wonders how many other aspects of the operation are also ineptly controlled so that company policies are ignored.

Discuss the kinds of controls MetLife could have imposed in 1990 that would have made compliance actual and not token.

An internal MetLife audit in 1991 also raised some questions about Urso's pre-approach letters. The term *nursing representative* was called a "made-up" title. The auditors also questioned the term *retirement savings policy* as not appropriate for the product. However, the report concluded by congratulating the Tampa office for its contribution to the company. Not surprisingly, such mixed signals did not end the use of misleading language at that time.

Allegations Intensify

In the summer of 1993, Florida state regulators began a more in-depth examination of the sales practices of the Urso agency. The crux of the investigation concerned promotional material Urso's office was sending to nurses nationwide. From 1989 to 1993, millions of direct-mail pieces had been sent out. Charges finally were leveled that this material disguised the product agents were selling. For example, one brochure coming from Urso's office depicted the Peanuts character Lucy in a nurse's uniform. The headline described the product as "retirement savings and security for the future a nurse deserves." Nowhere was insurance even mentioned, and it was alleged that nurses across the country had unknowingly purchased life insurance when they thought they were buying retirement savings plans.

As the investigation deepened, a former Urso agent, turned whistleblower, claimed he had been instructed to place his hands over the words "life insurance" on applications during presentations.

As a result of this investigation, Florida Insurance Commissioner Tom Gallagher charged MetLife with serious violations.

METLIFE CORRECTIVE ACTIONS, FINALLY

Under investigation by Florida regulators, the company's attitude changed. At first, MetLife had denied wrongdoing. But eventually it acknowledged problems. Under mounting public pressure, it agreed to pay $20 million in fines to more than 40 states as a result of unethical sales practices by its agents. It further agreed to refund premiums to nearly 92,000 policyholders who had bought insurance based on misleading sales information between 1989 and 1993. The refunds were expected to reach $76 million.

MetLife fired or demoted five high-level executives as a result of the scandal. Urso's office was closed, and all seven of his managers and several reps were also discharged. Life insurance sales to individuals were down 25 percent through September 1994 over the same nine-month period in 1993. Standard & Poor's downgraded MetLife's bond rating based on the alleged improprieties.

Shortly after the fines were announced, the Florida Department of Insurance filed charges against Urso and 86 other MetLife insurance agents, accusing them of fraudulent sales practices. The insurance commissioner said, "This was not a situation where a few agents decided to take advantage of their customers, but a concerted effort by many individuals to dupe customers into buying a life insurance policy disguised as a retirement savings plan."[4]

Now MetLife attempted to improve its public image by instituting a broad overhaul of its compliance procedures. It established a corporate ethics and compliance

---

[4] Sean Armstrong, "The Good, The Bad and the Industry," *Best's Review*, P/C. June 1994, p. 36.

department to monitor behavior throughout the company and audit personal insurance sales offices. The department was also charged with reporting any compliance deficiencies to senior management and to follow up to ensure the implementation of corrective actions.

In MetLife's *1994 Annual Report*, Harry Kamen, CEO, and Ted Athanassiades, president, commented on their corrective actions regarding the scandal:

> We created what we think is the most effective compliance system in the industry. Not just for personal insurance, but for all components of the company. We installed systems to coordinate and track the quality and integrity of our sales activities, and we created a new system of sales office auditing.
>
> Also, there were organizational changes. And, for the first time in 22 years, we assembled all of our agency and district managers—about a thousand people—to discuss what we have done and need to do about the problems and where we were going.[5]

Meantime, Rick Urso started a suit against MetLife for defamation of character and for reneging on a $1 million severance agreement. He alleged that MetLife made him the fall guy in the nationwide sales scandal.

The personal ramifications for Urso's life were not inconsequential. More than a year later he was still unemployed. He had looked for another insurance job, but no one would even see him. "There are nights he can't sleep. He lies awake worrying about the impact this will have on his two teenagers." And he laments that his wife cannot go out without people gossiping.[6]

WHERE DOES THE BLAME LIE?

Is Urso really the unscrupulous monster who rose to a million-dollar-a-year man on the foundations of deceit? Or is MetLife mainly to blame for encouraging, and then ignoring for too long, practices aimed at misleading and even deceiving?

The Case Against Metlife

Undeniably Urso did things that smacked of the illegal and unethical. But did the corporation knowingly provide the climate? Was his training such as to promote deceptive practices? Was MetLife completely unaware of his distortions and deceptions in promotional material and sales pitches? There seems to be substantial evidence that the company played a part; it was no innocent and unsuspecting bystander.

At best, MetLife top executives may not have been aware of the full extent of the hard-selling efforts emanating at first from Tampa and then spreading further in the organization. Perhaps, in the quest for exceptional bottom-line performance, they chose to ignore any inkling that things were not completely on the up and up. "Don't argue with success" may have become the corporate mindset.

---

[5] *MetLife 1994 Annual Report*, p. 16.
[6] Royal, p. 65.

At the worst, the company encouraged and even demanded hard selling and tried to pretend that it could be accomplished with acceptable standards of performance. If the standards were not met, the company's top executives could argue that they were not aware of any wrongdoing.

There is evidence of company culpability. Take the training program for new agents. Much of it was designed to help new employees overcome the difficulties of selling life insurance. In so doing, they were taught to downplay the life insurance aspects of the product. Rather, the savings and tax-deferred growth benefits were to be stressed.

New agents learning to sell insurance over the phone were told that people prefer dealing with specialists. It seemed only a small temptation to use the title *nursing representative* rather than *insurance agent*.

After the scandal, MetLife admitted that the training might be faulty. Training had been decentralized into five regional centers, and the company believed that this might have led to a less standardized and controlled curriculum. MetLife has since reorganized, so that many functions, including training and legal matters, are now done at one central location.[7]

The company's control or monitoring was certainly deficient and uncoordinated during the years of misconduct. For example, the marketing department promoted deceptive sales practices, while the legal department warned of possible illegality but took no further action to eliminate it.

AN INDUSTRY PROBLEM?

The MetLife revelations focused public and regulatory attention on the entire insurance industry. The insurance commissioner of Florida also turned attention to the sales and marketing practices of New York Life and Prudential. The industry itself seemed vulnerable to questionable practices. Millions of transactions, intense competition, and a widespread and rather autonomous sales force—all these afforded opportunity for misrepresentation and other unethical dealings.

For example, just a few months after the Tampa office publicity, MetLife settled an unrelated scandal. Regulators in Pennsylvania fined the company $1.5 million for "churning." This is a practice whereby agents replace old policies with new ones for which additional commissions are charged and policyholders are disadvantaged. Class-action suits alleging churning were also filed in Pennsylvania against Prudential, New York Life, and John Hancock.

But the problems go beyond sales practices. Claims adjusters may attempt to withhold or reduce payments. General agents may place business with bogus or insolvent companies. Even actuaries may create unrealistic policy structures.

With a deteriorating public image, the industry faced further governmental regulation from both state and federal agencies. But cynics, both within and outside

---

[7] "Trained to Mislead," *Sales & Marketing Management*, January 1995, p. 66.

the industry, wondered whether deception and fraud were so much a part of the business that nothing could be done about them.[8]

ANALYSIS

Here we have an apparent lapse in complete feedback to top executives. But maybe they did not want to know. After all, nothing was life-threatening here, no product-safety features were being ignored or disguised, nobody was in physical danger.

This raises a key management issue. Can top executives hide from less-than-ethical practices—and even illegal ones—under the guise that they did not know? The answer should be *No!* See the Information Box below for a discussion of management accountability.

INFORMATION BOX

THE ULTIMATE RESPONSIBILITY

In the Maytag case in Chapter 20 we examined a costly snafu brought about by giving executives of a foreign subsidiary too much rein. With MetLife the problem was gradually eroding ethical practices. In both instances, top management still had ultimate responsibility and cannot escape blame for whatever went wrong in the organization. Decades ago, President Truman coined the phrase "The buck stops here," meaning that in this highest position rests the ultimate seat of responsibility.

Any manager who delegates to someone else the authority to do something will undoubtedly hold them responsible to do the job properly. Still, managers must be aware that their own responsibility to higher management or to stockholders cannot be delegated away. If the subordinate does the job improperly, the manager is responsible.

Going back to MetLife, or to any corporation involved with ethical and illegal practices, top executives may try to escape blame by denying that they knew anything about the misdeeds. This should not exonerate them. Even if they knew nothing directly, they still set the climate.

In Japan, the chief executive of an organization involved in a public scandal usually resigns in disgrace. In the United States, top executives until recently often escaped full retribution by blaming their subordinates and maintaining that they themselves knew nothing of the misdeed. Is it unfair to hold a top executive culpable for the shortcomings of some unknown subordinate?

We are left with MetLife's top management grappling with the temptation to tacitly approve the aggressive selling practices of a sales executive so successful as to

---

[8] Armstrong, p. 35.

be the model for the whole organization, even though faint cries from the legal staff suggested that the practices might be subject to regulatory scrutiny and disapproval.

The harsh appraisal of this situation is that top management cannot be exonerated for the deficiencies of subordinates. If controls and monitoring processes are defective, top management is still accountable. The pious platitudes of MetLife managers insisting that they have now corrected the situation hardly excuse them for permitting it to have developed in the first place.

Ah, but embracing the temptation is so easy to rationalize. Management can always maintain that there was no good, solid proof of misdeeds. After all, where do aggressive sales efforts cross the line? When do they move from simple "puffing" to become outright deceptive? See the following Information Box regarding puffing, an admittedly gray area of the acceptable. Lacking indisputable evidence of misdeeds, why should these executives suspect the worst? Especially since their legal departments, not centralized as they were to be later, were timid in their denunciations?

INFORMATION BOX

WHERE DO WE DRAW THE LINE ON PUFFING?

Puffing is generally thought of as mild exaggeration in selling or advertising. It is generally accepted as simply the mark of exuberance toward what is being promoted. As such, it is acceptable business conduct. Most people have come to regard promotional communications with some skepticism—"It's New! The Greatest! A Super Value! Gives Whiter Teeth! Whiter Laundry! . . ." and so on. We have become conditioned to viewing such blandishments with suspicion. But dishonest or deceptive? Probably not. As long as the exaggeration stays mild.

But it can be a short step from mild exaggeration to outright falsehoods and deceptive claims. Did MetLife's "nursing representatives," "retirement plans," and hiding the reality of life insurance cross the line? Enough people thought so, including state insurance commissioners and the victims themselves. This short step can tempt more bad practices than if the line between good and bad were more definitive.

Do you think that all exaggerated claims, even the mild and vague ones known as puffing, should be banned? Why or why not?

Turning to controls, a major caveat should be posed for all firms: In the presence of strong management demands for performance—with the often implicit or imagined pressure to produce at all costs, or else—the ground is laid for less-than-desirable practices by subordinates. After all, their career paths and even job longevity depend on meeting these demands.

Such abuses are more likely to occur in a climate of decentralization and laissez-faire. A results-oriented structure suggests that it's not how you achieve the desired results, but that you meet them. So, while decentralization, on balance, is usually desirable, it can lead to undesirable practices in an environment of top-management laxity.

At the least, it leads to opportunistic temptation by lower- and middle-level executives. Perhaps this is the final indictment of MetLife and Rick Urso. The climate was conducive to his ambitious opportunism. For a while it was wonderful. But the abuses of accepted behavior could not be disguised indefinitely.

And wherever possible, top management will repudiate its accountability.

The Handling of the Crisis

MetLife responded slowly to the allegations of misconduct. A classic mode for firms confronted with unethical and/or product-liability charges is to deny everything, until evidence becomes overwhelming. Then they are forced to acknowledge problems under mounting public pressure—from regulatory bodies, attorneys, and the media—and have to scramble with damage control to try to undo the threats to public image and finances. In MetLife's case, fines and refunds approached $100 million early on. They would eventually reach almost $2 billion.

Being slow to act, to accept any responsibility, and, for top executives, exhibiting aloofness until late in the game, are actions that inflame public opinion and regulatory zeal. How much better for all involved, victims as well as the organization itself, if initial complaints are promptly followed up. And, if complaints are serious, they should be given top-management attention in a climate of cooperation with any agencies involved as well as the always-interested media.

LATER DEVELOPMENTS

On August 18, 1999, MetLife agreed to pay out at least $1.7 billion to settle final lawsuits over its allegedly improper sales practices. The agreement (in which MetLife admitted no wrongdoing) involved about 6 million life-insurance policyholders and a million annuity-contract holders. Essentially, these customers were expected to get one to five years of free term-life insurance coverage.

MetLife argued for years that it had done nothing wrong. It had previously dispensed with most of its litigation problems by settling rather than going to trial. The incentive for settling these final class-action suits even at the cost of a massive charge was to clear the way for MetLife's planned conversion to a stockholder-owned company from its current status as a policyholder-owned mutual company. "Clearly it's something they needed to put behind them before they demutualized," or went public.[9]

Harry Kamen, CEO of MetLife, brought Robert Benmosche, age 57, an ex–Wall Streeter, on board in 1995 to turn things around. Benmosche solved many of MetLife's problems and became chairman when Kamen retired in 1998. In April 2000, he took the company public, and the stock offering raised $5.2 billion.

[9] Deborah Lohse, "MetLife Agrees to Pay Out $1.7 Billion or More to Settle Policyholder Lawsuits," *Wall Street Journal*, August 19, 1999, p. B14.

In his relentless restructuring, Benmosche axed poor performers, some 1,300 including 154 assistant vice presidents and higher in 2001—and demanded better results and ethical standards. He required agents to work full-time, instead of part-time, as many had previously done: "I knew this was needed after I met someone who complimented one of my agents for his plumbing skills," explained Benmosche. He also compelled all agents to get securities licenses so they could sell investments like variable annuities. Bonuses were now tied into performance reviews and a division's financial results, and officers' bonuses were partly paid in stock that they were discouraged from selling: "If the top people . . . don't do what they have to do to make sure the company strongly survives, we should lose our shirts." MetLife's revenues in 2001 were $32 billion, up 18 percent since Benmosche became chairman.[10]

Demutualization, or taking a company public, has the powerful advantage of easier availability of funds due to stock offerings. But there are some drawbacks. The chief one is that public ownership exposes a firm to more visibility and criticism, as the following Information Box describes of alleged abuses of executive compensation for another big insurance company.

INFORMATION BOX

CRITICISMS OF PRUDENTIAL INSURANCE COMPANY

Prudential has long cultivated its image as the "Rock," using a logo of the Rock of Gibraltar, symbol of permanence and stability. But like MetLife, it faced investigations and litigation over deceptive sales practices that affected millions of policyholders in the 1980s and early 1990s, and its sales of life-insurance policies slowed markedly. The company set aside more than $2 billion to cover the costs of litigation, and took a $1.64 billion charge against 1997 earnings. To try to resurrect its tarnished image, it increased advertising expenditures to $130 million in 1996 and 1997.

In August 1998, it came under fire of another kind, with disclosures of hefty compensations paid its executives despite the performance downturn: the top 100 executives averaged $820,000 in 1997, up 30 percent from 1994. By contrast, MetLife's top hundred executives averaged $600,000 in 1997, and State Farm had fewer than three dozen earning $350,000 or more.[11]

The compensation criticisms probably would not have surfaced had Prudential not sought to end its mutual status and move to public ownership, which would enable it to raise money more easily for such purposes as acquisitions. But demutualization exposed Prudential to critical scrutiny by huge institutional investors, notably the California Public Employees' Retirement System, and TIAA-CREF, a giant pension fund. These

---

[10] Carrie Coolidge, "Snoopy's New Tricks," *Forbes*, April 15, 2002, pp. 100-102.
[11] Scot J. Paltrow, "As a Public Company Prudential May Find Pay Scales Draw Fire," *Wall Street Journal*, August 14, 1998, pp. A1 and A8.

major shareholders regularly examine executive-compensation records of publicly traded companies.

Should executives be richly compensated when their firms are not doing well? Is it right to criticize a firm whose executives are far more richly rewarded than others in the same industry? Is it right for institutional investors to criticize and try to change policies in firms they invest in?

* * *

Invitation to Make Your Own Analysis and Conclusions

Do you think Urso's career could have been salvaged? What could he have done? What could higher management have done to save this man's gifted but misguided career? Or was he worth saving?

* * *

WHAT CAN BE LEARNED?

Beware the head-in-the-sand approach to looming problems or public complaints.—Ignoring or giving only token attention to suspected problems and regulatory complaints sets a firm up for a possible massive crisis. Covering one's eyes to malpractices and danger situations does not make them go away; they tend to fester and become more serious. Prompt attention, investigation, and action are needed to prevent problem areas from getting out of hand. MetLife could have saved itself several billion dollars if it had acted on the early complaints of misrepresentation and misleading customers.

Unethical and illegal actions do not go undetected forever.—It may take months, it may take years, but a firm's dark side will eventually be uncovered. Its reputation may then be besmirched, it may face loss of customers and competitive position, and it may face heavy fines and increased regulation.

The eventual disclosure may come from a disgruntled employee (a whistle-blower). It may originate from a regulatory body or an investigative reporter. Or it may come from revelations emanating from a lawsuit. Eventually, the deviation is uncovered, and retribution follows. Such a scenario should be enough—but is not always—to constrain employees tempted to commit unethical and illegal actions.

What made MetLife's deceptive practices particularly troubling is that they were so visible, and yet were so long tolerated. Much of the sales organization seemed to lack a clear definition of what was acceptable and what was not. Something was clearly amiss both in the training and in the controlling of agent personnel.

The control function is best centralized in any organization.—Where the department or entity that monitors performance is decentralized, tolerance of bad practices is more likely than when centralized. The reason is simple. Where legal or accounting controls are decentralized, those conducting them are more easily influenced and are likely to be neither as objective nor as critical as when they are further from the situation. Reviewers and evaluators should not be close to the people they are examining. And they should report only to top management.

A strong sales incentive program invites bad practices.—The lucrative commission incentive for the whole-life policies—55 percent first-year commission—was almost bound to stimulate abusive sales practices, especially when the rewards for this type of policy were so much greater than for any other. Firms often use incentive programs and contests to motivate their employees to seek greater efforts. But if some are tempted to cross the line, the end result in public scrutiny and condemnation may not be worth whatever increases in sales might be gained.

Large corporations are particularly vulnerable to public scrutiny.— Large firms, especially ones dealing with consumer products, are very visible. This visibility makes them attractive targets for critical scrutiny by activists, politicians, the media, regulatory bodies, and the legal establishment. Such firms ought to be particularly careful in any dealings that might be questioned, even if short-term profits have to be restrained. In MetLife's case, the fines and refunds eventually approached $2 billion. Although the firm maintained, in its *1994 Annual Report*, that all the bad publicity was behind it, that there were no ill effects, some analysts wondered how quickly a besmirched reputation could truly be restored, especially with competitors eager to grab the opportunity presented.

Sometimes a tarnished reputation can be quickly restored.—Contrary to some experts, there is compelling evidence that customers tend to quickly forget misdeeds, as they apparently did with MetLife under the new management of Benmosche. We saw a similar restoration of reputation for Firestone after the Ford Explorer/unsafe tire debacle in Chapter 4. While the poor image of Continental Airlines was not due to product safety or deception, but rather to years of deteriorating service, it was quickly turned around with enlightened, fresh management. Perhaps these experiences should be comforting to a firm that incurs image damage, whether through its own fault, or maybe because of factors not directly under its control. It does help, however, if there is a change in top management. Still, in cases of unethical conduct, fines and perhaps a plethora of lawsuits are more immediate consequences of culpability.

CONSIDER

What additional learning insights to you see?

QUESTIONS

1. Do you think Rick Urso should have been fired? Why or why not?
2. Do you think the MetLife CEO and president should have been fired? Why or why not?

3. Why was it seemingly so desirable to avoid the term "life insurance"? What is wrong with life insurance?

4. Given the widespread publicity about the MetLife scandal, did you think the firm could regain consumer trust in a short time?

5. "This whole critical publicity has been blown way out of proportion. After all, nobody was injured. Not even in their pocketbook. They were sold something they really needed. For their own good." Evaluate.

6. "You have to admire that guy Urso. He was a real genius. No one else could motivate a sales organization as he did. They should have made him president of the company. Or else he should become an evangelist." Evaluate.

7. Do you think the arguments are compelling that the control function should be centralized rather than decentralized? Why or why not?

HANDS-ON EXERCISES
Before

1. It is early 1990. You are the assistant to the CEO of MetLife. Rumors have been surfacing that life-insurance sales efforts are becoming not only too high pressure but also misleading. The CEO has ordered you to investigate. You find that the legal department in the Southeast Territory has some concerns about the efforts coming out of Urso's highly successful Tampa office. Be as specific as you can about how you would investigate these unproven allegations, and explain how you would report them to your boss, assuming that some questionable practices seem apparent.

2. It is 1992. Internal investigations have confirmed that Urso and his "magnificent" Tampa office are using deceptive selling techniques in disguising the life-insurance aspects of the policies they are selling. As the executive in charge in the Southeast, describe your actions and rationale at this point. (You have to assume that you do not know the later consequences.)

After

3. The s__t has hit the fan. The scandal has become well publicized, especially on such TV programs as *Dateline* and *20/20*. What would you do as top executive of MetLife at this point? How would you attempt to save the public image of the company?

TEAM DEBATE EXERCISE

The publicity is widespread about MetLife's "misdeeds." Debate how you would react. One position is to defend your company, rationalize what happened, and downplay any ill-effects. The other position is to meekly bow to the allegations, admit wrongdoing, and be as contrite as possible.

INVITATION TO RESEARCH

Is MetLife still prospering under Benmosche? Can you find any information that contradicts that the situation has virtually been forgotten by the general public? Can you find out whether Rick Urso has found another job? Could you develop the pros and cons of a mutual (policyholder-owned) firm and a public firm owned by stockholders?

PART SEVEN

ENTREPRENEURIAL ADVENTURES

CHAPTER TWENTY-TWO

Boston Beer: Is Greater Growth Possible?

J im Koch was obsessed with becoming an entrepreneur. He wasn't quite sure where he should do his entrepreneuring. Maybe the brewing industry? Years before, his great-great-grandfather, Louis Koch, had concocted a recipe at his St. Louis brewery that was heavier, more full-bodied than such beers as Budweiser or Miller. However, it was much more expensive to produce than mass-market beers. It involved a lengthy brewing and fermentation process, as well as such premium ingredients as Bavarian hops that cost many times more than those regularly used by other brewers.

Jim had a well-paying job with the prestigious Boston Consulting Group. He had been with them for six and a half years already, but still he was haunted by the dream of becoming his own man. Of late, the thought pursued him that maybe the brewing industry might be ripe for a new type of product and a new approach, a good-tasting brew something like his ancestor's. He wondered if he might have a strategic window of opportunity in a particular consumer segment: men in their mid-twenties and older who were beer aficionados and would be willing to pay a premium for a good-tasting beer. What he couldn't be certain of was how large this segment was, and he knew from his consulting experience that too small a segment doomed a strategy. So, were there enough sophisticated drinkers to support the new company that he envisioned?

In 1984, he thought he detected a clue that this might indeed be the case: Sales were surging for import beers like Heineken and Beck's with their different tastes. Didn't this portend that enough Americans would be willing to pay substantially more for a full-bodied flavor?

As he studied this more, Koch also came to believe that the imports would be very vulnerable to well-made domestic brews. They faced a major problem in maintaining freshness with a product that goes sour rather quickly. He knew that the foreign brewers, in trying to minimize the destructive influence of the time lag between production and consumption, were adding preservatives and even using cheaper ingredients for the American market.

Some small local brewers offered stronger tastes. But they were having great difficulty producing a lager with consistent quality. And he sensed that they were

345

squandering their opportunity. Although they could produce small batches of well-crafted beer, albeit of erratic quality, what they mainly lacked was ability and resources to aggressively market their products.

He thought now that he had indeed found the right niche, a strategic window of opportunity, for becoming an entrepreneurial success. See the following Information Box for further discussion of a strategic window of opportunity and its desirable accompaniment, a SWOT analysis.

Koch decided to take the plunge, and gave up his job.

INFORMATION BOX

STRATEGIC WINDOW OF OPPORTUNITY AND SWOT ANALYSIS—REVISITED AGAIN

(We discussed this in Chapter 17, the Southwest Airlines case, but it is worth reviewing.) A strategic window is an opportunity in the marketplace, an opportunity that no competitor has yet recognized, and one that fits well with the firm's competencies. Strategic windows often last for only a short time before they are filled by alert competitors, but sometimes they may be more lasting if competitors deem it difficult to enter the particular niche. Potential competitors may pass because of price or image advantages they see the first firm as having, or perhaps because they judge—correctly or incorrectly—that the niche does not have sufficient potential.

SWOT analysis.—Strategic windows may be found by systematically analyzing the environment, examining the opportunities and threats it poses. The firm's competencies, its strengths and weaknesses, should be assessed. These competencies would include its physical and financial resources and, not the least, its people resources—management and employees. The objective is to determine whether the competencies of the firm might be appropriate for a particular course of action.

This then is the SWOT analysis:

Strengths and
Weaknesses of the firm, and
Opportunities and
Threats in the environment

Although SWOT analysis may be a formal part of the planning, it may also be informal and even intuitive. We suspect that Jim Koch, having worked six and a half years with a prestigious consulting firm, would have formalized this analysis. In the next case, OfficeMax, Michael Feuer may have been more informal and intuitive in his assessment of entrepreneurial opportunity.

Why do you think all the big brewers overlooked the possibilities of the higher-priced end of the market?

Amassing sufficient capital to start a new venture is the common problem with almost all entrepreneurs, and so it was with Koch. Still, he was better off than most.

He had saved $100,000 from his years with Boston Consulting, and he persuaded family and friends to chip in another $140,000. But while this might be enough to start a new retail or service venture, it was far less than the estimated $10 million or more needed to build a state-of-the-art brewery.

Koch got around this major obstacle. Instead of building or buying, he contracted an existing firm, Pittsburgh Brewing Company, to brew his beer. It had good facilities, but more than this, its people had the brewing skills coming from more than 20 years of operation. He would call his new beer Samuel Adams, after a Revolutionary War patriot who was also a brewer.

PROBLEMS

A mighty problem still existed, and the success of the venture hinged on this. Koch would have to sell his great-tasting beer at $20 a case to break even and make a reasonable profit. But this was 15 percent more than even the premium imports like Heineken. Would anyone buy such an expensive beer, and one that didn't even have the cachet of an import? See the Information Box: Competing on Price, Revisited.

INFORMATION BOX

COMPETING ON PRICE, REVISITED: THE PRICE/QUALITY PERCEPTION

In the Vanguard and Southwest Airlines cases, we examined the potent strategy of offering the lowest prices in an industry—if this could be done profitably due to a lower expense and overhead structure than competitors.

Here, Boston Beer was attempting to compete with some of the highest prices in the industry. Was this the height of foolishness? Why would anyone pay a higher price than for an expensive imported beer just for a different taste?

The highest price can convey an image of the very highest quality. We as consumers have long been conditioned to think this. With cars, we may not be able to afford the highest quality, such as an Infiniti, Lexus, or Mercedes convertible. But with beer, almost anyone can afford to buy the highest-price brew sometimes, maybe to impress guests or to simply enjoy a different taste that we are led to think is better.

Sometimes such a price/quality perception sets us up. It might be valid, or might not be. This is especially true where quality is difficult to ascertain, as with beer and liquor, with bottled water, with perfume, as well as other products with hidden ingredients and complex characteristics.

Have you have ever fallen victim to the price/quality misperception? How does one determine quality for an alcoholic beverage such as vodka, gin, and scotch, as well as beer? By the taste? The advertising claims? Anything else?

It fell to Koch as the fledgling firm's only salesperson to try to acquaint retailers and consumers with his new beer, this unknown brand with the very high price.

"I went from bar to bar," he said. "Sometimes I had to call 15 times before someone would agree to carry it."[1]

He somehow conjured up enough funds for a $100,000 ad campaign in the local market. Shunning the advertising theme of the big brewers, which almost without exception stressed the sociability of the people drinking their brand, Koch's ads attacked the imports: "Declare your independence from foreign beer," he urged. And the name Samuel Adams was compatible with this cry for independence. Foreign brews were singled out as not having the premium ingredients and quality brewing of Samuel Adams. Koch appeared on most of his commercials, saying such things as: "Hi, I'm Jim Koch ... It takes me all year to brew what the largest import makes in just three hours because I take the time to brew Samuel Adams right. I use my great-great-grandfather's century-old recipe, all malt brewing and rare hops that cost ten times what they use in the mass-produced imports."[2]

Gradually his persistence in calling on retailers and his anti-import ads, some of which garnered national attention in such periodicals as *Newsweek* and *USA Today*, induced more and more bartenders and beer drinkers to at least try Samuel Adams. Many liked it, despite the high price. (Or, perhaps, because of it?)

Now his problem became finding distributors, and this proved quite daunting for a new firm in this industry where major brands often had a lock on existing wholesalers. The situation was so bad in Boston—no wholesaler would carry Samuel Adams even though it was a local brand—that Boston Beer bought a truck and delivered the cases itself.

At Last, Slow Expansion

Koch slowly expanded his distribution one geographical area at a time, from Boston into Washington, D.C., then to New York, Chicago, and California, taking care that production could match the steady expansion without sacrificing quality. He brought in his secretary at Boston Consulting, Rhonda Kaliman, to assist him in building a sales organization. This grew from less than a dozen sales reps in 1989 to 70 nationwide by 1994, more than any other microbrewer and about the same number as Anheuser-Busch, the giant of the industry. Now, Samuel Adams salespeople could give more personalized and expert attention to customers than competitors whose sales reps often sold many beverage lines.

Sales soared 63 percent in 1992 when the company went national and achieved distribution in bars and restaurants in 48 states. In a continual search for new beer ideas, Boston Beer added a stout, a wheat beer, and even a cranberry lambic, a type of beer flavored with fruit. Adding to the growing popularity were the numerous industry awards and citations Samuel Adams had received since 1984. It was not only voted the Best Beer in America four times at the annual Great American Beer Festival, but also received six gold medals in blind tastings.

In April 1994, Jim Koch and two of his brewmasters were testing their entry in the Great American Beer Festival, "Triple Bock." They had not yet tried to market

---

[1] Jenny McCune, "Brewing Up Profits," *Management Review*, April 1994, p. 18.
[2] *Ibid.*, p. 19.

this creation, although their expectations were high. But this was so different. It boasted a 17 percent alcoholic content with no carbonation, and they planned to package it in a cobalt bottle with a cork. It was meant to be sipped as a fine brandy. "It's a taste that nobody has ever put into a beer," Koch said.[3] Too innovative? Jim and his colleagues pondered this as they sipped on this beautiful spring day.

THE BREWING INDUSTRY IN THE 1990s

In ten years, Boston Beer had forged ahead to become a major contender in its industry and the largest U.S. specialty brewer. But a significant change in consumer preferences was confronting the industry in the 1990s. The big brands that had been so dominant, to the extent that smaller brewers could not compete against their production efficiencies, now were seeing their market shares decline. The brand images they had spent millions trying to establish were in trouble. Many were cutting prices in desperate attempts to keep and lure consumers. For example, special price promotions in some markets were offering 12-packs of Budweiser, Coors, and Miller for just $1.99.

The shifting consumer preferences, and the severe price competition with their regular brands, were compelling the big brewers to seek the types of beers that would command higher prices. Imports were still strengthening, growing at an 11 percent rate between 1993 and 1994. But microbrews seemed the wave of the future, with prices and profit margins that were mouth-watering to the big barons of the industry.

Consequently, the major breweries came up with their own craft brands. For example, Icehouse, a name that conveys a fake microbrewery image to a beer was actually produced in megabreweries by Miller Brewing. So too, the pseudo-import Killian's Irish Red, was made by Coors in Golden, Colorado. Killian's, stocked in retailer's import cases and commanding a high price, muscled its way abreast of Samuel Adams as the largest specialty beer in the United States.

The brewing industry was desperately trying to innovate. But no one saw anything revolutionary on the horizon, not like the 1970s, when light beer made a significant breakthrough in the staid industry. Now, "ice" beers became the gimmick. First developed in Canada, these are beers produced at temperatures a little colder than ordinary beer. This gives them a slightly higher alcohol content. Whether because of this, or the magic of the name "ice," these products captured almost 6 percent of total industry sales in 1994, more than all the imports combined. But, still, the potential was limited.

Anheuser-Busch, with a still dominant 44 percent of U.S. beer sales despite its 9 percent sales volume slide in the early 1990s, asserted its reluctance to change: "The breweries that we have are designed to produce big brands. Our competition can't compete with big brands. That's why they've had to introduce lots of little brands."[4]

---

[3] *Ibid.*, p. 20.
[4] Patricia Sellers, "A Whole New Ballgame in Beer," *Fortune*, September 19, 1994, p. 86.

But even Anheuser, despite its words, was sneaking into microbrewing by buying into Redhook Ale Brewery, a Seattle microbrewery that sold 76,000 barrels of beer in 1993, versus Anheuser's 90 million. Anheuser's distributors applauded this move as a badly needed step in giving them higher-profit, prestige brands. When Anheuser tip-toed into this market, other giants began to look for microbreweries to invest in.

This troubled Jim Koch: "I'm afraid of the big guys. They have the power to dominate any segment they want." Then he expressed his faith and confidence: "Still, my faith is that better beer will win out."[5]

THE CONTINUING SAGA OF BOSTON BEER

In August 1995, Boston Beer announced an initial public stock offering (IPO) of 5.3 million shares, of which 990,000 shares would be made available directly to the public through a coupon offer. This selling of shares to the general public was unlike any other IPO and, as such, caught the fancy of the national press.

The company put clip-and-mail coupons on Samuel Adams six-packs and other beer packages. These offered customers a chance to buy 33 shares of stock at a maximum price of $15, or $495 total. Only one subscription was allowed per customer, and these were honored on a first-come, first-served basis. The success was overwhelming. First distributed in October, by the first of November the offering was oversubscribed. The company expected that the total funds generated from the IPO would be $75 million.[6] But when the new stock offering finally came out on November 20, 1995, heavy demand led to its being priced at $20 a share. Two days later it was selling on the New York Stock Exchange for $30. Interestingly, its stock symbol is SAM.

Boston Beer was riding a high. It reported an impressive 50 percent growth in 1994 over 1993, brewing 700,000 barrels and becoming the largest microbrewery in the country. The entire microbrewing industry was producing more than double the volume in 1990. By now Boston Beer had 12 different beers, including six seasonals, and was distributing in all 50 states through 300 wholesalers. Its newest beer, the 17-percent alcohol content Triple Bock, had been introduced to the market.[7]

Most of Boston Beer's production continued to be contract brewed. In early 1995, it encountered difficulties with Pittsburgh Brewing, the first of the three contract breweries it was now using. Because of an alleged overdraft of $31 million by its owner, Michael Carlow, who was accused of fraud, the brewery was to be auctioned off. Jim Koch stoutly professed having no interest in buying the brewery and that any problems of Pittsburgh Brewery would have no effect on Boston Beer.[8]

See the following Information Box for a discussion of contracting out rather than building production facilities.

---

[5] *Ibid.*
[6] "Boston Beer's Plan for Offering Stock," *New York Times* National Edition, August 26, 1995, p. 20.
[7] "Little Giants," *Beverage World*, December 1994, p. 26.
[8] "Sam Adams Brewer May Be on Block," *Boston Business Journal*, February 24, 1995, p. 3.

INFORMATION BOX

THE MERITS OF EXPANDING SLOWLY AND KEEPING FIXED COSTS TO A MINIMUM

There is much to be said for any enterprise, new or old, keeping its fixed overhead to a minimum. If it can escape having to commit large sums to physical plant and production facilities, its breakeven point is far less, which means that fewer sales are needed to cover expenses and interest payments, leaving more to go into profits. In the event of adversity, the firm can retrench much more nimbly than if burdened with heavy overhead. In every such decision of renting or buying, the economics of the particular situation need to be carefully analyzed.

Arguments against contracting out usually maintain that efficiency will be sacrificed because direct control is lacking. This argument would maintain that Pittsburgh Brewing could not do as good a job as Boston Beer could have done itself. Yet the empirical evidence is that Boston's contract brewers were giving it the high standards it wanted. Boston set the standards and insisted on their being met or it would find another contract brewery.

Still, the "edifice complex" tantalizes many top executives, as well as hospital and school administrators, who see the stone and mortar of their buildings and factories as conveying tangible evidence of their own importance and accomplishments. They will claim that this is important to the public image of their organization.

Given the approximately $100 million that Boston Beer received from its IPO, would you predict that some of this would go for "stones and mortar"?

TOWARD THE MILLENNIUM

By 1998, Samuel Adams had become the seventh-largest brewer overall, and was the largest independent craft brewer, in a sector that had grown 39 percent in a five-year period, while U.S. total beer shipments remained virtually flat. Samuel Adams Boston Lager, the company's flagship product, grew faster than the overall craft beer sector, and accounted for the majority of Boston Beer's sales in 1997.

For 1997, revenues were $184 million, down 3.8 percent from the year before, but a major increase from the $77 million in 1994, the year before Boston went public. Net income at $7.6 million was a decline of 9.9 percent from the year before, but this compared with $5.3 million in 1994.

Boston Beer produced more than two dozen styles of beer, and was selling in all 50 states and several foreign countries. Its sales force was still the largest of any craft brewer, and one of the largest in the domestic beer industry.

The acute disappointment had to be the stock-market valuation of its shares. An exuberant public reaction to the initial stock offering had bid the price up to $30 a share. Almost immediately, the share price began a slow decline. By late 1998, shares were trading around $8.

The situation had not improved significantly by the millennium. Indeed, the growth that had so bedazzled Koch and early investors seemed only an illusion. Samuel Adams had been the forefather of microbrews, but this specialty market had now spawned 3,000 microbrews, all competing within the $3 billion beer market—a market that represented just 3 percent of the U.S. beer market—with a mind-boggling array of ciders, ales, stouts, and so-called better beers. "After people got inundated with so many choices . . . they kind of stepped back," said one industry analyst.[9]

Koch drastically cut back his assortment of brews, concentrating only on best-sellers: the flagship lager and four seasonal brews. He went through four advertising agencies in six years trying to find the right pitch, but without much success. Experts were wondering if Koch would eventually sell out to a big brewer such as Miller. By mid-2001, the stock price ranged from $8 to $10 a share, still a disaster for its IPO investors.

UPDATE

Table 22.1 shows the trend in revenues and net income for 1998 through 2005. Sales and profits show little growth trend during this five-year period. The stock price ranged between $10 and $18 a share for 2003. 2005 had better results, with the stock price ranging from $20.71 to $27.27. Still, for those investors who bought at or near the initial offering in 1995, this was hardly a coup.

In August—National Beer Month—of 2002, Koch led a ten-city "Liquid Lunch" taste-test tour, pitting three Samuel Adams beers and local craft beers from each of the cities against leading international brews, such as Heineken, Corona, and Guinness. The beers were scored according to appearance, aroma, flavor, mouth-feel,

TABLE 22.1. Boston Beer Revenue and Net Income, 1998–2005 (in millions)

	1998	1999	2000	2001	2002	2003	2004	2005
Revenue	$183.5	$176.8	$190.6	$186.8	$ 215.4	$238.3	$239.7	$263.3
Net Income	7.9	11.1	11.2	7.8	8.6	10.6	12.5	15.6

Source: Company annual reports.

Commentary: Here we see a company with practically no growth from 1998 through 2003, even though revenue increased slightly during these five years. Net income, however, did not exceed that of 1999 and 2000 until 2004. Then 2005 finally looked like a banner year, giving hope of much better days to come. However, the stock market valuations for 2005 ranged from a low of $20.71 to $27.27. These statistics show a stable company, one comfortably established in its own niche. Unfortunately, this is little consolation for those investors who bought at the initial public stock offering (IPO) of $20 a share in late November 1995, or bought a few days later at $30 a share, expecting big growth.

[9] Hillary Chura, "Boston Beer Crafts Strategy: Slumping Brewer Abandons Some of Its Specialty Beers," *Advertising Age*, November 8, 1999, p. 20.

and overall impression. The taste testers included beer enthusiasts, consumers, journalists, and winners from local radio-station promotions.

In one-on-one taste tests, Samuel Adams was preferred over the imports in all 30 blind taste-offs. Many of the local brews also bested their foreign competition. Koch's crusade against imports received a good promotional push. He declared: "These imports have been considered the world standards . . . But I believe when you take away the fancy bottles and marketing mystique of imported beer, you discover that Samuel Adams and other American brewers simply make better tasting beers."[10]

In January 2005, Jim Koch announced that he would spend nearly $7 million modernizing an old brewery in Cincinnati to restore roots deep in Ohio's German heritage. Koch's father had once apprenticed in the brewery, and now the expansion would mean that nearly two-thirds of Samuel Adams beer would be produced and bottled in Ohio by the end of 2005. The mayor and other city officials downed bottles of beer with Koch to toast the economic coup of gaining 100 new jobs. Boston Beer's annual sales remained at about $208 million a year. "Anheuser spills more in a day than we make in a year," Koch quipped.[11]

ANALYSIS

Entrepreneurial Character

Although many entrepreneurial opportunities come in the retail and service industries, mostly because these typically require less start-up investment, Jim Koch saw the possibility in beer, even without a huge wallet. He started with $100,000 of his own money and $140,000 from friends and relatives. He had the beer recipe and determination. By contracting out the production to an existing brewery with unused production capacity, the bulk of the start-up money could be spent on nonproduction concerns, such as advertising.

His determination to gain acceptance of his beer, despite its high price and lack of foreign cachet, is characteristic of most successful entrepreneurs. They press on, despite obstacles in gaining acceptance. They have confidence that their product or concept is viable. They are not easily discouraged.

At the same time, Koch believed he had something unique, a flavor and quality that neither domestic nor imported brews could deliver. He had the audacity to make his product still more unique by charging even higher prices than the imports, thus conveying an image of highest quality.

His search for uniqueness did not end with the product. He developed an advertising theme far different from that of other beers by stressing quality and aggressively attacking the imports: "Declare your independence from foreign beer." And he was the spokesman on TV and radio commercials, giving a personal and charismatic touch.

[10] Boston Beer Company News, August 25, 2000, www.samadams.com.
[11] Bill Sloat, "Samuel Adams Brewer Expanding in Cincinnati," *Cleveland Plain Dealer*, January 7, 2005, pp. C1 and C3.

As Boston Beer moved out of regional into national distribution, Koch developed a sales force as large as Anheuser-Busch, the giant of the industry. His grasping of uniqueness even went to Boston Beer's initial public stock offering, in which customers were invited to buy into the company through coupons on six-packs. And it was oversubscribed in only a few weeks.

Controlled Growth (Aggressive Moderation)

The temptation for any firm, when demand seems to be growing insatiably, but especially for newer, smaller firms, is to expand aggressively: "We must not miss this opportunity." Such optimism can sow the seeds of disaster, when demand suddenly lessens because of a saturated market and/or new competition, leaving our firm with too much plant and other fixed assets, and a burdensome overhead.

Controlled growth—we might also call this "aggressive moderation"—is usually far better. Now our firm is not shunning growth, even vigorous growth, but is controlling it within its present resources, not overextending itself. Boston Beer showed this restraint by expanding within its production capability, adding several more contract brewers as needed. It expanded market by market at the beginning, only moving to a new geographical area when it could supply it. First was Boston, then Washington D.C., then New York, Chicago, California, and finally all 50 states.

Besides husbanding resources, both material and personnel, aggressive moderation is compatible with the tightness of controls needed to assure high-quality product and service standards. Even more than this, moderation allows a firm to build the accounting and financial standards and controls needed to prevent a dangerous buildup of inventories and expenses.

Limits on Potential

It is difficult for a new firm to perceive, in the heady days of growth, that its growth potential is sorely limited without drastic and risky changes. Limits on potential usually are due to two factors:

1. Ease of entry into the industry, which encourages a host of competitors. This turned out to be especially true with the influx of microbrewers, to 3,000 in just a few years.

2. Finite potential in demand. (This also affected the high-tech industry and the collapse of the NASDAQ at the turn of the millennium.) Demand for specialty beer, while at first robust and rising, was certainly not going to take over the mainstream beer market.

Given the rush to microbreweries in an environment of limited demand, the aspirations of Jim Koch to be a dominant force in the brewing industry had to be curbed. He could still be a profitable firm and do well in his niche, but he would never be a challenge beyond that. Perhaps that is enough for most entrepreneurs. They can hardly expect to grasp the golden ring of complete market dominance.

❖ ❖ ❖

Invitation for Your Own Analysis and Conclusions

We welcome your analysis of Jim Koch and his Boston Beer enterprise. Do you see any business plan that might have made him more successful, a bigger factor in the market?

❖ ❖ ❖

WHAT CAN BE LEARNED?

The price-quality perception, again.—We have a curious phenomenon today regarding price. More consumers than ever are shopping at discount stores because they supposedly offer better prices than other retailers. Airlines competing with lowest prices, such as Southwest and JetBlue, are clobbering higher-cost carriers. Yet for many products, especially those that are complex and have hidden ingredients, a higher price than competitors is the major indicator of higher quality. Boston Beer certainly confirms that higher price can successfully differentiate a firm. Especially if the taste is robustly different, and if the theme of highest quality is constantly stressed in advertising.

Perhaps the moral is that both low prices and high prices can be successful. A strategy of lowest prices, however, tends to be more vulnerable, since competitors can so easily and quickly match the low prices (not always profitably, of course), while a high-price strategy stressing quality tends to attract fewer competitors. But it will also attract fewer customers, as with higher-priced goods such as Herman Miller's office furniture. The high-price strategy should generally be more successful with products that are relatively inexpensive to begin with, such as beer, and ones where the image of prestige and good taste is attractive.

The challenge of the right approach to growth.—In the analysis section we discussed the desirability of *controlled growth*, also known as *aggressive moderation*, and noted that Boston Beer practiced this well. There are some who would challenge such slowness in grabbing opportunities. *Exuberant expansion* instead is advocated, when and if the golden opportunity is presented (some would call this "running with the ball"). Operations should be expanded as fast as possible in such a situation, some would say. But there are times when caution is advised.

Risks lie on all sides as we reach for these opportunities. When a market begins to boom and a firm is unable to keep up with demand without greatly increasing capacity and resources, it faces a dilemma: Stay conservative in the expectation that the burgeoning demand will be short-lived, and thereby abdicate some of the growing market to competitors, or expand vigorously and take full advantage of the opportunity. If the euphoria is short-lived, and demand slows drastically, the firm is left with expanded capacity, more resource commitment than needed, high interest and carrying costs, and perhaps even jeopardized viability because of overextension. Above all, however, a firm should not expand beyond its ability to maintain organizational and accounting control over the operation. To do so is tantamount to letting a sailing ship brave the uncertainties of a storm under full canvas.

Keep the breakeven point as low as possible, especially for new ventures.—Fixed investments in plant and equipment raise the breakeven point of sales needed to cover overhead costs and make a profit. (For a review of breakeven, see the Breakeven Box in Chapter 11, Euro Disney.) Boston Beer kept its breakeven point low by using contract breweries. Now this would have been a mistake if the quality of production at these breweries was erratic or not up to Boston Beer's expectations. Excellent and dependable quality were vital requirements if it was to succeed in selling its high-priced beer. But by working closely with experienced brewers, quality control apparently was no problem.

Certainly the lower breakeven point makes for less risk. And the future is always uncertain, despite research and careful planning. Mistakes will be made. The environment is constantly changing as to customer attitudes and preferences, and particularly in actions of competitors.

When a decision involves high stakes and an uncertain future—which translates into high risks—is it not wiser to approach the venture somewhat conservatively, not spurning the opportunity, but also not committing major resources and efforts until success appears more certain?

The importance of maintaining quality.—For a high-priced product, a brief letdown in quality control can be disastrous to the image. The story is told of Jim Koch ordering a draft of his own Samuel Adams at a restaurant across from Lincoln Center in New York City. He was horrified at the taste. He called the manager, and they went to the basement and looked at the keg. "It was two-and-a-half months past its pull date." The manager quickly changed the past-its-prime keg, which the distributor, intentionally or not, had sold the restaurant.[12] Sometimes a lapse in quality is not the fault of the manufacturer, but of a distributor or dealer. Whoever is at fault, the brand image is tarnished. And it is difficult to resurrect a reputation of poor or uncertain quality.

For investors, consider the risk of initial public offerings (IPOs).—IPOs are often bid up to unreasonable prices because of public enthusiasm over new offerings. While Boston Beer did well as a niche brewer, and dominated its niche, it had to be a major disappointment to its investors who bought in at the beginning. Perhaps the better investor strategy is to wait for public enthusiasm to calm down before taking a stake in a new enterprise.

CONSIDER

Can you think of other learning insights?

QUESTIONS

1. Have you ever tried one of the Boston Beer brews? If so, how did you like the taste? Did you think it was worth the higher price?

---

[12] McCune, p. 16.

2. The investment community evidently thought Boston Beer had great growth probabilities to have bid up the initial price so quickly. Why do you suppose so many fell into this trap? Or was Jim Koch a poor executive in not bringing Boston Beer up to their expectations?

3. "The myriad specialty beers are but a fad. People will quickly tire of an expensive, strong-flavored beer. Much of it is just a gimmick." Discuss.

4. What problems do you see retailers facing with the burgeoning number of different beers today? What might be the implications of this?

5. Playing the *devil's advocate*, critique the strategy of charging some of the highest prices in the world for your beer.

6. We saw the detection of a problem with the freshness of a beer at a restaurant by Jim Koch himself. How can Boston Beer prevent such incidents from happening again? Can distributor negligence or shortsighted actions be totally prevented by Boston Beer?

7. Do you think Boston Beer can continue to compete effectively against the giant brewers, with their infinitely greater resources, who are now moving into the specialty beer market with their own microbrews? Why or why not?

8. In 1998, Boston Beer produced more than two dozen styles of beer. Now it is down to just a few. Do you see any problems with this?

HANDS-ON EXERCISES

1. You are Jim Koch. You have just learned that Michael Feuer, founder of OfficeMax, described in Chapter 23, has grown his entrepreneurial endeavor to a $1.8 billion enterprise in just seven years. It has taken you ten years to grow Boston Beer to a $50 million firm. You are depressed at this but determined to greatly increase your company's growth. How would you go about setting Boston Beer on this great growth path? Be as specific as you can. What dangers do you see ahead?

2. It is 1986 and Boston Beer is beginning its growth after hiring Pittsburgh Brewery to produce its beer. Jim Koch has charged you with coordinating the efforts at Pittsburgh Brewery, paying particular attention to assuring that your quality standards are rigidly maintained. How would you go about doing this?

TEAM DEBATE EXERCISE

Debate how Boston Beer should commit the $100 million it received in late 1995 from the public stock offering. In particular, debate whether the bulk of the proceeds should go to building its own state-of-the-art brewery, or something else.

INVITATION TO RESEARCH

How is Boston Beer faring today? Has its expansion accelerated or stalled? Is it facing any particular problems? Has the stock price risen to the $30 initial issuance price? Are any merger rumors circulating?

CHAPTER TWENTY-THREE

OfficeMax: To the End

$\textbf{\textit{M}}$ichael Feuer had a passion to be an entrepreneur. He knew that this passion was rather late in coming, but by age 42 he was bored with the corporate life. Still, perhaps it had been there all along, this passion.

He had started with Fabri-Centers of America, a 600-store chain, 17 years before, and quickly rose through the ranks. He liked to describe himself in those days as suffering from the Frank Sinatra syndrome—"I wanted to do it my way." And he got tired of what he called CYB, "covering your backside," which he saw most executives spending too much of their time trying to do, at the expense of total effectiveness. If only he had his own business, he could escape these drains on career satisfaction and constraints on his potential. However, he couldn't accept the common notion of the true entrepreneur as someone who has enormous self-confidence, enough to give up the security of the paycheck and go off on his or her own. "I'm not a true entrepreneur because I suffer acutely from what I call 'F of F,' the fear of failure."

In his pursuit of entrepreneurship, Feuer turned down a number of big-money corporate jobs and the perks that go with them. Increasingly he felt an overwhelming urge to be his own man, to succeed or fail on his own terms. He soon achieved the reality of starting a small business from scratch, however, and experienced something quite in contrast with what might have been if he had chosen the corporate option.

THE START

OfficeMax officially began on April Fools Day, April 1, 1988.[1] Its most precious asset at the time was a blank sheet of paper. But the concept, laid out that day on paper, was simple: Create an exciting office-products superstore that featured breadth and depth of merchandise, present it in a contemporary manner with professional, friendly service, and then offer prices 30 to 70 percent less than those at more traditional office-supply retailers.

---

[1] Until late 1993, little was written about the success of OfficeMax. Much of the early material and quotations come from speeches Feuer made to business groups and graduate business school classes.

Michael Feuer and his partner had recognized a flaw—another of those strategic windows of opportunity (see Chapters 17 and 22)—in the existing system for marketing office products, and they resolved to exploit it, if they could convince enough investors to give them the resources needed. The traditional channel of distribution for this merchandise was from manufacturers to wholesalers or distributors, and finally to stationers, who were usually small retailers. This rather lengthy channel imposed markups at each stage of the distribution and resulted in relatively higher prices for the end-user. Feuer saw this as archaic, akin to the "old-time mom-and-pop groceries on every corner," which were eventually replaced by more efficient and much lower-priced supermarkets. These for the most part bypassed wholesalers and distributors and went directly to manufacturers. While Feuer was not unique in recognizing the flawed method of distributing office products, he was in the forefront.

Feuer and his partner, Robert Hurwitz (who ceased to be active in the firm on a full-time basis), were able to mass $3 million from 50 investors, some friends and family members as well as a number of doctors and lawyers. The two partners did not use debt financing, nor did they seek venture capitalists. They shunned these most common sources of capital for new firms, not wanting to give up any control of their enterprise; neither did they want to answer to skeptics and defend every major decision. However, for many promising small businesses, venture capital can provide needed startup funds difficult to obtain otherwise. See the following Information Box for more discussion of venture capitalists and their role in fostering small enterprises.

INFORMATION BOX

VENTURE CAPITALISTS: AID TO ENTREPRENEURS

The biggest roadblock to self-employment is financing. Banks tend to be unreceptive to funding unproven new ventures, especially for someone without a track record. Given that most would-be entrepreneurs have limited resources from which to draw, where are they to get the financing needed?

Feuer and Hurwitz bypassed conventional sources of financing by finding 50 willing investors. For many other would-be entrepreneurs, venture capitalists may be the answer.

Venture capitalists are wealthy individuals (or firms) looking for extraordinary returns for their investments. At the same time, they are willing to accept substantial risks. Backing nascent entrepreneurs in speculative undertakings can be the route to a far greater return on investment than is possible otherwise—provided that the venture capitalist chooses wisely whom to stake. The decision is much easier after a fledgling enterprise has a promising start. Then venture capitalists may stand in line for a piece of the action. But until then, the entrepreneur may struggle to get seed money.

How do these sources of funding choose among the many business ideas brought to them? "They look at the people, not the ideas," says Arthur Rock, one of the foremost venture capitalists. "Nearly every mistake I've made has been because I picked the wrong people, not the wrong idea."[2]

For a would-be entrepreneur seeking venture capital, then, the most important step may be selling yourself in addition to your idea. Intellectual honesty is sometimes mentioned by venture capitalists as a necessary ingredient. This may be defined as a willingness to face facts rigorously and not be deluded by rosy dreams and unrealistic expectations.

Those who win the early support of venture capitalists will likely have to give away a good piece of the action. Should the enterprise prove successful, the venture capitalist will expect to share in the success. The funds provided by a venture capitalist may well be crucial even to starting, or they may mean the difference between being adequately funded and so poorly funded that failure is almost inevitable.

Selling a definitive business plan to a prospective venture capitalist is usually a requirement for financing. In the process, of course, you are selling yourself. You may want to do this exercise: Choose a new business idea, develop an initial business plan, and attempt to persuasively present it to a would-be investor.

While Feuer and Hurwitz recognized what seemed an attractive market opportunity, they were not the only ones to do so. In May 1988, an industry trade paper listed all the embryonic firms in the emerging office-products superstore industry. OfficeMax rated number 14 on a list of 15. "We would have been dead last, but another company had started a week later than we did, although neither one of us had any stores."[3]

Feuer and Hurwitz established headquarters offices in a tiny 500-square-foot brick warehouse. It had little heat or air-conditioning. The company owned only a few pieces of office furniture, a coffeemaker, and a copy machine, but no fax. The restroom had to be unisex since there was only space for one toilet. They had recruited seven people, who were only half-jokingly told that they needed to have small appetites because there was little money to pay them. But Feuer promised that they would share in the financial success of the company, and for these seven their faith and hope for the future were enough. Feuer liked to tell the story of how he reinterviewed a candidate for a vice-president's position who had turned him down in 1988. Had he accepted the job then, he would have been a multi-millionaire by 1993.

THE FIRST YEAR

Even with $3 million of seed money from the 50 investors, OfficeMax had limited resources for what it proposed to do. A major problem now was to convince manufacturers to do business with this upstart of a firm in Cleveland. Most manufacturers

[2] John Merwin, "Have You Got What It Takes?" *Forbes*, August 3, 1981, p. 61.
[3] John R. Brandt, "Taking It to the Max," *Corporate Cleveland* September 1988, p. 17.

were satisfied with the existing distribution channels and were reluctant to grant credit to a revolutionary newcomer with hardly a store to its name.

The key to winning the support of the manufacturers lay in convincing them that OfficeMax had such a promising future that it could offer them far more business potential than they would ever have with their present distributors—that OfficeMax would be a 30-, 50-, even 300-store chain in a few years. "We explained to them that it was in *their* best interest to help us today—to guarantee a place with us tomorrow."

To make its message credible, OfficeMax needed to create an image of stability and of a firm poised to jump-start. To help convey this image, Feuer convinced a major Cleveland bank to grant it an unsecured line of credit. There was only one condition: OfficeMax had to promise never to use it. But this impressive-looking line of credit, bespeaking the faith that a major bank seemingly had in the embryonic firm, brought respect from suppliers. (Note: Do you see this as entirely ethical?) Then OfficeMax went so far as to ask sellers for unheard-of terms of sale—such as 60, 90, even 120 days to still get a cash discount.

Xerox was somehow persuaded to grant a year's payment delay for purchases. Many other manufacturers also accepted the outlandish requests. The bold promise of growth was realized, as many manufacturers five years later found OfficeMax to be their best customer. OfficeMax became so important at Xerox that the account was handled by a divisional president and chief financial officer.

The first store was opened July 5, 1988, three months after the enterprise itself was started. This was an amazingly short time to fine-tune the concept, find a site, remodel as needed, and merchandise and staff the store. Feuer explained that the firm urgently needed some cash to survive, hence the desperate efforts to bring the first unit on line. In addition to providing needed cash flow, they needed the first store to confirm the viability and promise of the superstore concept to investors and suppliers alike.

This the first store quickly did. Customers eagerly embraced the great variety but lowest prices of the superstore for office products, more commonly known today as a *category-killer store*. The only publicity had been a newspaper story two days before. Yet the store racked up $6,400 in sales that first day.

In the next 90 days, stores two and three were opened, also in metropolitan Cleveland. The fourth store was opened in Detroit, not far from the executive offices of Kmart, destined a few years later to become a majority shareholder. Within six months the company was breaking even before corporate expenses.

As Feuer described his work schedule in those early days, he typically was in the corporate office from 7:00 a.m. to 7:00 p.m., stopping at his home just long enough to change into nondescript clothing before going to the first store, where he could inconspicuously observe the shopping activity there and talk to customers, asking them what they liked and didn't like about the store. He liked to recount how he would even follow customers who left without buying anything out to the parking lot to ask them why OfficeMax did not meet their needs.

Following Feuer's example, the company from its inception had a strong commitment to its customers. For example, OfficeMax accepted collect calls from customers. Any complaints had to be resolved in less than 24 hours, complete with an apology from OfficeMax. The company's objective was to build loyalty. "We're not embarrassed to say that we were wrong—and the customer was right."

As the company began making a small profit, Feuer's worst nightmare was that the accounting had been "screwed up," and that OfficeMax was on the verge of bankruptcy without realizing it. With this tormenting thought, he went back to the existing shareholders after six months to raise additional capital. The early success of the enterprise enabled them to raise the per-share price 75 percent over the original placement.

By the end of the first full year, OfficeMax had six stores operational in Ohio and Michigan, with total sales of $13 million. The stores were profitable thanks to an undeviating cost-consciousness.

GROWTH CONTINUES

By early 1990, two years into the operation, OfficeMax had 17 stores in operation. Unexpectedly, Montgomery Ward proposed a merger between OfficeMax and Office World, a similar operation that Ward had funded along with a number of venture capitalists. Office World had been started with what seemed to Feuer to be almost a king's ransom. But it proceeded to lose $10 million in a very short time. In the negotiations, OfficeMax was in the power position, and it acquired Office World and its seven Chicago locations on rather attractive terms: Its major concession was to relinquish two of its ten board seats to Montgomery Ward and the venture capitalists, but along with the stores it acquired several million dollars in badly needed cash.

By the summer of 1990, OfficeMax had about $25 million in cash, with 30 stores in operation. It raised another $8 million in a third private placement, at a share price 600 percent higher than the original investors had paid just two years before. Corporate offices were now moved into a building with space for both men's and women's restrooms.

Feuer began an aggressive new expansion program, calling for opening 20 additional stores. Competition was heating up in the new superstore industry, and several competitors had gone public to raise funds for more rapid expansion. Several others had gone bankrupt.

The Kmart Connection

The biggest threat facing OfficeMax now came from news that Kmart was poised to roll out its new Office Square superstore chain, which would be a direct threat to OfficeMax. Given Kmart's huge financial and managerial resources, and its real estate expertise and influence, Feuer and company saw themselves being crushed and driven into Lake Erie. Feuer consoled himself that being left penniless would at least be character building.

Mostly as a defensive strategy, Feuer sought to open talks with Kmart. The company's executives proved to be receptive, and in November 1990 an agreement was negotiated in which Kmart made an investment of about $40 million in return for a 22 percent equity stake in OfficeMax. As part of the agreement, the feared Office Square became a possession of OfficeMax, and Kmart received one seat on the OfficeMax board.

Now the expansion program could begin accelerating, with Kmart's full cooperation and support. So good was the rapport that within ten months of the initial transaction, discussions were started concerning a broader business relationship with Kmart.

As the original goals of the business were being realized, it was perhaps time to cash in some of the chips, so Michael Feuer thought. Two options seemed appropriate for the original investors: (1) go public, or (2) structure a new deal with Kmart. The company decided to go with Kmart. Kmart agreed to buy out all of the shareholders, with the exception of 50 percent of the shares of Feuer and partner Hurwitz, for a total market capitalization of about $215 million. This was up from zero just 42 months earlier. What made the deal particularly attractive was the fact that while 92 percent of OfficeMax was sold to a well-heeled parent, it could still retain total autonomy.

Onward and Upward, Without Kmart

By the end of July 1995, OfficeMax had 405 superstores in more than 150 markets in 41 states and Puerto Rico. The typical store was 23,500 square feet and had 6,000 items. Faster growth had been achieved through two major acquisitions: the 46-store Office Warehouse chain and the 105-store BizMart chain.

Sales were primarily to small and medium-sized businesses employing under 100 employees, home-office customers, and individual consumers. But institutions such as school boards and universities were also targets, and the low prices at OfficeMax were powerful inducements. A new program was established for next-day delivery of office supplies, based on calls to telephone centers with toll-free lines.

The company was planning to open up to 20 new FurnitureMax stores, which were to be 8,000- to 10,000-square-foot additions to existing OfficeMax stores devoted to office furniture. It was also testing five to ten new CopyMax stores. Along with a multimedia advertising strategy, the company now had a 220-page merchandise catalog featuring about 5,000 items with toll-free telephone ordering.

Meanwhile, Kmart was seeking additional money to provide badly needed facelifts for its stores in a desperate attempt to hold off the mighty Wal-Mart. This led Kmart to sell its share of OfficeMax, as well as some of its other subsidiaries, in order to raise a needed $3 billion in cash. The sale was finalized in July 1995. OfficeMax netted $110 million to be used to fund its store expansion. Its future as a public company rather than a subsidiary of Kmart now presented a heady dream to Feuer and his investors. The following Information Box discusses the prescription for great wealth in going public.

In fiscal 1995 (year ending January 31) revenues were over $1.8 billion. Net income was $30.4 million, up 181 percent from the year before. Figures 23.1 and 23.2 show the growth in sales and in number of stores.

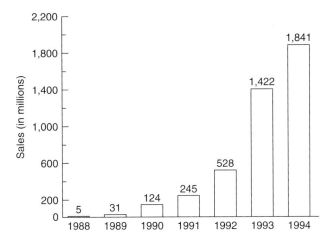

Figure 23.1. Sales growth (fiscal years ending Jan. 31 of the next year). In 1988, OfficeMax projected 1993 sales of less than $100 millon; actual 1993 sales were 14 times larger.

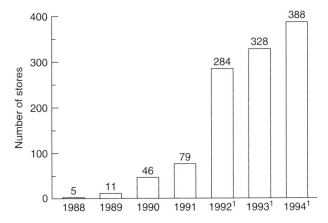

Figure 23.2. Growth in number of stores (fiscal years ending Jan. 31 of the next year). OfficeMax's 1988 business plan called for 50 stores by 1993; the company ended the year with nearly seven times that number.
[1] Includes BizMart stores.

INFORMATION BOX

THE PRESCRIPTION FOR GREAT WEALTH FOR ENTREPRENEURS

An entrepreneur often has much to gain by going public with an enterprise after a few years if it shows early success and a promising future. The entrepreneur keeps a portion of the stock and offers the rest to the public. With an attractive new venture, the offering price may be high enough to make the entrepreneur an instant multimillionaire.

Take Office Depot, for example. This was the largest office-supply superstore chain in North America, although not that much bigger than OfficeMax. It was listed on the New York Stock Exchange, with its 94,143,455 shares of common stock selling for about $39 a share, giving a total market value of about $3.7 billion. If OfficeMax went public and had a similar relative market value, and if Feuer and Hurwitz held 8 percent of the total capitalization, they would be worth about $296 million, or almost $150 million apiece.

What rationale do you see for Feuer's decision to structure a new deal with Kmart rather than go public? Do you agree with his rationale?

STORM CLOUDS

In 1996, OfficeMax became only the fourth company up to that time to exceed $3 billion in revenues in less than nine years. As of September 1998, it had 769 stores in 48 states and Puerto Rico. Through joint ventures, it also had nine stores in Mexico and a first store in Japan. In addition, there were 129 CopyMax outlets targeting the estimated $9 billion print-for-pay industry, as well as 129 FurnitureMax stores tapping the estimated $12 billion office-furniture industry.[4]

In 1999, it planned to open 120 new superstores in the United States on top of the 150 opened in 1998. Revenues had steadily climbed to $3.765 billion in 1997, while net income had grown to $89.6 million, an increase of 30 percent from 1996.[5] Over the three-year period from January 31, 1994 to January 31, 1997, OfficeMax's market share, compared to its largest competitor, Office Depot, rose from 30.1 percent to 35.9 percent, as shown below:

	Fiscal 1997	Fiscal 1994
Office Depot revenues	$6.716 billion	$4.266 billion
OfficeMax revenues	3.765	1.841
Market share of OfficeMax relative to Office Depot	35.9%	30.1%

By September 1998, however, OfficeMax's stock price had fallen precipitously to under $10 a share. Later that year, analysts began attacking OfficeMax because of its poor showing against competitors Office Depot and Staples. In particular, sales were lagging at its older stores, and OfficeMax warned that third- and fourth-quarter

[4] 1998 OfficeMax Annual Report.
[5] Ibid.

earnings would not hit expectations, mostly because of heavy price-cutting on computers. Critics were quick to point out that Office Depot and Staples were not so adversely affected.[6]

The situation worsened as businesses began cutting back in a slowing economy in 2000, and the office-supply industry faced a saturated market—too many stores from years of vigorous expansion in the 1990s.

The fourth quarter of 2000, which should have been the strongest quarter of the year, was particularly nasty. OfficeMax posted an $85 million loss, while Office Depot and Staples posted $168 million and $112 million losses respectively. All announced sharp cuts in expansion and closings of underperforming stores. OfficeMax, now grown to 995 stores, planned 50 store closings. Company stock was trading around $2 a share.

THE END

On July 14, 2003, OfficeMax announced that it had agreed to be acquired by Boise Cascade Corp., a big lumber and paper company. In a $1.15 billion buyout, OfficeMax shareholders would get $9 a share, about a 25 percent premium over the current share price. Feuer himself would stand to make $22.3 million from the shares he held, in addition to at least five years of his $983,000 salary for having a consulting role in the new operation.

Feuer had been actively seeking a buyer since the fall of 2002, having concluded that he had taken the company about as far as he could with his resources, and with its being the smallest firm in office-products retailing. In spite of all his efforts, OfficeMax had had eight losing quarters before regaining profitability in late 2002. He felt worst about the investors who had enthusiastically joined him when he took his enterprise public in 1994. Their faith in him was largely unrewarded, and many of these investors were his friends, and they had paid $19 a share then. In the bad days of 2000 and 2001, their shares had sunk 92 percent to $1.56 at the lowest point. Perhaps he had been too ambitious, had opened too many stores, more than OfficeMax was able to assimilate. These brought a hefty debt load that became an unhealthy burden. Now he had finally turned the company to profitability, but the stock price remained only a fraction of what it had been a few years earlier, well below what many of these people had paid.

Feuer reflected on the drawbacks of being a distant third in a strongly competitive industry. He had never been able to gain a foothold with the large customers his rivals had. No, his main customer base was consumers and small businesses; the profitable volume was just not there.

Boise had been endeavoring to move away from the severe price competition of being a commodity supplier to distributors and wanted to get into the more profitable business of selling paper products to end-users. It had already made more than

---

[6] For example, "OfficeMax Opens New Stores While Sales Lag at Old Ones," *Cleveland Plain Dealer*, October 29, 1998, p. 2 C.

40 acquisitions in recent years to expand its office-products business, and this offered the potential of tapping into the larger customer base.

Would this turn out to be one of the few mergers "made in heaven" or another of the ill-fated ones? At least Feuer came out of his 15 years of entrepreneurship a very wealthy man.[7]

Late-Breaking News

Boise had to have been disappointed by its acquisition of OfficeMax and its total commitment to a retail operation and abandonment of its lumber and paper manufacturing. On February 14, 2005, the company announced the resignation of CEO Christopher Milliken, on the job for less than four months. He was the third senior executive to leave OfficeMax that year, amid a growing accounting scandal. Investigation had uncovered improper billings, as well as errors in rebates and other payments from vendors in 2004 that necessitated restating operating income for three quarters. The scandal came to light after the firm posted disappointing Christmas season results and lowered its profit forecast.

ANALYSIS

Here we see what initially was an outstanding entrepreneurial success. The growth rate in only a few years rivaled the best at the time. In the same year that OfficeMax was started, 685,095 other new businesses were also founded in the United States, but more than half of them eventually failed. Of the survivors, only a small percentage would ever achieve a net worth over $50 million. Only a handful would ever reach $200 million. What made OfficeMax so uniquely successful?

It was not that it had identified a great idea and nurtured it exclusively. While OfficeMax launched a business opportunity arising from the archaic distribution structure of the office-products industry, it was far from the first to do so. Indeed, the concept of category-killer stores was in the ascendancy for all kinds of retail goods.[8]

The competition could become intense when category-killer stores competed with each other. Eventually, only three chains of superstores remained in the office-products industry, and OfficeMax was one of them, although the smallest. Why did OfficeMax succeed so well, while most of its competitors failed or were acquired?

Much of the success was due to the efforts of the principal founder, Michael Feuer. His vision was to retain control of the nascent enterprise by shunning venture capitalists and debt financing. While the money initially raised, $3 million, would seem adequate for most ventures, for a category-killer chain it was barely sufficient.

---

[7] Jim Carlton, "Boise Cascade Expects OfficeMax to Shore Up Profit," *Wall Street Journal*, July 15, 2003, p. B5; Teresa Dixon Murray and Janet H. Cho, "Michael Feuer Drove OfficeMax and Himself," *Cleveland Plain Dealer*, July 20, 2003, pp. A1 and A10.

[8] A category-killer store gets its name from the strategy of carrying such a huge assortment of merchandise at good prices in a particular category of goods that it practically destroys traditional merchants of such goods.

But severe austerity combined with the promise of great future rewards motivated both employees and suppliers. This required optimism and an enthusiastic selling job by Feuer. And it also required a trusting relationship with investors, employees, and suppliers.

Great attention to customer service, to cost containment to the point of austerity, to the myriad details needed for opening stores with adequate employees and merchandise in severe deadline situations—all these were part of the success package. Building on the growth without losing sight of the austerity heritage was perhaps even more important as the enterprise grew from a few stores to 20, 50, and more.

Of particular interest for any growing enterprise is the opportunity to make attractive acquisitions of former competitors who have fallen into desperate straits. The successful firm is in a position to quickly build on the bones of former competitors who could not make it.

Alas, some of the early virtues of austerity and moderate borrowing (and consequent modest interest expenses) were disregarded in the heady rush to expansion in the late 1990s. In the eagerness to open ever more stores, the debt burden became a lodestone. A saturated market and an economic slowdown forced retrenchment, not only for OfficeMax but for its bigger competitors as well.

◦ ◦ ◦

Invitation to Make Your Own Analysis and Conclusions

What do you see as accounting for Feuer's great success going bad? How could he have handled things better?

◦ ◦ ◦

WHAT CAN BE LEARNED?

Successful entrepreneurship is not easy.—Not many who opt to go into business for themselves expect it to be an easy road, a comfortable and lazy lifestyle. Yet the work ethic of successful entrepreneurs can be awesome, even for those prepared for long hours and worries in the night. Michael Feuer customarily put in 12- to 18-hour days between corporate headquarters and keeping in close touch with stores and customers and suppliers. He would wake up at 3:00 a.m. to stare at the ceiling while wondering whether he made the right decision. He felt a responsibility to his employees, even after they had grown from the seven original ones whose jobs depended on his decisions. By the end of 1993, he had more than 19,000 reasons to worry in the night.

Would he have been less successful with a more moderate work ethic? Maybe. But the personal stake in a growing business drives many entrepreneurs to become workaholics even to the point of sacrificing other aspects of their lives, including family.

There is power in a growth image, even if it is only an illusion.—In one of the most crucial moves taken in the early and most vulnerable months of the embryonic enterprise, Feuer and his people were able to sell both bankers and manufacturers on the great growth prospects for the company, that "we would rapidly become a 20-, 50-, or even 300-store chain. We explained that it was in their best interest to help us today—to guarantee a place with us tomorrow."

What makes a strong growth company so attractive to investors, creditors, suppliers, and employees? Part of the attractiveness certainly is that everyone likes to be associated with a winner. The greatest appeal of growth companies is their economic promise. This embraces investors, of course, because their investment grows with the business. Creditors and suppliers see more and more business coming their way as the company grows ever larger. And employees see great career opportunities continually opening up in a rapidly growing organization.

Perhaps, in creating the image of OfficeMax as a company on the threshhold of great growth, Feuer was simply very persuasive. But perhaps many of the people he talked with were so eager to be convinced, and to be offered the opportunity to get in on the ground floor of what might be the stuff of dreams, that they would accept even grandiose conjecture.

Go the extra mile in customer relations.—It is easy for an organization to proclaim its dedication to customer service and good customer relations. Too often, however, such talk is only lip service, pious pronouncements without real substance. OfficeMax went far beyond lip service. Feuer and his executives, at least in the early years, sought close contact with customers in stores, even to the point of following them to the parking lot to see what might have been lacking in the merchandise or service that discouraged a purchase. The company accepted collect calls from customers who might have problems or complaints or special needs. The promise of satisfaction of all complaints within 24 hours, the guiding "How can we make you happy?" question in all customer dealings, and the readiness to apologize, attest to a customer commitment beyond the ordinary. With few exceptions, all businesses depend on customer loyalty and repeat business for their success. In office products, where many customers are businesses, customer loyalty may be all the more important. But it is easy to delude yourself and an organization that the loss of any single customer is not all that important, and that the firm must guard against being taken advantage of by unreasonable customers. Where should a firm, particularly a retailer, draw the line? Can a retailer be too liberal in the handling of customer complaints?

Again, the power of "lean and mean."—In several earlier cases we noted problems of bloated bureaucracy and/or uncontrolled spending, and the dire effect on profitability. We examined several highly successful firms, notably Southwest Airlines and Vanguard, that followed a policy of continued frugality despite increasing size. The temptation with great growth is to let down the barriers and open the spending spigots. OfficeMax resisted this urge in the early years, but then got caught up in the frenzy of opening stores as fast as it could.

Again, dedicated employees can give a powerful advantage.—As with Southwest Airlines, OfficeMax in its early years was able to stimulate employees to move beyond individual concerns to a higher level of performance, a true team approach. This dedication, and the vague promise of future great expectations, brought employees to OfficeMax for very low wages, some turning down much higher paying jobs for the dream that might or might not come to pass. The dedication of these employees made it possible to open the first store from scratch barely three months after the company was founded, with other stores quickly following.

The hope for great growth, a trusted leader, and an organization geared to a team effort seem to be most compatible in producing dedicated employees. One suspects there is also a close relationship in lean-and-mean organizations, where the limited bureaucracy and management levels foster easy communication. Unfortunately for a maturing OfficeMax, these motivational factors began to wan. The hope for great growth had to be more soberly appraised in a competitive environment where OfficeMax was number three behind two other aggressive competitors and a market rapidly becoming saturated.

Beware market saturation.—How many office-supply superstores can one metro area handle and still enable all outlets to prosper? Especially when there is little to choose from among the major competitors? OfficeMax, Staples, and Office Depot all have large box stores, the widest possible assortment of goods, reasonably low prices, and all push employees to be friendly, knowledgeable, and provide the best-possible service. In such an environment, with little distinctiveness possible, market saturation or overstoring becomes a real problem. It hurts profitability, until weaker competitors leave the market, and certainly curbs the growth potential.

CONSIDER

Can you identify other learning insights coming from this case?

QUESTIONS

1. In the hiring process, how would you identify the candidates who are most likely to become dedicated employees?
2. Can a firm be too liberal in handling customer complaints?
3. "OfficeMax is number three in its industry. This is a severe disadvantage, as it can never match the resources of its two larger competitors." Evaluate this assertion.
4. Do you think Feuer was being entirely ethical when he sold manufacturers on the desirability of doing business with OfficeMax in the very early days of the company? Why or why not?
5. Do you see any limitations to the future of category-killer stores?

6. Can you think of some types of merchandise where category-killer stores are unlikely to be successful?

7. Feuer regularly put in 12- to 18-hour days in the early years. Do you think he would have been as successful with less of a work ethic? Why or why not?

8. Be a *devil's advocate*. Argue against Feuer's plans to sell out to Boise.

9. Would you personally have been willing to work for OfficeMax in the early days, with very low pay, primitive accommodations, long hours—but maybe for a dream?

HANDS-ON EXERCISES

1. You own a small office-supply store. Business has been steady and sufficient for a good living for you and your family up to now. Now an OfficeMax has opened less than a mile away. Discuss how you possibly can compete against such a superstore when you cannot come close to matching its variety of goods or its prices.

2. You are the assistant to Feuer. He wants you to draw up plans for targeting large institutions and businesses. Be as specific as you can, making assumptions where needed, and persuasively support your recommendations.

TEAM DEBATE EXERCISE

On October 25, 1995, the largest office-products retailer, Office Depot, announced it was planning to open a dozen stores on OfficeMax's home turf, metropolitan Cleveland, where OfficeMax has its headquarters and 17 stores. "When we enter a major market, our usual policy is to go in rather quickly and saturate the market with six to a dozen to twenty stores within the first couple of years," Office Depot said. Michael Feuer was unfazed. "We think the advantage we have is such a fierce sense and focus of local pride. I don't think there will be much of a test," he said.[9] Debate the challenge OfficeMax now faces: it should be badly worried, because the market already is close to saturation; it should not be worried, because the market potential is still increasing and it can outcompete Office Depot. Then lay out business plans to compete in this environment.

INVITATION TO RESEARCH

What is the situation with OfficeMax and its acquisition by Boise? From what you can ascertain, has it been a fairly successful merger? What is Feuer doing?

---

[9] Bill Lubinger, "Office Depot Is Taking on OfficeMax," *Cleveland Plain Dealer*, October 25, 1995, p. C1.

CHAPTER TWENTY-FOUR

Gateway Computer's Efforts to Stay Alive

*T*he mettle of a person, or a firm, is best tested and judged, not in the euphoria of prosperity and boom conditions, but in the bleakness of adversity. The several years before and after the millennium provided the testing ground in the marketing wars among PC (personal computer) makers.

By 2002, the lower-price PC market had narrowed to two main adversaries, both the founders of their firms: Michael Dell of Dell Computer and Ted Waitt of Gateway. Both had started their ventures in the mid-1980s on a shoestring. One was 19 years old; the other 22. Both became billionaires. But by 2002, the PC boom was over, spending for technology was stagnant, and high-tech was in the vanguard of the stock-market collapse. Once mighty and highly valued names like Lucent, Cisco Systems, and Compaq were only grim reminders of lost chances to cash out in the heady days of 50 percent annual growth.

Some analysts saw the PC market as saturated, with everyone who needed and could afford a desktop or laptop already having one. Technological advances had slowed because the current generation of machines was already fast enough for most uses, thus lessening incentive to replace or trade up. The economic downturn further supported tightened rather than extravagant spending. With the product life cycle for PCs lengthened, long-term growth prospects dimmed for computer makers. The high stock multiples of only a few years before were hardly sustainable in a low-growth era. Furthermore, as the market became saturated, not all firms were likely to survive.

TED WAITT OF GATEWAY

In the fall of 2002, Ted Waitt, chairman and CEO of Gateway, had to be concerned. It would have been bad enough if the computer collapse were affecting all firms equally, with their market shares staying about the same. But this was not happening. While Gateway and most others were suffering, one firm—Dell—seemed somehow to be profiting and picking up great chunks of market share, much of it at Gateway's expense.

Waitt's thoughts went back to the beginning, to the farmhouse where in 1985 he and friend Mike Hammond had put their dreams to the test with a used computer, a three-page business plan, and a loan of $10,000 guaranteed by his grandmother. Waitt had dropped out of the University of Iowa to devote full time to this fledging endeavor, this dream. The business plan was simple and had not changed much even by 2002: offer products directly to customers and build to their specifications, with the goal of providing the best value for the money by bypassing middlemen. The enterprise grossed $100,000 in its first year, and was on the way to becoming a multibillion-dollar company.

Now Waitt's thoughts turned to the heady years of growth and unbelievable promise. In 1989, he began selling computers online, taking pride in being the first in the industry to do so. Even mighty Dell did not use the Internet for sales until 1996. In 1991, Waitt got the idea of introducing the cow-print boxes, which brought wide acclaim for Gateway and made its products distinctive. He was then on a roll and, in 1992, began offering customers a choice of software at no additional cost. It was with a great sense of achievement that he learned in 1993 that Gateway had become one of the *Fortune* 500 biggest firms, one year after Dell had joined these prestigious ranks. Not bad for an Iowa farm boy. But that same year, something even more momentous happened. Waitt took the firm public, and investor enthusiasm was so great that he became an instant multimillionaire, and not long after, a multibillionaire. A person can get used to these accomplishments. In 1996, Waitt introduced a nationwide network of what he called Gateway Country stores—after all, he was a country boy—where customers could try out his products, get advice from technical experts, and learn more about the technology in high-tech classrooms. With things going so well, he felt he could ease up a bit, and confidently chose a successor.

Problems

He shrugged his shoulders in disgust. In 1999, his one-third share of the business had been worth $9 billion. Now, in 2002, it was worth $400 million, and still falling, an unbelievable personal loss of over $8.5 billion. He felt flummoxed.

At first Waitt blamed his handpicked successor, whom he ousted when he returned as CEO. But his magic touch now seemed to elude him. He faced a battle for market share in a down market and, to boot, a price war with Michael Dell, his nemesis. Dell had somehow gotten his costs so low that he could undersell all competitors and still make money. In desperation, Waitt slashed Gateway's workforce by 10 percent. But it was not enough. Then he scaled back the company's international ambitions by exiting Europe and Asia, and reduced the workforce by another 25 percent. But Gateway's U.S. market share dropped from 7.4 percent in 2001 to 5.6 percent in 2002.

Waitt turned his attention to Apple Computer. If he couldn't match Dell on price, maybe he could attack Apple. On August 26, 2002, he launched a nationwide TV brand battle against Apple, with a new computer, the Profile 4, which resembled Apple's iMacs but was $400 cheaper (albeit with fewer features). For years Waitt had struggled to establish Gateway as a cult brand (hoping his rural Holstein theme with the black-and-white cow spots would convey an image of heartland honesty and dependability), one that would appeal to Apple's cult-like followers as well as others. But that had not happened, and he was thinking of putting the cow to rest. See the Information Box: Trying to Upgrade an Image, Maybe to a Mystique for a report on Gateway's efforts to change its image, hopefully to one that might have more potential for a cult following than its cow spots.

INFORMATION BOX

TRYING TO UPGRADE AN IMAGE, MAYBE TO A MYSTIQUE

For years, the Gateway brand had been symbolized by a Holstein cow—its white boxes speckled with black cow spots—and the company carried over this theme to its Gateway Country stores. CEO Ted Waitt even appeared in television commercials with a bovine co-star. He had hoped the homespun flavor might appeal to many buyers, perhaps conveying an image of integrity and frugality. But as the computer war intensified, with Gateway steadily losing market share, Waitt thought an upgrade was needed, and he killed his beloved cow. "I'm calling it the de-prairiefication" of the company, he said. The change to sleek black-and-silver PCs and laptops went beyond the product to the stores and advertisements.

Analysts were divided in their view of the shifting strategy. "I don't think consumers will hold it against them that they don't have the cow. Any campaign gets old after a while," said one.

Others disagreed: "The cow motif was one of those odd, quirky, counterintuitive trademarks that succeeded in spite of themselves."

"Odd and quirky" sounds like getting close to a mystique. Do you think Ted Waitt made a good decision in de-prairiefication? Why or why not?[1]

Apple had nourished its cult with magazines, chat groups, and a storied 20-year battle against the standard PC. But could Gateway gain some of this following? Critics were not very complimentary, citing Profile 4's lack of a rewriteable DVD drive and upgraded graphics, its boxiness compared with Apple's sleek design, and a screen that did not swivel as smoothly. Well, critics be d___d; his model was still $400 cheaper.

But the price war with Dell could not be ignored. Trying to reduce costs was cutting into muscle, hurting market share, and still not yielding profits. The loss in the quarter ending June 30, 2002 tripled to $61 million on revenues of $1 billion. By contrast, Dell was prospering with a $501 million profit on sales of $9.5 billion, up 11 percent from the previous year. To add salt to the wounds, one of its executives gloated in a prominent business journal: "It hasn't been a tough market for us."[2]

---

[1] Adapted from Frank Ahrens, "Gateway Changing Its Spots to Create an Upscale Image," *Washington Post*, as reported in *Cleveland Plain Dealer*," November 10, 2002, p. G3.
[2] Arlene Weintraub, "Gateway: Picking Fights It Just Might Lose," *Business Week*, September 9, 2002, p. 52.

Now analysts were picking at Gateway's bones, like jackals on the prowl. They were speculating that many of Gateway's 274 stores would have to be closed, and more production outsourced to foreign manufacturers, if there was any hope of returning to profitability.[3]

Doggedly, Waitt predicted, as 2002 drew to a close, that Gateway would show a quarterly profit at some point during 2003. But he was disconcerted to learn that both the Council of Institutional Investors and the huge California Public Employees Retirement System had added Gateway to their lists of underperformers.[4]

DELL COMPUTER

In 1984, a year before Waitt started Gateway, Michael Dell, a tall curly-haired youth of 19, started Dell Computer in a dorm room at the University of Texas with $1,000. He too had the idea that computer systems could be sold direct to customers rather than going through middlemen. He thought the manufacturer could better understand the needs of customers and provide them the most effective computing systems at lower prices. This direct marketing would also do away with retailers and their high margins.

Three years later, in 1987, Dell began his international expansion by opening a subsidiary in the United Kingdom. The next year, Dell took his enterprise public, with an initial offering of 3.5 million shares at $8.50 each, and became an instant multimillionaire. By 1992, Dell was included in the *Fortune* 500 roster of largest companies. In 1997, the pre-split price per share of the common stock reached $1,000, and Michael Dell was a multibillionaire.

With the bruising industry downturn, Dell's stock price fell along with all the rest, its shares by mid-2002 down 55 percent from the early 2001 peak of $59. So Michael Dell bought 8.5 million shares of his company to add to the 300 million he already owned.

Competition in 2002

In this troubled environment, Dell's revenue grew 2.6 percent in 2001 while that of the PC industry fell 14 percent. For the quarter ended May 3, 2002, Dell reported $457 million in earnings on sales of $8 billion. These figures were flat from the year-earlier figures, but far better than Dell's competitors.

Compaq, once the master of the PC business, found its stock collapsing from $50 to below $10, and was forced into a merger with Hewlett-Packard (HP) since it could not compete profitably with Dell. Gateway was on the ropes, and even high-end manufacturers like Silicon Graphics and Sun Microsystems were losing sales to Dell. Only IBM seemed insulated from Dell's competitive strength, due to its huge mainframe and services businesses, which were not directly in competition.

---

[3] *Ibid.*

[4] Gary McWilliams, "Gateway's Loss Shrinks, But It Sees Gloomy Year," *Wall Street Journal*, October 18, 2002, p. A7.

In the fall of 2002, with the Christmas season looming, PC makers dropped prices to new lows. Big names like IBM and HP, which usually catered to the higher-end market, went squarely after low-price leader Dell. Other makers dropped their already-low prices even more. For example:

- HP and eMachines had models starting at $399.
- Gateway announced its own $399 desktop.
- Microtel Computer Systems brought out a bare-bones machine for $199.
- HP cut prices for its new HP Compaq Evo to $899, from $1,100 a few months before.
- Even laptop prices plummeted—for example, IBM's ThinkPad notebooks were reduced to $950.

The severe industry price-cutting soon extended beyond PCs. HP reduced operating costs by $800 million by consolidating suppliers and shutting factories. It sought to increase selling direct to customers, thus bypassing middlemen, and expected such direct methods to reach one-third of all sales by November 2003. To be competitive, HP cut prices on computers aimed at business buyers by 10 percent to 15 percent. Dell entered the switch market (the technology linking computer networks) with prices one-half to two-thirds those of comparable models from 3Com and Cisco. 3Com promised "aggressive discounts to meet Dell pricing."[5]

To counter the severe price-cutting by its rivals, Dell started selling unbranded PCs through computer dealers that it had traditionally shunned. This program was aimed at small- and medium-size businesses.

THE SITUATION WORSENS FOR GATEWAY

By the end of the Christmas season 2002, Ted Waitt's hopes that this might be a turnaround year were dashed. He had stocked his 274 retail stores with cash-and-carry PCs and broadened the merchandise assortment to include hot sellers such as digital cameras and plasma TVs, and he spent dearly for advertising. Waitt tried to build PC sales by price matching, everyday low prices, and even daily specials, but all these only added to Gateway's losses. Now he had to contemplate restructuring again, with the retail chain foolishly created in the heady days of 1996 coming under close scrutiny for new cost cuts. The *Wall Street Journal* noted, however, that Waitt was in no danger of losing his job, since he was the largest stockholder.[6]

The situation worsened in latter 2003, despite Waitt's dogged prediction of at least one profitable quarter for 2003. On October 24, Gateway's stock price plunged 24 percent after it reported a third-quarter loss of $136.1 million and issued a dour

---

[5] Pui-Wing Tam, Gary McWilliams, and Scott Thurm, "As Alliances Fade, Computer Firms Toss Out Playbook," *Wall Street Journal*, October 15, 2002, p. A8.
[6] Gary McWilliams, "Under Gateway's Tree, Another Shake-up," *Wall Street Journal*, January 6, 2003, pp. A13 and A15; "Slaughterhouse," *Forbes*, January 20, 2003, p. 34.

forecast for the fourth quarter. Waitt's push into consumer electronics had failed to offset his PC woes. Still, a few analysts saw hope for the company in its having no debt and $1 billion in cash and securities (most of the current assets came from big income tax refunds, but these ended in the first quarter of 2003). But even a good-sized cash horde would not long endure with over $100 million in quarterly losses.

Dell, meantime, in August 2003 again slashed PC prices, this time aiming more specifically at HP, which had just reported that its PC unit had slipped into the red in its fiscal third quarter ended July 31 because of overly aggressive price-cutting. Dell had a monstrous advantage in its low-cost structure: Dell's overhead in the second quarter of 2003 was 9.6 cents, while HP's was 21.3 cents per dollar of sales.[7] Ted Waitt could take some perverse satisfaction in seeing that Gateway was not alone in being savaged by Dell: even much larger HP was just as vulnerable.

Still, Gateway was Dell's most direct competitor. Both firms sold PCs direct to customers by phone or on the Internet, thereby bypassing dealers. A point of difference was the several hundred Gateway Country stores, where customers could "test drive" PCs in the store. Both companies geared their offerings to the low end of the price range, but Gateway was having serious problems competing with Dell on price. Gateway had lost $1 billion on $6 billion in revenues in 2001, and the company was on the ropes. See Table 24.1 for the trend in operating results from 1994 through 2003 for Dell, Gateway, and Hewlett-Packard, and the relative shifts in market shares for these three major PC competitors. Table 24.2 shows net income comparisons and trends for the same three competitors.

A NEW STRATEGY FOR GATEWAY

The Acquisition of eMachines

In early 2004, Gateway acquired privately held eMachines for $290 million in stock and cash. At the time of the acquisition, eMachines employed only 138 workers to achieve its $1 billion in annual sales. And it was consistently profitable. Along with the acquisition, Gateway got Wayne R. Inouye, who agreed to serve as CEO of Gateway, while Waitt would remain chairman.

Wayne Inouye

Inouye, 51, had a reputation for frugality. For example, he never spent more than $6 for lunch, bought the cheapest gas for his car, and was known to be a coupon clipper even for such staples as soap. Not surprising, he came from modest means, the son of a tomato and peach farmer in the Central Valley of California. He had dropped out of the University of California at Berkeley in the 1970s and, for a time, sold guitars to rock musicians. Then he switched to selling electronic goods to dealers and built close relationships with such key PC retailers as Best Buy, CompUSA, Circuit City,

---

[7] Gary McWilliams and Ann Zimmerman, "Dell Price Cut Put a Squeeze on Rival H-P," *Wall Street Journal*, August 21, 2003, pp. B1, B7.

**TABLE 24.1.   Market Shares of Top Three Competitors (Million $),
1994–2003**

	2003	2001	2000	1998	1996	1994
Dell						
Revenue	41,440	31,168	31,888	18,243	7,759	3,475
Market Share	35.1%	37.8	35.3	25.1	15.2	11.2
Gateway						
Revenue	3,402	6,080	9,601	7,468	5,035	2,701
Market Share	2.9%	7.4	10.6	10.3	9.8	8.7
Hewlett-Packard						
Revenue	73,061	45,226	48,782	47,061	38,420	24,991
Market Share	62.0%	54.8	54.1	64.6	75.0	80.1

Note 1: The market shares are computed as the revenue relative to the total of these three leading competitors. For example, in 2001 the total revenues of Dell, Gateway, and HP were $82,474 (millions). Dell's market share, then, was its own revenues divided by the total revenues for the year:

$$\frac{31,168}{82,474} = 37.8\%$$

Note 2: The three competitors had slightly different fiscal years. I have adjusted them all to the same calendar years.

Note 3: The 2003 figures for HP reflect the merger with Compaq. HP is also more diversified than Dell and Gateway, especially with its printer and ink division. Hence, its market share is biased upward for PCs.

Source: Company annual reports.

Commentary: The trend information of these statistics is the major significance. It shows over these nine years that Dell has increased its market share relative to its major competitors from 11.2 percent to 35.1 percent, a major feat in a competitive market. In the same years, HP has had a steady decline in market share from 80.1 percent to 54.8 percent in 2001, then a spike after the acquisition of Compaq to 62.0 percent in 2003. Gateway, after gaining market share steadily up to 2000, had a precipitous decline in its competitive position.

Wal-Mart, Sam's Club, Costco, and Office Depot among others in the United States, as well as key dealers in the U.K. and Japan.

Inouye planned to turn Gateway around by employing the same strategy he had used with eMachines. There he slashed expenses by eliminating waste and consolidating suppliers. At the same time, he made eMachines attractive to dealers by improving quality and providing prompt order filling—all this with some of the lowest prices in the industry.

A Turnaround?

At Gateway, Inouye announced plans to return to the firm's original mission of marketing personal computers. He would do away with most of the consumer electronics, such as big-screen TVs, DVD recorders and digital cameras, that Waite

TABLE 24.2. **Net Income Comparisons of Gateway and Its Major Competitors (Million $), 1994–2003**

	2003	2001	2000	1998	1996	1994
Dell						
Net income	$2,645	1,246	2,236	1,460	531	149
% of three competitors	51.0%	66.6	37.0	30.9	15.8	8.1
Gateway						
Net income	(515)	(1,014)	253	346	251	96
% of competitors	NM	NM	4.2	7.3	7.5	5.2
HP						
Net income	2,539	624	3,561	2,946	2,586	1,589
% of competitors	49.0	33.4	58.8	61.8	76.7	86.7

Note 1: The net income percentage of competition is computed similarly to Note 1 in Table 24.1 Instead of relative market share based on revenues, we have compared individual net incomes as a percentage of the total of the three firms.

Note 2: See Note 2 and Note 3 in Table 24.1. NM means Not Meaningful, in this case because of the net loss.

Source: Company annual reports.

Commentary: Here again, trend information is very revealing of the shifting competitive strengths in this market. Dell's profitability compared to its two main rivals shows steady gains, with a huge jump in 2001. HP's relative profitability has been steadily declining since 1994, and took a real hit in 2001. Even in 2003, after the major costs of the Compaq acquisition should have been out of the way, HP's profitability was less than Dell's on greater than 40 percent more revenue. Gateway's profitability, which had a nice trend in the boom days of the industry, suffered badly in the industry downturn, and with the huge loss in 2001 and a $500 million loss even in 2003, has to be considered in extreme difficulty. Its viability as a separate entity may be in doubt.

had plunged into only four years before. "Our first objective is to fix our core business. People talk about multitasking, but in real life you have to focus on one thing at a time," he said.[8]

Inouye closed the last 188 of the original 274 Gateway Country stores across the United States, Europe, and Japan—a diversification that Waitt had never been able to bring into profitability. Paradoxically, these closings came just after Gateway had spent some $35 million to remodel the stores and reposition them as one-stop shops for all sorts of consumer electronics.

Inouye moved to outsource manufacturing and customer service. The firm would continue to direct-market PCs and related products via the Internet and telephone sales. But it would also market through the big retailers that Inouye had so successfully courted in his years with eMachines.

---

[8] Gary McWilliams, "Gateway CEO Presses Restart: Back to PCs," *Wall Street Journal*, September 13, 2004, p. B5.

By the end of 2004, Inouye expected to reduce overhead costs, which had been the highest in the industry at 26 percent of revenues, to below Dell's 9.6 percent. Much of this would come from closing the Country Stores. By the end of October, the number of employees would be reduced from 7,500 to 1,800. With this restructuring, Inouye expected Gateway to return to profitability even with thin PC margins of about 8 percent.

He boldly announced three- to five-year goals to unseat Hewlett-Packard as the leading seller of home PCs after its merger with Compaq, and to become a $10 billion business by expanding U.S. and overseas sales to at least 1 million PC sales a quarter, up from 795,000. "I don't think it's a big stretch," he insisted.[9]

Critics questioned Inouye's abandonment of the higher-markup consumer electronics that contributed 75 percent of the company's gross margin (i.e., the profit margin before expenses) even though they generated just 22 percent of revenue. (Compared with consumer electronics, PCs produced 78 percent of total company revenues but only 25 percent of gross margin.) They also questioned Inouye's prediction of besting HP's share of the home PC market. "We're going to vigorously protect our market position," HP said.[10]

LATEST DEVELOPMENTS—2006

2006 was proving to be a watershed year for Gateway—and, surprisingly, also for its nemesis, Dell. Early in February, Wayne Inouye abruptly resigned, less than two years into his effort to restructure Gateway. His departure came just a week after the company reported disappointing fourth-quarter results. Higher-margin corporate sales continued slumping, from $3 billion in 1999 to only $1 billion now. Direct-sales business, where PCs were sold through its Web site and by phone, also steadily declined. The one bright spot was Gateway's retail business, the consumer PCs sold through retail stores (reflecting Inouye's efforts), and here market share increased over the year before. The disappointing fourth quarter drove common stock down 2 percent, to $2.46 a share. Over the next six months of 2006, the share price was to fall to $1.43, before rising toward $2.00 on rumors of bids to buy the company from two investor groups that now saw Gateway as attractively valued. Scott Galloway, founder of Firebrand Partners, in an interview described Gateway as "grossly undervalued," and well positioned to target teenagers and young adults because of its reputation and retail presence. He suggested that shareholder value could be increased by separating Gateway's successful retail business from the struggling corporate and direct-sales businesses.[11]

Dell was also seeing a change in its fortunes. In late July 2006, its stock plummeted to the lowest level in four and a half years, with earnings per share projected to fall nearly 50 percent. Dell blamed aggressive PC pricing (while it had been the instigator of aggressive PC pricing, in the last few years its cost advantage has lessened and

---

[9] *Ibid.*, p. B1.
[10] *Ibid.*, p. B5.
[11] Christopher Lawton, "Gateway Gets Bid for Retail Group," *Wall Street Journal*, August 24, 2006, p. B3.

new Far Eastern firms had entered the market as low-price competitors). The company had also been confronted with poor customer service (see the following Information Box about the perils of outsourcing), personnel defections, and the recall of 4.1 million laptop batteries that potentially could overheat and burst into flames. Criticisms mounted against Kevin Rollins, who became Michael Dell's hand-picked successor as CEO in July 2004, when Dell stepped away from active management.

INFORMATION BOX

PERILS OF OUTSOURCING CUSTOMER SERVICE

To save money, Dell had moved toll-free customer service and tech support to India in 2001. Consumers soon started complaining about foreign voices and communication problems. At first, Dell executives ignored the complaints, pointing out that the corporate clients who represented 85 percent of Dell's business seemed satisfied. Evidently that satisfaction was either misread or had changed, because in 2004, Dell shifted support for business clients, but not for consumers, back to the United States. In a November 2005 semiannual survey of its own employees, the criticism was clear: "They felt we might not have been listening enough and that they didn't think we were positioning the company for success," Rollins recalled. "We felt terrible. We thought we could do better." In late 2005, Dell hired 2,000 people for its U.S. call centers and stepped up training for 5,000 other reps—making a $150 million commitment to shift customer support back to the United States. The company was spending an additional $100 million in 2006 to improve customer service, and call-wait times were down 50 percent.[12]

Is Dell's experience with outsourcing customer service the tip of the iceberg? Today, even medical diagnoses are being outsourced despite patient discomfiture. Might we be seeing a reversal of non-manufacturing outsourcing?

ANALYSIS

Were the Gateway Stores the Crucial Mistake?

With hindsight, this issue seems hardly controversial. The stores created a massive overhead that led to unremitting losses, despite their contributing 75 percent of the firm's gross margin. But the expenses of the stores could not be brought down enough to yield a net profit. Gateway had three options in dealing with the stores: (1) increase sales substantially, (2) reduce expenses drastically, (3) get rid of the stores. Let us briefly examine each possibility.

1. *Increase store sales substantially*. Waitt and Gateway had no real experience in retailing. Furthermore, with the Gateway stores they were up against seasoned,

---

[12] Elizabeth Corcoran, *Forbes*, June 19, 2006, pp. 44–46.

well-heeled competitors like Office Depot, Best Buy, Wal-Mart, and Circuit City. The effort to increase sales substantially was probably doomed from the start. Adding more stores would only make the drain on profits worse.

2. *Reduce expenses significantly.* This possibility seems even more remote than increasing sales substantially. Perhaps some operations could have been made more efficient, so that expenses would be reduced. But it is doubtful that substantial expense reduction would be possible in an environment of aggressive, highly efficient competitors.

3. *Get rid of the stores.* Why did it take Waitt so long to recognize the futility of the store operation? In desperation, he even poured another $35 million into rejuvenating the stores, just before Inouye came on board and then got rid of them.

Expanding the Product Line?

This issue goes hand in hand with the Gateway Stores dilemma. Gateway's expanding the product line beyond PCs in order to make the stores more attractive compounded an untenable situation, lacking as the company did the resources to compete with other electronics and appliance competitors. While the possibility of higher markups for such goods seemed attractive, any firm's priority has to be net profit and not gross margin. Higher profit margins for some goods must be weighed against the increase in overhead required to sell them.

Is There Any Defense Against a Master Price-Cutter Like Dell?

A firm has only two real defenses in competing on a price basis: (1) If it is able to build on an image of higher quality or service, this would allow a price premium; (2) If it can cut its expenses and perhaps be willing to accept a lower profit margin, it may be able to match the price-cutter's prices.

Waitt could hardly change Gateway's image to one of higher quality or service, especially as the industry was becoming more mature, with technological break-throughs unlikely. Developing a mystique and cult following for his Gateway brand might have permitted a price premium. But few firms are able to do this, and cult followings are more fortuitous than planned.

Still, Waitt might have come close to matching Dell's low overhead by strenuous efforts at streamlining and a willingness to accept less profit. Certainly, he could hardly do this saddled with the millstone of the stores. Perhaps more aggressive outsourcing might have brought production costs closer to Dell's. We are told that Inouye, when he came on board, moved to outsource some production and service. This apparently had not that much effect on Gateway's cost structure.

One other possibility remains: Don't try to match the lowest prices in the industry. While many customers will be lost to the lower-price competitors, enough may be interested in something more than the lowest prices, and may even perceive higher prices as denoting higher quality.

❖ ❖ ❖

Invitation to Make Your Own Analysis and Conclusions

What is your assessment of Ted Waitt's mistakes?

Short of accepting a buyout, do you see any business plan that might salvage Gateway's fortunes?

❖ ❖ ❖

WHAT CAN BE LEARNED?

A firm ignores its basic core business at its peril.—Every reasonably successful firm has a basic core of its operation that is unchanging, and should be the final bastion to fall back on for regrouping, if necessary. This is often, but not always, the product or strategy with which the firm got its successful start. In an age of diversification, mergers, and acquisitions, the core is often ignored in the quest for greater growth opportunities. But sometimes the diversifications do not work out, or become vulnerable. Sometimes a firm finds itself in a crisis situation, and viability may depend on retrenchment back to the core. Retrenchment back to the core could save Gateway.

Cut your losers and those operations where your competence does not match competitors'.—The Gateway retail stores certainly fall into this situation. Probably no amount of time and training would make Gateway stores competitive with the powerful Best Buys, Circuit Citys, and Wal-Marts. While the decision to venture into retail stores seemed reasonable early in the growth stage of marketing PCs to consumers— where the computers could be demonstrated and customers given hands-on training and service—the decision should have been reexamined years before it was. Waitt stayed too long with a losing operation that had little likelihood of ever succeeding.

A price war can be disastrous.—A price war developed toward the end of 2002. An economic downturn and uninterested customers were background factors, but Dell initiated it. Generally a price war is detrimental to all participants because of its effect on profitability, and is shunned by mature industries (though gasoline wars do flare up from time to time). Most firms in a mature industry have similar costs, and innovations are scarce. So all firms suffer from price wars, even though revenue may increase some because of the lower prices.

In new industries, price wars are more common as technology advances and production economies develop, and as inefficient firms are weeded out. But the computer industry has matured, and most of the marginal firms are long gone. Dell, alone among its competitors, stood to gain from a price war in the 1990s, and Michael Dell had no qualms about starting one. But by 2005, Dell's cost advantage was becoming muted.

Survival of the fittest—power of lower costs.—If a firm has managed to reduce its operating costs and overhead significantly below its competitors, and if they are not able to quickly match these cost reductions, then a price war can be a shrewd business strategy. While it may reduce profits somewhat, market-share gains could be significant, and might be lasting. In two previous cases, Southwest Airlines and Vanguard, we find similar instances of firms having significantly lower costs than the rest of the industry; their advantage has not been matched because few competitors could cut costs sufficiently to meet their prices and still be profitable. The power of lower costs can make for a survival-of-the-fittest environment and result in greater efficiency and price benefits for customers.

It is difficult but not impossible to match the price-cutter's low prices.—The key to matching a competitor's low prices lies in reducing your overhead to nearly that of the competitor. This may be achieved by severe cost cutting, by weeding out inefficient and cost-draining operations (sometimes referred to as running a tight ship), or, as is becoming more prevalent albeit controversial, outsourcing some operations to foreign countries where labor costs are much cheaper.

If our firm is burdened with heavy fixed costs, such as mortgages and other borrowings that reflect profligate expansion efforts in the past, then overhead can never be reduced to be competitive with leaner competitors. The best course of action in this scenario is to divest the poor profit-performing operations, even if this must be done at a loss. Overhead loads may also come from a cumbersome organization, such as too much bureaucracy, too many layers of management, too many staff people, and the like. Some weeding may well need to be done.

Matching an aggressive competitor's low prices may mean being willing to accept less profit, at least in the near term.

A firm may not need to match a competitor's low prices if it has a unique product and/or marketing strategy.—Differentiation may come from a unique product; it may also come from a good reputation, perhaps for quality and service, with this usually fostered by advertising and branding over the years. Such nonprice competition insulates a firm from the worst of price competition. Certainly if Gateway could come up with such uniqueness, it could worry less about a price war with Dell. But in the mature PC market, distinctiveness and/or innovation may not be achievable.

Is it possible to develop a cult following?—A cult following usually depends on a company or brand developing (or acquiring) a mystique of some sort. Few brands have been able to do this. Coors beer did back in the 1960s, when it became the brew of celebrities and the emblem of the purity and freshness of the West. Marlboro rose to become the top seller on a somewhat similar image, the Marlboro man. The Ford Mustang had a mystique at one time, and Apple also had its devoted followers. But no one has beat Harley Davidson in capitalizing on the mystique of its big motorcycles, as we described in Chapter 6.

How does a firm develop a mystique? There is no simple answer, no guarantee. Certainly a company's product has to be distinctive, even if only psychologically. But it takes more than a distinctive product—many firms strive for this, and few achieve a mystique. Image-building advertising, focusing on the type of person the firm is targeting, may help. Even better is image-building advertising of people whom customers might wish to emulate, as Nike did so well with athletes.

Perhaps, in the final analysis, acquiring a mystique is more fortuitous than deliberate. Two lessons, however, can be learned about mystiques. First, they seldom last forever. Second, once gained, the company may be able to exploit them by extending the name or logo to other goods, even unrelated ones, through licensing.

The prescription for great wealth.—Great wealth can come from going public with a successful format. We saw in this case how Michael Dell and Ted Waitt both became, not only millionaires, but billionaires, when they took their enterprises public. They had prior examples and inspirers: Bill Gates of Microsoft, and Steve Jobs of Apple.

While these are extraordinary success stories, on a smaller scale many small businesses can find themselves attractive to investors seeking growth companies that may offer better potential than existing firms. If the founder of the business keeps a substantial block of the company's stock, the payoff from investors' positive appraisal of the enterprise can be mind-boggling.

CONSIDER

Can you identify additional learning insights that could be applicable to other firms in other situations?

QUESTIONS

1. "Tradition has no place in corporate thinking today." Discuss this statement.

2. Discuss the pros and cons involved in Dell's decision to start a price war as the downturn worsened in 2000.

3. Discuss the options Gateway faced with an industry price war.

4. "The computer industry—and most high-tech as well—is saturated. This is no longer a growth area, and investors should look elsewhere for growth." Evaluate this statement.

5. "Gateway, with its Holstein cow image, was on the verge of developing a cult following. Now they're doing away with it. I'm selling my Gateway stock." Evaluate this attitude.

6. "I see no one in the foreseeable market who can compete with Dell." Evaluate.

7. How do you judge the quality of a product, whether a computer or something else? Is it mostly on price? Discuss your perception of price and quality, as well as any ramifications.

8. Do you think Gateway will still be around in five years? Give the rationale for your prediction.

HANDS-ON EXERCISES

1. Be a *devil's advocate*. Argue against Ted Waitt's decision to abandon the cow. Be as persuasive as you can.

Before

2. You are Ted Waitt of Gateway just before the slide of the high-tech industry. What might you have done to prevent the profit collapse and market-share erosion that occurred? Defend your position.

After

3. You are Ted Waitt of Gateway near the end of 2002, with your firm on the ropes. What restorative program do you propose? Defend your ideas.

TEAM DEBATE EXERCISES

1. Debate Inouye's strategy to shift away from higher-margin consumer electronics and concentrate on PCs and related items.

   I would suggest dividing into two groups, with one being as persuasive as possible in arguing for the drastic cutback, while the other strongly contests this, and proposes a more conservative approach to regaining profitability. Be prepared to attack your opponents' arguments, and defend your own.

2. "There is no need to be unduly concerned with Dell's price war. Our products are higher quality than Dell's, and consumers and business customers alike will quickly recognize that they get what they pay for." Debate this statement, with one group supporting it, the other contesting it.

INVITATION TO RESEARCH

What is the situation in the PC industry today? Is Dell still the lowest-cost producer of PCs, or have Asiatic competitors become major factors in the low-price market? Has Gateway been acquired, or is it still independent? What has happened to Waitt?

CHAPTER TWENTY-FIVE

Conclusions: What Can Be Learned?

In considering mistakes, three things are worth noting: (1) All organizations make mistakes, even the most successful, but they will survive as long as they maintain a good "batting average" of satisfactory decisions; (2) Mistakes should be effective teaching tools for avoiding similar errors in the future; and (3) Firms can bounce back from adversity, and turnaround.

We can make a number of generalizations from the mistakes and successes treated in this book. Management is, of course, a discipline that does not lend itself to laws or maxims, so, examples of exceptions to every generalization can be found. Nonetheless the decision maker will do well to heed the following insights. For the most part they are based on specific corporate and entrepreneurial experiences and should be transferable to other situations and other times.

INSIGHTS REGARDING OVERALL ENTERPRISE PERSPECTIVES

Importance of Public Image

The impact, for good or bad, of an organization's public image was a common thread through a number of cases—for example, Southwest Airlines, Vanguard, United Way, Disney, Gateway, Wal-Mart, Maytag, Perrier, Harley-Davidson, and Boston Beer.

Southwest's image of friendliness, great efficiency, and unbeatable prices propelled it to an unassailable position among short-haul airlines. Now it seeks to expand its image to longer hauls. Vanguard has used its image of frugality and great customer service in the mutual fund industry to propel it to the top with relatively little advertising. Harley-Davidson was able to develop its image one step further—to a mystique with a devoted cult following. Boston Beer was able to capitalize on its image of highest quality to go along with its highest price beer. Gateway Computer tried to upgrade its Holstein cow image to a mystique, but without success.

Some images were less favorable. Disney found that its image did not travel well to Paris, nor did Maytag's quality image to the United Kingdom. Perrier responded aggressively to a contamination problem by making a major product recall, but lost its image of quality. The not-for-profit United Way was brought to its knees by revelations about the excesses of its longtime chief executive, William Aramony. While Wal-Mart's image of lowest prices remained attractive to many, its image of not exactly a good citizen was bringing it concern.

The importance of a firm's public image should be undeniable. Yet some companies continue to disregard their image, and either act in ways detrimental to their reputation or else ignore the constraints and opportunities that it affords.

Power of the Media

We have seen or suspected the power of the media in a number of cases. Firestone and Ford, Vanguard, Perrier, and United Way are obvious examples. This power is often used critically—to hurt a firm's public image. The media can fan a problem or exacerbate an embarrassing or imprudent action. In particular, media focus can trigger a herd instinct in which increasing numbers of people join in protests and public criticism. But in Vanguard's case, positive media attention minimized the need for much advertising.

We can make five generalizations regarding image and its relationship with the media:

1. It is desirable to maintain a stable, clear-cut image and undeviating objectives.
2. It is difficult and time-consuming to upgrade an image.
3. An episode of poor quality can leave a lasting stigma.
4. A good image can be quickly lost if a firm relaxes in an environment of aggressive competition.
5. Well-known firms are especially vulnerable to critical public scrutiny and must use great care in safeguarding their reputations.

No Guarantee of Continued Success

That success does not guarantee continued success or freedom from adversity is a sobering realization from examining these cases. Many of the mistakes occurred in notably successful organization, such as Ford and Firestone, Harley-Davidson, IBM, Disney, Boeing, Maytag, MetLife, even United Way. How could things go so badly for organizations so conditioned to success? The three C's mindset offers some explanation for this perversity.

The Three C's Mindset

We can also call this the "king of the hill" syndrome. In a three C's organizational climate, success actually brings vulnerability. The three Cs—complacency, conservatism, and conceit—can blanket leading organizations. To avoid this, an attitude of never underestimating competitors can be fostered by

- Bringing fresh blood into the organization for new ideas and different perspectives
- Establishing a strong and continuing commitment to customer service and satisfaction—this should be more than just lip service
- Conducting periodic corporate self-analyses designed to detect weaknesses as well as opportunities in their early stages
- Continually monitoring the environment and being alert to any changes (more about this later)

The business environment is dynamic, sometimes with subtle and hardly recognizable changes, at other times with violent and unmistakable changes. To operate in this environment, an established firm must be on guard to defend its position.

Adversity Need Not Be Forever

Just as a dominant firm can lose its momentum and competitive position, so can a faltering organization be turned around. If a firm can at least maintain some semblance of viability, then there is hope. Continental Airlines, IBM, and Harley-Davidson are examples of such comebacks.

PLANNING INSIGHTS

What Should Our Business Be?

An organization's business, its mission and purpose, should be thought through, spelled out clearly, and well communicated by those involved in policy making. Otherwise, the organization lacks unified and coordinated objectives, which is akin to trying to navigate without a map.

Good judgment suggests choosing safe rather than courageous goals. But in the heady optimism for high-techs in the 1990s, few such firms could resist the temptation to go for the moon, and spend and plan accordingly with no semblance of frugality. Rather, we suggest controlled growth (aggressive moderation) for firms as they plan their growth, and Boston Beer and Southwest exemplify this.

Determining what a firm's business is or should be gives a starting point for specifying goals. Several elements help with this determination.

A firm's resources and distinctive abilities and strengths should play a major role in determining its goals. It is not enough to wish for a certain status or position if resources and competencies do not warrant this. To take an extreme example, a railroad company can hardly expect to transform itself into an airline, even though both may be in the transportation business. A Wal-Mart is hardly likely to successfully imitate a Neiman Marcus.

Environmental and competitive opportunities ought to be considered. The initial inroads of foreign carmakers in the United States stemmed from environmental opportunities for energy-efficient vehicles at a time when U.S. carmakers were ignoring this area. Vanguard found opportunity in lower expense ratios for its mutual funds than the rest of the fund industry was willing or able to match. The same for Southwest Airlines. The recent emergence of aggressive hedge funds, armed with huge war chests from wealthy investors and looking for faltering companies with depressed stock prices, such as Kmart and Sears, represents the new wave in the business arena.

Need For Growth Orientation—But Not Reckless Growth

The opposite of a growth commitment is a status quo philosophy, one uninterested in expansion or the problems and work involved. Harley-Davidson was content, despite being pushed around by foreign competitors, until eventually a new management reawakened it decades later. Sunbeam's lack of growth led to the ill-fated choice of "Chainsaw Al" Dunlap to get things moving again.

In general, how tenable is a low-growth or no-growth philosophy? Although at first glance it seems workable, such a philosophy sows the seeds of its own destruction. More than half a century ago the following insight was made:

> Vitality is required even for survival; but vitality is difficult to maintain without growth, at least in the American business climate. The vitality of a firm depends on the vigor and ambition of its members. The prospect of growth is one of the principal means by which a firm can attract able and vigorous recruits.[1]

Consequently, a firm not obviously growth-minded finds it difficult to attract able people. Customers see a growing firm as reliable, eager to please, and constantly improving. As we saw with OfficeMax, suppliers and creditors tend to give preferential treatment to a growth-oriented firm because they hope to retain it as a customer when it reaches large size.

But emphasizing growth can be carried too far. The growth must be kept within limits that the firm can handle. Cases such as Southwest, Boston Beer, Vanguard, and Wal-Mart show how firms can grow rapidly without losing control. But we also have the bungled growth efforts of Maytag's Hoover Division in the United Kingdom, where controls were loosened far too much for a foreign subsidiary. And Boeing and Newell Rubbermaid show the fallacy of reckless growth. Not to be outdone, we saw the unethical growth climate at MetLife. Good financial judgment and decent ethical behavior must not be sacrificed to the siren call of growth. With relatively new firms, growth can easily outpace management competence and the ability to effectively utilize mass infusions of investment capital. OfficeMax, in its desire to become a bigger factor in its industry, destroyed its profitability, as did Gateway Computer.

Therefore, an emphasis on growth can be carried too far. Somehow the growth must be kept within the capabilities of the firm.

---

[1] Wroe Alderson, *Marketing Behavior and Executive Action*, Homewood, IL.: Irwin, 1957, p. 59.

In our championing of aggressive moderation, we can make these generalizations about the most desirable growth perspectives:

1. Growth targets should not exceed the abilities and resources of the organization. Growth at any cost—especially at the expense of profits and financial stability—should be shunned. In particular, tight controls over inventories and expenses should be established, and performance monitored closely.

2. The most prudent approach to growth is to keep the organization and operation as simple and uniform as possible, to be flexible in case sales do not meet expectations, and to keep the breakeven point as low as possible, especially for new and untried ventures. The great competitive advantages of Vanguard, Southwest Airlines, and Wal-Mart were in their having much lower overhead than anyone else in their industries. Boston Beer is another example of giving priority to a low breakeven point.

3. Rapidly expanding markets pose dangers from both too conservative and overly optimistic sales forecasts. The latter may overextend resources and jeopardize viability should demand contract; the former opens the door to more aggressive competitors. There is no right answer to this dilemma, but management should be aware of the risks and the rewards of both extremes.

4. A strategy emphasizing rapid growth should not neglect other aspects of the operation. For example, older stores should not be ignored in the quest to open new ones.

5. Decentralized management is more compatible with rapid growth than centralized, because it puts less strain on home-office executives. However, delegation must have well-defined standards and controls as well as competent subordinates. Otherwise, the Maytag Hoover fiasco may be repeated.

6. The safety and integrity of the product and the firm's reputation must not be sacrificed in pursuit of growth and profits. This is especially important when customers' health and safety may be jeopardized, as Ford and Firestone discovered with the Ford Explorer.

The Rush to Merge

Some have called the rush to merge *merger mania*. Mergers and acquisitions often work out badly for employees, communities, even stockholders. Only the top executives and the lawyers, bankers, and consultants usually come out ahead. The payday for a top executive can be awesome. The recent huge merger of Procter & Gamble and Gillette resulted in a payday for James Kilts, CEO of Gillette, of at least $185 million.[2]

[2] Charles Forelle and Mark Maremont, "Gillette CEO Payday May Be Richer," *Wall Street Journal*, February 3, 2005, p. B2.

We have seen three cases where acquisitions turned out horrendously: Newell Rubbermaid, Snapple, and Maytag. The unfulfilled promise from the Hewlett-Packard merger with Compaq, contributed to Carly Fiorina's firing in February 2005. The ultimate success of the Kmart and Sears merger remains questionable, although the hedge fund headed by Edward Lampert is reaping the rewards of cutting costs to the bone with negligible reinvestment. While Kmart and Sears are losing market share, investors are salivating at the cash flow.

Forbes magazine reported on some recent large mergers that were losers:

Daimler-Benz buys Chrysler, May 1998, for $46 billion.
"A perfect fit," said Juergen Schrempp, CEO of Daimler
Outcome: Combined market value down 50 percent.

AT&T buys Tele-Communications, June 1998, for $48 billion.
"Undisputed leader in . . . the fastest-growing segments of the communications services industry."
Outcome: Cable businesses sold for half the original price.

America Online buys Time Warner, January 2000, for $173 billion.
"We did wrestle a little bit with valuations . . . but most of the time was spent on social issues."
Outcome: Times Warner stock off from $73 to $18.[3]

Some cautions: Don't rush into the merger or acquisition.
Beware of optimistic projections for mergers.
Assumptions in merger decisions should be defended.
Really examine the compatibility of the two firms.
Beware overpaying for an acquisition.

Strategic Windows of Opportunity

Several of the great successes we examined resulted from exploiting strategic windows of opportunity. Southwest found its opportunity by being so cost-effective that it could offer both cut-rate fares and highly dependable short-haul service that no other airline could match. Similarly, Vanguard found its strategic niche with the lowest expense ratios and overhead in the mutual fund industry. Sam Walton certainly found a strategic window in the small towns of rural America in the early decades of Wal-Mart. Jim Koch found a narrow opening for some of the highest-priced beer in the industry.

We make these generalizations regarding opportunities and strategic windows:

1. Opportunities often exist when a traditional way of doing business has prevailed in the industry for a long time—maybe the climate is ripe for a change.

2. Opportunities often are present when existing firms are not entirely satisfying customers' needs.

3. Innovations are not limited to products but can involve customer services as well as such things as methods of distribution.

[3] "Seemed Like a Good Idea at the Time," *Forbes*, February 28, 2005, p. 38.

4. For industries with rapidly changing technologies—usually new industries—heavy research and development expenditures are generally required if a firm is to avoid falling behind its competitors. But heavy R & D does not guarantee being in the forefront, as shown by IBM, Hewlett-Packard, and other competitors of Dell Computer.

Power of Judicious Imitation

Some firms are reluctant to copy successful practices of their competitors; they want to be leaders, not followers. But successful practices or innovations may need to be copied if a firm is not to be left behind. Sometimes the imitator outdoes the innovator. Success can lie in doing the ordinary better than competitors.

OfficeMax achieved its initial success by imitating the successful practices of a few other category-killer chains, notably Office Depot and Staples, which had already been on the scene for a few years. Unfortunately, it was never able to expand beyond third place in the industry and was vulnerable when the market became saturated.

For 50 years, Boeing was the innovator in the commercial-jet industry, sometimes taking big risks to do so. Its biggest risk was in the 1960s, when it almost bankrupted itself to build the 747, which was twice the size of any other plane in commercial use. Now Airbus is the innovator with its huge plane, the 600-seat A380. Boeing decided not to follow Airbus's lead, and at present this looks like a wise decision.

We can make this generalization:

> It makes sense for a company to identify the characteristics of successful competitors (and even of similar but noncompeting firms) that brought their success, and then adopt these characteristics if they are compatible with the imitator's resources. Let someone else do the experimenting and risk taking. The imitator faces some risk in waiting too long, but it usually is far less than the risk of being the innovator.

LEADERSHIP AND EXECUTION INSIGHTS

Managing Change and Crises

Crises are unexpected happenings that pose threats, moderate to catastrophic, to the organization's well-being. We described three crisis cases in Part I: Firestone/Ford, Perrier, and Scott Paper/Sunbeam. Other cases also involved crises: Boeing, Euro Disney, Maytag, Herman Miller, United Way, Gateway, MetLife, Continental, and Rubbermaid Newell. Some firms—United Way, Herman Miller, Continental—handled their crises reasonably well, although we can question how such crises were allowed to happen in the first place. However, Firestone/Ford, Maytag, and Perrier either overreacted or underreacted and badly failed to salvage the situation. And Al Dunlap's savaging of Sunbeam and Scott Paper can be condemned.

Most crises are preventable if a company takes precautions. This suggests being alert to changing conditions, having contingency plans, and practicing risk avoidance. For example, it is prudent to not have key executives travel on the same air flight; it is prudent to insure key executives so that their incapacity will not endanger the organization; and it is prudent to set up contingency plans for a strike, an equipment failure or plant shutdown, the loss of a major distributor, unexpected economic conditions, or a serious lawsuit. Some risks, of course, can be covered by insurance, but others not. The mettle of any organization may be severely tested by an unexpected crisis. Especially is this true after 9/11: In an age of terrorism, anything is possible.

Crises and significant environmental changes—as Gateway faced in the volatile PC market, and Herman Miller in the office furniture market—may necessitate some shifts in the organization and the way of doing business. Firms should avoid making hasty or disruptive moves or, at the other extreme, responding too late and too grudgingly. The middle ground is usually best. Advanced planning can help a company to minimize trauma and enact effective solutions. This advanced planning should include worst-case scenarios.

Environmental Monitoring

The dynamic business environment may involve changes in customer preferences and needs, in competition, and in the economy and environment. It may involve changes on the international scene—such as nationalism in Canada, NAFTA, OPEC machinations, continuing problems in the Middle East, changes in Eastern Europe and South Africa, advances in productivity and quality control in the Pacific Rim countries, and, of course, the new threat of terrorism. For example, Harley-Davidson and Boeing failed to detect and act upon significant changes in their industries. Disney encountered customer attitudes in Europe different from anything it had experienced before. More recently, Maytag was slow to join the trend of the industry to shift production jobs to cheaper overseas workers, and found itself unable to compete with competitors like Whirlpool.

How can a firm stay alert to subtle and insidious or more obvious changes? It should have *sensors* constantly monitoring the environment. The sensor may be a marketing or economic research department, but in many instances a formal organizational entity is not necessary to provide primary monitoring. *Executive alertness* is required. Most changes do not occur suddenly and without warning, though we know the possibility exists. Feedback from customers, sales representatives, and suppliers; the latest news and projections in business journals; and even simple observations of what is happening in stores, advertising, prices, and new technologies can provide information about a changing environment. Unfortunately, in the urgency of handling day-to-day operating problems, managers may miss clues of imminent changes in the competitive environment.

Following are generalizations regarding vulnerability to competition:

1. Initial market advantage tends to be rather quickly countered by competitors.

2. Countering by competitors is more likely when an innovation is involved than when the advantage comes from more commonplace effective management, such as superb cost controls or customer service.

3. An easy-entry industry is particularly vulnerable to new and aggressive competition, especially if the market is expanding. In new industries, severe price competition usually weeds out marginal firms.

4. Long-dominant firms tend to become vulnerable to upstart competitors because of their complacency, conservatism, and conceit (the three C's). They frequently are resistant to change and myopic about the environment.

5. Careful monitoring of performance at *strategic control points* can detect weakening positions before situations become serious. (This point is discussed further in the next section.)

6. In expanding markets, increases in sales may hide a deteriorating competitive situation. More important is market share data, how our firm is doing relative to its competitors.

7. A no-growth policy, or a temporary absence from the marketplace, even if fully justified by extraordinary circumstances, invites competitive inroads. Example: Perrier.

Effective Organizations

We can identify several characteristics of the most effective organizations:

Management by Exception

With diverse and far-flung operations, and as a firm becomes larger, it becomes difficult to closely supervise everything. Successful managers therefore focus their attention on performance that deviates significantly from the expected norms at *strategic control points*. Such points should include market share, profitability measures, turnover ratios, expense ratios, and the like, broken down by individual operational units. Trend information is important: is performance getting better or worse? Subordinates can be left to handle ordinary operations and less significant deviations, so that the manager is not overburdened with details.

Management by exception failed, however, with Maytag and its overseas Hoover division. Seemingly, no budget restraints and approvals were required for expenditures of any amount. The lack of such approval requirements could be directly blamed for the reprehensible promotional plans. By the time results came in, it was too late.

The Deadly Parallel

As an enterprise becomes larger, a very effective organizational structure is one made up of operating units of comparable characteristics. Sales, expenses, and profits can then be more readily compared, enabling strong and weak performances to be identified so that appropriate action can be taken. Besides providing control and performance evaluation, this *deadly parallel* structure fosters intrafirm competition that can stimulate best efforts. For the deadly parallel to be used effectively, operating units must be fairly equalized, perhaps by size or through quotas or similar categories of sales potential. This is not difficult to achieve with retail units, since departments and stores can be divided into sales volume categories—often designated as A, B, and C units—and operating results compared within the category. The deadly parallel can also be used with sales territories and certain other operating units for which sales and applicable expenses and ratios can be directly measured and compared with similar units.

Lean and Mean

A new climate is sweeping our country's major corporations. In one sense it is good: It enhances their competitiveness. But it can be destructive. Vanguard, Southwest Airlines, Wal-Mart, Boston Beer, and OfficeMax (in its formative years) are all examples of the lean-and-mean movement. Lean-and-mean firms develop flat organizations with few management layers, thus keeping overhead low, improving communication, involving employees in greater self-management, and fostering an innovative mindset.

In contrast, we saw the organizational bloat of Boeing and IBM with their many management levels, entrenched bureaucracies, and massive overhead. A virtual cause-and-effect relationship exists between the proportion of total overhead committed to administration/staff and the ability to cope with change and innovate. It is like trying to maneuver a huge ship—bureaucratic weight slows the response time.

The problem with the lemming-like pursuit of the lean-and-mean structure is knowing how far to downsize without cutting into bone and muscle. As thousands of managers and staff specialists can attest, productivity gains are not always worth the loss of jobs, the destruction of career paths, and the possible sacrifice of long-term potential. The extreme example of this is Dunlap's decimating of Scott Paper and Sunbeam.

Coping with Resistance to Change

People, like organizations, do not embrace change well. Change is disruptive; it destroys accepted ways of doing things and muddles familiar authority and responsibility patterns. Previously important positions may be downgraded or even eliminated, and people who view themselves as highly competent in a particular job may be forced to assume unfamiliar duties amid the fear that they cannot master the new assignments. When the change involves wholesale terminations in a major downsizing, as with Kmart and Sears, Scott/Sunbeam, and Boeing in its down cycles, the resistance and fear of change can become so great that efficiency is seriously jeopardized.

Normal resistance to change can be eased by good communication with participants about forthcoming changes to dampen rumors and fears. Acceptance of change is helped if employees are involved as fully as possible in planning the changes, if their participation is solicited and welcomed, and if assurances can be given that positions will not be impaired, only changed. Gradual rather than abrupt changes also make a transition smoother.

In the final analysis, however, making needed changes and embracing new opportunities should not be delayed or canceled because of possible negative repercussions on the organization. If change is desirable, as it often is with long-established bureaucratic organizations, then it should be done without delay. Individuals and organizations can adapt to change—it just takes some time.

The Power of Giving Employees a Sense of Pride and a Caring Management

The great turnaround of Continental from the confrontational days of Frank Lorenzo has to be mainly attributed to the people-oriented environment fostered by Gordon Bethune. The marvel is how quickly it was done, starting with such a simple thing as an open-door policy to the executive suite, and full communication with employees.

Still, Continental was not unique in the enlisting of employees to the team. Other successful firms have done so, starting with Sam Walton in the early days of Wal-Mart. Herbert Kelleher fostered this as Southwest Airlines began its great charge. Michael Feuer gained dedicated employees in the startup of OfficeMax, and John Bogle imbued Vanguard with his concept of frugality and customer service.

Then we have the other extreme, the mechanistic handling of employees by Al Dunlap. Any temporary improvement of profits obtained by cutting expenses to the bone with vast layoffs finally came home to roost as he himself was fired at Sunbeam. Frank Lorenzo, the predecessor of Bethune, devastated Continental with his confrontational labor-management relations.

Boeing's problems with its peaks and valleys of layoffs and hiring destroyed the pride and esprit de corps of employees, except perhaps for a nucleus. A sense of pride was certainly latent with such a prestigious product, but without workplace stability a great opportunity was lost to cement employee morale.

In addition to a people-oriented management, another key factor in cultivating employee teamwork lies in the perceived growth prospects of the firm. Where growth prospects look good, even coming back from the adversity of Continental, employees can grasp that extra measure of enthusiasm and motivation.

CONTROL INSIGHTS

Delegation Overdone

Good managers delegate as much as possible to subordinates. Giving them some freedom and as much responsibility as they can handle develops future leaders. More than this, delegation allows higher executives to concentrate on the most important matters. Other areas of operation need come to their attention only where performance deviates significantly from what is expected at strategic control points—thus we have *management by exception*.

Management by exception failed, however, with Maytag and its overseas Hoover division. The flaw lay in failing to monitor faulty promotional plans. Admittedly, with diverse and far-flung operations it becomes more difficult to closely monitor every aspect, but still there should be strategic control points to warn of impending dangers. At the least, home office approval of expenditures above a certain amount must be enforced.

We found delegation problems in other cases. The ridiculous acquisition of Snapple—a product at the end of its faddish life cycle and incompatible with Gatorade's existing distribution structure—smacks of dependence on incompetent researchers to whom too much authority had been delegated.

The Euro Disney difficulties may have resulted from not enough autonomy. The European operation did not adjust well to a somewhat different playing field, in which customers were far more price-conscious than had been experienced before.

At the top executive level, United Way found the excesses of its chief, William Aramony, to be unacceptable. Here, the board of directors could be faulted for being far too tolerant of a chief executive's questionable behavior. This raises another issue: How closely should the board exercise control?

Board of Directors Patsies

A board of directors can monitor top management performance closely and objectively. Or it can be completely supportive and uncritical. In the latter situation, the board exercises no controls on top management; in the former, it becomes an important control factor at the highest level.

Given the potential control power of the board, top executives find their own interests best served by packing the board with supporters. Aramony of United Way had such a sympathetic and supportive board that his excesses went unmonitored until investigative reporters blew the whistle.

Instead of assuming the status of watchdogs for investors' best interests, patsy boards disserve them.

Systematic Evaluations and Controls

Organizations need feedback to determine how well something is being done, whether improvement is possible, where it should occur, how much is needed, and how quickly it must be accomplished. Without feedback or performance evaluation, a worsening situation can go unrecognized until too late for corrective action.

As firms become larger, the need for better controls or feedback increases, because top management can no longer personally monitor all aspects of the operation. Mergers and diversifications, which often result in loosely controlled, decentralized operations—for example, again, Maytag and its overseas unit—need systematic feedback on performance all the more.

Financial and expense controls are vital. After all, if costs and inventories get severely out of line—and, worse, if this is not recognized until late—then the very viability of the firm can be jeopardized. Many exuberant high-tech enterprises found that heedless extravagances hastened their demise, leaving the field to stalwarts like Hewlett-Packard and Dell.

Performance standards are another critical means of control for widespread operations. Unless operating standards are imposed and enforced, uniformity of performance is sacrificed, resulting in unevenness of quality and service and a lack of coordination and continuity among the different units. Even unethical and illegal practices may ensue, as we saw with MetLife. Instead of running a tight ship, managers face a loose and undisciplined one.

INSIGHTS REGARDING SPECIFIC STRATEGY ELEMENTS

Can Advertising Do the Job?

The cases provide several insights regarding the effectiveness of advertising, but they also present unanswered questions and contradictions. Vanguard became the star of the mutual fund industry with virtually no advertising; unlike its competitors, it relied instead on word-of-mouth and free publicity. In recent years, Wal-Mart has resorted to extensive institutional advertising in an attempt to improve its public image. But its image, instead of improving, seems to be worsening. Such outcomes raise doubts about the power of advertising. Then we have a case where promotional efforts were too effective: Maytag Hoover's promotional campaign created more customer demand than it could possibly handle.

Thus we see the great challenge of advertising. One never knows for sure how much should be spent to get the job done, such as to reach a planned objective of increasing sales or market share by a certain percentage. However, despite the inability to measure directly the effectiveness of advertising, it is the brave—or foolhardy—executive who stands pat in the face of increased promotional efforts by competitors.

We draw these conclusions:

1. There is no assured correlation between expenditures for advertising and sales success. But the right theme or message can be powerful.

2. In most cases, advertising can generate initial trial purchases. But if the product or service does not meet expectations, customers will not buy again.

3. It is quite difficult to evaluate the effectiveness of institutional (nonproduct) advertising. Such ads are almost akin to advertising on faith.

The Importance of Price as an Offensive Weapon

Price promotions are the most aggressive competitive strategy and the one most desirable from the customer's viewpoint. We saw three notable marketing successes that geared their major strategy on lower prices than competitors: Vanguard, Southwest Airlines, and Wal-Mart. Euro Disney found its European customers resisting its high prices. Low-price competitiors cut into the profits of Herman Miller, Maytag, Gateway, Snapple, and even IBM. Still, for Perrier a high-price strategy was key to its marketing success before the crisis, because consumers perceived the high price as indicative of high quality. The high-price strategy—higher even than most imports—was also a positive differentiation for Boston Beer. Hewlett-Packard so far has been able to milk its printer ink business with exorbitantly high prices.

The major disadvantage of price competition is that other firms, if they can, are almost forced to meet the price-cutter's prices—in other words, the strategy is easy to match. Consequently, when prices fall for an entire industry, no firm has any advantage and all suffer diminished profits. Thus, price-cutting gives no competitive advantage, so goes the conventional thinking. We saw three major successes with price competition, but these came from greater operating efficiencies and lower overhead costs that still permitted good profits, whereas most competitors could not match the price cuts without losing money.

In general, other strategies are better for most firms,—such as better quality, better product and brand image, better service, and improved warranties—all of which are aspects of nonprice rather than price competition.

Still, in new industries characterized by rapid technological change and production efficiencies, severe price competition is the norm, and this weeds out marginal operations. Even a larger firm in such an industry may not be insulated from price competition that can jeopardize its viability.

Analytical Management Tools

We identified several of the most useful analytical tools for decision making. In Euro Disney we discussed *breakeven analysis*, a highly useful means for making go/no-go decisions about new ventures and alternative business strategies. In the Maytag case, we described the *cost-benefit analysis* that might have prevented the bungled promotion in England. The Southwest and Boston Beer cases introduced us to SWOT (strengths, weaknesses, opportunities, threats) analysis. While these management tools do not guarantee the best decisions, they bring objective and systematic thinking into the art of decision-making.

A Kinder, Gentler Stance?

In several cases, we could identify an arrogant mindset as leading to difficulties. The French did not appreciate the arrogance of Disney, and the Euro Disney project was almost a disaster. Arrogance played a role in the Firestone/Ford Explorer disaster, and the size of Wal-Mart has sometimes led to arrogance in its dealings with others.

At the other extreme, is there room in today's competitive environment for a kinder, gentler stance by business firms? Any firm is in contact with numerous parties, but let us consider this question with regard to suppliers and distributors, customers, and employees.

Relations with Suppliers and Distributors

With the movement toward just-in-time deliveries in the search for more efficiency and cost containment, manufacturers and retailers are placing greater demands on suppliers. Those who cannot meet these demands will usually lose out to competitors able to do so. The big manufacturer or retailer can demand ever more from smaller suppliers, since it is in the power position, and the loss of its business could be overwhelming. We saw the problems Rubbermaid had when it was unable to meet the service demands of Wal-Mart. At the least, the big customer deserves priority attention because its business is so important to any supplier.

Some of the big retailers today, such as Wal-Mart and Home Depot as well as supermarket chains, impose "slotting fees." A slotting fee is essentially a toll charged by the retailer for the use of its space; suppliers pay this up-front if they wish to be represented in the retailer's stores. Other demands include driving cost prices down to rock bottom, even if this destroys the supplier's profits, and insisting that the supplier take responsibility for inventory control, even to the point of stocking shelves and providing special promotional support. It is common for big customers to make suppliers wait longer to be paid but nonetheless take the cash discount for prompt payment.

While organizations such as Wal-Mart argue that the use of clout leads to greater marketing efficiencies and lower consumer prices, it can be carried too far. The term *symbiotic relationship* describes the relationship between the various channel-of-distribution members: All benefit from the success of the product, and it should be to their mutual advantage to work together. The manufacturer and the dealers and distributors thus should represent a valued partnership. They are on the same side; they are not in competition with one another.

Relations with Customers

Most firms pay lip service to customer satisfaction, but some go much further in this regard than others. The participation of Harley- Davidson at rallies and other events helped develop a cult following. While not exactly gaining a cult following, Vanguard has created a loyal and enthusiastic body of customers. A symbiotic relationship can also be seen as applying to manufacturer-customer relations: They both stand to win from highly satisfied customers. And again, isn't a kinder, gentler relationship a positive?

Giving Employees a Sense of Pride and a Caring Management

Kelleher of Southwest Airlines certainly developed esprit de corps, and this helped account for Southwest's great cost advantage. On the other hand, Boeing's problems with its peaks and valleys of layoffs and hiring destroyed any hope of widespread pride and esprit de corps among most of its employees. A latent sense of pride was certainly present for a firm with a strong national symbol, but management did not cultivate it at present-day Boeing.

Herman Miller has been a paragon in environmental protection and employee relations for many decades. Of late, its profitability had not matched that of its closest competitors, and it was forced to downsize to remain competitive—in violation of its long-held policy. Despite this, it still has a caring management.

Ethical Considerations

A firm tempted to walk the low road in search of greater short-run profits may eventually find that the risks far outweigh the rewards. Even more risky is a refusal to admit mistakes and product-safety risks, as characterized Ford and Firestone, with product-safety deficiencies that cost hundreds of lives. While we cannot delve very deeply into social and ethical issues,[4] these insights are worth noting:

- A firm can no longer disavow itself from the possibility of critical ethical scrutiny. Activist groups often publicize alleged misdeeds long before governmental regulators get involved.

[4] For more depth of coverage, see R. F. Hartley, *Business Ethics, Mistakes and Successes*, New York: Wiley, 2005.

- Trial lawyers are quick to pounce on anything that might bring big payoffs from deep-pocketed defendants.
- The media will help fan public scrutiny and criticism of alleged misdeeds.

Should a firm attempt to resist and defend itself? The overwhelming evidence is to the contrary. The bad press, the continued adversarial relations, and the effect on public image are hardly worth a confrontation. The better course of action may be to back down as quietly as possible, repugnant though that may be to a management convinced of the reasonableness of its position. Better rapport with the media may be gained by corporate openness and cooperation, with company top executives readily available to the press.

GENERAL INSIGHTS

Impact of One Person

In many of the cases, one person had a powerful impact on the organization. Sam Walton of Wal-Mart is perhaps the most outstanding example, but we also have Herb Kelleher of Southwest Airlines, tormentor of the mighty airlines, and Gordon Bethune, who brought Continental Air back from the depths. Let us not forget John Bogle, the founder and crusader of the Vanguard Fund Family, and his gospel of frugality. For turnaround accomplishments, virtually unknown is Leonard Hadly, who quietly turned Maytag around after the disaster with its United Kingdom subsidiary.

One person can also have a negative impact on an organization. How can we forget "Chainsaw Al" Dunlap. The impact of one person, for good or ill, is one of the recurring marvels of history, whether business history or world history.

Prevalence of Opportunities for Entrepreneurship Today

Despite the maturing of our economy and the growing size and power of many firms in many industries, opportunities for entrepreneurship are more abundant than ever. Opportunities exist not only for the change-maker or innovator, but also for the person who only seeks to do things a little better than existing, and complacent, competition.

Most entrepreneurial successes are unheralded, although dozens have been widely publicized, such as Bill Gates of Microsoft, and Michael Dell and Ted Waitt, founders of major computer firms. Wal-Mart and Southwest Airlines, and even McDonald's and Vanguard, are not so many years away from their beginnings. Opportunities are there for the dedicated, with venture capital to support promising new businesses helping many fledgling enterprises. As a new business shows early promise, initial public offerings (IPOs)—i.e., new stock issues—become important sources of capital, and of great wealth for the entrepreneurs.

But entrepreneurship is not for everyone. The great venture capitalists look at the person, not the idea. Typically they distribute their seed money to resourceful people who are courageous enough to give up security for the unknown consequences of their embryonic ventures, who have great self confidence, and who demonstrate a tremendous will to win. Our two entrepreneurs in the Boston Beer and OfficeMax cases exemplify this (although Michael Feuer claimed he never had any self confidence—"he always had an acute fear of failing.")

CONCLUSION

We learn from mistakes and from successes, although every management problem and opportunity seems to have been cast in a unique setting. One author has likened business strategy to military strategy:

> Strategies which are flexible rather than static embrace optimum use and offer the greatest number of alternative objectives. A good commander knows that he cannot control his environment to suit a prescribed strategy. Natural phenomena pose their own restraints to strategic planning, whether physical, geographic, regional, or psychological and sociological.[5]

He later adds:

> Planning leadership recognizes the unpleasant fact that, despite every effort, the war may be lost. Therefore, the aim is to retain the maximum number of facilities and the basic organization. Indicators of a deteriorating and unsalvageable total situation are, therefore, mandatory ... No possible combination of strategies and tactics, no mobilization of resources ... can supply a magic formula which guarantees victory; it is possible only to increase the probability of victory.[6]

Thus, we can pull two concepts from military strategy to help guide business strategy: the desirability of flexibility in an unknown or changing environment, and the idea that a basic core should be maintained in crises. The first suggests that the firm should be prepared for adjustments in strategy and business plans as conditions warrant. The second suggests that there is a basic core of a firm's business that should be unchanging; it should be the final bastion to fall back on for regrouping if necessary. Harley-Davidson stolidly maintained its core position, even though it let expansion opportunities slither away. Gateway also moved back to its basic PC core, shedding its retail stores and other electronics; whether this basic core will keep Gateway viable remains to be seen.

In regard to the basic core of a firm, every viable firm has some distinctive function or *ecological niche* in the business environment:

> Every business firm occupies a position which is in some respects unique. Its location, the product it sells, its operating methods, or the customers it serves tend to set it off in some degree from every other firm. Each firm competes by making the most of its individuality and its special character.[7]

Woe to the firm that loses its ecological niche.

---

[5] Myron S. Heidingsfield, *Changing Patterns in Marketing*, Boston: Allyn & Bacon, 1968, p. 11.
[6] *Ibid.*
[7] Alderson, p. 101.

QUESTIONS

1. Design a program aimed at mistake avoidance. Be as specific, as creative, and as complete as possible.

2. Would you advise a firm to be an imitator or an innovator? Why?

3. "There is no such thing as a sustainable competitive advantage." Discuss.

4. How would you build controls into an organization to ensure that similar mistakes do not happen in the future?

5. Array as many pros and cons of entrepreneurship as you can. Which do you see as most compelling?

6. Do you agree with the thought expressed in this chapter that a firm confronted with strong ethical criticism should abandon the product or the way of doing business? Why or why not?

7. We have suggested that the learning insights discussed in this chapter and elsewhere in the book are transferable to other firms and other times. Do you completely agree with this? Why or why not?

8. Do you agree or disagree with the author's contention that a kinder, gentler stance toward channel members would be desirable and profitable? Why or why not?

HANDS-ON EXERCISE

1. Your firm has had a history of reacting rather than anticipating changes in the industry. As the staff assistant to the CEO, you have been assigned the responsibility of developing adequate sensors of the environment. How will you go about developing such sensors?

TEAM DEBATE EXERCISE

Debate the extremes of forecasting for an innovative new product: conservative versus aggressive.

Index

X

Y

Z